THE RECURRENCE OF FATE

Studies in Theatre History & Culture

Edited by Thomas Postlewait

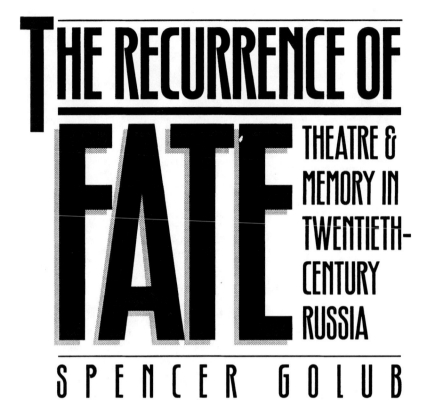

THE RECURRENCE OF

FATE

THEATRE &
MEMORY IN
TWENTIETH-
CENTURY
RUSSIA

SPENCER GOLUB

UNIVERSITY OF IOWA PRESS Ψ IOWA CITY

University of Iowa Press, Iowa City 52242

Copyright © 1994 by the University of Iowa Press

Printed in the United States of America

Design by Richard Hendel

Printed on acid-free paper

Library of Congress Cataloging-in-Publication Data
Golub, Spencer.

The recurrence of fate: theatre and memory in
twentieth-century Russia / Spencer Golub.

p.   cm. — (Studies in theatre history and culture)

Includes bibliographical references and index.

ISBN 0-87745-457-4, ISBN 0-87745-458-2 (pbk.)

1. Theater and society—Russian S.F.S.R.

2. Theater—Russian S.F.S.R.—History—20th
century.   3. Russian S.F.S.R.—Intellectual life—20th
century.   4. Russian drama—20th century—History
and criticism.   I. Title.   II. Series.

PN2724.G56   1994

792'.0947—dc20   93-23631

                                                       CIP

01   00   99   98   97   96   95   94   C   5   4   3   2   1
01   00   99   98   97   96   95   94   P   5   4   3   2   1

To Jeanie, Rachel, and Ethan,

for the adventure of real life

We must be proud of not being needles and thread

in the hands of fate as it sews the motley stuff

of history.

— *Aleksandr Herzen*, My Past and Thoughts

Suddenly . . .

But about suddenly, we shall speak later.

— *Andrey Bely*, Petersburg

CONTENTS

ACKNOWLEDGMENTS

Before I knew that my interests and research might become a book, Tracy Davis told me that they should and they would. For this, I thank her. From its inception, the book's guardian angel has been its activist editor and self-designated "resisting reader" Thomas Postlewait, who liked the manuscript even before it was written and as he knew it eventually would be written. I could not have asked for a more perfect reader not only of my text but of my mind. Expert copy editor Kathy Lewis supported and helped develop th project.

A sabbatic leave granted to me by Brown Universit was instrumental in bringing the book to completion, and funding ｜ ｏm the office of Dean of Faculty Bryan Shepp helped ensure that the ｏook would be illustrated. I was aided in my research by the following individuals, who ｐrovided me at one time or another with advice and/or source materials: Marie-Françoise Christout and her staff at the Bibliothèque de l'Arsenal (Paris), Vladislav Ivanov, Katherine Lahti, Alma Law, Irena R. Makaryk, Larry May, Michael McLain, Jeanne Newlin and her staff at the Harvard Theatre Collection. An earlier version of chapter 3 appeared in Laurence Senelick, ed., *Gender in Performance: The Presentation of Difference in the Performing Arts* (Tufts/University Press of New England, 1992); chapter 4 in Sue-Ellen Case and Janelle Reinelt, eds., *The Performance of Power: Theatrical Discourse and Politics* (University of Iowa Press, 1991); chapter 6 in Judith Milhous, ed., and Walter Meserve, guest ed., *Theatre Survey* (American Society for Theatre Research, May 1991); and chapter 7 in Dennis Kennedy, ed., *Foreign Shakespeare: Essays on Contemporary Performance Outside of English* (Cambridge University Press, 1993). I wish to thank the publishers and editors of these collections for allowing me to alter and expand the thoughts in my original essays for publication in this book.

There remain some special thanks for contributions which include and transcend the present study. The students in my Russian Theatre and Drama course and Theatrical Modernism seminar, as well as those to whom I have taught performance and theatre history, have helped me to understand and articulate more clearly what I and they knew. My colleagues and the students in the Department of Theatre, Speech and Dance at Brown University make this a uniquely exciting place to be. I am especially grateful to Don B. Wilmeth, who brought me into the department, and to John Emigh, who has chaired it during my tenure there. I value greatly the dialogue we share. I wish to thank as well the faculty of the Department of Comparative Literature for inviting me into their home. I owe the most professionally to Laurence Senelick, who has imbued this study and my career as a scholar with the information, recommendations, caveats, criticisms, advice, and insights of an expert close reader and a friend. He has played the role of "Mr. Memory," often for him (as for his fictional counterpart in *The Thirty-Nine Steps*) at the most inopportune moments, but for me always with the most enlightening results.

My greatest personal debt is owed to Jeanie Golub, whose real-life genius has run interference between me and the world and helped to define the world for me through her friendship, her curiosity, and her theatricality. As a truly gifted person, she bears the burden of others' dependence upon her talents and their vicarious living through her example. This makes the value of her personal contribution to my life and work even more generous, singular, and immeasurable. Our children, Rachel and Ethan, to whom this book will remain for some time a mysterious, unread chapter in their lives, are for me the most important part of that reality from which and for which other realities are invented. My family, my always supportive parents and sister, and my wife's family have given me more than can ever be said or even written in appreciation.

NOTE ON TRANSLITERATION

I have for the most part employed what I feel is the most readable system of transliteration: System I, in J. Thomas Shaw, *The Transliteration of Modern Russian for English-Language Publications* (Madison: University of Wisconsin Press, 1967). I have dropped all soft signs (') for the benefit of the general reader in the main text. Soft signs are included in parenthetical references in the text as well as in the endnote references for the information of the Russianist reader. In some cases in the notes, publishers have employed different systems in rendering authors' names and the titles of their works. Unless otherwise indicated, all translations are mine.

THE RECURRENCE OF FATE

‖NTRODUCTION

The Methodology of Cultural Mise en scène

The theme of this book is Russian theatrical memory in the period circa 1900–1980. I intend to illustrate how, by creating rather than simply retrieving memory, the Russian state and intelligentsia directed history to conform to the recurring patterns and tragic conventions of fate. The (self-)martyred artist-intellectual is the true protagonist in this cultural *mise en scène* of messianic self-fashioning. The lionized and long-suffering "people" (*narod*), who have historically understudied the protagonist's role, stand in the wings, (still) awaiting their entrance cue.

While I invoke a cast of characters in this study, I am most concerned with a "cast of mind" (from the Russian *oblik*) or *mentalité*. Specifically, I demonstrate how the intelligentsia evolved a romantic code of iconic self-entrapment through its interactive "revolutionary dreaming" with the state about self and society.[1] In relating this theatrical narrative, I place great stock in images and correspondences, deployed as the stage props of history. Each chapter composes from a combination of elements—actor/icon/archetype; geographic, cultural, and scenic design; theatrical and societal *mise en scène*; dramatic, narrative, and historical text—the always elusive picture of stage figures imbued with the assumption of spectatorship and a stage seen from an audience's shifting point of view.

Conceptually and methodologically, this study owes much to the historical models presented by members of the Moscow-Tartu School of Cultural Semiotics, especially those of Yury Lotman. Theatricality—that is, performative motives, masks, and norms—interests Lotman more than theatre, which he regards as a "translation-code" through which society and the other representational arts can be more evocatively read.[2] Lotman's ongoing concern has been with what his colleague Boris Gasparov calls "the dynamic relationship between the social norm and its violation in individual behavior." In Lotman's construction, "the real life of a society" is "a text ('parole') organized according to a specific cultural code (its language)." This coded social text amplifies or silences for the purpose of its structural cohesiveness the dissenting, self-dramatizing voice or personality.

Lotman argues that theatricalized behavioral norms, like "Decembrism" (rebellious self-dramatization) and "khlestakovism" (inspired lying), both of which I discuss, developed in Russia owing not only to its long history of ritualistic and oral traditions but to the fact that the culture's natural evolution has been artificially inhibited "or, at some instant, completely halted."[3] Cultural fetishism and historical improvisation arose from such interruption(s), redefining romantic and realistic behavioral and societal norms so that they became in places not merely symbiotic but identical. Lotman and other Russian cultural historians point to Peter the Great's early-eighteenth-century "theatrical" fiat requiring Russian nobles to act like Europeans as the primary cultural interruption. Lotman contends that this interruption is characteristic of "a polarity expressed in the binary nature of its structure," from its beginnings to the early nineteenth century.

Together with a "sacral semantics," the mythologizing in literature, and performance of the tsar's rule over the nobility and the nobility's power over their serfs, culturally inorganic behavior and class authority were ritualized and life theatricalized. Priscilla R. Roosevelt has demonstrated, for example, that beyond supporting serf theatres, some late-eighteenth-century Russian estates were "little more than stage sets," complete with false façades, *trompe l'oeil* properties and scenic elements, mirrors deployed so as to distort and magnify depth and scale, and "shams," or "adroitly painted, oil-on-wood, two-dimensional, life-sized figures." Nobles even "assumed different roles in different areas of the house, altering their behavior to fit the setting."[4] Still, it is the public rather than the private performance of Russian culture which, owing to a three-quarter-century legacy of revolutionary interruption and ruler-worship, has defined the theatricality of Russia in the twentieth century. Following the "utopian apocalypse" of 1917, the state, initially led by intellectuals, sought, through the mythical fixing of space and time, "to make the extraordinary repeatable."[5] Memory alone could not accomplish this. However, memory, in concert with theatre and theatricality, which regularly rehearse and perform what Stanislavsky called "the illusion of the first time," could and did.

Following Lotman's example, the latter parts of chapters 1, 2, 5, and 7 of this book are extended case studies which illustrate textually (via play analysis and/or examination of theatrical *mise en scène*) the intersection of theatre and life. I suspend this strategy in chapters 3, 4, and 6, which focus on the intelligentsia's and the state's theatricalization of their roles in their courtship of the people.

In chapter 1, I discuss how in *The Cherry Orchard* (*Vishnyovy sad*, 1904) Chekhov demythologized the Russian cultural condition of internal (temporal) and external (spatial) exile, which Lenin revised after 1917. Revolutions in history and time, circa 1900–1917, conspired with Russian culture's spatial (geographic) and temporal (apocalyptic) paranoia to recalibrate assumptions and expectations in the minds of the intellectual "class." *Fin de siècle* Russia was caught up in the historical-scientific-philosophical debate over such issues as neovitalism (extra-spatiotemporal motive force) and mechanistic determinism (causality), cultural messianism (symbolism), and evolutionary biologism (Darwinism). This argument concerned not only notions of immutability and relativity but the relative importance of the dominant social code versus an inner absolute moral code derived from the experiencing of subjective time. This revolution in consciousness anticipated the conscious revolution of 1917. Lev Tolstoy suggested that human history could be regarded as a continuous process, deducible with the aid of calculus, from "the huge mass of world historical incidents." Russian scientists and mathematicians developed probability theory to deal with the relationship between "mathematical expectation" (sequence) and "variance" (randomness) in predicting events at roughly the same time that dialectical materialism became a universal calculus for the solution of history.[6]

Chekhov's introduction of simultaneist and relativist space-time into *The Cherry Orchard* through the medium of an unseen train coincided with the arrival of the railroad in the Russian countryside, where the great mass of people lived. The Communist belief that Marx discovered "history's 'laws of motion'" was reaffirmed for the faithful in 1917 by the arrival of the exiled Lenin's revolutionary train.[7] Lenin's arrival destroyed existing social myths, reordered cultural time and space, and proclaimed a new certainty which legitimized created over remembered history and promoted the present-future over the past.

In chapter 2, the discussion shifts to myth-making of a more individual nature. I examine the masks of female otherness which male

artist-intellectuals of the Silver Age (ca. 1894–1917, following the
Golden Age of Russian literature, ca. 1820–1880) devised and sometimes wore in order to express their feelings of social impotence
and spiritual disquietude. The concepts of the _femme fatale_ and the
femme fragile are discussed in relation to symbolist literary models,
scenic design, and theatrical iconography. I relate these paradigms
and strategies to two contrasting theatrical icons of the period, actresses Ida Rubinstein and Vera Kommissarzhevskaya. My general
discussion of male self-(en)gendering in conceptual and perceptual
space touches upon semiautobiographic painting, poetry, and narrative fiction. My analysis of Aleksandr Blok's modernist harlequinade
The Little Showbooth (_Balaganchik_, 1906), which concludes this
chapter, proceeds thematically from the treatment of _The Cherry Or-
chard_ in chapter 1. In his play, Chekhov parodied mythically defined
exile by alternatively defining intellectual self-absorption as a higher,
integrated consciousness. In his _balagan_, Blok ironically exposed the
limits of intellectual self-absorption in art, which was coded according to divisive gender politics after 1905. By that time, whatever optimism the _fin de siècle_ had engendered in the creative intelligentsia
had been eroded by a humiliating national defeat in a war with Japan and a suppressed revolution at home. Blok's play performed the
authorial and "class" agony of the intellectual masks—Harlequin-
Columbine-Pierrot, Hamlet-Ophelia—which recur throughout this
study.

Chapter 3 inverts the theme of male-female disguise. The Bolsheviks' ostensible and ostentatious equalization of the sexes following the revolution masked their attempt to syncretize and degender
woman as part of the masculinized "new person." The "woman
question" (women's rights, liberation, and feminism) was folded into
the "class question" (the rights and powers of "the people"). Women
were punished for exercising the new-found freedoms which the
revolution claimed to have made available to them. This chapter introduces the "gynoid," created from misogynistic fear and male self-
loathing. The gynoid cruelly parodied new personhood and machine-
culture through the soulless mask of independent and destructive
female robotism.

In chapter 4, I discuss how the postrevolutionary intelligentsia's
and state's _mentalité_ transformed the iconically ambiguous tramp
persona of Charlie Chaplin into an ideological symbol. Chaplin
uniquely embodied the division between romantic individualism (humanist civilization) and utopian collectivism (machine-culture), a col-

lision which preoccupied Soviet society in the 1920s. The speed, strength, resourcefulness, resiliency, and optimism of American popular culture, vested in Chaplin by the Soviet cultural avant-garde, helped define a democratic aesthetic of proletarian self-creation. In particular, these same qualities fueled the escapist fantasies of that alienated and disillusioned segment of the creative intelligentsia which Leon Trotsky dubbed the Fellow Travelers (*poputchiki*) in 1923. This somewhat speculative chapter continues the spiritual biography of the Russian intelligentsia by mimicking its (and secondarily the state's) appropriation of Chaplin as a test case for imaginative reconstruction.

Chapter 5 reveals the hidden presence of totalitarianism, the culmination of utopic hope and messianic-catastrophic dread, underlying modern Russian culture's iconomania and iconophobia. Abstraction, the first necessary step in the Soviet cultural project of distancing the ontologically material past, has perennially been in conflict with Soviet power's attraction to unequivocal materialism. Modern Soviet culture transformed the concreteness of actual participation in the historical past into the passive spectatorship of mythic identity in the timeless future. Such spectacle, asserts Guy Debord, "obliterates the boundaries between true and false by driving all lived truth below the *real presence* of fraud ensured by the organization of appearance."[8] This chapter examines the embodied paradox of totalitarianism's measureless surveillance and control over unquantifiable, immaterial cultural fate. I locate theatrical images of spatiotemporal and protagonistic paralysis in the work of stage directors Vsevolod Meyerhold and Aleksandr Tairov. Their productions of *The Inspector General* (*Revizor*, 1926), *Woe to Wit* (*Gore umu*, 1928), and *Phèdre* (1922) contain revelatory signs of the unmaking of both revolutionary romanticism and historical truth by the state's and the intelligentsia's mythologizing processes. The discussion of silence and stasis in this chapter is the antinarrative to the first chapter's treatment of revolutionary pronouncement and cultural change.

Russian culture was built upon the interlocking bases of prescience and imposture. The tsars, the nation's prerevolutionary political and sacred rulers (they were likened to and even called "Christ"), were the people's preordained deliverers. But even those anointed leaders engaged in masquerade and falsification and were often challenged by pretenders to their authority and to their history. A false Tsarevich Dmitry arose during the Time of Troubles (*Smutnoe vremya*) in the early seventeenth century, and later the peasant revolutionary Emelyan Pugachyov (ca. 1742–1775) passed himself off as Tsar Pyotr III.[9]

The political unmasking of secular pretenders accelerated with the rapid erosion of authority and authenticity by historical discontinuity and revolutionary totalism after 1917. A new tradition of charismatic leadership, predicated upon the reinvention of history through editing and erasure, was engineered under Stalin. Chapter 6 analyzes how Stalin extended the curtainless stage of revolutionary culture, while more narrowly and formally constructing the Procrustean bed of authoritarian socialist realist aesthetics.

Russian drama and theatrical culture have spoken cross-generationally of intellectual values and have helped to create an unofficial history of the intellectual class, as well as performative roles for this class to play. Still, by far the most ubiquitous and compelling role, Hamlet, was appropriated from abroad and translated into Russian cultural terms. Russian history has validated the artist-intellectuals' worst fears of spiritual entrapment and social marginality, while testing their resolve for moral action in the face of impossible odds. To be Hamlet in Russian theatre and culture means entering the "*Hamlet* gulag" of socially and self-imprisoning meanings, values, traditions, and assumptions. Chapter 7, like those which touch upon Lenin and Stalin, addresses the problem of personality in a culture which distrusts the "metaphysical contradictions" promoted by individualism.[10] Russian and Soviet culture have both unequally configured the one against the many, and, in the case of artist-intellectuals, against themselves. This chapter's centerpiece is the individual and shared iconicity of creative intellectuals Vladimir Vysotsky, Yury Lyubimov, and Boris Pasternak, whose *Hamlet* premiered at Moscow's controversial Taganka Theatre at an especially propitious historical moment.

While this study invariably invokes images of intellectual heroism and cultural and self-martyrdom, it stops short of indulging the bathos of the mythic "martyred nation" (or class) trope, in which, in Isaiah Berlin's definition, the government "jack-boot" treads upon a "sullen" and "brutalised" populace. There is unarguable value in Sheila Fitzpatrick's efforts to de-romanticize the "totalitarian model" of historical scholarship in Russia and the West, which depicts the intelligentsia in perpetual conflict with the Soviet state and Communist Party apparati. Fitzpatrick notes, for example, that for all its feelings of "powerlessness, humiliation and even martyrdom," the intelligentsia remained a privileged socioeconomic elite even under Stalin, who was included in their number. However, even though some artists and intellectuals benefited from the Soviet system, the persistence of victims and of a "victim mentality" among members of the intelligentsia cannot be dismissed and justifies continued documentation and analysis of this historical phenomenon.[11]

In this study, "Russian" and "Soviet" are used to designate temporal and political-cultural (that is, pre- and postrevolutionary) difference, as well as to suggest a not always tacit republicanism. "Russia" denotes the geographic and cultural centrality of Moscow and St. Petersburg (the nation's two historical capitals), arrived at in intellectual history by imaginative and emotional consensus. The theme of the omnipotent Russian center recurred most recently and most dramatically in the dissolution of the Soviet Union and in the advent of the Russian republican leader Boris Yeltsin. Even as I was completing this book, Yeltsin, who became the new embodiment of national authority following the failed coup of August 1991 and the subsequent ouster of Mikhail Gorbachev, was struggling for his political life. This study does not strive to be topically relevant to these momentous events but may claim to understand at least in part the mythic-historical dynamics which precipitated them and which will determine Russia's future. "History, no doubt, is bound to repeat itself," the exiled poet Joseph Brodsky has written with his homeland in mind; "after all, like men, history doesn't have many choices."[12] In a culture that is overly infused with created or theatrical memory, history has fewer choices still.

This book's epigraphs clarify two aspects of Russia's cultural problem, one historical and the other thematic. The sense of individual will's and democratic choice's inevitable defeat in the struggle between Russian history and fate was already apparent in Herzen's day (ca. 1850s). That is, the problem is long-standing, like much else in modern Russian culture antedating the 1917 revolution that was credited by the state (prior to 1991) with having delivered a new, predetermined history. The certainty that interruption defines a normative, recurrent pattern in Russian history and consciousness was noted by Bely in the form and idea of his novel *Petersburg* (1916; revised edition 1922), long before Lotman took up this theme on the other side of the 1905 and 1917 revolutions.

Is it possible to honor the history of class and cultural memory without succumbing to the siren song of a constructed fate, the allure of a singular destiny? What are the moral consequences, not so much of forgetting, which the state periodically prescribes and the intelligentsia appropriately reviles, but of opting out of the high tragedy of remembrance as a rehearsed rite? History has shown if not taught

Russia the peril of always awaiting the whirlwind rather than embracing reality.

The Intelligentsia and the Drama of Fate

In his "First Philosophical Letter" (1836), Pyotr Chaadayev outlined Russia's fate scenario: "We belong to none of the great families of mankind; we are neither of the West nor of the East, and we possess the traditions of neither. Somehow divorced from time and space, the universal education of mankind has not touched upon us." Russia had been singled out, Chaadayev and many other of his kin before and since have maintained, "to teach the world some great lesson." Russian culture's messianic self-fashioning and its belated exposure to Western humanism under Tsar Peter the Great (reigned 1682–1725) helped develop its sense of extratemporal (mythic) legitimacy and temporal (historical) illegitimacy. This condition has in turn engendered the tacit cultural belief among both intellectuals and ideologues that Russia was somehow minimally accountable to the past but maximally accountable to the future. Chaadayev wrote of Russia, "We walk through time so singly that as we advance, the past escapes us forever." Russian and foreign scholars alike still passionately argue the question of whether this slippage or erasure of history and memory in Russian culture are the by-products of a real or manufactured fate, part of a spiritual mission or merely a rationale for sociopolitical omission.[13]

The "gift for prophecy" ceded to Russia by its intellectuals and ideologues in part may be a function of its Christian tradition and cultural backwardness. Until the period between 1861 (the year serfdom was abolished) and 1917 (the year of the revolution), Russian popular culture was more dependent on oral traditions than on "common literacy." By 1900, about one-third of the population (2.2 percent of which belonged to the intelligentsia) was literate, marking a dramatic increase but leaving considerable unfulfilled potential.[14] Lotman has remarked that "written culture is oriented towards the past, while oral culture is oriented towards the future. Predictions, fortune-telling and prophecy play an enormous part in it."[15] The predictive nature of modern Russian culture springs from a desire to commandeer fate's determinacy while suppressing the indeterminacy of chance. In so doing, choice and consciousness in the fullest sense are excluded from the historical process.

For over a century, the intelligentsia has sought to translate "moral passion" and "critical thought" into an active social ideology which addresses life's "cursed questions" on behalf of Russian society. Like the state, the intelligentsia has tended to embrace a directional orthodoxy of timely and timeless cultural rebirth and to superimpose a spiritual geography of moral certainty through conscious history upon "the immensity, the vagueness, the infinitude of the Russian land." The state and the intelligentsia have congealed the theme of imminent revolutionary change into the iconography of unchanging appearance and inevitable return. Nevertheless, the complicity of the intelligentsia in this process seems almost insignificant when compared with the personal and collective price it has had to pay.[16]

The state and the intelligentsia's conceptualizing of history embodies the paradox of a temporally obsessive culture which is at once committed to staging the utopian future and reenacting the "genuinely real" past in the present.[17] Long before the state theorized a new quasi-moral order in 1917, the intelligentsia dreamed of returning to a "nonhistorical, transcendental Russia," Holy Russia, a real moral locus beyond the reach of central authority. The term "Holy Russia" (*Svetlaya Rossiya*), which was originally coined in the fourteenth century to distinguish the country's Christian "chosenness" from the paganism of foreign peoples, gradually became a sign of both difference and communion, expressive of a class's thwarted social aspirations and vaulting moral ambition. In the latter half of the seventeenth century, the concept embodied the noble class's attempt to wrest from the tsar the sole authority of "orthodoxy and purity."[18]

By the late eighteenth century, the proprietorship of Holy Russia began to change hands from the nobility to the evolving "class" which Vissarion Belinsky and Aleksandr Herzen, in their social criticism of the next century, dubbed "the intelligentsia." Defined in the period 1825–1861 in terms of its geographic isolation on gentry estates, the intelligentsia was later characterized by itself and others in terms of spiritual and political alienation. This alienation helped precipitate the intelligentsia's commitment to moral values and the need for social change. The iconoclastic 1860s in Russia saw the transformation of the intelligentsia's socio-spiritual disengagement into a full-blown class martyrology. Those who included themselves among its number distinguished the intelligentsia from the generally more conservative, middle-class intellectuals, the academics and custodians of highbrow culture. The intelligentsia believed itself to be "above class" and considered its culture of truth, mercy, and conscience to transcend that of society.[19] By the late nineteenth and early twentieth century, the self-contained mythic "reality" of Holy Russia signified both the stateless intelligentsia and "that perpetual and universal mass inertia [embodied by the intelligentsia] which it was the task of the state mechanism to conquer."[20]

Politically speaking, the prerevolutionary intelligentsia (ca. 1900–1917) included significant liberal and radical contingents. The first group sought legal reforms which would further human rights regardless of class. The second group promoted class interests and the violent overthrow of the state authority that opposed it. The radical intelligentsia of this period updated the theoretical activism of the generation of the 1860s. The modern radical *intelligenty* quoted the writings of Nikolay Chernyshevsky, which Lenin valued over Marx's. They also positively invoked the populist and terroristic activities of the People's Will (*Narodnaya volya*) Party of the 1880s. The Russian Marxist Social Democratic Workers' Party (the Social Democrats), which bore the radical mantle into the twentieth century, split in 1902 into the Mensheviks (Minoritarians) and the Bolsheviks (the Majoritarians), the latter led by Lenin. One year earlier, the Social(ist) Revolutionary Party was formed, which, unlike the Social Democrats, saw the peasants rather than the industrial proletariat as the popular base for future revolutionary upheaval. Both the SDs and the SRs called for the creation of a classless socialist society, but the SRs were more firmly committed to terrorism as a means to this end.

The Liberation (that is, liberal) Movement was founded in 1901 by legal philosopher Pavel Novgorodtsev and was developed in the period 1902–1904 by ex-Marxists such as Pavel Milyukov, Pyotr Struve, and Sergey Bulgakov. Included among the liberals were nobles, urban professionals, university professors, and former members of the local elective assemblies (the *zemstva*). Out of this group emerged the Constitutional Democratic Party, also known as the Party of National Freedom and informally as the Kadets. This group was generally characterized by its incipient bourgeois civic-mindedness. An exemplary CD was the liberal jurist V. D. Nabokov, father of the famous novelist, who championed a variety of unpopular but humane and progressive causes.

The Kantian Idealism of the CDs was antipositivist, antimonist (and anti-Marxist), and opposed by the majority of Russian intellectuals. In 1904, Bulgakov, together with fellow philosophers Nikolay Berdyayev and Vladimir Solovyov, broke with the CDs, shifting from secular liberalism to Christian socialism. This group believed that the integration of the individual's total being and the solution to social, political, and economic problems could only be found in Orthodox Christianity and by sacrificing "egoistic individualism" to a higher and more essential concept of "human personhood."

This shift in focus from social to spiritual transformation was still insufficient for the "God-seekers" (*bogoiskateli*), among whom were numbered creative intellectuals Dmitry Merezhkovsky, Zinaida Gippius, and Vasily Rozanov. They viewed the Russian Orthodox Church as a soulless, outmoded institution which slowed rather than hastened their cause—the liberation of the spirit through the senses, including the flesh. The members of this group merged Nietzschean individualism with sexual experimentalism. They were denounced by both the liberals and the radicals for their overintellectualized and elitist aestheticism and by the church for their freethinking and their apparent desire (true only in the case of Rozanov) to make a religion out of sex.[21]

After 1905, Kantian-based Russian symbolism, which incorporated Christian socialism, especially Solovyovian mysticism (discussed in chapter 2), and the God-seekers' erotic aestheticism, further isolated creative individuals from the rank-and-file intelligentsia, as well as from the general population. Essays and lectures proliferated on the theme of the (non)relationship between the intelligentsia and the people and on the connection between religion and socialism. In 1904–1905, the symbolists split along generational and "decadent" versus "mystical" (religious-philosophical) lines. Valery Bryusov was the leading theorist of the first group, which also included Konstantin Balmont. The second group was led by Vyacheslav Ivanov, whose theories of myth-creation (*mifotvorchestvo*) and communal or choral action (*sobornost'* or *khorovoe deystvo*) related Nietzsche's interactive Apollonian-Dionysian philosophy to Russian scythianism.

R. V. Ivanov-Razumnik (pseudonym of Razumnik Vasiliyevich Ivanov), an SR who later became a Bolshevik partisan, promoted the term "scythianism" to acknowledge Russia's Asiatic barbarism and God-seeking tendencies. Scythianism was one of several utopian searches among Russian intellectuals in this period for "mythic wholeness," the "lost unity in contemporary civilization," and the reconciliation of the mystical (Dionysian) and rational (Apollonian) aspects of Russian identity. Scythianism attracted self-conscious, self-critical members of the symbolist generation, most notably Andrey Bely and Aleksandr Blok, who were concerned with the future of the culture, and more particularly of the intelligentsia.

The neo-mythic, Hellenic, and liturgical dramas of Vyacheslav Ivanov and fellow symbolists Innokenty Annensky, Fyodor Sologub, and Valery Bryusov linked Dionysian and Christian mysteries and rituals in an effort to discover a theatrical corrective to Russia's (or at least the creative intelligentsia's) spiritual crisis. Ivanov's philosophy confronted what he called "the pathos of individualism" afflicting his generation of intellectuals. According to Ivanov, the Dionysian "ecstasy of personal happiness" was a means by which to liberate the individual from "the prison of the ego."[22]

Ivanov's philosophy renewed the intelligentsia's preoccupation, expressed in the nineteenth century in the literary work of Aleksandr Pushkin, with the relationship between "the poet and the crowd" (from Pushkin's poem of the same name). Blok took up Pushkin's theme in his 1908 essay "On Theatre" (*O teatre*). Pushkin's dream of a people's theatre was furthered in the prerevolutionary period by the translation into Russian of Friedrich Nietzsche's *The Birth of Tragedy from the Spirit of Music* in 1903, Richard Wagner's *Art and Revolution* in 1906, and Romain Rolland's *Theatre of the People* in 1910. The Bolsheviks, led by the playwright and first education minister Anatoly Lunacharsky, appropriated from Ivanov and the symbolists the idea of cultic reconciliation of the tragic antinomy between yearned-for self-assertion and collective belonging.[23]

Both the symbolists and the Bolsheviks theoretically sought to discover or restore a common language with which the literate and the illiterate, the initiated and the uninitiated, could communicate. Via their quasi-theurgic impulses and theories, both groups hoped to deepen the individual and collective experiencing of reality and to close the philosophical and practical gap between realism and idealism. Actually, the symbolists created an arcane poetic language which further isolated the poet from the crowd. The Bolsheviks devised a proletarian language through which they sought to conceal their own intellectual origins and to remove the creative and liberal (as opposed to radical) intelligentsia from the sources of power. The state, which the liberals viewed as a historical necessity and the Marxists considered to be only a transitional historical phase, became a monument to the bureaucratization of the radical intelligentsia and its class ethics.

In their self-conscious and increasingly abstract art and culture, the creative intelligentsia internalized what Andrey Bely called the "invisible idol of fate."[24] The intelligentsia's level of education and literary discourse inevitably distanced it from the peasants and the workers. However, the intelligentsia needed to conscript "the unenlightened and unconscious" masses into its battle for survival with the state, even if the people could not comprehend the issues at stake and the intellectuals could not comprehend the people. It was sufficient for the intelligentsia that the people, like Holy Russia, were eternal, inherently moral, and beyond the control of the state. In 1917, the Bolsheviks succeeded in assuming the historical burden of the people's suffering, and the old intelligentsia lost a measure of its identity. The (old) intelligentsia became synonymous with the Russian cultural fetish of reinvention and Hamletian self-questioning, while the state formalized the countervailing cultural aversion to self-definition and other matters of the self.[25] Ironically yet inevitably, members of the disempowered creative intelligentsia advertised their disappointment with and even rejection of self and class. At the same time, the state confidently erased all categories of thought and being outside its own.

CHAPTER I

ARRIVALS AND DEPARTURES

Of time, too, it can be said: no thinking being has set

foot there. If not even all the most powerful trains could

move everything that mankind has written about space,

then everything written about time could easily be lifted

by any pigeon in a letter hidden under its wing.

— Velimir Khlebnikov[1]

Russian consciousness has historically been more comfortable predicting time (messianism, eschatology, and utopianism) than fathoming space. In so vast a nation, a mythically empowered center imagines a dark, impenetrable, and devouring peripheral emptiness, and a mythically innocent rural periphery imagines a far distant demonic core, radiating a paranoid energy. The pre-sixteenth-century administrative term for "separate territory" in Russian (*oprichnina*) soon came to mean "outer darkness" (*kromeshny*), in the sense of the demonic in Russian culture.[2]

On his grand tour of Russia in 1839, the Marquis Astolphe de Custine noted that "every Russian city has its Kremlin" or walled fortress designed to repel outside invaders and to keep inner space inviolate.[3] Russian national consciousness and the sense of a cultural destiny came to be defined in opposition to internal and external manifestations of foreign otherness. The causes for this can be found in the sheer size of Russia and the great distances socially, ethnically, and geographically separating town and country and their inhabitants. Orthodox traditions, which dominated village life, blended with Slavophile cultural assertiveness and xenophobia, especially after Peter the Great's program of enforced Westernization in the early 1700s, to deepen and solidify this tendency. Russia's frequent and dramatic historical transformations (from a pagan culture to a Christian, secular, and finally atheistic civilization) suggested to both rural priests and urban philosophers the journey and trial of a beleaguered Russian soul.

The nineteenth-century narrative and dramatic fiction of Nikolay Gogol, Ivan Turgenev, Aleksey Pisemsky, Mikhail Saltykov-Shchedrin, and Anton Chekhov reaffirmed the belief in Russian readers that geographic distance from the cultural center produced social and political irrelevance, existential uncertainty, spiritual inertia, and even moral decay. The town depicted in Gogol's stage comedy *The Inspector General* (*Revizor*, 1836) is not miles but (three) years from civilization. In this play, Gogol twice mentions Siberia, the peculiarly Russian metonym for the utmost interiority of geographic and personal disappearance. Gogol's protagonist, the liar-nonentity Ivan Khlestakov, escapes at play's end to "Lord knows where," into a Russia which, like Siberia, contains unimaginable, immeasurable space and time and the promise of eternal anonymity. The steppe was the primary text of nineteenth-century Russian writers' spatial demonology of geographic vastness and physio-spiritual isolation. However, Siberia, which symbolized the state's social engineering, its transformation of chance (where you were born) into fate (where you were sent), isolation into exile, became this demonology's metatext, its doubled consciousness.[4]

While the literature which linked physical and spiritual isolation with inertia did not actually bring about social alienation and internal exile, it ceded to these conditions a sort of legitimacy among members of the intelligentsia. This legitimacy was ultimately self-defeating. Similarly, the purposeful recycling by the state and its writers of this cultural myth of internal exile to empower the radical intelligentsia while disempowering the liberal, creative intelligentsia reinforced the predisposition of many artists influential within their social and intellectual class to conceive history as fate.

In *Beyond Good and Evil* (*Jenseits von Gut und Böse*, 1886), Nietzsche popularized the image of Russia as the "gigantic and mysterious enigma in the East," the spatiotemporal antithesis of the rationalist West's vanished frontiers and exhausted history.[5] The currency of this belief among members of the Russian intelligentsia at the *fin de siècle* was parodied in Chekhov's *The Cherry Orchard* (*Vishnyovy sad*, 1904), in which the quasi-intellectual misfit Yepikhodov remarks that "everything has long since been settled abroad."[6] Nietzsche's statement reinforced a long-standing belief among Russian intellectuals that national geography somehow contained the mystery and the certainty of cultural destiny. In the foreword to his poetry cycle *Ashes* (*Pepel*, 1909), Andrey Bely likened the condition of his lost soul to "the remote, unawakened expanses of the Russian land."[7] Creative intellectuals of Bely's generation, who read Nietzsche in German between 1872 and 1898 and in Russian thereafter, internally balanced two fears. They feared losing the self in the labyrinthine inner darkness of private consciousness and in the outer darkness of a social reality whose existence compels it to evict the dreamer from the refuge of a personal Kremlin.[8]

In his plays, particularly *The Cherry Orchard,* which is this chapter's primary focus, Chekhov sought to dissolve the very intellectual malaise of inaction and self-criticism he is now generally (dis)credited with having sustained or even created. Furthermore, he offered a positive, culturally revolutionary solution to the intelligentsia's acceptance of (its) history as fate. On the one hand, Chekhov exposed the debilitating theatrical roles played by the gentry and intelligentsia in response to their social isolation. On the other hand, he legitimized the private consciousness which nominally deepened their sense of exile but likewise granted them a measure of freedom.

Chekhov's plays only appear to be about physical distances and personal isolation from a geographic center. His characters parody serious regard for real physical places by transforming these places— a lake in *The Seagull* (*Chayka*, 1896), Moscow in *Three Sisters* (*Tri sestry*, 1901), and some blossoming trees in *The Cherry Orchard*— into metaphysical abstractions. The lake is "magical." Moscow and the orchard are even more magical, because they have been lost, save in memory and in dreams. The centrifugal and centripetal forces created by time, like those produced by the spinning top that Rode and Fedotik bring to Irina Prozorov's name day party in *Three Sisters,* direct Chekhovian reality. These forces, along with arrivals and departures and other literal and figurative echoes in Chekhov's plays, are part of a complex pattern of recurrence, in which time and people return to imaginary places without ever leaving where they really are. The pathos of this externally static condition is balanced by the internal temporal liberation of Chekhov's dramatic protagonists from the spatially encoded demonology of self, class, and society.

While *The Cherry Orchard* was premiering at the Moscow Art Theatre in 1904, V. I. Lenin was navigating the European underground on what would later be perceived as his long revolutionary path to Petrograd (as St. Petersburg was renamed in 1914). Lenin (formerly Ulyanov) had taken his pseudonym from the Lena, the longest of the great Siberian rivers. In so doing, he had absorbed the otherness of exile which his return to the center as "Lenin" conquered.[9] The arrival of Lenin's train at the Finland Station in 1917 consummated the defeat and fatalism of the old intelligentsia which Chekhov's plays depicted and defined new terms for cultural (re)memory. In other words, assumptions about exile and the demonology of exterior and interior space that were subverted by Chekhov in 1904 were revised but remythologized after 1917 according to Lenin's personal example. To note this parallel is not to suggest that the creative intelligentsia or a particular representative of it (for example, Chekhov) had a direct impact on Russia's political destiny. Instead, it indicates the ways in which the art of these intellectuals personalized and antagonized the concept of cultural destiny as it developed in this century.

Historians and political scientists have borrowed the term "charismatic authority" from religious studies to describe the aura and influence of secular leaders who have (re)made their nations' cultural destinies. Charismatic authority "repudiates the past," ritualistically assuages the social "distress" or "acute malaise" that characterizes the present, and confidently predicts a secure and healthy future. Lenin's relationship to charismatic authority, vested in him by a disaffected radical intelligentsia and "proved" by the revolution, was, like his relationship to the historical past and the messianic future, complex and paradoxical. Physically unprepossessing, Lenin, whom Max Eastman likened to "a granite mountain of sincerity," derived his personal aura from his unwavering belief in and commitment to a cause greater than himself.[10] Lenin's belief that the common man or woman could become a "new person" and that the proletariat could rule usurped the charismatic authority not only of the ruler and the state but of the self-absorbed liberal and conservative intellectuals who opposed them. When, after interviewing him in 1920, H. G. Wells dubbed Lenin "the dreamer in the Kremlin," he inadvertently linked him to an intellectual condition and tradition he had sought to disown.[11]

Chekhov's dramatic characters project the anticharismatic authority of personal and social insecurity and unfulfilled desire. They unwittingly discourage and undermine the very attention and support they hope to attract. Chekhov offers a consistent critique of self-obsessed personality (along with messianic time), creating a world devoid of real personal charisma and of a human response to it. This critique effectively targets the performance of otherness that deepened and recast as fate the gentry intellectual's (sense of) exile. The self-images of Chekhov's protagonists especially parody romantic, melancholic archetypes like Hamlet. Masha's opening line in *The Seagull*, "I am in mourning for my life," directly acknowledges this anti-charismatic motif.[12] Her habitually black attire symbolizes unacknowledged personal charisma, a life that no one notices and Treplyov in particular refuses to save. Treplyov plays Masha's role of the anti-charismatic melancholic, the anti-Hamlet, in his relationship with Nina Zarechnaya. He symbolically offers a seagull's corpse to forestall her inevitable first departure from the country to the town and his own corpse after her inevitable return and final exit. Like Masha, Treplyov has been in mourning for his life and a potential suicide for too long to warrant serious attention. As Laurence Senelick has noted, Dorn tells Trigorin at play's end that Treplyov "has *finally* shot himself" (*zastrelilsya*).[13] Chekhov has Treplyov kill himself in the wings as further punishment for his intellectual role-playing.

Chekhov's "former people," as Lenin's "new people" conceived the gentry and non-Marxist intellectuals whom the playwright depicted, lived only theoretical lives, filled with speculative past and future time and devoid of honest labor. The monotony of Chekhovian provincial life exaggerated and intensified internal time and self-consciousness. It has been eleven years since Sonya's mother, Vanya's sister, died in *Uncle Vanya* (*Dyadya Vanya*, 1899) and since Doctor Astrov first became a regular visitor to the estate. "But," the family's elderly nanny Marina remarks, "it may be even more . . ." (*A, mozhet, i bol'she . . .*). "Father was given command of a brigade, and we all left Moscow eleven years ago," says Olga, the eldest of Chekhov's "three sisters." "Eleven years have passed but I remember it all as though we left there yesterday."[14] Characters like Vershinin and Tuzenbach philosophize about life in the distant future, and Treplyov about an equally distant past. Treplyov's playlet within *The Seagull* creates a symbolist anamnesis or remembering of life before human life as we know it, the intuited past before the historical past.

The self's response to the charismatic authority of the past—sainted parents in *Three Sisters* and *The Cherry Orchard*, sacred places like Moscow and sacred objects like Gayev's bookcase—is one of childlike wonder and reverence. This response is geared not solely to these icons but to the world they anchored, a world in which the child's, now the dreamer's, centrality was assumed. Ranevskaya's first line in *The Cherry Orchard* is "The nursery!" (*Detskaya!*), which linguistically is closer to "childhood" (*detstvo*) and "childish" (*detsky*) in Russian than in English.[15] The play begins and ends in this room. The characters in both *Three Sisters* and *The Cherry Orchard* attempt to recreate festive parties in which their charismatic authority centripetally draws ardent suitors and past time to them. The irony is that the guests at these parties are no longer the stuff of youthful dreams, but, as is the case with the Postal Clerk and Stationmaster in *The Cherry Orchard*, human chronometers of modern, linear time, the time that has passed and is passing the protagonists by.

The memory-making and selective memory loss of Chekhov's characters, their utopian and nostalgic reveries, are consistent with their compulsion to role-play. Chekhov's modernist "simultaneism" (Guillaume Apollinaire's term) is embodied in dramatic characters, who, like Gogol's liar Khlestakov, conflate and misquote times and texts.[16] In *The Cherry Orchard*, for example, Lopakhin commands Varya, "Okhmelia, get thee to a nunnery" (226). In this misquoting of *the* classic intellectual text, Chekhov underscores the class slippage and confusion and attendant self-conscious role-playing of his day, which keeps the anti-Hamletian Lopakhin and the nunlike Varya from building a real future together.

In order to impress the maidservant Dunyasha, who is poorly acting a role from French romantic fiction, Yepikhodov drops into his conversation a reference to H. T. Buckle's *The History of Civilization in England*. Buckle's history, published in two volumes between 1857 and 1861, was popular with young Russian intellectuals of the 1860s and early 1870s but was woefully outdated by the *fin de siècle*. In his quasi-scientific history, Buckle denounced human reliance upon chance and subjectivity. He posited a possible linkage of historical process with "the progressive affirmation of personality," a theory which Chekhov displaced from character to time. The period 1861–1904 saw the breakup of the old class system (serfdom) and the beginnings of a process which would vest spectral authority in the lower classes. Eschewing both social illusionism and romantic individualism, Chekhov trained his "objective" gaze on an ineffable constant which the turn of the century, the scientific community, new philosophy, and perhaps his own pressing intimations of mortality brought more clearly into focus—the "complete personality" of time.[17]

Nineteenth-century historicism claimed to know real time. Modernist time proclaimed a new reality of its own. One year *after* the Moscow Art Theatre (MAT) premiered *The Cherry Orchard*, Einstein observed in his Special Theory of Relativity that "time and space are not only relative for the movement of objects, but also for the observer who carries his own time and space with him."[18] Henri Bergson, whose work on human perception and consciousness was popular among Russian intellectuals ca. 1900–1910, would eventually say (in *Durée et simultaneité*, 1922) that relativity destroys nominally "universal" time, producing and revealing a multiplicity of inner or subjective times. These inner or subjective times only reconstitute themselves into a unity of time in a fourth dimension of space-time.[19] In *The Cherry Orchard*, Chekhov anticipated this, as well as P. D. Uspensky's insight, expressed in *The Fourth Dimension* (*Chetvyortoe izmerenie*, 1909) and in *Tertium Organum* (1911), that while relativity empowered the human perception of time and space our finite and incomplete experiencing of these dimensions created an illusion of motion and change which conditioned expectations and reconditioned human fate. The true reality is constant and immobile, a historical and conditional montage of actualities and possibilities.

Vladimir Alexandrov contextualizes Uspensky's theories in terms of "the broad stream of syncretic mysticism that appeared in Europe during the last quarter of the nineteenth century with the theosophy of Yelena Petrovna Blavatskaya ('Madame Blavatsky')." The theosophic movement, writes Alexandrov, "fed into the revival of religious and mystical speculation in Russia around the turn of the century." Uspensky's credo of transcendence from the material world to the "higher dimensions" of being, that is, the noumenal world, was also in part intended as a critique of Darwinian evolution. Mimicry, and all else in Uspensky's construction, demonstrates human uniqueness and spontaneity, and not the logical result of an unfolding biological plan. Uspensky's view of humankind is epiphanic and theatrical (he acknowledged the influence of Nikolay Yevreinov's studies of the theatricalization of life), rather than linear and Euclidean.

Chekhov answered Uspensky's call for science "[to] come to mysticism." Drawing on Russian symbolism and no doubt on Nikolay Lobachevsky's non-Euclidean "imaginary geometry" (first published as "On the Principles of Geometry," in *The Kazan Messenger* in 1829), Chekhov sought to escape not to reinforce old (notions of) time. Although Uspensky rejected Lobachevsky's work for ignoring the higher dimensions of time, Chekhov was able to reconcile the two men's temporal and spatial dynamics on the stage, which temporalizes the individual and immobilizes time in a recurring spatialized present.[20] At a time in Russian culture when "reality" was not only suspect but becoming increasingly unknowable (or, conversely, knowable in a plethora of conflicting forms and conceptual strategies),

Chekhov sought, as would Proust, to comprehend the indivisible reality of "his whole mind."

Proust viewed the railway station as an objective correlative to the wholeness of the mental journey, a locus of universal symbology and quotidian particulars. In *The Cherry Orchard*, Chekhov did the same, allowing the temporal flow of the railroad journey to frame and pervade visible space, while deploying its visible form, the railroad and the station, offstage. *The Cherry Orchard* captures what Roger Shattuck, in reference to Proust's art, calls "coenesthesia," that is, "the organic sensation of existence, released by a full encounter with music." Music is the most direct artistic notation of time, an awareness also expressed by Vsevolod Meyerhold in his critical interpretation of *The Cherry Orchard*'s third-act "symphonic" movement and structure. In this act, news of the offstage sale of the cherry orchard to the merchant Lopakhin intrudes upon the onstage party being held on Ranevskaya's estate. Chekhov's most prominent symbolic linkage of music and time, the sound of the breaking or snapped string (*zvuk lopnuvshey struny*), bisects and concludes the play. Like his other symbolic notations of time, the train and the orchard, it pervades scenic space without being physically contained by it.

Chekhov affords the breaking string, which is also his most grandiose purely temporal notation, a full range of alternative responses by both Euclidean and non-Euclidean thinkers in the play and in the theatre auditorium. Lopakhin rationalizes the sound in terms of space and causality, the result of a bucket falling down a mineshaft, "somewhere very far away" (224). Firs links the sound to personal and historical memory, to the time before "the troubles," that is, before the freeing of the serfs. Gayev and Trofimov regard it as a portent organic to nature, a heron or an owl's cry. Ranevskaya thinks it "unpleasant somehow" (*nepriyatno pochemy-to*, 224), by which she means unsettling. Gayev and Ranevskaya possess the "emotional clairvoyance" which Uspensky ascribed to the "non-Euclidean" mind.[21] Gayev's and Ranevskaya's metaphysical self-possession makes up for their material dispossession, their money and linear time running out. Their evocation of and response to other hidden sights and sounds in the play suggest that without their presence the breaking string could not be heard by any of the other characters.

The breaking string embodies the *fin de siècle*'s peculiar energy and identity of eventful noneventfulness.[22] Like the orchard, it is an image of time that is unfixed in history and unfixed as a symbol. In this, it is unlike Chekhov's earlier pervasive symbol, the seagull, which becomes stuffed and self-parodying within its dramatic context. The breaking string and the cherry orchard are metonyms of the destruction of history and the suspension of real time by private consciousness. This consciousness is likewise conveyed through the play's dominant color, white (white blossoms, rooms, billiard ball), which at the *fin de siècle* signified apocalypse. Chekhov used his sound, color, and temporal symbols to express the transformation of reality into the "dazzling, brutal energy" of abstraction. This abstraction may in turn symbolize *fin de siècle* anxiety over the subversion and inversion of concrete or known and accepted categories of time and space, class, self and other.[23] Chekhov managed to quote this condition symbolically, without succumbing, as had Treplyov, to the charismatic authority of his symbols. Chekhov realized in advance Proust's formula of being "real without being actual, ideal without being abstract."[24] This formula presumed and expressed a linkage between the "whole mind" of the self and "the complete personality of time," which together obviated otherness.

Chekhov's plays refract rather than reflect social reality. In his work, the provincial estate serves as a locus for a multiplicity of class and character memories and myths, including the timeless idyll of gentry life. Nineteenth-century memoirs, the fiction of Aleksandr Pushkin, Sergey Aksakov, Ivan Goncharov, and Ivan Turgenev, and the social criticism of Vissarion Belinsky, Nikolay Chernyshevsky, Nikolay Dobrolyubov and Aleksandr Herzen established the gentry home as the Kremlin of "superfluous" people and unproductive or dream time. Nabokov described the gentry home as having been one huge dream: "the masses slept—figuratively; the intellectuals spent sleepless nights—literally—sitting up and talking about things, or just meditating until five in the morning and then going out for a walk." Aleksandr Blok likened the timeless reality of his family estate at Shakhmatovo to a "landscape of the soul," symbolic of Russia, with her songs ringing with "prison despair."[25]

These impressions were conditioned by real historical circumstances. The tsars traditionally dispersed properties granted to the gentry for administrative service in order to guard against conspiracy and insurrection. Landowners were often kept on the move between their widely scattered properties to prevent them from becoming rooted in a particular area and overly familiar with the local population. This geographic and social isolation, together with the memory of enforced, lifelong state service from which they were gradually freed in the 1730s–1750s, made the landed gentry largely apolitical.

The dissolution of the socioeconomic caste system based on serfdom impoverished the gentry and transformed the lack of initiative conditioned by former wealth into fatalism.[26]

Chekhov employs the otherness of estate life, floating free from a broad social and precise temporal context at the *fin de siècle*, to represent the otherness of time. This usage is clearly focused in the brief scene between the gentry (and their visitors and retainers) and the Passerby (an exact translation of *Prokhozhy* in Russian) in act 2 of *The Cherry Orchard*. Critics argue in general that the Passerby embodies either an unemployed former serf or a dispossessed landowner. Laurence Senelick suggests that the Passerby's quotation of an N. A. Nekrasov poem ("Brother of mine, suffering brother . . . ") is meant to draw the other characters back to real time in the real present. Although Lenin later labeled Nekrasov's poetry "classic," Chekhov, Senelick notes, employed it as a "sign of insincerity and fake social conscience." Herbert Blau theorizes that the Passerby represents the revolutionary prescience or future-inscribed reality that was announced two years earlier in Gorky's *The Lower Depths* (*Na dne*, 1902). Whatever the character himself represents, his appearance frames in a particular historical moment the otherness of estate life to the outside world (in society and the theatre auditorium) and the otherness of the world outside to the estate's residents. However, in the same moment, the Passerby, whose entrance is cued by the sound of the breaking string, introduces unprecedented, unfamiliar, messianic-apocalyptic time. This may explain why the antimessianic Chekhov is so quick to get rid of him. The presence of the Passerby alerts, stimulates, and terrorizes the present with static images of the past and the future, while also suggesting, along with his name, that time passes by.[27]

The Cherry Orchard begins and ends with two former serfs, the *nouveau riche* Lopakhin and the still voluntarily indentured Firs, performing the habit of sleep. This action appears to embody the "typically Russian" condition of sluggishness or "oblomovism" (*oblomovshchina*), Nikolay Dobrolyubov's critical coinage derived from Ivan Goncharov's 1859 novel *Oblomov*. The book's slumbering antihero continuously relives in dreams the nostalgic childhood idyll of innocently happy egoism and all-consuming mother-love, instead of confronting the frustrations and disappointments of adult social life.

Slumbering in their chairs, Firs and Lopakhin embody social myths—the sputtering, erratic myth of the past and the not yet fully evolved or tested myth of the future. At the same time, they perform oblomovism secondhand—as a literary convention rather than as a social norm—consistent with the role-playing that occurs throughout the play. However, by allowing the future (Lopakhin) to sleep while the past (the family) arrives offstage at the beginning of the play, Chekhov subverts social assumptions about productive and unproductive time.[28] The agents of "the past" surprise the agent of "the future," who is not alert enough to anticipate or understand the recurrence of the past in the internal time of subjective consciousness. In the logic of the play, Lopakhin's attempt to rouse the gentry from their dreams to save the orchard is doomed by the social reality in which time passes. However, that social reality is obviated by the inner life of dreams in which time does not so much pass as pool. In *The Cherry Orchard*, Chekhov transforms the antisocial oblomovism of the gentry home, a possible metaphor for the "introverted egoism" of the intelligentsia (which historically derived from the gentry), into a rapprochement between the self and the world. In so doing, Chekhov anticipated by three years Bergson's *Creative Evolution* (*L'Evolution créatrice*, 1907), one of whose goals was "to show that the Whole is of the same nature as the self, and that we can understand it by achieving a deeper and more complete understanding of the self."[29] In *The Cherry Orchard*, Chekhov offers the dreaming self of the exile, the intellectual, or gentry estate-dweller as a possible conduit through which to achieve a revolutionized socio-spiritual "Whole."

Lopakhin's dream of the future and the gentry's dream of the past both seem to radiate from the orchard. But the orchard facilitates rather than determines the fates of the characters by solidifying their experience of time. The cherry orchard is a false mnemonic device, a memory which erases history. The orchard's destruction—it is destroyed because its *immaterial* (that is, incorporeal) value is not transferable—does not destroy the past, which Chekhov saw more as a renewable lease than as a historical foreclosure. Likewise, the destruction of the orchard does not seal the future, which would require either destroying the past or mythically reconfiguring it as the Bolsheviks did after 1917.

The Cherry Orchard's two performance modes of personal fate—chance and choice—reveal the spectral presence of an ineffable universe, a universe of time, whose *a priori* meaning is neither capricious nor fully subject to existential control. Chekhovian fate is not, as Robert Louis Jackson suggests, a largely negative capability, that is, an autonomous presence affirmed by his characters' abnegation of personal responsibility for their lives and the lives of others (the conventional "loss of the cherry orchard" theme).[30] The category of chance includes Gayev's and Ranevskaya's fiscal irresponsibility and Simeonov-Pishchik's consignment of his life to luck. His estate *is* saved when white clay is fortuitously discovered on his land. The category of choice includes Lopakhin as an agent-issue of natural selection, who pursues Ranevskaya in order to bring the future within the characters' collective grasp. Charlotta Ivanovna's existential life performance (the *salto mortale* or leap for life) and magic act seek to domesticate chance, to transform it into a game, a card trick, where the odds can be fixed and the results predicted. Charlotta's uncomprehending assistant in this "trick" is Pishchik, who chases after her in a state of amazed eroticism or, in Nietzschean terms, aroused will.

After Chekhov admitted having failed as a Tolstoyan optimist, Tolstoy feared that he (Chekhov) had become a Nietzschean pessimist. Such was not the case.[31] Chekhov's plays parodically transmuted Nietzschean *amor fati*, much as they did symbolism, which their author similarly could neither wholly reject nor embrace. In *The Cherry Orchard*, the perennially fundless and irresponsible landowner Simeonov-Pishchik plans finally to take control of his life by forging banknotes, because his daughter Dashenka read in Nietzsche that "it is possible" (339). Pishchik draws the Queen of Spades, the "fate" card in Russian culture (after Pushkin's fatalistic gambling tale "The Queen of Spades," *Pikovaya dama*, 1833), from the deck of Charlotta Ivanovna, the German governess.

The true dialectic in Chekhov's plays, according to Bert O. States, is between the single voice of the "disorganized soul" and the "reactionary echo of silence in reality," the universal and ironic "nonresponse of the world." Indeed, one finds this in Gayev's bookcase, in the breaking string, and in the past which theoretically refuses to revive, except through the experiencing of personal loss (for example, the drowning of Ranevskaya's son Grisha). However, Chekhovian "whiteness" denotes not absence and nonresponse so much as what Vasily Kandinsky called in painting "the harmony of silence . . . pregnant with possibilities." Echoes in which the solitary voice hears only itself, like recurrence, in which arrivals and departures seem to reframe monotony to deepen the awareness of things that do not change and people who do not move, reveal the profound reciprocity between the self (private consciousness) and the world. Personal objects and family heirlooms like Gayev's bookcase are metonyms of time's and the play's retentive consciousness, which the breaking string more broadly contains. Within this landscape of time, people actively retrieve and create memory, opening a gap between what is said and done, dreamed and accomplished, between what fate determines and what determines fate. Chekhov was not a fatalist, but he did not disown fate as a self-made component of the natural and human condition. We make our fates as we make our time(s). Fate is not sealed time, unless we make it so.[32]

For Chekhov, time was the half-raised curtain which refuses to fall or rise, to predict the past or the future as a sealed fate. In *The Cherry Orchard*, past, present, and future are theoretically contemporaneous. This condition is illustrated in the "myth-historical design," the moving of space's temporal borders, which opens act 2.[33] In act 2, Lopakhin broaches his plan to partition the estate and to erect summer cottages, an idea made possible, as Gayev suggests, by the proximity of the railway line. The train, as physical presence and as the invisible trajectory of new time, intersects Chekhov's largely figurative space and reveals its hidden order of human intention and mythic design. Accordingly, Chekhov rejected V. A. Simov's original scenic design at MAT, which favorably suggested to Stanislavsky the traditional landscape paintings of I. L. Levitan (1860–1900). Chekhov was particularly insistent that the road and the field look real and that the urban vista look unusually distant for the stage, undoubtedly to contextualize the abstract, disquieting fracture of the breaking string's first sounding in this act. Chekhov also insisted that if the train appeared onstage, as Stanislavsky suggested, it must be soundless. But although Chekhov defined a railroad presence onstage in the earlier play we now call *Platonov* (1878), which ends with a character collapsing upon the rails, it made no such appearance in *The Cherry Orchard*.[34]

Chekhov's opening stage directions for act 2 depict the town in the background encroaching upon the country in the foreground. Telegraph poles in the distance roughly echo the trees and conceivably the crosses which would be found in the small cemetery and chapel that are also visible onstage. In *Platonov*, the images of the railroad and the telegraph poles were scenically juxtaposed. Chekhov's scenic elements, like the cherry orchard, are extracted and abstracted from life. Ivan Bunin pointed out that orchards of uniformly regular, beautiful, perennially blossoming cherry trees proximate to gentry homes were the stuff of literary myth-making. Bunin knew that his friend Chekhov had quoted this myth in order to dispel not reinforce it. By defining the orchard as the center of a virtual reality, Chekhov was able to recast the components of the visible landscape into changeable and removable symbols. This allowed space to participate more fully in time's overall recasting of reality and identity than the psychological realist Stanislavsky realized was possible.[35]

Also seen in the near distance at the start of act 2 is the road to Gayev's house, the road suggesting what Laurence Senelick calls the "uncongenial vacancy" of dispossession, of spatiotemporal indeterminacy "between past and future, birth and death, being and nothingness." The road, which recurs in Gogol's work as a symbol of freedom, in Chekhov's world represents the perennially unrealized hope of arrival and dread of departure. Into this picture moves the unseen train, evoked by Gayev. It dissects Chekhov's time-lapse image of rural foreground (the past) and urban background (the future), reframing foreground and background together in the audience's mind as a new, harmonic "middle landscape," that is, "a middle ground somewhere 'between,' yet in a transcendent relation to the opposing forces of civilization and nature."[36] This artistic "master image" connotes the modernist moment, in which memory and prediction coexist in the present and urban and rural consciousness interpenetrate without fully dissolving into one another.

Chekhov's figurative landscape also reflected the historical moment in which his play was written. The migration from country to town in Russia was far from complete in 1904. Even those peasants, workers, and foreign landowners who had already moved to town had not yet abandoned the consciousness formed in the country. Despite the radicalizing of the peasantry following the 1905 revolution, the peasants and workers who had moved to the city continued to treat nobles (dvoryane), that is, country-based gentry of any rank or status, with the deference owed to the barin, or lord, "the representative and symbol of privileged Russia."[37] The peasants who brought their class-based deference to the towns and cities, however, left behind them a social order which was already breaking up and a landscape which had already been invaded by urban industry.

By 1900, two-thirds of the gentry in forty-five Russian provinces no longer owned land. The population living in cities and towns grew by 97 percent against a general population increase of 53.3 percent between 1863 and 1897. The "deserted gentry houses and estates" were soon occupied by those enriched by the new urbanization and industrialization, including merchants like Lopakhin and the railroad builders, such as MAT financier Savva Morozov, who helped to realize these merchants' dreams.[38] Therefore, the arrival of the machine or *mashina* (machine; train or car in Russian colloquial speech) in the figurative landscape of Chekhov's play is far more important than the nonarrival of the *deus ex machina* of a financial windfall. This non-arrival was, historically speaking, a *fait accompli*, as was the purchase of the orchard by a merchant or railroad builder. The missed deadlines in the play—the family's late arrival by rail and failure to save the orchard—are less important than the revolutionary but invisible timetable on which the unseen train runs. The train serves as "the moving skeleton" of the play's spatiotemporal form, its analogical net. The railroad timetable, like Einstein's theory of relativity (in Boris Pasternak's analogy), discovers the hidden pattern of a new temporal order in the apparently discrete and discontinuous components of modern life and modernist art.[39]

Again contemporary developments in Russian society yielded Chekhov his dramatic metaphor. In the period between 1898 and 1913, railway traffic increased by two and one-half times in Russia, reaching 128 million people in 1904, the year of *The Cherry Orchard*'s premiere and the 4,000-mile Trans-Siberian Railroad's completion. The great increase in railroad building, especially betweeen 1895 and 1905, was part of an overall national push toward industrialization and owed much to the efforts of Tsar Aleksandr III's minister of finance, Sergey Witte, who had been the minister of transport.[40] The vast majority of passengers (83 million) on all commuter railroads, unsurprisingly, traveled third class, although first-class passengers tended to travel greater distances. The *dachniki* (seasonal country-home dwellers), whom Chekhov depicted in his plays, retraced their former town to country carriage routes by rail in increased numbers during the summer months. All told, Russia produced only 40,000 miles of usable railway line in this period, placing it well behind Europe and the United States.[41]

In Chekhov's short stories, nearly all of which were written prior to 1900, the novelty of railway travel did not compensate for its assorted difficulties—breaks in the lines, tracks, and bridges, delays, great distances from the stations to the towns, and the poor quality of the roads which connected them. Not all of the evidence for railway hardship in Russia at this time is literary. Wooden railroad bridges froze during the long Russian winters, derailing trains and contributing to some 1,500 railroad fatalities in 1900 alone. One-third of this number were railway workers.[42]

In *When Russia Learned to Read*, Jeffrey Brooks notes that in Chekhov's short story "The Criminal" a peasant, accused of causing a train wreck by removing a bolt from the rails to use as a fishing sinker, is unable to comprehend the relationship between cause and effect.[43] The railroad's inscription of a new causality upon the countryside represented a denaturing of rural reality by urban industrial consciousness. The modernization of the largely rural Russian population required the objectification of time, the "mechanization of awareness," which the railway schedule could partially accomplish.

In contributing to demographic shift, the railroad widened the discrepancy in Russian culture "between the supernatural perfection of an imaginary environment and the natural limitations of human life as it is."[44] The introduction of the railroad into the Russian countryside in 1837 had confounded and discomfited many of the simple, God-fearing peasants. Rural folk were accustomed to traveling either overland along difficult dirt roads (on foot and by means of the primitive "drowska," a small carriage) or by boat along the nation's many rivers. Nineteenth-century Russian literature contains images of peasants who perceived the train engine and the series of strung-together carriages and wagons it pulled as an infernal force bent on destroying everything in its path. Thus, the peasant woman Fyoklushka in Aleksandr Ostrovsky's play *The Storm* (*Groza*, 1859) anthropomorphizes the railroad as an iron devil, whose arrival signals to her the end of the world. However, it was not only illiterate, superstitious peasants who reacted in this way. Tolstoy was literally nauseated by train rides, drove his heroine Anna Karenina to suicide "on the rails of progress," and died in a railway station in Astapovo in 1910.[45] He and Dostoyevsky both likened the self-contained, self-powered railroad to atheistic logic. The railroad brought this logic, which the two writers associated with Western materialism, foreign otherness, from the town to the country.[46]

Actually, the Russian government, bearing in mind the invasive potential of the foreign other, originally designed railways to avoid towns, which for purposes of defense had been built on hills and across bodies of water. Thus, the fact that the railway station is twenty versts (one verst equals about two-thirds of a mile) from the town where the Prozorov family lives in *Three Sisters* is not as "strange" as Lieutenant Colonel Vershinin suggests (128). What is strange, Chekhov intimates, is that the Prozorovs never ride this train anywhere, least of all to Moscow.[47]

In Chekhov's world, appearances and apparent motives are deceiving. In his tale "My Life: A Provincial Story" (*Moya zhizn': Rasskaz provintsiala*, 1896), a station is built five versts outside of town not, as noted above, for strategic purposes, but because the engineers responsible sought to inconvenience the local population for failing to offer them a sufficient bribe. A station cut off from the life of a town serves to underscore the isolation of the person responsible for operating it. Similarly, the presence of the railroad which seemingly can go anywhere dramatizes the futility of human beings who cannot or will not travel, except perhaps in consoling dreams.[48]

Chekhov understood this firsthand. In 1898, Chekhov, whose tubercular condition exiled him to Yalta in the Crimean section of southern Russia during the MAT premieres of his plays, wrote a hopeful letter to his brother Mikhail. In it, he repeated a rumor he had heard that a railway line connecting Yalta with Moscow and himself with civilization would soon be built. But although Chekhov's brother-in-law, railroad engineer Konstantin Knipper (Chekhov's wife was MAT actress Olga Knipper), was responsible for approving proposed railway sites through the Crimea, the railroad did not come to Yalta in Chekhov's lifetime. Stuck in internal exile, four to five days *by mail* from Moscow, he dreamed of recapturing his good health and with it Moscow. Chekhov reached Moscow for the last time as a corpse in a railroad car marked "Fresh Oysters,"[49] an anticharismatic arrival which he might have conceived for himself.

Even at the outset, railroads and railway travel had their ardent supporters in Russia. Catriona Kelly has illustrated that the advent of the railroads was celebrated in Russian popular culture (for example, *balagan* or fairground entertainments) as a miracle. The railroad seemed equally miraculous to intellectuals of the politically pivotal generations of 1840, 1860, and 1910. Belinsky recognized the railroad as a harbinger and agent of economic progress.[50] Lenin viewed railroads and electric power stations as the magical agents in Russia's transformation into a modern nation. Like Chekhov, Lenin's opinion of the railroad was formed from personal experience. In his years in exile between 1904 and 1917, Lenin shuttled by rail from St. Petersburg/Petrograd to Kuokkala (site of a Russian artists' colony, two hours away in Finland), Stockholm, Berlin, Munich, Geneva, London, Paris, Prague, Cracow, Berne, and finally Zurich. Here the rumor of revolution reached him from Petrograd.[51] Lenin's deviously heroic journey helped define an underground network for modern revolutionaries and helped foster a body of Russian railway literature, extending from the early 1900s through the 1950s, in which trains themselves were sometimes heroes.[52] Lenin's journey into exile and secret return to Petrograd in a sealed train car recalled Russian folktales in which the hero is "carried away through the air," generally on a horse or a goose and returns home "unrecognized." At the conclusion of *The Seagull*, Treplyov has a premonition of Nina Zarechnaya's secret return. Nina has registered, one assumes anonymously, at a railway hotel. Affordable and accessible to the train which will quickly bear her away, Nina's lodgings parody in their homelessness her earlier escape in search of love and fame. Nina's return from exile, like Chekhov's but unlike Lenin's, is anticharismatic.[53]

Lenin mastered exile and the road. He embodied the optimistic, outward-looking reversal of the romantic author and literary antihero as "fated man," who, like Turgenev's nihilist Bazarov in *Fathers and Children* (*Ottsy i deti*, 1862), not only fails to change society but dies and is buried in one of Russia's "far corners."[54] Lenin, who derived his "fated man" status retrospectively from history rather than prospectively from literature, was successful in his journey through the disjointed, universalized space and time of exile, in the timeliness of his arrival and the timelessness of his life beyond physical death (a theme to which I return in chapters 5 and 6).

Wherever it traveled, the railroad disrupted social logic, inviting subjective, even mythic reconstructions of time. In post-Victorian England, Sherlock Holmes's adventures were often timed to the arrivals and departures listed in *Bradshaw's Guide* (*to Railway and Steam Navigation for Great Britain and Ireland*). In France, Proust's narrative persona in *A la recherche du temps perdu* (1913–1927) would later note that "since railways came into existence, the necessity of not missing trains has taught us to take account of minutes, whereas among the ancient Romans, who not only had a more cursory acquaintance with astronomy but led less hurried lives, the notion not only of minutes but even of fixed hours barely existed."[55] In Russia, Pasternak saw the railroad as an image of historical time reshaping itself "in a period of national crisis and heightened consciousness." In 1922, he declared the railway schedule to be "grander than Holy Scripture."[56]

In the Russian country(side), where time and distance were more a matter of imprecise oral communication (the Russian word *seychas* denotes an indeterminate "now") than of "objective authority," the experiencing of time differed among classes but also between individuals of the same social class. Chekhov demonstrated in his short stories and plays that although a person's methods of relocating the self in dislocated time may be class-conditioned and class-coded, the primary factor in all cases remains how the individual imaginatively reconstructs and reexperiences time. By employing the arrival and departure of a train linking town and country as the framing action of *The Cherry Orchard*, Chekhov grounded his meditation upon the nature of time in a set of social and historical circumstances which foreground the passage of time.

The major temporal dialogue in *The Cherry Orchard* is between the urban timetable of the railroad, which begins and ends the play, and the rural timetable of the agrarian seasonal cycle, which gives the play its act structure. Lopakhin, whom historian Richard Stites calls an "ineffectual Taylorist" (after Frederick Winslow Taylor, 1856– 1915), cannot get the characters in the play to conform to the new schedule. Despite Lopakhin's warning to them that "time waits for no one," he must conform to their expanded schedule of waiting and desultory action and inaction.[57]

Lopakhin is anxious over the family's train being late (a motif that echoes the opening of *Fathers and Children*). The fact that the train is two hours late may discomfit Lopakhin, but it can hardly surprise him. Ranevskaya has already illustrated to his dissatisfaction her indifference or insensitivity not only to schedules and deadlines but also to the passage of time. He believes that Lyubov's return to the estate five years after the drowning of her son Grisha is *five years late*. Her lateness conflates in Lopakhin's mind with the imminence of the cherry orchard's sale and her avoidance of this topic. The play's first two major temporal statements are Lopakhin's concerning the train and Varya's concerning the estate's sale.

Gayev wonders aloud how a train whose temporal being is directed by a system, a timetable, can be two hours late. One may easily read in this statement Gayev's dissatisfaction with modern technology—or rather his satisfaction in noting the failure of modern technology to conform to its own schedules. More significantly, Gayev is expressing his and Ranevskaya's internal experiencing of time which cannot be precisely calibrated in a linear fashion, as a chronology of discrete past and future events filling and emptying space. Ranevskaya "mistakes" a white sapling bent over in the orchard for the figure of her dead mother. In her world, a parent's death naturally conflates with an orchard's imminent loss, and the living presences of both are great within her.

In order to assess the two major temporal modes, linear and durative, which Chekhov employs in his play, consider this brief piece of

seemingly misdirected dialogue between Gayev and Lopakhin, which
occurs in act 1 (203):

> Lopakhin: Yes, time passes.
> Gayev: What's that?
> Lopakhin: Time, I say, passes.
> Gayev: And this place smells of patchouli.

Lopakhin's observation concerning time interrupts Gayev's remembrance of how as children he and Ranevskaya used to sleep in the
nursery, which has not changed, although he has. He has grown up.
Gayev, who was led into this remembrance by his imaginary game of
billiards, is playing a four-dimensional game in time and will not enter
into the less compelling three-dimensional game that Lopakhin offers.

Chekhov demonstrates in the structure of this brief passage that
Lopakhin's statement concerning time should be self-evident and requires no direct response. Gayev's absentminded "What's that?"
compels Lopakhin to enact the passage of time through his reworking of the statement "time passes" as "Time, I say, passes." In the
process, Lopakhin unknowingly imbues time with personal consciousness, present time flowing to the past ("Time passes" [*Vremya
idyot*]) and past time flowing to the present ("Time, I say, [that is,
I repeat/have already said] passes" [*Vremya, dogovoryu, idyot*]).
Gayev's sensory reference to patchouli not only undercuts Lopakhin's
quasi-philosophical musing, which is consistent with the merchant's
anti-Hamlet line of business in the play, but also suggests the synesthesia which the play creates and in which Gayev participates. Time
not only passes; it recalls the past in a smell. In his play, Chekhov
retains the pathos of time's passage, remembrance, loss, and difference, the drama of past, present, and future, played out in objects—
bookcases and orchards—people and events. However, he overlays
this with the coenesthesia of recurrence, recreation, and reexperienc-
ing. Individual characters represent an impatience with one or the
other temporal conception to illustrate what we deny ourselves in understanding for the sake of nominal coherence.[58]

All of Chekhov's characters embrace what is necessary to them and
with this some measure of self-delusion. In fact, there sometimes appears to be little difference between the delusion about self and the
higher intuition about time that Chekhov vests in his dramatic protagonists. Consider Chekhov's three sisters, who cannot see themselves

accurately, but whose surname, Prozorov (from *prozorlivy*, meaning "perspicacious"), tells us that they see beyond the present. Their name is both ironic and appropriate. "The removal of the desired object to an enormous distance," in their case Moscow, is achieved by journeying into a self-consciousness that is more profoundly desired and real than real life. Real life becomes bathetically self-confessional and inert. The physical act of leaving is only "accomplished in intent," and goals seem attainable only "by fate: through omen and portent." The subjective self-empowerment of human consciousness and insight becomes absolute.[59]

In *The Cherry Orchard*, Chekhov clarified time as a theatrical problem by giving a harder edge to unseen or only partially seen physical elements. Of these elements, only the train, a "self-enclosed ensemble of origin and destination," captured society's mixture of hope and dread at the advent of modern times and modern time. The train mechanically denatured material reality and "cut off nature from the outside world." Inherently "sealed" (as myth says that Lenin's train was in 1917), it is absolute, yet renders all else relative in spatio-temporal terms. The train's lateness in *The Cherry Orchard* suspends narrative (that is, chronological time) and with it "the coercive nature of plot," in favor of Bergsonian *durée*, which transpires outside the narrative flow of history. Despite the Soviets' co-opting of *The Cherry Orchard* as part of their (proto)revolutionary canon, Chekhov here denied plot, prescience, and directional time.[60]

The gentry's language of indecision and distractedness in *The Cherry Orchard* is symptomatic of an inner negotiation of individual times and spaces to which they do and do not belong, out of which they are configuring a new whole. Their apparent fixation on the universal myth of the past signals their process (at which they will eventually succeed) of becoming unstuck from the historical past as a discrete spatiotemporal unit of lingering and debilitating memory. This process internalizes the play's central action and overall design, which in turn embodies the *fin de siècle* dialectic between nineteenth-century historicism and twentieth-century modernism. Chekhovian reality sought to embody "the Absolute which contains a world of differences" and which opposes the Russian and later the Soviet messianic "culture of last things."[61]

Lenin, who in 1917 realized this "culture of last things," read Chekhov's short stories, first published in journals as early as 1892, while working as a lawyer in the village of Samara. This was five years after his expulsion from the University of Kazan for participating in a revolutionary student circle and his subsequent internal exile under police surveillance. Lenin was attracted to Chekhov's serf origins and provincial upbringing. Chekhov, like Lenin, denounced "bourgeois *poshlost'* [gaudy bad taste born of moral indolence], boorish egoism, greed." Like Lenin's favorite authors, Goethe and Gorky, Chekhov lyrically extolled human value. Above all, Lenin appreciated "the experiential truth and precision of [Chekhov's] language."

Lenin's letters home during his early exile, circa 1892–1904, requested information and newspaper clippings regarding Chekhov's MAT premieres and expressed regret at being unable to attend them personally. In the first two years following his return from exile (1917–1919), Lenin became a regular visitor to MAT, catching up with the Chekhov productions he had missed. *Uncle Vanya*, which Lenin saw at MAT on 24 February 1920, was the most frequently performed of Chekhov's plays in Russia, 1917–1920. Some memoirs, especially those by Russian emigrés, have suggested that, in spite of Nadezhda Krupskaya's testimony to the contrary, her husband actually disliked Chekhov's plays at MAT after 1917. There are several possible explanations for this apparent discrepancy. The utilitarianism of Lenin's taste in art may have been sharpened by exile to the exclusion of apolitical *belles lettres*. Also, his mental image of Chekhov's fictional world may have been too acute for MAT or any theatre to realize in production. Finally, it is possible that Lenin's true opinion of Chekhov's plays and/or MAT's productions of them was misread by some or all of his interpreters. Whatever the case, Lenin took from Chekhov's work the politically "useful" characters and plots he needed and ignored the more profound subtext of nonpartisan revolutionary time.[62]

Both Chekhov and Lenin dramatized the themes of exile's return and liberation from the confines of history as old time. However, Chekhov also derailed myth, whereas Lenin set it back upon its course. Lenin's journey to Petrograd from Berlin on 3 April 1917 brought the future (utopian time) to the past (historical time), the outside to the inside, the border to the center, and in March 1918 shifted the center itself from Petrograd back to the old capital of Moscow. Arriving a decade earlier than Lenin, Chekhov's train sought to release the intelligentsia from myth and memory in a play which counterfeited historically driven social evolution. Chekhov's parodic ritual of repeated arrival (and departure) subverted historical eventfulness, whereas Lenin's extraordinary arrival monumentalized it. Chekhov's road veered sharply away from the Russian tradition of debilitating romanticism and messianism, while Lenin's road turned even more sharply back to it.

Lenin's train transformed Russians into temporal indicators of either the recalcitrant past or the glorious future (a process later co-opted by Stalin). By 1917, those members of the intelligentsia who optimistically welcomed the Bolshevik revolution all but thoroughly demonized the self as being an inner void. Aleksandr Blok, whose play *The Little Showbooth* (*Balaganchik*, 1906) was a "mea culpa" for intellectual self-absorption, dreamed of being able to stop thinking, thus erasing the intellectual's *raison d'être*. Blok wrote in April 1917, "If I were they [the state leaders], I'd hang the whole lot of us [the intelligentsia]."[63] Another of Blok's images from 1917 depicted members of the intelligentsia, stranded for so long on a freezing railway platform that "when their train at last came in, they had hardly the strength to board it and no desire left to travel." Although true from a Marxist-Leninist historical perspective, this image is more important as an example of intellectual self-loathing, which had been carried over from the last years of the previous century.[64]

History as linear time and revolutionary engine seemed to validate the Bolshevik path (*put'*) as a modernization of romantic thought.[65] The train came literally to embody the revolution and the whistle on the train to represent "the new person." "When the trains stop," Lenin proclaimed, "that will be the end!" That *was* in fact the end for Tsar Nikolay II, whose train was stopped on its tracks by Russian railway workers in 1917, forcing him to abdicate by telegram. The Nikolayev Railway, which ran between St. Petersburg and Moscow and which had derailed the first Nikolay in 1856, was renamed the October Railway after the 1917 revolution. The first railway plan approved by the tsar was ironically called the 1917 Five-Year Plan, anticipating in its terminology both Lenin and Stalin.[66]

The journey of the center from St. Petersburg/Petrograd to Moscow is marked at its point of origin both by Falconet's statue of Peter the Great on horseback overlooking the Neva River and by the statue of Lenin standing atop his armored car (*bronevik*) at the Finland Station (fig. 1). David M. Bethea has noted that artists raised in the shadow of Falconet's apocalyptic statue of Peter (the centerpiece of Pushkin's narrative poem "The Bronze Horseman," *Medny vsadnik*, written 1833, published 1837) wrote self-consciously of imminent border crossings and of expected unexpected arrivals. In 1917, the machine-man (Lenin/the Bolshevik) unseated the mounted rider (tsar) as heroic icon, and the railroad arrived as revolutionary symbol.[67] The myth of

FIGURE I
Statue of Lenin at the Finland Station, St. Petersburg, 1926.
Courtesy of Sovfoto/Eastfoto.

human incapacity in the face of immeasurable distance, which Russian writers like Chekhov had addressed, was seemingly dispelled. But in the same instant a new myth of superhuman agency capable of collapsing and even erasing distances in space, time, and consciousness and replacing them with a universal sociopolitical logic arrived.

CHAPTER 2

ARTISTS AND MODELS

Again — to love Her in heaven

And betray Her on earth . . .

— Aleksandr Blok

There are two Hamlets — one is called Hamlet,

the other Ophelia.

— Michael Chekhov[1]

In the epilogue to Andrey Bely's *Petersburg*, a novel which looked back at the period of the failed 1905 revolution, the radical *intelligent* Nikolay Apollonovich Ableukhov traveled to Egypt, where he sat reading the *Book of the Dead* at the base of the sphinx. There he realized that, as an Asiatic European, he was "himself a pyramid, the summit of a culture which will crash into ruins." The former Egyptian capital of Alexandria, named after Alexander of Macedonia, whom Nikolay Berdyayev credited with uniting the East and the West, represented for Russian poets a culturally syncretic model which they could apply to their divided personal and national (European-Asiatic) character.[2] Silver Age intellectuals, who regularly gathered at the stone replicas of the ancient sphinxes bordering Petersburg's Neva River, did more than conflate the necropolises of Alexandria and Petersburg, Eastern mysticism and Western rationalism. They acknowledged the watchful presence of fate in their culture and in the self-conscious construction of their creative and class personae, poised upon the brink of extinction.[3]

Petersburg, which Bely described as "the meeting [place] of Greece and Christ," was the stage upon which the less cynical among the Russian intelligentsia played the role of the divided and reconstituted "suffering god." Their inspirational text was Vyacheslav Ivanov's treatise "The Hellenic Religion of the Suffering God" (*Ellinskaya re-*

ligiya stradayushchego boga), which legitimized existential agony as an elitist communal myth. Those like Aleksandr Blok who were unable to perform anything but their disillusionment found their models not in Dionysus and Christ but in Hamlet and Pierrot.[4]

Blok seemed to construe the sphinx's instruction "Guess, or I devour you" not as an intellectual challenge but as a sign that the time for self-absorbed contemplation was at an end.[5] Blok, whose first diary entry for 1901 read, "I have split in two," "feared the two-facedness of [his] soul," which made him feel socially irrelevant, like "a corpse . . . among people." He quoted and identified with Heinrich Heine's expression of the sophisticated, paradoxical, self-questioning, and self-imprisoning mind: "I do not know where irony ends and heaven begins."[6]

By the time Blok wrote, "We are awaiting a whirlwind; I want reality" (25 June 1905), Russia had weathered a storm. Between 1902 and 1905, two consecutive interior ministers, Sipyagin and Plehve, along with the tsar's second cousin and brother-in-law the Grand Duke Sergey, the governor-general of Moscow, were assassinated. Russia had suffered a series of humiliating defeats in its war with Japan. Soldiers, sailors, and peasants revolted. Railway, factory, newspaper, and electrical workers, as well as students, went out on strike. On what came to be known as "Bloody Sunday" (22 January 1905), tsarist police massacred 130 workers, wounding several hundred more, who, under the influence of the charismatic priest and "adventurer" Father George Gapon, had come to petition the tsar at the Winter Palace in St. Petersburg for increased civil liberties and economic relief. The revolution of 1905, "the first mass rising against the [tsarist] regime in the history of Russia" and a "dress rehearsal" for 1917, brought terrorism into twentieth-century Russian politics, often perpetrated by and against the intelligentsia. The beleaguered self and state circa 1905 reflected and precipitated divided loyalties and negative unities among intellectuals, who both hoped for reintegration into a new society and were resigned to political and especially spiritual defeat.[7]

For creative intellectuals who felt entitled by the *fin de siècle* to know and even choose their personal and cultural fates, 1905 was a year of profound disappointment.[8] The poet Osip Mandelstam compared "Bloody Sunday" to a medieval mystery play. For Blok, whose future friend and rival for his wife's love, Andrey Bely, arrived in Petersburg on this day, the memory of "Bloody Sunday" combined tragedy with irony. To Blok, who led the descent into irony among creative intellectuals beginning in 1905, it seemed clearer than before that, although the life of his society was phenomenologically real, it lacked spiritual meaning for the artist. Conversely, although art was meaningful to its creators, it was not real to its society. It did not reach the people. It did not change anything. A general feeling of helplessness among Russian intellectuals, exacerbated by the political repression which followed Nikolay II's disbanding of the Second Duma on 3 June 1907, produced a wave of suicides in 1907–1908. To the members of intellectual elite fell the seemingly unnecessary burden of creating sphinxlike questions and symbolic mysteries that only they could decipher.

The creative intellectual, who cast himself in the role of suffering actor/god, cast as his nemesis the self-deluding, self-consuming (female) muse. The beneficent (divine) and malevolent (carnal) faces of the muse, the *femme fragile* and the *femme fatale*, were conceived by men and often adapted and subverted by the women who played them. These roles expressed the creative intelligentsia's fatalistic "will to death" disguised as beauty, engendered by the conflicting influences of the *fin de siècle* and the delayed *mal du siècle* of 1905.[9]

Male artists of the Silver Age translated their social disempowerment into a hopeful/hopeless metaphysics of passive expectancy. This condition in part arose from and was embodied by one particular image of the *femme fragile* or Eternal Feminine, the Divine Sophia (Sophia, the Divine Wisdom). Vladimir Solovyov first sighted Sophia, in the form of an ethereal woman, in an eleventh-century icon in Novgorod, then in the library of the British Museum, and finally near the pyramids in the desert outside Cairo. Later, he fashioned this recurring vision into a theoretical construct of messianic deliverance, a Second Coming in female form. Solovyov asserted that the Divine Sophia promised to break the mortal "habit" of human life on earth. This habit was set in motion when "the created world" of human autonomy broke away from "the uncreated world" of God's direct spiritual dominion.

Aside from representing another mask of the Eternal Feminine, the Divine Sophia was a paraphrase of elements in the Holy Trinity. She also embodied the ideal of androgyny as a sign of spiritual wholeness (the reintegration of the self and the other), derived from the Kabbala and Christian gnosticism and coincident with Vyacheslav Ivanov's Dionysiac cult. Dionysus, the androgynous god of revelry, excess, and madness, "liberates the female in the male, the male in the female, thus undermining traditional gender identity." Euripides' play *The*

Bacchae, which was translated into Russian in 1894 by Innokenty Annensky, illustrated this theme with masculinized women (Dionysian maenads) and a man (Pentheus) who witnesses their revels, dresses as a woman, and is destroyed by them.

Sophia represented the productive dream of spiritual activism or "God-seeking." She was the medium through which symbolist artists sought to reconstitute themselves out of doubles and to rediscover both a unified consciousness among the fragments of humanity and "the humanity in man" at a time when their world appeared to be breaking apart. For scythians like Bely, the Divine Sophia became after 1917 "the Woman Clothed with the Sun," a "good" Mother Russia, a nurturer, consoler, and reconciler of Eastern myths and dreams and Western reason and abstract philosophy.[10] The persona of a pronouncedly Asiatic, "bad" Mother Russia, who like the sphinx devours its questioners (that is, artists and intellectuals), appeared one year later in Blok's poem "The Scythians" (*Skify,* 1918): "Grieving, jubilant, / and covering herself with blood / she looks, she looks, she looks at you—her slant / eyes lit with hatred and with love."[11]

Iconic women synthesized the questions which male and also female artists asked about the stability and legitimacy of the self and its artistic projections. By effectively transferring female victimization to the male (for example, through the personae of Dionysus, Christ, Hamlet, and Pierrot) and recasting the *femme fragile* as the *femme fatale* and the social other (Salome, Cleopatra, Columbine), the male artist-intellectual engendered a peculiarly mixed martyrology of the self. Female artists, who confronted the same social conditions and existential questions as their male counterparts, negotiated their own provisional solutions through an iconography which they had to co-opt in order to control. Silver Age culture offers examples of many casualties of cross-gendered consciousness, of male and female intellectuals projecting themselves and being projected through art as their gender opposites, the self as other. There are perhaps an equal number of cases of intellectuals who used artistic gender recasting to their advantage. The creative intellectual knew that, although the negotiation of such roles could prove to be inconsequential to society and the people at large, this process might be fateful if not fatal to himself or herself personally.

The erotic aestheticism of the *femme fatale* Ida Rubinstein (Lidiya Lvovna Rubinshtein) and the ascetic eroticism of the *femme fragile* Vera Kommissarzhevskaya defined the two extremes of female iconicity in Silver Age culture. Rubinstein's Beardsleyesque decadent

FIGURE 2

Portrait of Ida Rubinstein, *1910, by V. A. Serov. Courtesy of Aurora Art Publishers, St. Petersburg.*

thinness inverted and eviscerated the voluptuous sensuality of contemporaneous Duncanesque dancers (after Isadora Duncan's first Petersburg appearance in 1904) and the ubiquitous Columbines and rival Salomes depicted in Russian theatre and drama of the period. Whether on the stage or recumbent upon a sea of blue, as in V. A. Serov's famous nude portrait (1910, fig. 2), Rubinstein brazenly presented her body to her audience, engaging them with her direct harlot's gaze. The fact that Rubinstein commissioned the painting and that it was executed on the site of a former monastery on the Boulevard des Invalides in Paris following Rubinstein's *succès de scandale* in the Diaghilev Ballet production of *Cléopâtre* (premiere 2 June 1909) speaks to the actress's mastery of her own sexual-theatrical *mise en scène*. Since Rubinstein, who was bisexual, appealed to both heterosexual and homosexual audiences, the composite gaze which her "ideal spectator" returned was, in a sense, as sphinxlike as her performance. By presenting herself in various portraits and stagings as a spectacle of celebrated physical features—dark, hollow eyes; elongated, languid, anorexic, androgynous body; long, dark hair (women's hair having been a common *fin de siècle* fetish)—Rubinstein conspired with male painters and directors to appropriate her "identity as cultural fetish" from her audience. In Silver Age Russian culture, the demonstrably (un)self-conscious (*uslovny*) subject,

FIGURE 3
The Marquise's Bath, *1906, by Aleksandr Benois. Courtesy of Izdatel'stvo izobrazitel'noe iskusstvo, Moscow.*

whether body, text, or stage, expressed the anonymous authority of outside spectatorship (see, for example, fig. 3).

Romaine Brooks's painting *Dead Woman* (*Le trajet*, ca. 1911) presented Rubinstein as an iconic "silent, white and still" bridal corpse, like Ophelia, Desdemona, and Nina in *Masquerade* (*Maskarad*, 1836), Mikhail Lermontov's Russian *Othello*, who were punished as imagined social and sexual transgressors.[12] The transformation of fallen women into dead princesses in Russian folklore and in literary fairy tales by Pushkin and others created in death a visual symbol of both Hamlet's and Ophelia's unrealized life and the realization of their solitary paths to death. Brooks, who was engaged in a lesbian affair with Rubinstein at the time of this painting's execution, was as quick as male artists to project her own psychological fetishes upon a subject/object whose androgyny encouraged, accepted, and intensified the tendency to universalize desire as an end in itself. However, Rubinstein's appropriation of the corpse's role in her artistic presentation of her vampiric physiognomy articulated her refusal to remain the *Hamletmachine* of the creative intelligentsia. Nikolay Kalmakov reappropriated the corpse as a self-fetishizing male role in his *Self-Portrait as Adonis* (*Autoportrait en Adonis*, 1924), which likewise adopted the recumbent posture, emaciated physiognomy, and dramatic hair (here ample but curled) of Brooks's "Rubinstein."

Like Oscar Wilde's popular *fin de siècle* icon Salome, a role which she performed, Rubinstein could be said to have "fantasized in a male manner," co-opting the aggressive gaze.[13] Although Rubinstein's bisexuality invited this gaze, her androgyny, especially framed in her performance of Gabriele d'Annunzio's St. Sébastien in Paris (1911), invoked an ancient myth of purity and integrality. The androgyne, who like Salome was linked to the moon, further reinforced the eschatology of the period in its extratemporality and nonprocreative sexuality. The androgyne was regarded by some Russian symbolists as "the perfect human being," a victory of the spirit and human will over social oppression and discord. This bisexual but asexual ideal represented a Nietzschean self-overcoming, which paralleled and reinforced humanity's God-building (*bogostroitel'stvo*), embodied in and announced by the Divine Sophia. However, Rubinstein recalled the moon more through the Phoenician sexual goddess Astarte, to whom she was compared, than through the Divine Sophia, to whom she was not. Rubinstein's androgyny likewise invoked the two-sidedness of the period's two cultic females, Cleopatra as queen and concubine and Salome as virgin and harlot.[14]

The Petersburg Cleopatra cult derived from Pushkin's story "Egyptian Nights" (*Egipetskie nochi*, written 1835, published 1837), which stressed the character's sphinxlike carnality. In the story, men draw lots from an urn to determine who will spend the night with Cleopatra and, by so doing, die. Cleopatra inspired a number of works of Silver Age literature, beginning with Mikhail Kuzmin's unfinished opera *Kleopatra* in the early 1890s. Male artists fetishized her not only as a *femme fatale* but as a divided self, who like them could not help but kill the thing she loved (a Wildean coinage). Cleopatra's beautiful body, Dostoyevsky wrote, "concealed the soul of a darkly fantastical horrible reptile." In the Silver Age, Valery Bryusov called Cleopatra "a soulless incarnation of beauty and temptation" and "a symbol of passionate, exalted woman, unable to master her passions." Blok, who wrote a poem entitled "Cleopatra" in 1907, compared her in 1910 (in his essay "On the Contemporary State of Russian Symbolism," *O sovremennom sostoyanii russkogo simvolizma*) to Russian artists who chose "submissive death" over "heroic struggle."[15]

Whether or not creative intellectuals actually believed the *femme fatale* to be personally and culturally apocalyptic, they rendered her so, often as part of a scenario of transfiguration. Lev Bakst's 1908 painting *Terror Antiquas* (*Antichny uzhas*) represented the Eternal Feminine as the mythic Pandora, Aphrodite, and perhaps even the Russian Orthodox Virgin Mary, loci of apocalyptic destruction and messianic rebirth.[16] Salome killed a holy man and Cleopatra innocent youths. The *femme fatale* seemed purposely to confuse sex with love and embodied the paradox of love and death, romantic and carnal yearning as one. She was the antimuse, incarnating sex as fate at a time when decadent hedonism was being treated in such works as Mikhail Artsybashev's novel *Sanin* (1907; dramatized as *How to Live*, 1911), Kuzmin's homoerotic novella *Wings* (*Kryl'ya*, 1907) and Lidiya Zinovyeva-Annibal's lesbian sketch "Thirty-Three Abominations" (*Tridtsat'-tri uroda*, 1907). Zinovyeva-Annibal was the Dionysian cultist Vyacheslav Ivanov's wife. Renato Poggioli sees mirrored in this Silver Age decadence the paradoxical condition of a culture and presumably an intellectual elite which was (to paraphrase) spiritually sensual, sacredly profane, perversely masochistic, and omnipotently sadistic.[17]

Critical responses to Rubinstein's performance as the predatory Cleopatra noted her "vacant eyes" and "pallid cheeks" but especially fetishized her "open mouth." One reviewer wrote that "her lips, scarlet, like a wound, gave one an odd sensation of mingled fascination and repulsion."[18] One year earlier in St. Petersburg, Nikolay Yevreinov and his designer Nikolay Kalmakov set Wilde's *Salome* (translated by N. I. Butkovskaya) inside a giant scenic vagina, stripping away all pretense of illusion and metaphor. This *mise en scène*, performed for a "Sphinxian Herod" with powder blue hair, literally made a spectacle of gender consumption (the vagina dentata) and artistic self-consumption.[19] Later, in his painting *The Spanish Dancer* (*Plyashushchaya ispanka*, 1916; fig. 4), Yevreinov contorted a neo-maenad's frenzied body, so that like a human uroboros, her own sex was placed in jeopardy of being consumed by her painted lips and

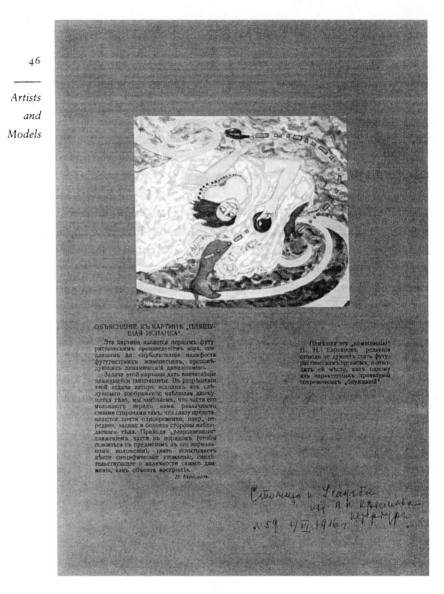

FIGURE 4

The Spanish Dancer, *1916, by Nikolay Yevreinov. Courtesy of the*
Bibliothèque Nationale, Paris, Département des arts du spectacle,
Collection Nicolas Evreïnoff.

toothy smile. Here the doubled self, consumptive self-absorption, and androgynous and bisexual self-containment linked the male subject and the female object, the artist and his antimuse. Here Salome, who for Russian artists suggested the folkloric *rusalka* (by way of Push-kin's dramatic poem "The Rusalka"), a mermaid-siren, an "unclean

FIGURE 5

Salome Sphinx, *1928, by Nikolay Kalmakov. Courtesy of a private collection, Switzerland.*

spirit," danced herself and her prey to their deaths, their shared fate.[20]

Yevreinov's Silver Age plays, often derived from *commedia dell'arte* conventions and themes, were works of self-portraiture, which at times depicted the author in female masquerade and in the act of (monodramatic) self-consumption. Kalmakov's self-demonizing *oeuvre*, which like Yevreinov's was defined in the Silver Age but extended beyond 1917, affixed the painter's face to the sexually predatory bodies of Salome and the sphinx (*Salomé sphinge*, 1928, fig. 5). In a 1921 painting, Kalmakov appeared as Salome's victim John the Baptist with women's breasts, constituting with the Salome-sphinx a fitting interactive referent both to Wilde's *Salome* and to his poem "The

Sphinx" (1874). Wilde compared his sphinx's eyes to "fantastic moons that shiver in some stagnant lake," anticipating Pierrot's gender- and self-mirroring celestial orb in Blok's play *The Little Showbooth* (*Balaganchik*, 1906).[21]

The moon, of course, inverts the order and reason of Apollo, the god of the sun, and defamiliarizes reality in its silvery light. It was, as Konstantin Treplyov realized in staging the quasi-symbolist playlet at the heart of *The Seagull*, the perfect means of evoking mood and invoking the spirit of the Silver Age.[22] In Wilde's play, Salome saw her reflection in "the dark mirrors, the black lakes of Jokanaan's [John the Baptist's] eyes" (588), completing the male monodramatic inscription of female narcissism and inertia. In *Against Nature* (*A Rebours*, 1884), Huysmans's dandy Des Esseintes described Gustave Moreau's *Salome* (in his paintings of the 1870s) as an "unfeeling and unpitying statue," an "innocent and deadly idol," who danced without really moving.[23] Salome's counterfeiting of male desire was here exposed as a bad male impersonation of the female. Her empty mystery likewise confounded the "ecstatic expectancy" of the male viewer who hopes beyond arousal for some self-realization that never comes. Members of the creative intelligentsia of the Silver Age regarded Salome, like Hamlet, as a casualty not only of her environment but also of what Dmitry Merezhkovsky called the "internal fate" of heredity, a likely metaphor for directed consciousness, or intellectual self-victimization.[24] Symbolist poet Konstantin Balmont saw in Salome not only the human face of love, but its divine and its demonic visage, its ecstasy and madness, and a mystery greater than (albeit at times synonymous with) death.[25]

Rubinstein bordered on being a parodic *femme fatale*, a necrophiliac's dream, who invited an artistic response that both objectified her and made a mockery of objectification. The analytical perception of Rubinstein's "decadent" physical qualities, her "curveless lines," "slender flanks," and "long thighs," helped foster a critical intuition concerning her soullessness, her "disturbed inner depth." Even an obituary notice set aside the person to remember the "body that once thrilled the Western World." Aleksey Radakov's 1912 caricature of Serov's portrait of Rubinstein presented her androgyny not as sexual perfection but as sexual friction, even combustibility, in a configuration of matchbox torso, matchstick arms and legs, and heavily made-up doll head.[26]

This simultaneously rigid and broken object-montage no doubt expressed what many male critics actually deemed to be Rubinstein's absurd antieroticism, what Stanislavsky called her "shameless," "vapid" nakedness, as well as their resentment of her dilettantish celebrity. Rubinstein's body, untrained both in dance and in acting, and her underprojected voice, which "limped in the area of diction," did not prevent Vsevolod Meyerhold, Lev Bakst, Aleksandr Benois, Michel Fokine, Sergey Diaghilev, Gabriele d'Annunzio, Igor Stravinsky, and Claude Debussy from working on the vanity productions which she financed and in which she starred. Some of Rubinstein's contemporaries felt that the perception of her as a dilettante was a function of her versatile, uncategorizable talent and ambiguous persona. The failure, argue(d) Rubinstein's supporters, was not hers but her critics', who were too limited or resistant to understand her. Others found Rubinstein's frankly acknowledged narcissism to be as distasteful as the wealth that exposed it to the world. Rubinstein's brazen sexuality, which debased the androgynous ideal she counterfeited, attracted some and repelled others, as did her "exoticism," a code word for her Jewishness. Rubinstein's androgyny, which caricatured corrupted innocence, recalled the case of the adolescent boy Sasha in Fyodor Sologub's novel *The Petty Demon* (*Melky bes*, 1907), who is seduced, perfumed, and sent to a masquerade ball by his older female lover in the costume of a geisha. Rubinstein simultaneously performed the roles of the cross-gendered seducer/seduced.

Rubinstein's largely silent, plastic performances of androgynes and *neznakomki*, such as St. Sébastian, Salome, and Cleopatra, suggested the voguish cult of *tableaux vivants* or "living statuary" in Russia and Western Europe. Unveiling nude and seminude female "statues" to musical accompaniment was a feature of the eighteenth- and nineteenth-century Russian serf, private, and variety theatres. Priscilla R. Roosevelt retells one incident in which naked male and female serfs, who were painted white and posed motionless to resemble Venus and Hercules, descended from their garden pedestals to blind their master with sand and then to beat him to death. The living statues unveiled at St. Petersburg's/Petrograd's Crooked Mirror Theatre (Teatr Krivogo Zerkala) during Yevreinov's tenure as artistic director (1910–1917) were far more benign. Mayakovsky's giant papiermâché "Girlfriend" (*Znakomka*) in *Vladimir Mayakovsky: A Tragedy* and Blok's "Unknown Woman" (*Neznakomka*), in the play of the same name, both of whom first appeared in performance in 1913, were variations on this theme.[27] The self-fetishizing striptease which introduced Rubinstein's Cleopatra on the stage of the Théâtre du Châtelet in Paris eroticized the equivalent of an androgynously smooth, hairless epidermis (as in Kalmakov's paintings), a statue's cold skin.

Rubinstein was an amateur performer whose persona was largely a formal pose calculated to shock and entice through aggressive ambiguity. Vera Kommissarzhevskaya, by contrast, was a talented professional actress capable of suggesting psychological depth of character and evoking an audience's empathic response. Her ethereal presence, combining a contemplative quality with the impression of vulnerability, inspired romantic dreams rather than sexual fantasies, especially in the symbolists whose plays she produced at her theatre. Kommissarzhevskaya's thin, pale, and nervous countenance (fig. 6) and the stage settings in which she was placed—a blue-lit window for her Hilda Wangel in *The Master Builder* (staged in 1905), a blue-green Hedda Gabler harmonized with a similarly hued background in Ibsen's play (premiere 10 November 1906)—suggested another bridal corpse, a drowned Ophelia consumed by male authorial, directorial, and spectatorial consciousness.

While Rubinstein built her performance of "the abominable little Salome" around a "dance of the seven veils" which culminated in full nudity, Kommissarzhevskaya dreamed of playing Salome as a tragically suppressed personality.[28] Although she never played Salome, the role figured prominently in her fate. The Holy Synod's censoring and subsequent closing of the Yevreinov-Kalmakov *Salome* in 1908 indirectly ruined Kommissarzhevskaya, at whose theatre it had premiered. In order to recoup her financial losses, Kommissarzhevskaya, one of the most popular and respected actresses of her day, toured the provinces, where she contacted smallpox and died in Tashkent in 1910. In a remembrance of the actress written shortly after her death, Blok evoked Kommissarzhevskaya the "clear-sighted total artist, who saw simply and profoundly like a child." In her eyes, Blok saw "the small shard [which broke free from] the magic mirror" in Hans Christian Andersen's fairy tale "The Snow Queen." Blok identified Kommissarzhevskaya with Hilda Wangel, the builder Solness's muse and destroyer. Hilda/Vera first appeared onstage at Kommissarzhevskaya's theatre faintly at twilight, a radiant figure "with passionate hope and expectation in her blue eyes."[29] In this moment, symbolists, who by 1905 despaired that the Divine Sophia might never come, saw their faith (*vera* in Russian) rewarded and renewed their claim to be master builders of a new spiritual order.

Kommissarzhevskaya originated in performance the *femme fragile*

FIGURE 6
Portrait of V. F. Kommissarzhevskaya, *ca. 1906, by E. S. Zarudnaya-Kavos.*
Courtesy of Aurora Art Publishers, St. Petersburg.

Nina Zarechnaya in the unsuccessful premiere of Chekhov's *The Seagull* (Aleksandra Theatre, St. Petersburg, 17 October 1896). In specifically Russian terms, Nina was both a *rusalka* and a *ptitsa-sirin*, a bird-maiden, hero-helper, avenger/self-victimizer, foreteller/embodiment of death and rebirth. Nina fused the *femme fragile*'s passive, childlike ethereality with the *femme fatale*'s moral frailty and emotional shallowness in the minds of her male "creators," the writers Boris Trigorin and Konstantin Treplyov. Like Tonya Zhivago, whose poet-husband Yury in Pasternak's novel likens her body (in the act of giving birth) to his stand-up writing desk, Nina is the metaphoric stage for which Treplyov writes as well as the metaphoric text which Trigorin creates.[30] Her performance of self cannot at first successfully compete with the performative text others have made of her. Her identity as "seagull" encapsulates her in an endless self-mirroring of what is really an evacuated self, a male head placed atop a female body. Nina's hollow, ventriloquistic impersonation of Treplyov's quasi-symbolist World Soul, itself a symbol of death and rebirth, is finally replaced by a successful performance of her own life. This self-created performance silences Treplyov's voice, and he dies just out of earshot of his emotionally absent actress mother. Woman's apparent will and willingness to counterfeit her emotions and even herself conspires with the male desire to oversee such recreation and to live vicariously through this alternative self.[31]

Despite her affinity for and association with Chekhov's Nina, Kommissarzhevskaya was a far more pragmatic and powerful woman than her self-victimizing performances suggested. Prior to founding her own theatre (15 September 1904), with a company of Stanislavsky's disciples (including I. A. Tikhomirov, A. P. Petrovsky, and N. N. Arbatov), Kommissarzhevskaya rejected Vladimir Nemirovich-Danchenko's concerted effort (in 1902) to add her to the acting corps of the Moscow Art Theatre. Kommissarzhevskaya had proved herself to be a tough negotiator with MAT, demanding to play no fewer than five major roles per season in St. Petersburg as well as in Moscow and to receive no less than ten thousand roubles per season. She rejected the principle of "directorial dictatorship" (the Treplyov-Nina-Trigorin scenario) and conditioned her own theatre's audiences to come primarily to see her and to be able to distinguish between her skillful performances and the often less accomplished performances of her company members. Many in her audience could likewise distinguish between the actress and the roles she played in the unpopular symbolist plays she insisted upon producing. The symbolists in the audience saw Kommissarzhevskaya through the filter of the muse's role, which transcended any given play or performance.

It became a subject of concern and some mystification for theatre-goers and critics when the new artistic director of Kommissarzhevskaya's theatre, Vsevolod Meyerhold (MAT's original Treplyov), transformed their icon into a living statue in service to his personal vision. In the bas-relief "silhouetteness" (flattened, depthless pictorialism) of Meyerhold's symbolist stagings, Kommissarzhevskaya became more an *objet d'art*—her Hedda Gabler was compared to a pawnshop green bronze figure in the *style moderne*—than a human sufferer.[32] Meyerhold's attempt to create Hedda's watery "spiritual abode" (*zhilishche dukha*), for example, framed by a proscenium hung with silver lace and by a giant window, figuratively evoked the drowned Ophelia. Meyerhold's production of *Hedda Gabler*, designed by Nikolay Sapunov, was criticized for failing to make manifest the bourgeois world which imprisoned the heroine and against which she rebelled, offering her instead as part of the scenic resolution of a purely painterly problem. Here and elsewhere in his pre- and postrevolutionary work, Meyerhold's unconscious male prejudice threatened to overwhelm his conscious artistic agenda to "repulse the beastliness of the bourgeois."[33]

Throughout 1906, Meyerhold was caricatured in the press as Kommissarzhevskaya's evil genius, Coppelius to her soulless automaton Olympia. Taken from the story "The Sandman" by the popular German fabulist E. T. A. Hoffmann and popularized in Offenbach's opera *Contes de Hoffmann*, the Coppelius-Olympia iconography transformed the female eroticism of the barefoot dancer Salome into the male autoeroticism of the mechanically programmed, self-destructive female robot, which I will discuss in detail in chapter 3. The caricatured seductiveness of Kommissarzhevskaya's twisted and attenuated antierotic body expressed its compliance to male will (fig. 7). Within the space of eight days in 1906, Kommissarzhevskaya played, under Meyerhold's direction, two of Ibsen's class- and gender-suppressed heroines, Hedda and Nora (*Nora, or A Doll's House*, the subject of the caricature; premiere 18 November 1906). Critics praised her Nora for being the only performance in the production which broke free of Meyerhold's bas-relief style of staging. However, the concurrence of these plays in production promoted the image of the actress as a mummified body, in iconic opposition to the erotic cocoons from which the period's Salomes, Cleopatras, and Columbines were then emerging.

FIGURE 7

Caricature of Meyerhold and Kommissarzhevskaya by N. Kalibanovsky, from the journal Splinters *45, St. Petersburg, 1906. Courtesy of Vserossyskoe teatral'noe obshchestvo, Moscow.*

Once Meyerhold was fired from his position as artistic director and replaced in 1908 by Yevreinov, his detractors sought to "bare the device" of what they considered to have been his malevolent direction. Meyerhold's art was "exposed" as theatrical sham, a puppet show (a less precise English translation of *Balaganchik*, or *The Little Show-booth*). Meyerhold was revealed as being not the master but rather the real subject of this puppet show, whose need to control Kommissarzhevskaya's performance concealed an inability to control his own fate and artistic identity. Meyerhold, his detractors might say, persisted in this fashion. In 1912, he welcomed Blok's wife, Lyubov Mendeleyeva, to his troupe and aided in her transformation from the Beautiful Lady of the symbolists into a pantomimic Columbine.[34]

The seductiveness of theatrical magic, especially that of the *commedia dell'arte*, was revealed in a harlequinade with Dionysian overtones witnessed as a child by Aleksandr Benois. In this scenario, Pierrot murdered, dismembered, and juggled Harlequin, who was then revived and reconstituted by a female fairy and finally chased through a house by servants and a chef. Harlequin popped out of a pot of "real" boiling water ("real" steam was produced), the case of a grandfather clock, and a flour tub. He then vanished through a trapped floor, flew through an open window, jumped inside a mirror, rode across the stage on a dragon, and pursued his pursuers in a large cupboard in which they had entrapped him. Suitably impressed by this action, which transpired in the second act alone, Benois declared, as would Yevreinov, "I wanted to become Harlequin myself."[35]

The cruel harlequinades written and performed in the period 1905–1917 reflected a general instability in which even character masks could not always be counted on to act true to form or, perhaps more accurately, revealed in their actions dark (sexual) possibilities which other generations had not needed or were unwilling to explore.[36] In Kuzmin's play *The Venetian Madcaps* (*Venetsianskie bezumtsy*, written 1912, produced 1914) Harlequin, a young bisexual male, murders Columbine, his disguised male lover, over another (real) woman whom the male Columbine hates.

Vasily Rozanov believed that the relationship of a writer to a woman might "reveal the hidden mechanism of his creative imagination." Silver Age male artists were especially fascinated with the marriages, real and imagined, of artists and their muses/demons, including those of Dante, Pushkin, Lermontov, Turgenev, Dostoyevsky, Lev Tolstoy, and, in a somewhat different vein, the fictional Anna Karenina. Creative intellectuals saw in these marriages the struggle between spirit and flesh, and (male) self and (female) other, whose (re)integration held life and death in the balance. Blok, whose marriage invites such study, wrote of Ibsen that "the soul of every artist is filled with demons." These demons were sometimes dispersed, as in the case of Dante, by the inner voice of the female muse. However, Blok, whose thirteen-page entertainment *The Little Showbooth* was the period's great modernist harlequinade, fell into the category of those artists whose real muse was agony. Along with other Russian symbolists, Blok identified to a degree with August Strindberg, for whom (Blok wrote in 1912) fate was gendered feminine and the suffering soul masculine.[37]

In 1896, sixteen-year-old Blok courted his then seventeen-year-old future wife by playing Hamlet to her Ophelia in her parents' barn theatre at Boblovo. Blok extended their *emploi* into life, hoping through a Hamlet-Ophelia concordance to reconstitute himself out of his doubleness (*dvoystvennost'*). In 1902, Mikhail Vrubel, who sought visually to translate "perception into consciousness" in his *Hamlet* and *Ophelia* (1884, 1888) and *Demon* cycle of paintings (ca. 1890–1902, after Lermontov's classic poem) went mad. Vrubel superimposed his own face upon his first *Hamlet*. The *Demon*, who in one incarnation unintentionally resembled Blok, embodied self-isolating, self-victimizing artistic-intellectual consciousness which rejected "human wholeness of spirit" (Ophelia as the Solovyovian Divine Sophia) and mind (Hamletian awareness of in/finitude). Blok's disillusionment with symbolism and life after 1905 strengthened his association with Vrubel's Demon and with Hamlet, especially the Hamlet described in 1837 by Aleksandr Herzen, whose life somewhat paralleled Blok's own. "I have read *Hamlet* ten times," wrote Herzen. "Each word of his breathes cold and fear. . . . And just what was the matter with him after his first despair? He began to laugh, and this laughter, hellish and horrible, continues through the whole play." After 1848, Herzen confronted both his wife's infidelity and revolution's broken promises, as did Blok after 1905.[38]

Blok's wife was the daughter of the famous chemist Dmitry Mendeleyev, inventor of the periodic table of elements. Surrounded by famous men, Mendeleyeva fought to discover her reality not only as a self-possessed and sinless body but also, like Nina Zarechnaya, as an unmediated voice. She sought to divorce herself from the theoretical womanliness ascribed to her by Blok as Ophelia and by the symbolists as the Divine Sophia. Shortly after Blok-Hamlet married Mendeleyeva-Ophelia, in August 1903, his "Verses on the Beautiful Lady" (*Stikhi o prekrasnoy dame*, 1898–1904), imbued with what Bryusov called "the pathos of expectation," ceased and a puppet show of another sort began. The role which Blok played in this spectacle combined the creative intellectual's *emploi* of theatrical savior (Harlequin-Christ in Yevreinov's coinage) and suffering god/suffering fool (Dionysus-Pierrot).[39] Blok's theatrical role of male sphinx, with the body of a clown and the head of a deity and the recasting of Mendeleyeva's Beautiful Lady as Columbine transformed Vyacheslav Ivanov's mystical rite of theatre into a tragi-farcical *balagan* (theatrical grotesquerie).

The Blok-Mendeleyeva union soon became a *mariage blanc*. But although he abstained from sex in his conjugal relationship, Blok continued to frequent prostitutes. The symbolists tried to see in Blok's denial of Mendeleyeva's sexual desire and desirability the paradoxical condition of loving but being unable to possess the Divine Sophia.[40] However, Blok's consorting with prostitutes actually subverted the very idea and efficacy of the Divine Sophia. Blok's separation of sex and love expressed his disgust with his former naively idealistic individualism, with collective and personal efforts to fuse the self and the world/the other. This separation also expressed Blok's rejection of the symbolist philosophy which depended upon these self-important assumptions.

Blok likened the earth to "a universal prostitute" and sex to an "overturned, disfigured heaven," the decaying of spiritual life by time, flesh, and matter, the violation of the Divine Sophia. In this Blok echoed Gogol, for whom woman embodied "moral fatigue" (*nravstvennaya ustalost'*), demanding physio-spiritual resuscitation (*ozhivotvorenie*) by the male, in what was clearly meant as a sexual metaphor. In his essay "Woman" (1830–1832), Gogol compared the artist's futile attempt to "transform his immortal idea into crude matter" to the effort to "embody woman in man." Gogol's grotesque art, built upon the psychic and moral terror of sexual inversion, prefigured Blok's "overturned, disfigured heaven" in the concept of *poshlost'*, the profane coarsening of life by deathlike form (matter, art, woman/the feminine), which derived from but was no longer synonymous with life.[41] Blok realized that for him marriage could not match the androgynous self-sufficiency of art. However, self-sufficiency/self-fulfillment through art proved to be only an alternative, self-imprisoning myth for the creative intellectual.

In Blok's marriage, the idealized reconciliation of sex and love, posited by Rozanov among others, quickly fell apart. In Blok's stage world, the destructive power of sex is less significant than that of self-love, and infidelity is symptomatic of more profound self-deception. Blok's *The Little Showbooth*, which sought to parody Solovyovian ideals and ideologues, proved Solovyov's thesis that when egoism motivates human behavior the tenuous realities of the self and the world are in mortal peril.[42]

Meyerhold's direction and Sapunov's design of *The Little Showbooth* at Vera Kommissarzhevskaya's theatre (premiere 30 December 1906; fig. 8) rejected "the abstract culture" of symbolist consciousness by "baring the device" of symbolist staging, at which Meyerhold had recently excelled. The production began with the prompter climbing into his onstage box in full view of the audience. Scenery and property changes were similarly exposed to audience view, as were the ropes for hoisting the curtain (designed by Lev Bakst). The play's action was framed by the dark sound of a drum and by the plaintive sound of Pierrot's flute (the music was composed by Kuzmin). Meyerhold, who moved and spoke like a wooden puppet in the role of Pierrot, sought to confront his audience with the reality of the stage rather than with the symbolists' hopeful "window on another life."

FIGURE 8

The Mystics scene in Nikolay Sapunov's design for Blok's The Little
Showbooth, *1906. Courtesy of Ardis, Ann Arbor.*

By exposing the stage, Meyerhold, like Blok, hoped to reveal "the
essential unity of art, life and politics." However, except as a remedy
for symbolist obscurantism, the theatrical solution represented by
modernist *balagan* was not particularly optimistic.

Like his *Hedda Gabler* set, Sapunov's *Little Showbooth* design
stressed socio-spiritual entrapment in its semiotic dialogue—the spectral unsteadiness of life's realia-realiora. The Mystics, representing the
symbolists who were awaiting the arrival of the Divine Sophia, met in
a tastelessly wall-papered room in a provincial house bathed in blue
light (a visual reference to Meyerhold's symbolist stagings). A real
window versus a painted one represented actual versus *uslovnaya*
(that is, conventional) reality. Surface painterliness, which forced
action into a narrow downstage playing area, contrasted with the
picture-frame illusion of depth in space. Overall, the design depicted
a stage world which became most spiritually delimiting at the moment
that its openness was revealed.[43] This spatial context rendered beauty
and belief irrelevant, if not impossible.

Blok composed *The Little Showbooth* during a period when he felt
himself vainly shouting to be heard over the din produced by the artistic egoism of those writers who refused to be "bigger than them-

selves" and by the whistling and clanking of the dawning machine age. Blok wrote in despair that he no longer heard the sound of the people's soul. One could glimpse in the puppet show being performed by Russian culture between the revolutions of 1905 and 1917 the masked terror of *le Grand Néant*, the Great Nothingness, the transparent theatrical mask of fate and fatality.[44]

All three of Blok's lyrical dramas of 1906—*The Little Showbooth*, which featured a cardboard bride, *The King in the Town Square* (*Korol' na ploshchadi*) with its unrealized Pygmalion-Galatea theme, and *The Unknown Woman*, with its beautiful star fallen to earth as a prostitute—bitterly debunked the author's one-time faith that (male-imagined "female") beauty (the Divine Sophia; art) has the power to transform life. Konstantin Somov, who linked Harlequin, Death, and Nothingness in his 1907 painting of the same name, added Woman to this equation in his cover for Blok's *Lyrical Dramas* (*Liricheskie dramy*, 1906). John E. Bowlt suggests that Somov's 1907 portrait of a lifeless-looking Blok against a light background (fig. 9) figuratively pictured the poet in "the pale vacuum" of the void into which he as Harlequin leapt at the conclusion of *The Little Showbooth*.[45]

In addition to the Mystics, the cast of *The Little Showbooth* includes a Pierrot whose beloved is transformed by these Mystics into a cardboard bride and, as Columbine, is inevitably stolen away from him by Harlequin; male and female maskers at a ball, who mirror each other and represent the progression of the author's spiritual disillusionment via their expression of romantic, fatalistic, and ironically self-referential perspectives on love; and a meddlesome Author who loses control of and misunderstands his play. The play is defined by Harlequin's climactic leap out a painted window in a paper wall. This action was undoubtedly suggested by Gogol's play *Marriage* (*Zhenit'ba*, 1835), in which a nervous bridegroom named Podkolyosin (Under the Wheel) leaps out a window on his wedding day rather than marry an aging and foolish spinster with whom he has been matched. This limited experiential leap may have been existentially reinforced in Blok's mind by Charlotta Ivanova's *salto mortale* or leap for life, of which Chekhov wrote in 1904. Harlequin's rupturing of the set's paper wall reveals Death in the person of a long-haired woman shouldering a scythe, an image possibly derived by Blok from Andrea Orcagna's *The Triumph of Death*, one of the frescoes of the cloister at Campo Santo in Pisa.[46]

In an ironic foreshadowing of this moment, the Mystics earlier mistook Columbine's shoulder-length braid for Death's shouldered

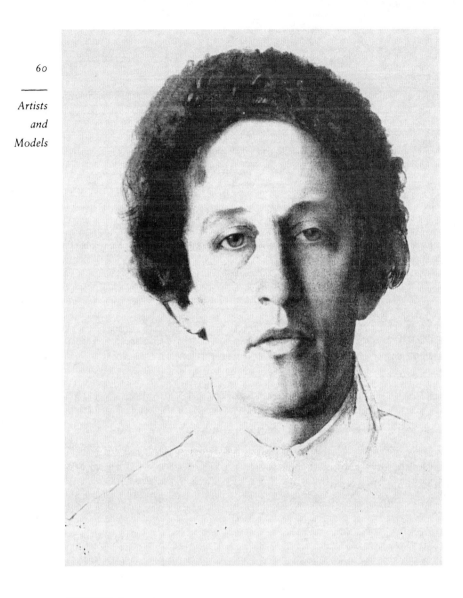

FIGURE 9

Portrait of the Poet A. A. Blok, *1907, by Konstantin Somov. Courtesy of
Izdatel'stvo izobrazitel'noe iskusstvo, Moscow.*

scythe (*kosa* means both "braid" and "scythe" in Russian), much as
the symbolists mistook the carnal Mendeleyeva for the incarnate Divine Sophia. Traditionally in Russia the single braid signified an unmarried maiden. During the Silver Age, however, it came to represent
the wearer's participation in a *mariage blanc*. No doubt Blok had in
mind the marriage of symbolist writers Dmitry Merezhkovsky and

Zinaida Gippius (who wore her hair in a single braid), whom the Mystics in *The Little Showbooth* are meant to parody. Gippius and Merezhkovsky participated in a similarly sexless *ménage à trois* with Diaghilev's lover Dmitry Filosofov.[47] The ascetic *ménage* was the relational counterpart of androgyny and a reflection of Gippius's and Merezhkovsky's belief in Otto Weininger's "theory of the bisexuality of life." Weininger's misogynist study *Sex and Character* (*Geschlecht und Charakter: Eine prinzipielle Untersuchung*, 1903), which theorized gender ambiguity, was translated into Russian in 1909.[48] Blok's use of the single braid in *The Little Showbooth* parodied both the chastity of the Eternal Feminine (Mendeleyeva) and his own nonparticipation in a *ménage* with his wife and her lover, Blok's friend Andrey Bely.

Blok's play likewise parodied the pursuit by Gippius and Rozanov of what Olga Matich calls "the unsolved mystery of sex and its relationship to God." Gippius and Rozanov agreed that such a relationship existed but disagreed on the role played in it by Christ and Christianity. Gippius argued that the asceticism of Christ represented the spiritual transformation of sex and not its negation. Rozanov, "the Russian Nietzsche," embraced love for "excluding the lie" but rejected the Christian idea of love for condemning sex and so embracing death.. Still, Rozanov viewed Christ as the primary model for what Vladimir Solovyov called "Godmanhood," the theoretically "harmonized" human being (Pyotr Uspensky's coinage), the realization of human personality's potential as a divine, creative force. Christ, the reconciliation of spirit and flesh and of masculine and feminine being, represented new human authenticity achieved through new personhood. He exemplified the Solovyovian ideal of individuality asserted through the sacrifice of egoism. Sergey Bulgakov called this "spiritual Dionysianism," that is, the affirmation of subjective feeling in service to an ideal that transcends the self. In *The Little Showbooth*, the melancholy narcissist Pierrot, the creative intellectual who has been betrayed by his would-be sexual and spiritual deliverers Columbine and Sophia, remains trapped in the subjective theatre of the self, from which Harlequin nominally escapes.[49]

In Blok's play, mortality consumes both flesh and the spirit in the person of Woman as Death, the hoped for and dreaded *belle dame sans merci*, whose sphinxlike gendered mystery devours the artist in the moment that he guesses her secret. At play's end, the veil of mystery/scenery flies up, and the Author is chased off the stage for the last time. Pierrot, in an homage to the Mayor, who (at the conclusion of

The Inspector General) denuded spectatorship with direct address, exclaims to the audience, "I'm very sad. You think it's funny?" (175).

The plaint of this passive, "feminized" mask expressed the social and spiritual alienation not only of Blok but of the intellectual class to which he belonged.

Blok's original notebook sketch of *The Little Showbooth*'s plot embodied his personal doubleness but not yet the full expression of its dramatic irony. It was composed on two sides of white unlined paper, on one side in black ink and on the other in crayon. Pierrot, here called "No one" (*Nekto*), had not yet emerged from the chorus of Mystics, and his final line to the audience had not been scripted. Blok's inspiration for the Mystics was the work of Belgian symbolists Maurice Maeterlinck and Emile Verhaeren, especially Maeterlinck's play *Death of Tintagiles* (*La mort de Tintagiles*, 1894), which Meyerhold staged at the Theatre Studio in Moscow in summer 1905. Blok's Pierrot resembles the character of Mikhail in Bely's play *The One Who Comes* (*Prishedshy*; originally published in the journal *Northern Flowers* in 1903), who alone among the characters in the play questions whether to wait for the end of the world and the Last Judgment. The end of the world as terminal stasis theme had a precedent in Russian drama in *The Inspector General*, in which ideological content and the mechanics of fate simultaneously expose one another in a final tableau. In *The Little Showbooth*, the Divine Sophia is the inspector who does not arrive, and Death is the inspector who does. The arrival of Death/the Inspector marks "the ultimate point of discontinuity for the individual" and the ultimate delimiting of what had appeared to be boundless consciousness and the endless chaos of inner time and space. The mystical reverencing of Death as deliverer from life's turmoil and frustrations was also a theme of Bryusov's play *Earth* (*Scenes from the Future*) (*Zemlya: Stseny budushchikh vremyon*, 1904). Blok never admitted consciously parodying Bely's and Bryusov's works.[50]

The Blok-Mendeleyeva-Bely relationship on which *The Little Showbooth* is said to have been partially based may actually have commenced several months *after* the play was written. This chronological ambiguity effectively frames the shadowy relationship of art to life and their co-creation of new cultural possibilities in the Silver Age. Similarly, by purposely generalizing the characters called for in this play—for example, "Mystics of both sexes" and a Pierrot "like all Pierrots" (9)—Blok, like Chekhov before him, sought to speak through the typical traits of the intellectual class to his own spiritual and actual biography and through his biography to the typical traits of intellectuals. The shift from Chekhovian parody to Blokian irony (of which gender ambiguity was a sign), from self-affirming internal exile to the self-destroying internal void, dramatized the growing pessimism of the intellectual class after 1905. The unmasking of the unreliable Author may have been derived from the play *Fantasia* (*Fantaziya*, 1851) by parodist "Kozma Prutkov" (pseudonym of Count Aleksey Tolstoy and Aleksey, Vladimir, and Aleksandr Zhemchuzhnikov), but its prototypes could also be found in the works of Shakespeare, Christian Dietrich Grabbe, and Ludwig Tieck, which were familiar to Blok. The act of authorial unmasking, the mirror image of pretendership, revealed the presence of personal and cultural biography.[51]

While Meyerhold's production of *The Little Showbooth* had Harlequin appear from under the Mystics' table, Blok's finished text called for him to emerge from a chorus with torches, following the scenes in which the three pairs of couples speak of love and fate. Blok juxtaposed the happy dancing maskers with the melancholy Pierrot, seated "on the same bench where Venus and Tannhäuser usually kiss" (14). While Blok's naming of this bench may only allude to a scenic convention of the Russian stage, the associations it evokes are significant, given the anguished, self-revelatory message of his play. In his essay on Wagner's *Tannhäuser*, Charles Baudelaire wrote that the great poet's inevitable romantic self-critique logically begins and ends with the Tannhäuser legend, which mediates between the poet's longing for an ideal world beyond social restraints and guilt-driven nostalgia for the real world of social responsibility. In this scenario, woman, the artist's muse and tormentor, embodies the cruel paradox of his condition—the desire to create a timeless yet temporally controllable and complete(d) work of art. Out of this legend, retold by Hoffmann, Tieck, Keats, and Heine, as well as by Wagner, was born the romantic image of *la belle dame sans merci*. The "physical perfection and immortality" of *la belle dame* cruelly mocks and, like the female sphinx (that is, the ancient Greek model), may destroy the male artist whose life and language are unable to possess her mystery via sensuous description. It is while seated on his Tannhäuser bench that Blok's Pierrot bemoans the loss of his own beloved Venus, his muse, who fell to earth out of Harlequin's sleigh, therein transforming into a "cardboard girlfriend" (15). Sergey Bulgakov argued that Solovyov's inspiration for the Divine Sophia was not in heaven but on earth, in the person of his "eternal girlfriend" (*vechnaya podruga*), the writer Anna Schmidt. Blok-Pierrot's "cardboard girlfriend" lowered the Divine Sophia further, from the real to the base.[52]

Pierrot's romantically ironic uncoupling discourses with Venus and Tannhäuser's synthetically romantic coupling, much as *The Little Showbooth*'s overall action of breaking apart and subverting unified artistic vision destabilizes the Wagnerian notion of the *Gesamtkunstwerk* (total artwork). In later essays, Blok would mourn "the lost unity" of ancient Greece, a unity which Nietzsche sought and partially achieved through music (personified as humankind's "mother") by Wagner. In *The Little Showbooth*, Blok demonstrated how the exaggerated Nietzschean individualism and the self-directed obscurantism of the Russian symbolists was a recipe for personal and class, if not cultural, extinction. Blok's statement that Wagner's work, like that of Marx and Engels, was "directed to the whole *intellectual* proletariat" (my emphasis) revealed the paradoxical agony of the artist who in seeking to deny the self inadvertently and indirectly reaffirmed it through its iconic double.

The theme of Wagnerian rhythmic ecstasy, which Blok cited and valued, could also be found in the writing of symbolists Vyacheslav Ivanov and Georgy Chulkov, the ballet choreography of Mikhail (Michel) Fokine, and specifically in Bely's *Rhythm as Dialectic and "The Bronze Horseman"* (*Ritm kak dialektika i "Medny vsadnik"*, 1928). Blok's *The Little Showbooth* set the theurgic impulse of inner (actor/individual) and outer (spectator/the people) musical necessity against the blasphemy of what Bely called "mechanical symbolism." Pantomime, which Wagner, Blok, and Meyerhold believed clarifies for the spectator the world of the inner person, in *balagan* revealed the void. *Uslovnoe* or self-unmaking art exposed self-unmaking life.[53]

Blok's *uslovnaya* play fulfilled the overall intention of the *balagan*, which Blok described in a letter to Meyerhold as being "to punch a hole in temporal mystery." As the apologist for matter, who claimed to have written the "most real of plays" (*realneyshaya p'esa*, 14), and as the exemplar of divisive external pressure, Blok's Author is most cruelly mocked. The Author's retro-revolutionary tirades, reminiscent of a stale Chatsky (from *Woe from Wit*, discussed in chapter 5), are interrupted repeatedly by Blok's modernist stagecraft. In production, Blok called for a carpet to be laid across the stage to muffle the steps of the characters on the small showbooth stage and by contrast to amplify the ponderous footsteps of the Author on the larger stage's apron. While some critics saw fate imaged in the disembodied hand which "is thrust through the curtain, grabbing the Author by the scruff of the neck" and dragging him "shrieking offstage" (14) just prior to the ball scene, it more likely represents the union of the real author's will and the creative will of *balagan*. Far from desiring to fix fate, as does the Author, *balagan* affirms life's ambiguity and unpredictability.

The Author's joining of Pierrot's and Columbine's hands near play's end, his final attempt to fix fate through the typification of character and scenic action, is thwarted by Harlequin's leap, which precipitates the small stage's scenery flying up (21), exposing the real theatre's rear wall. Harlequin's leap through a painted square into the void smashed the idol of symbolist faith with the force of creative will. It released the full implosive power of theatrical absence, meaning consumed by performative contrivance, and the "terrifying marionetteness" of play.[54] In displacing his suffering at play's end onto the audience's bemused response ("I'm very sad. You think it's funny?"), Pierrot eschews Hamlet's "hellish laughter." He seeks instead to armor his pain against audience (and his own) derision. Pierrot thus curtails the artist's agitational action, placing him in an ironic and ultimately self-defeating relationship to the world at large. Pierrot's fear seeks comfort in self-absorbed inertia. Like the creative intelligentsia which Blok represented, to which he belonged and which he critiqued, Pierrot no longer played Hamlet but was consumed by Hamletism. His most self-defeating tendency overcame his most triumphal role.

In a play in which a dead mannequin may seem alive (a possible borrowing by Blok from his friend and fellow writer Yevgeny Ivanov), *commedia* masks abstracted from social reality are concretized in theatrical performance. Ironically, the play's *uslovnaya* theatrical form, which subverted Authorial and authorial intentions (Blok's hope of harmonizing his doubleness through art and quest for a "reality" beyond "the whirlwind"), fixed the two authors' fates as one. Authorship and agency in *The Little Showbooth*, as in *Hamlet*, are both transparent masks, "unities of fixed qualities" which fail to conceal the "callousness and inner disintegration" which "lend unity to everything." The Mystics vacate their cardboard bodies, much as one scene after another precipitously vacates the stage. Harlequin leaps into an unseen but scripted abyss. Elsinore's castle walls, solid only as a theatrical habit and not as a social reality (they are riddled through with society's eyes and ears), are turned to paper and fly away, revealing the stage and auditorium as a Gogolian spatio-spiritual panoptic void.[55]

Sergey Makovsky noted that the Blok he saw at rehearsals for Meyerhold's production of his play was visibly fatigued and changed. At the curtain call on opening night (the play opened after ten rehearsals to generally unfavorable reviews), a sadly grinning Blok stood hand in hand with his spectral Pierrot, as had Woman and Death in his play. This presented a doubled image of authorial suffering in the ever ending, ever recurring fatalistic world which theatre uniquely conveys.

The Little Showbooth, like a dead Harlequin miraculously reviving behind a final curtain, experienced a sort of theatrical afterlife. At a post-premiere ball entitled the Evening of Paper Ladies (*Vecher bumazhnykh dam*), cast members appeared in paper costumes that might have been salvaged from the production's torn-up walls. The maskers in this fragile performance mirrored "the unhappy masks" on the streets of St. Petersburg, whom Blok described in his essay "Troubled Times" (*Bezvremen'e*, October 1906). This was the theatricalized world of swirling maskers and historical events which Bely depicted in *Petersburg*. It was a world in which "the integrality of things" had seemingly disappeared. In Bely's novel, "the boundaries between things and the fixed identity of individual objects fell away into cosmic infinity," leaving the intellectual protagonist alone to ponder morosely and perhaps futilely his class and culture's fate at the foot of the Egyptian sphinx. By 1906, the world of the Silver Age intellectual had become a tragic *balagan*. It seemed that in the confusion of the historical moment, the self-mirroring intelligentsia, divorced from the people, could do no more than leap from one stage onto another, without hope of exiting, save through death.[56]

In his essay "Gogol's Child" (*Ditya Gogolya*, 1909), Blok described how the author of many sudden and magical literary escapes hallucinated one final flight on his deathbed. Harlequin's Gogolesque leap through a painted paper window onto a bared stage in Blok's play exposed the inescapability of life as a theatrical mode of being and of theatre as a compulsion to freeze time (and fix fate) rather than "to punch a hole" in it, as Blok (and Meyerhold) had hoped.

Harlequin's life publicizes the unrealizable impulse to leap out of himself after his laughter at death turned inward. Harlequin resembles the False Dmitry in *Boris Godunov* (written 1825; produced 1870), Pushkin's play about historical pretendership. Having failed to convince his interlocutors at a border crossing (significantly) that he is not the pretender to the Russian throne (an existential double negative), the monk Grigory Otrepev/False Dmitry leaps out of a window (scene 8). In so doing, he leaps back into his false identity and out of himself (that is, out of his true self). Blok knew Pushkin's play and remembered the Petersburg harlequinades and puppet shows of his youth that were originally staged in front of the Tsar's Winter Palace (site of "Bloody Sunday") and later on various parade grounds. Blok fashioned his Harlequin's leap as just such a vexed action in a play which he said emerged from "the depth of my soul's police department."[57] Harlequin's leap, which is subverted by the removal of context (scenery/social relevancy) and the appearance of Death, is the existential negative of Charlotta Ivanovna's "leap for life" in *The Cherry Orchard*.

Unable to leap out of himself or to realize his social causes as social change, the Silver Age Harlequin repeatedly leapt into his existential other, into what Oskar Kokoschka, in 1907, called the "ever more enticing abyss of Eros": "woman." In *The Little Showbooth*, woman as *mise en abîme*, the Gogolian anthropomorphized abyss, carries upon her shoulder a scythe, which Blok likened to "an overturned moon expiring in the morning light" (20). The scythe, like the open window through which "the night flows out" (20) but through which nothing escapes, was a metonym of woman's inversion and ultimately of man's inversion as "woman." The death's head of the Beautiful Lady/Divine Sophia in *The Little Showbooth* wore the artist-intellectual's crown of thorns, woven from his limitless (dis)belief and expressive of his voided self.

In 1917, Aleksandr Golovin painted Meyerhold as Blok's Pierrot, reflected in a mirrored background and foreground (fig. 10). This captured what Vera Verigina, an actress in Meyerhold's production of Blok's play, described as the actor-director's fixed gaze at the audience and into himself. The sphinxlike gaze from within the portrait belonged to Harlequin-Pierrot in and out of control of his fate, a condition to which the caricatures of Meyerhold during his tenure as Kommissarzhevskaya's alter ego and nemesis indirectly alluded. Golovin presented Meyerhold in Blok's role as Blok had presented himself, trapped in a doubled, cross-gendered theatre of exile. Neither Blok nor Meyerhold realized in the period 1905–1917 that the pervasive co-opting of female iconicity by male artist-intellectuals to express their own rather than women's social and existential dilemmas would soon conspire with the state's desire to marginalize and silence the creative intelligentsia. In fact, by 1917, this class of gender-charged, unreconstructed individuals—Hamlet and Ophelia, Harlequin-Pierrot and Columbine, the groom and his cardboard bride, the male and female sphinx—had conducted a lengthy wedding rehearsal for their *mariage blanc*.[58]

Portrait of the Actor and Director V. E. Meyerhold, *1917, by Aleksandr Golovin. Courtesy of Izdatel'stvo izobrazitel'noe iskusstvo, Moscow.*

On 22 October 1917, the Kamerny Theatre's production of *Salome*, staged by Aleksandr Tairov and starring his wife Alisa Koonen, opened a new era. The play's heroine was presented not as an unbalanced, decadent girl infantilized and eroticized by what we today call the "male gaze" but as a woman seeking personal liberation in an emotional state of revolutionary undress. The de-eroticizing and re-socializing of Salome as an "intensely impersonal" and "passionately intimate" icon, bathed in red light in Tairov's production, affirmed the earliest introduction of the new concrete poetry of ideological clarity and socially ordered passion. Ultimately, though, the residual ambiguity, the cross-gendered desire stimulated by Salome, proved to be too much for the Soviet state. This new Herod, which had little tolerance for gender ambiguity and female metaphors, ordered the proletariat, its fetishized spear carriers, to fall upon Salome and the other iconic artists and models of the Silver Age with their shields and to crush them.[59]

CHAPTER 3

REVOLUTIONIZING GALATEA

Each of us represents a kind of disunited being. But the

perfect person is not a man, not a woman, nor even a

man and a woman together, and is neither man nor

woman.

— *Fyodor Sologub* [1]

In Soviet culture after 1917, male hands often roughly sculpted the female image. The Soviet Pygmalion, who remade *himself* historically, viewed his Galatea with suspicion, while desiring her with a combination of private obsession and revolutionary fervor. Meanwhile, Soviet women, who often appeared as dramatic characters and theatrical performers, political revolutionaries, and party workers in pre- and postrevolutionary society, rarely if ever served as playwrights, stage directors, or members of the government or the party's inner elite. But although women's roles were only occasionally authorial, they were far more than merely participatory in defining the life and image of the new Soviet culture. Woman was for the Soviets a necessary and significant object through which a wider discourse was conducted.

The nineteenth-century "woman's bible," August Bebel's *Woman under Socialism* (originally, *Woman in the Past, Present and Future*, 1878), along with Friedrich Engels's *The Origins of the Family, Property and the State* (1884), based upon Marx's ethnographic research, formally set the tone and limits for the Marxist discourse on the "woman question." The Marxists located the basis of socio-sexual inequality in the family, the source and model of bourgeois economic oppression. After 1917, the Bolsheviks nominally reconstructed women as proletarians, wielding increased power in economic production, rather than as "bourgeois feminists," who separated sexual relations from "the economic relations of production." In this way,

the Bolsheviks could claim to have liberated woman from her bourgeois imprisonment, while effectively folding the woman question
into the "class question." The revolutionizing of Galatea by the patri-

archal Soviet state's Pygmalion coincided with the "feminized," politically uncommitted, and disempowered artist-intellectuals being
cast in the statue's role. This development ironically recast the expressed desire of decadent prerevolutionary Russian culture, which
equated woman and art with inertia and death. As such, the Soviet
aesthetic reaffirmed a counterrevolutionary concept dressed up in the
trappings of a new style and a new, more enlightened way of seeing.
This tragic theme emerged only gradually from the historical drama
whose announced plot was the reconfiguration of man and woman as
political and cultural equals bonded together by a common cause.[2]

In the prerevolutionary period, behavioral and artistic codes of
male and female self-engenderment (sexual role reversal, androgyny,
and bisexuality) defined a performative and metaphorical solution to
personal and national identity crises, even as it illustrated the problem. "Systematic duality," entertaining difference while predicting
spiritual union, was effaced, after 1917, in the Bolsheviks' promotion
of the anonymous, largely degendered proletariat and the resolution
of history into Communism's all-encompassing revolutionary moment. The new Soviet state-designed collective monolith of material
utopianism celebrated its victory over the prerevolutionary aesthetes'
nostalgically envisioned spiritual communities. Rather than attempt
the impossible, the inscription of "the feminine . . . in common language," the Bolsheviks forged a syncretic vocabulary of group-speak
and official acronyms. The Bolsheviks revolutionized Galatea in theory, while absorbing her into a syncretic model of new personhood
for the new society. However, while the male party leadership and
Soviet culture celebrated the "new man" for his toughness and hon-
esty, they characterized the "new woman" as "grim, mannish, plain,
and armed." Masculine consciousness continued to cast a watchful
eye on feminine spontaneity.[3] Woman was attendant at the birth of
the revolution. According to Soviet history, however, man was its
birth mother.

The new Soviet regime wanted to see itself expressed in images of
mastery—invention and production—rather than in terms of mystery
and identity crisis. Machines and machine-men defined a man-made
world of objects and materials whose rational, orderly perfection
shamed "the capriciousness of [Mother] Nature." Man's universal
fear of female otherness was quelled by absorbing the woman ques-

tion into the class question. Sex and gender issues were demystified, even as they were pushed onto the national stage by politics and more often discussed.[4]

The new Soviet culture inscribed masculine values and forms, promoting the athletic body over the aesthetic eye, spatial mass, density, and dynamism over the static painted surface which masked the prerevolutionary symbolists' inner world. This tendency was ironically predicted by elements in the prerevolutionary avant-garde. A character called "A Time Traveler" in the "transrational" (*zaumnaya*) cubo-futurist opera *Victory over the Sun* (*Pobeda nad solntsem*; St. Petersburg premiere December 1913), proclaimed: "Look / Everything has been masculinized / The lake is harder than iron / Don't trust the old gauges." Artist El Lissitsky's (Lazar Markovich Lisitsky) *The New One* (*Novy chelovek*, fig. 11), a lithographic representation of an "electro-mechanical production" for an unrealized staging of *Victory over the Sun*, captured the new constructed mystery of the machine age. This two-legged, two-headed "dynamic figure built up of nonobjective shapes," with its red-square heart and overall red and black revolutionary color code and metallic frame, suggested the new order's resolved dualism, a reconstructive, dialectical consciousness, which extended to gender.[5]

This new order and its artistic representation passed from the abstract to the concrete under Stalin in Vera Mukhina's statue *Worker and Collective Farm Woman* (fig. 12). Commissioned to crown Boris Yofan's Soviet pavilion at the 1937 Paris exhibition, the statue celebrated the union of Soviet industry and agriculture in the straining musculature and resolved stride of its giant hammer-wielding man and sickle-bearing woman. While El Lissitsky's avant-garde piece capitalized on the confusion of the Civil War years (1917–1923), Mukhina's heroic symbol of unified, patriotic production masked the Great Terror of the 1930s.

In the 1920s, artistic montages in various media broke up the homogeneity of visual space, and, within that space, woman's body continued to disrupt social consciousness. Judith Mayne suggests that woman's image was used in the early Soviet cinema to represent "the difficulty of articulating a new narrative and cinematic consciousness for socialism." The example she gives, from Friedrich Ermler's film *Fragment of an Empire* (1929), rapidly alternated images of objects with close-ups of a woman in the window of a speeding train.

The new Soviet order "presupposed socialist fellowship as a fellowship of men" and continued to distrust women as being inherently

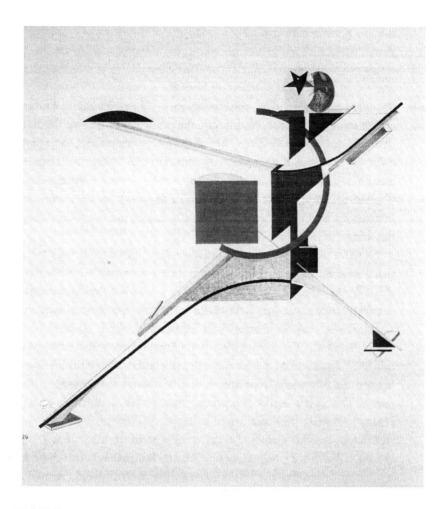

passive, inconsistent, and uncommitted to any political ideology.
While few male party leaders were as openly misogynistic as Joseph
Stalin, who referred disparagingly to female intellectuals as "herrings
with ideas," all sidestepped the question of complete equality between
the sexes. This attitude prevailed despite the fact that it was the riot-
ing of socialist factory women which ushered in the February 1917
revolution.[6]

Lenin, who believed that "a woman can never give herself a hundred percent to the party," certainly had the many illiterate and socially conservative citizens of his country in mind when he proclaimed

that "a person who can neither read nor write is outside politics."
Fewer women than men were politically indoctrinated in the early
stages of the revolution, and those who were (along with a high percentage of artists and Jews) soon became responsible for improving
the literacy and political consciousness of Bolshevik men. Women
commissars headed the Politotdely, the political sections of the Red
Army during the Civil War. These functions were under the general
direction of Varya Kasparova, who directed the Agitational Department of the Bureau of Military Commissars in Moscow. Women also
directed the Central Executive Committee's School for Agitators and
Instructors. Still others worked in the Cheka, the secret police, during
this same period (1917–1921).

Yet there were many other women whose "support positions" consisted of little more than making the beds, cooking the meals, and
cleaning the apartments of male activists. Lenin, for example, sought
to cast his wife Nadezhda Krupskaya in the role of domestic madonna
to counterbalance his mistress Inessa Armand's role of revolutionary
muse. Armand, "the French-born daughter of two music-hall enter-
tainers," later chaired the Moscow Provincial Economic Council and
headed the Women's Department of the Central Committee of the
party.[7] This ironic replay of prerevolutionary decadent iconic stereotyping backfired, however, when Lenin discovered, much to his con-
sternation, that his domestic skills were superior to his wife's. Krupskaya's self-defined role was, at first, largely limited to doing whatever
was necessary to free her husband to do his political work. Armand,
however, was Lenin's soulmate and political confidante and, on at
least one occasion, his alter ego. Lenin sent her to represent him at
a revolutionary Presidium under the female variant of his pseudonym "Petrov(a)," telling her: "So, through our pseudonyms, we shall
face the public united in one person—openly yet secretly. You will
actually be me." This conflation of male-female identity modeled
what was to be the new fashion of anonymous revolutionary collectivism which would nominally replace the celebrity of prerevolutionary individualism.

In the meantime, Krupskaya, whose frumpishness and unexcep-
tional nature embarrassed her husband, evolved from being a nurtur-
ing wife to being a skilled educational propagandist. Yet she continued to be plagued by shyness, which was misread as passivity. Even
leading female revolutionaries helped on occasion to reinforce male
stereotypes of women. The widely admired revolutionary Mariya Spi-
rodonova (she killed a provincial governor at the age of nineteen) told

FIGURE 12

Vera Mukhina, Worker and Collective Farm Woman, *1937.*
Courtesy of Popperfoto, London.

the American Communist writer Louise Bryant that women are better martyrs than administrators, because "it needs temperament and not training to be a martyr." Spiridonova and fellow revolutionary Angelika Balabanova suggested that women are held back by conscience and a lack of inner freedom, qualities of character that do not impede most men.[8]

"We are weak," reflected Vera Pavlovna, the protofeminist heroine of Chernyshevsky's novel *What Is to Be Done?* (*Chto delat'?* 1863), "because we consider ourselves so." However, this negative self-assessment is inconsistent with the historical profile of female revolutionaries developed in part from the testimony of their male counterparts. The men saw them, again romantically, as being more ruthless than men, with an "almost reverent" attitude toward terrorism. Historian James H. Billington, citing examples of female revolutionaries of the nineteenth and early twentieth centuries, writes that "their distinctive role . . . was to purify and intensify terror, not to articulate ideas." "This passion for purity," he continues, "fueled a growing desire among women revolutionaries to be the one to throw the bomb, to be sentenced to death, or even to immolate one's self in prison." One such revolutionary, Yevstoliya Rogozinikova, "heavily perfumed in an elegant black dress," blew up the director of the main prison administration in St. Petersburg with "thirteen pounds of high explosives that she had packed into her bodice and used to enhance her bust."[9] Such self-empowered women were the prototypes for a revolutionary *belle dame sans merci* that male Soviet leadership feared and respected enough neither to encourage nor to develop.

Russian men in general still considered women to be objects, even as Bolshevik Party leadership extended to them limited partnership as revolutionary subjects. Lenin, who spoke to the first All-Russian Congress of Women, was a sympathetic listener in the discussion of the woman question; nevertheless, in "On the Emancipation of Women" (1919), he stated that working women must liberate themselves without creating their own separate political organizations, which he feared would divide the party and subvert the class question. Accordingly, Aleksandra Kollontay tried to make the Women's Section or Department of the Party's Central Committee Secretariat (Zhenotdel, 1919–1930), which she headed from 1920 to 1922, appear to be less separatist and more gender-neutral. Feminism was regarded by most Soviet men and women as a bourgeois enterprise. As Billington notes, "Women tended to be more revolutionary than feminist in Russia." Evidence to the contrary was provided by Yakov Protazanov's 1924 film *Aelita*. Aelita, Queen of Mars, seduces a brave Soviet engineer into aiding her in fomenting a workers' revolt on her planet. This plot having been accomplished, Aelita seeks to destroy the engineer, thus betraying a feminist agenda hidden within her revolutionary plan. This scenario embodied a male and party paranoia which never really abated.

The extent to which this paranoia had evolved since the prerevolutionary period is demonstrated by comparing the foregoing example to an earlier work of Russian science fiction, Aleksandr Bogdanov's 1908 novel *Red Star* (*Krasnaya zvezda*). Bogdanov's story presented a positive socialist union between the "male" and "female" civilizations of earth and Mars, the latter being far more advanced. The Martian language lacks gender distinctions, indicating only whether a person is living or dead. Bogdanov, a one-time ally and later an adversary of Lenin, was less concerned with vilifying women than with sifting through general apocalyptic unease, inflammatory, destabilizing romantic passion, the fear of revolutionary terrorism, and the "cult of personality" (Martian monuments honor events, not people) in order to discover "the unity of Life."

The number of prominent Bolshevik women placed close to the centers of political power, while small in the period between the advent of the revolution and the years directly following the Civil War (1917–1923), thereafter dropped precipitously. In 1922, only 8 percent of party members were female, a proportion that rose to 12 percent by 1927. Overall, only three women, Yelena Stasova (functioning secretary of the party during and immediately after the revolution), Varvara Yakovleva (director of the Petrograd branch of the Cheka in 1918), and Aleksandra Kollontay (commissar of public welfare, the first female member of the Party's Central Committee, and director of Zhenotdel, 1920–1922) belonged to the party's highest ranks. Only four women—Klavidya Nikolayeva, Aleksandra Artyukhina, Krupskaya, and Anna Kalygina—served on the party's Central Committee between 1924 and 1939.[10] The role of women in the government was only slightly better.

Politically talented women occupied mainly mid-management positions in the new regime and competed for Lenin's attention. His benign but aloof paternalism replaced the patriarchy of the church fathers and reinforced that of the husbands who ruled the traditional family unit. Although the political equality which radical women had expected since the nineteenth century and which the Soviet Constitution guaranteed never came about, Lenin could justifiably proclaim in

"Soviet Power and the Status of Women" (1919): "In the course of two years of Soviet power in one of the most backward countries in Europe, more has been done to emancipate woman, to make her the equal of the 'strong sex,' than has been done during the past 130 years by all the advanced, enlightened, 'democratic' republics of the world taken together." Still, the Bolsheviks were concerned with liberating working-class women, more for their social class than for their gender, and woman remained "an appendage to a broader labor problem."[11]

The "sex question" was a symbolic means for the Bolsheviks to maintain the characterization of woman as politically recalcitrant other, so as to separate her from the goal of political common cause. A statement made by a character in Fyodor Gladkov's Soviet novel *Cement* (*Tsement*, 1925) that romance required "the muscles of a bull," "healthy nerves," and cold, calculating minds reflected the Bolsheviks' attempt to abstract sex from the realm of private emotion, to transmute it into an objective, anonymous (that is, collective) political desire. The Bolsheviks at least publicly asserted that abstinence rather than sex with contraception was most conducive to effective party work.

Aleksandra Kollontay's removal as minister of welfare was made inevitable by what Lenin viewed as her mixing of sex and politics. Kollontay was specifically reprimanded for defending her husband Fyodor Dubenko, leader of the Kronstadt fleet, against the charge of trading with the Germans. Louise Bryant suggests, however, that the unspoken charge against Kollontay was her "excessive theatricality." To this description one might ascribe her advocacy of free love, her marriage to a man some years her junior, her "feminine" insincerity and irresponsibility (the ability to play-act and the desire to do so), and her iconicity. The political patriarchy preferred the maternal "heavy, earthy figure of Eve" to "the slim, inspired unmaternal figure" of the new woman—the autonomous revolutionary Salome which Kollontay embodied.[12] Kollontay put the party too much in mind of the decadent Columbines who graced the stage of prerevolutionary culture, in which ironic *commedia dell'arte* plays and motifs were extremely popular among the "feminized"—that is, the ambivalent, alienated, and paradoxical—intelligentsia.

The Bolsheviks disliked and distrusted renegade theatricality, which escaped their design and control, whether in the form of free love or gender role reversal. For this reason, Provisional Government leader Aleksandr Kerensky, whom Edmund Wilson described as being "an emotional and ornamental orator . . . badly spoiled by the ladies of Petrograd," saw his vanity and self-importance parodied. Nikolay Yevreinov, in the mass spectacle *The Storming of the Winter Palace* (*Vzyatie Zimnego Dvortsa*, 7 November 1920) depicted Kerensky escaping from the Winter Palace in drag to the exclamations of his Women's Battalion. (The real Kerensky was actually disguised as a Serbian officer.) Sergey Eisenstein, in his film *October* (*Oktyabr'*, 1927), presented Kerensky as a preening Napoleon, perhaps intentionally recalling the Russian people's legendary association of the vainglorious emperor with the Antichrist. As recently as the 1970s, Yury Lyubimov offered a "hysterical" Kerensky to a new theatregoing public at Moscow's Taganka Theatre.[13]

Kerensky's theatrically flamboyant figure contrasted unfavorably with the unprepossessing Lenin, "who never said more than he meant" and who refused to purchase new clothing en route to the Finland Station to take command of the revolution. Nevertheless, both Lenin's and Kerensky's personae were developed from legitimate revolutionary models. Lenin's revolutionary asceticism—the mythical Lenin who ate only what was within reach of the common people and engaged in "nothing but the necessary"—derived from Rakhmetov, who slept on a bed of nails to strengthen his will in Chernyshevsky's *What Is to Be Done?* Kerensky, with his self-dramatizing tendencies, his love affair with language, costume, and self-affirmation, could claim as his prototype the Decembrist revolutionaries of the 1820s. But the syllogistic logic which equated theatricality with femininity, femininity with weakness, and thus theatricality with weakness proved to be too ingrained to be easily effaced. The developing Soviet state sought to "defemininize" and detheatricalize men and women, to strip them of all vanity and pretense (code words for individualism) in order to create the appearance of a uniform and a uniformly strong political collective.[14]

Romantic egoism was replaced officially by comradeship, predicated upon the assumption that "nobody is *one*, but *one of*." The subjective "I" was symptomatic of and conducive to bourgeois nostalgia and petty sentiment. In Yevgeny Zamyatin's dystopic parody *We* (*My*, 1920), the male protagonist D-503, a worker on the space project Integral ("the endless equalization of all Creation," 168), rejects the sentimental and compliant O-90 for the "new woman" E-330, who helps him to develop a soul (*dusha*, feminine in Russian). The new man's and the new woman's sense of having invented one another, the ideal embodied in El Lissitsky's *The New One*, and partially in the D-503/E-330 relationship, is shadowed in *We* by an image from/of the past. In a glass cage, suspended in midair, a man and woman stand frozen in a kiss, "her whole body . . . bent backward, as if broken. This for the last time, for all time" (332).[15]

Bolshevism was threatened by nonpolitical romantic union and by separatist politics. In particular, the party hierarchy feared the autonomous Amazon, characterized by her detractors as a "psychological freak," an unnatural hybrid of male will and female desire.[16] The model of Amazonian autonomy was the Women's Death Battalions (fig. 13), commissioned by the Provisional Government as "stopping detachments" in the struggle to capture army deserters and dissuade would-be defectors during the Civil War. Of the 250 members of the Women's Battalion who unsuccessfully defended the Winter Palace from Bolshevik attack in 1917, 6 were killed and 30 wounded. Their commander, Mariya Bochkarova, the daughter of a former serf, hated men and distrusted women in equal measure. She trained her all-female unit separately from the male soldiers, which deepened the suspicion and resentment already caused by the battalion's link to a right-wing feminist organization. Bochkarova recruited her soldiers by appealing to their and society's ideals of "sexual purity" (they took a vow of chastity for the duration of their military service) and "maternal self-sacrifice," as protectors of the nation's children and defenders of "Mother Russia," which they embodied. When one of Bochkarova's female charges clandestinely sought sexual union with a man, Bochkarova allegedly bayoneted her to death in the act.

In the film *October*, or *Ten Days That Shook the World* (*Oktyabr', Desyat' dney, kotorye potryasli mir*, 1928), Eisenstein depicts the members of the Women's Battalion in a moment of repose inside the Winter Palace. They proceed to remove their masculine uniforms, revealing their female undergarments, and to apply cosmetics. This action parodies both femininity, via homoerotic association, and the depth of female resolve to enact the male's activist role, a resolve the Bolsheviks considered to be suspect. At least in the fictional retelling, the Winter Palace as symbol of the decadent past became the stage upon which both Kerensky and his female defenders engaged in crossdressing. Once the honest, healthy Bolshevik workers seized control of the government, the Amazons of the Women's Battalion "were ordered home and told to put on female attire because they were considered enemies of the revolution."[17]

The amount and intensity of criticism, gossip, and parodic abuse of the Women's Battalions in Russia and abroad constituted nothing

short of a ritualized public humiliation. These masculinized women had not only co-opted a male social role but a male artistic prerogative. Prerevolutionary male artists expressed their embedded femaleness in female characters whom they both idealized and destroyed. The Women's Battalions transformed the female role from artistic object to artistic subject and dared to fetishize and perform *male* identity in the process. The fictional Kerensky's donning of female garments, while under the protection of his trousered female defenders, signified that the only women's skirts left to hide behind were his own. Male desire was thrown back upon itself. The anti-Bolshevik prerevolutionary artist-intellectuals director Nikolay Yevreinov and designer Yury Annenkov, who staged Kerensky's "historical" action in the mass spectacle, would soon emigrate, their political and cultural disempowerment vested in the symbolic images they had helped to create.

The vast majority of the approximately five thousand women who fought in World War I and the eighty thousand who served in the Civil War, many of whom filled the noncombatant roles of laborer, health- and food-service worker, teacher, and spy, were individuals teamed with men and celebrated in wartime propaganda.[18] The Bolsheviks produced their own heroic Amazon in the person of Larisa Reysner, the prototype for the Commissar who saves the fleet from anarchy in Vsevolod Vishnevsky's 1933 drama *An Optimistic Tragedy* (*Optimicheskaya tragediya*). The daughter of a St. Petersburg law professor who helped draft the first Soviet Constitution, Reysner was a twenty-two-year-old beauty when she joined the Red Army in the Civil War. As head of the intelligence section of the Volga Fleet, she conducted spying missions behind enemy lines, but later she could not accept the moral turpitude precipitated by the Soviet experiment in free market economy, the New Economic Policy (1921–1928).

The traditional hagiographic Soviet view, echoed by feminist scholars in the West, sees Reysner as the "Revolutionary Pallas," a paragon of self-discipline and a charismatic heroine during the Volga Flotilla's engagement at the Svyazhsk front. There she helped restore the health and spirit of the then nineteen-year-old Vishnevsky and his fellow seamen after their near drowning in a skirmish. In a lecture to the Kamerny Theatre company during their rehearsals for his play, Vishnevsky reverentially intoned that the simple kiss Reysner placed upon his forehead during his recovery would burn in his memory for the rest of his life. This same view holds that Reysner, who may have served as a model for Lara in Pasternak's *Doctor Zhivago*, was herself an important, somewhat overlooked author, championed by Andreyev and conversant with if not entirely hospitable to the avant-garde. Her one play, *Atlantida* (Shipovnik, 1913), presented a young (male), self-sacrificing would-be savior of Atlantis as a metaphor for social- ist heroism. Interestingly, Reysner, who offered actor critiques and penned dramatic criticism, wrote her first literary analyses on Ophelia and Cleopatra. A recent essay by Alla Zeide indirectly suggests a ten- sion in Reysner's real character between the insecurity and determi- nation that these two roles embody. Unable to live up to her parents' intellectual and artistic example (her father worked with the Meyer- hold Theatre in the early 1920s), Reysner declared herself to be an enemy of her class, the intelligentsia, and recreated herself as a heroic orphan via the 1917 revolution.

Alisa Koonen, the lead actress of Moscow's Kamerny Theatre and wife of its artistic director, Aleksandr Tairov, counted Vishnevsky's Commissar among her most successful professional roles (Kamerny Theatre premiere 1933). In her performance, Koonen stressed the partially revealed feminine qualities in the Amazon, Reysner the poet as well as the member of the Soviet "cult of power" and the self- designated "woman of the Russian Revolution." Reysner had sought to intercede with Lenin to stay the execution of her lover, the Acmeist poet Nikolay Gumilyov, whose sentence was carried out in 1921. Here and elsewhere, she manifested the empathic, "contradictory and unrestrained" (that is, feminine) aspects of her otherwise Amazonian character. By reconstructing the Salome-sphinx's negative female la- conism as constructive, Lenin-like, positive male laconism, the fiction- alized Amazon Reysner could become the "heroine" of Vishnevsky's play. Vishnevsky wrote of the Commissar: "She does more observing than speaking because there is so much that she will have to do."[19] The silent woman had been presented by prerevolutionary male art- ists in a deadly or deathlike state, the (male) artist-destroying symbol- ist sphinx, who "rules [words] by stopping them, stillborn, in the throat," and by the drowned Ophelia, the artistic object who enacts the artist's (Hamlet's) self-destructive self-adulation. In *An Optimistic Tragedy*, the translation of the female's penchant for "untransformed cruelty" and self-victimization into a thoughtful prelude to heroic ac- tion was accomplished simply by masking a male character with a woman's face.[20]

If the Bolsheviks were in conflict concerning dramatically expressed female autonomy, they were likewise uncertain as to whether and how the family unit could be made responsive to woman's and the party's nominally shared ideals. The Bolsheviks, citing *The Commu-*

nist Manifesto, believed that bourgeois family life would disappear along with capitalism. Marx linked women's liberation with the abolition of the patriarchal family structure. Lenin, however, associated the family with orderliness and orderliness with the party cause. Neither the Bolsheviks nor the average Soviet citizen wanted to see family life abolished, and only the Bolsheviks wanted to see it redefined. The revolutionaries did tap into a traditional cultural sense of spiritual community which often transcended the biological family.[21]

Leon Trotsky warned that the revolutionary woman, in particular the *zhenotdelovka* (member of Zhenotdel), owing to her preoccupation with the women's movement, would act as a dissolvent of family life. Throughout the country and especially in the provinces, men fought (sometimes with the aid of other women) Zhenotdel's efforts to organize and politicize their wives. For the most part, Zhenotdel concerned itself with family issues such as child and orphan care, school service and inspection, food distribution and housing supervision, preventative medicine, and public health and education. Still, by investing civil powers in strong women and by giving women in general a sense of personal and collective identity independent of their husbands, Zhenotdel helped to undermine the traditional patriarchal family structure. The assertion of an even more dominant, centralized patriarchy under Stalin, made necessary by the demands of intensified industrialization, led to the elimination of all secondary loyalties and associations, including Zhenotdel. With this development, the woman question, born in Russia in the late 1850s and early 1860s, was officially considered "resolved." Paradoxically, Zhenotdel was originally founded by the male party leadership (and staffed in part by their wives and relatives) as part of a propaganda campaign aimed at winning women over to the Communist cause.[22]

The prototypical new Soviet woman, the *zhenotdelovka* Dasha Chumalova in *Cement*, was "a woman with a red kerchief about her head . . . burn[ing] like a flame" (60), an image suggestive of Lenin's revolutionary newspaper the *Spark* (*Iskra*, founded 1900). She seemed "strange, not womanly" to her husband Gleb, just returned from serving in the Civil War. Whereas in Rakhmetov's "spiritual autobiography" in *What Is to Be Done?* reading precedes experience, Dasha is first brutalized by life and only then becomes a "woman at the table," a student of self-denial/self-fulfillment via revolution. This new activist sociopolitical character type sought to replace the poetically adored but personally co-opted and disenfranchised prerevolutionary woman, a male-dependent, passive nonparticipant in life. The "woman at the table" actually first appeared toward the end of the last century in paintings such as Vladimir Makovsky's *Evening Meeting* (1875–1897) and Ilya Repin's *Revolutionary Meeting* (1882) whose titles suggest her movement out of the house and into a more public, active, even activist domain. This new role did not, however, represent a clean break with the past. When the student revolutionary Mariya Vetrova was lionized for immolating herself with kerosene from her reading lamp, her martyrdom to a self-determined fate simply recast the decadent icon of woman as the bride of death.[23]

In *Cement*, one of Dasha Chumalova's fellow *zhenotdelovki* announces her intention to cut her braid, likening it to a noose on which women hang and which men hang onto as a romantic symbol. The cutting of the braid, a likely reference to Blok's *The Little Showbooth* (discussed in chapter 2), represents the new Soviet woman's consignment of the virgin-harlot personae to obsolescence. The semiotics of altered and confused identity—bobbed-haired women and cleanshaven men—reflected the changing face of the party, as surely as Peter the Great's shaving of his nobles' beards in the early eighteenth century signified the shift from an old, insular Slavic order to a new Westernizing one.

Aleksandra Kollontay proclaimed in 1918 that "a class conscious mother should achieve the spiritual level at which she would no longer make a distinction between 'my child' and 'your child,' but would remember that all children are 'ours,' children of a Communist, toiling Russia." A nonnurturing and sexually liberated mother and wife, Dasha gives her young daughter to the collective to be raised and withholds herself physically from a husband, whose inability to listen to her she calls "unmanly." The Chumalovs' child dies in the care of the Children's Home "Krupskaya" (where all the girls have their hair cut like boys), symbolically leaving the future in the hands of the party workers, while tacitly fulfilling Trotsky's explicit and the other Bolsheviks' implicit warning of a separate feminist agenda. The recent consolidation of Bolshevik power in spring 1921 and the intraparty factionalism that commenced with Lenin's death in January 1924 required the appearance of unity that a bonded male-female model could iconically represent. Thus, Dasha, with the aid of her politically reconstructed husband, reopens the derelict cement factory, a space of shared male-female authority and activity. Yet as Judith Mayne illustrates in her analysis of Soviet silent films of the 1920s, public life and space remained largely male preserves. Women were still relegated to and trapped in private (domestic) space.[24]

In his 1928 drama *Inga*, Anatoly Glebov employs the mechanization of the factory as a metaphor for the suppression of woman's emotional desire and independence.[25] The proletarian Inga, a member of what a male character calls "the class of paradoxical women," is unmarried and physically unable to bear children. Her enthusiasm is for elevating the work process to an aesthetic realm, introducing art into production. This art-into-production ideal and the reference in the play to "the figure of a woman-mannequin draped in 'a new model dress'" (376) recall the "Amazons" of art and design of the 1920s. Varvara Stepanova, Aleksandra Ekster, Lyubov Popova, and Vera Mukhina applied the constructivist principle of "the organic entry of art into life" to the factory-inspired rhythmic design and mass production of functional clothing (*prozodezhda*) and sports clothes (*sportodezhda*). They, along with fellow Amazons Natalya Goncharova, Valentina Kulagina, and Olga Rozanova, brought an "aggressive enthusiasm" to all aspects of design, including theatre, that helped dispel the association between female passivity and aestheticism/nonutilitarian art.

A number of the so-called Amazons were closely associated with male artists of various sorts: Goncharova with Mikhail Larionov, Kulagina with Gustav Klutsis, Popova with Aleksandr Vesnin, and Rozanova with Aleksey Kruchenykh. Stepanova often co-created artistic projects in a single studio with her husband, Aleksandr Rodchenko. Rodchenko designed the set and costumes for the 1929 production of *Inga* at Moscow's Theatre of the Revolution.[26]

Lacking a domestic and a sexual life, Inga forfeits her status as role model for the new Soviet woman to Glafira, who learns to balance child-rearing with sociopolitical work after her husband leaves her. Ultimately, implies Glebov, the new Soviet woman must satisfy the new Soviet man, who is threatened by a proletarian Joan of Arc like Inga, who makes no allowance for family life. The limits of female autonomy were continuing to be defined by male revolutionary culture.

Concurrently, nearly instantaneous, no-fault divorce was legislated in 1917, and in 1918 a new code recognized marriage as a matter for civil rather than religious authority. The Family Law of 1918 allowed each party in a marriage to take "that property earned by his/her labor," while the Family Code of 1926 established community property and legally recognized domestic labor as a valid claim on property rights. The 1926 code also permitted adoption, which the revolution had abolished as a legal right. In 1920, hospital abortions performed by physicians were declared legal (this law was repealed in 1936), and throughout the 1920s maternity benefits for working mothers were improved.

Although Glebov's Glafira rejects alimony payments from her ex-husband, most Soviet women continued to depend on male incomes. The experimental New Economic Policy (NEP) resulted in devastating unemployment among women, who represented the major part of the nation's unskilled labor force.[27] Mikhail Bulgakov's NEP dramatic satire *Zoya's Apartment* (*Zoykina kvartira*, 1926) depicts resourceful and desperate women operating a seamstress shop/brothel, a parodic reworking of Chernyshevsky's seamstress collective/revolutionary cell, established by his heroine Vera Rozalskaya. Kollontay called prostitution "a scourge which falls chiefly upon the women of the working class" and sought via Zhenotdel propaganda to keep the family as social building block intact. Bulgakov's brothel madam is a survivor. She calls her prostitutes "mannequin," cloaking them metaphorically in the modesty of the seamstress's profession. These "mannequin"/prostitutes are both male-manufactured and male-fetishized objects and revolutionary subjects.[28] They model figuratively the Stepanova-designed and Glebov factory-produced *prozodezhda* of the real Soviet woman, who is actively engaged in her profession. In Zoya's apartment the collective ideal yields to economic necessity; in turn, Soviet society's illegitimacy, which the state had attempted to bury with law and propaganda, is revealed.

In the early postrevolutionary years, Galatea, in the person of woman and the marginalized "formalist" artist, was examined by the state in light of the "legitimacy question." In this scenario, historical legitimacy, which confers political authority, was determined by ideology masquerading as an objective point of view. This theme was represented in official art and critiqued in the countervailing perspective-seeking art of the Fellow Travelers, who were thrice damned for being nonproletarians, non-Communist Party members, and formalists. These artists revealed in their work how, in the postrevolutionary period, the decadent theme of male voyeurism in relation to female anatomy had come to symbolize the panoptic reality conditioned by an increasingly paranoid collectivism. Although the national plan for communal housing began in earnest in 1929 under the slogan "For the socialist reconstruction of daily life," this Gogolian profanation of the collective ideal started earlier. As in *The In-spector General* (discussed in detail in chapter 5), spatial compression foreshortened individual perspective in Soviet society, so that, while external authority could peer in, the anonymous Galateas shaped by the state's voyeuristic Pygmalion gaze could not look out with any accurate sense of distance or context.[29]

The dramatic satires of Fellow Travelers Nikolay Erdman and Yury Olesha demonstrated how the state's emasculation of both intellectual and proletarian culture in its bid to consolidate all power in its own hands conditioned a resurgence of prerevolutionary stereotyping of woman by men. In Soviet drama, Galatea guiltily confessed the male artist-intellectual's powerlessness to reconstruct his own image as a new Soviet man, while also encoding his resentment of the Pygmalion state, which sculpted him in the female statue's image.

In Erdman's play *The Suicide* (*Samoubytsa*, 1928), the iconically named Mariya embodies the residual, longed-for yet profaned soul of "Mother Russia," upon whom her unemployed husband Podsekalni-kov leans for support while still casting blame for his weakened state. She is in turn objectified by the proletariat in the person of Yegor the Postman, who spies on her through the keyhole in the bathroom door of their collective apartment. This voyeurism is sanctioned by the state, Yegor assures her, because it represents a "Marxist point of view."[30] Meanwhile, Podsekalnikov's decision to commit suicide (an idea inadvertently suggested to him by his wife) has brought forth a plague of Gogolian "sluts" and "witches," preying women and femi-nized men (that is, artists, dilettantes, and intellectuals). These "for-mer people" (*byvshie lyudi*), disenfranchised by the revolution, are anxious to legitimize themselves by claiming Podsekalnikov as a mar-tyr to their individual causes. Finally recognizing that "I can imagine myself without a wife," but not "without me" (51), Podsekalnikov unheroically chooses life.

Goncharova, a Soviet actress playing Hamlet in Olesha's drama *A List of Blessings* (*Spisok blagodeyany*, 1931), embodied the existen-tial dilemma of the individual being policed by the social collective.[31] The political irresponsibility of the artist's individual agenda is repre-sented in the protagonist's "femaleness," which others perceive both in her anatomy and in her dreamy frivolousness. Olesha clearly iden-tified with his protagonist, who leaves Russia to perform the role (Hamlet) that she, as an alienated female artist-intellectual, has in fact already been playing in life for some time.

While publicly asserting that "women must think like men now"

(69), Goncharova depends privately upon fairy tales to bolster her low self-esteem. She sustains the anti-Soviet dream of freedom from the oppressiveness of social type embodied by Cinderella, the Ugly Duckling, and Charlie Chaplin. She co-opts the fairy-tale hero's role, generally reserved in Russian fables for men, but simultaneously assumes woman's traditional role as the witch who impedes the hero in his quest.[32] She generates two lists—of Soviet power's blessings and crimes—that together symbolize her Hamletian self-contradiction. Having been played upon by capitalists, Communists, and anti-Communist emigrés, Goncharova ends as an accidental martyr to the Marxist cause, when she intercepts a bullet meant for a strike leader in Paris. Although she asks to be covered with a red flag, her corpse, as is appropriate to her ambivalence in life, is left uncovered.

Goncharova, like the Commissar in *An Optimistic Tragedy*, is, in a sense, a man disguised as the new Soviet woman. She was based, in part, on the famous Soviet Hamlet and emigré actor Michael (Mikhail) Chekhov and on Olesha, whose biography reveals his obsession with fairy tales and images of flight. Chekhov sought to play Hamlet for Max Reinhardt in Berlin in December 1928, but instead Reinhardt's agent offered to make him into "the second Grock" (a famous Swiss clown). While performing the role of the clown Skid in *Performers* (*Artisten*) for Reinhardt, Chekhov experienced a Hamletian dual consciousness of simultaneously being and not being inside his role.[33] The impediment to the fulfillment of her "masculine" goals which Goncharova's biological femaleness created likewise represented a male fantasy imposed upon woman. The play struck an ambivalent cautionary note, warning Soviet culture that biology cannot be undone and that the masculinized woman may prove as "freakish" as the feminized man (a "freakishness" the playwright himself experienced). Although Soviet power had, in effect, legislated alienation and difference out of existence, Olesha's representation of a woman impersonating a man (Hamlet/Michael Chekhov/Olesha) suggests that the Soviet male artist's romance with the self, a legacy derived from prerevolutionary times, required the continued services of the other.

The state insisted that the capacity for change, for development toward the Soviet collective ideal, must be unimpeded by the paradox of self-love/self-hatred. Individuals and personal relationships were legitimized by their political, social, and cultural iconicity. Goncharova's failure to remake herself into a new Soviet citizen is signaled by her attachment to a politically incorrect icon, Hamlet, the symbol of the intelligentsia's disenfranchisement and its romance with alienation. The artist-icon affinity reveals the more profound problem of social class. Not being a proletarian by birth, Goncharova cannot be remade. In Aleksandr Afinogenov's drama *Fear* (*Strakh*, 1931), a play generally studied for the political conversion of its male protagonist, the female character of Valya likewise remains untransformed, despite her marriage to a new Soviet man.[34] A member of the intelligentsia, Valya is guilty of iconic incorrectness: she is working on a sculpture of Venus, the goddess of love.

The woman who is remade in *Fear*, Yelena Makarova, is, by contrast, not an artist but a scientist and "a rough-hewn, proletarian young woman, vital, energetic, and handsome in an unadorned style" (407). Her apartment, like Dasha Chumalova's, reflects the semiotic laconism of the true revolutionary: "Its furnishings are simple, almost severe, consisting of bare necessities" (407). The workplace is the locus of her passion for experimentation. She champions an art "sired" by the flesh-and-blood new Soviet man, rather than "the clay sculpted 'Proletarian in Science'" (151), which the newly "converted" Valya has prepared. Valya's dependence on others to recreate her (for example, a new proletarian husband) transforms this sculptress-Pygmalion into a Galatea and underscores the moral weakness of her social class. Her clay-footed intellectual father's recantation of his theory that fear rules the new Soviet order coincides with his newly sculpted proletarian daughter's crumbling into dust. Makarova's transformation is announced unintentionally in her ex-husband's statement: "You were born a woman by mistake" (116).

The sculptor Michelangelo's words (Sonnet XXIV) preface Aleksey Arbuzov's play *Tanya* (1938): "And so I first appeared in life as a rough draft of the more perfect creation I would later become. . . ."[35] Tanya's solipsistic love for her husband and young son requires that they both be taken from her as punishment. Thereafter, she remakes herself into a country doctor and a socialist heroine. She is, in a sense, a regendered mirror image of Chatsky, the protorevolutionary hero of Griboyedov's classic dramatic satire *Woe from Wit* (1824). Chatsky, newly arrived in Moscow bourgeois society from European revolutionary culture, is sent away by his beloved Sofiya, an act partially justified by his misanthropic individualism, expressed in his anti-bourgeois critique. Conversely, Tanya is welcomed in from the storm by her future love, who later joins her in the pursuit of a romanticized socialism. Where Sofiya's dream fearfully predicted the arrival of Chatsky as a rampaging beast, Ignatov's (Tanya's lover's) frames

Tanya in a heroically "vivid flash of lightning" (455)—as the spontaneous yet inevitable advent of the revolutionary moment.

By the 1930s, the new Soviet man and woman had apparently dreamed one another into existence. But even before the nightmare of Stalinist terror and the mythologized pedestrianism of socialist realism killed the dream, artists and the state had separately and together sown the seeds for the destruction of the marriage between the new Soviet man and woman. The tragic irony that was for a long time implicit and now became explicit in this drama was that Pygmalion and Galatea were being merged into the statue's role by the state. By engineering a merger which vested in itself virtually all power to create art and iconicity, the state concluded its plan, not to revolutionize Galatea, but to rob her of all eminence as well as of autonomy.

Prior to Stalin's creation of the machine-man in the thirties, the male creative intelligentsia revamped romantic fiction's (E. T. A. Hoffmann's and Jean Marie Villiers de l'Isle-Adam's) machine-woman.[36] The passive gynoid armed the superfluous intellectual with the Amazonian power and feminine compliance of an imaginary new Soviet woman in his struggle with the aggressive android, the new Soviet man.

Originally, the gynoid was designed as "humane technology," symbolic of degendered comradeship and equality between man and woman.[37] Even here, however, there were aspects of Amazonian "shaming" of Soviet men. Such was surely the case with the Phosphorescent Woman in Mayakovsky's play The Bathhouse (Banya, 1930), who visits the bureaucratic Soviet state, circa 1930, from the twenty-first century and exposes the shallow and self-serving ineptness of its male leadership. Like the factory-produced "woman-mannequin draped in 'a new model dress'" in Inga, the gynoid encoded a mixed message.

Ivan Babichyov, the counterrevolutionary hero of Olesha's novel Envy (Zavist', 1927; dramatized as The Conspiracy of Feelings, Zagovor chuvstv, 1929), "dreamed of Woman as the flowering of a dead civilization blinding the new man with her light." Having lost his adopted daughter Valya to the new Soviet machine-man Volodya, Babichyov invents "Ophelia" (borrowing the name of the prerevolutionary Hamlet's romantic victim), a "universal machine" programmed to corrupt Soviet technological order with bourgeois, emotional chaos. His gynoid combines the aggressiveness of the "vulgar bitch" (for example, Salome) with the passivity and propensity for self-victimization "of a girl who lost her mind for love and from despair" (Ophelia). Even in Grigory Kozintsev's much later Soviet film version of *Hamlet* (1964), Ophelia was presented as "a will-less marionette, laced into the iron corset of court etiquette." On hearing the news of her father Polonius's death, "her puppet mechanism breaks down."

In Olesha's work, the plaited hair of the virgin-harlot had become steel-plated and sharpened to a point. Instead of avenging the male inventor against the new order, Ophelia emasculates Babichyov by stripping him and pinning him squealing to the wall with a shining needle. Babichyov's Ophelia (whom he has dreamed about but not actually produced) is the product of a self-emasculating male imagination. She directly recalls the inventor Rotwang's "machine-vamp," in Fritz Lang's utopian film fantasy *Metropolis* (1926), who is cast in the image of the protagonist's beloved "Maria," an idealized and idealistic proletarian. Indirectly, the recalibration of the Pygmalion-Galatea relationship predicted a machine of another sort, Heiner Müller's *Hamletmachine* (1977), a play in which, as Elizabeth Wright states, "Hamlet's failure to become a revolutionary subject is contrasted with Ophelia's refusal to remain a pathetic victim of male oppression."[38]

Beginning in the 1920s, Soviet culture displayed a "yearning for machines [which was] stronger than that for a sweetheart." As part of this yearning, artists such as Meyerhold, whose career spanned the prerevolutionary and postrevolutionary periods, staged and enacted the growing cultural confusion between the production and romantic functions of woman and gynoid. Meyerhold did so in part via the constructivist design work of so-called Amazons Popova and Stepanova on Fernand Crommelynck's *The Magnanimous Cuckold* (*Le cocu magnifique*, 1921) and Aleksandr Sukhovo-Kobylin's *Tarelkin's Death* (*Smert' Tarelkina*, 1869). The productions' stage machinery expressed and exacerbated the impotence and self-torture of the plays' male protagonists in relation to women and machines and to women as machines. *Cuckold's* jealous husband Bruno transforms his innocent young wife Stella into an adulteress. In the process of this recreation, Bruno becomes enamored of his role as passive observer, of his wife's role as "vulgar bitch," compliant to his "inventor's" role, and of the machinery (his jealousy) that effected the transformation. Bruno plays Pygmalion to his wife's Galatea and Galatea to his own Pygmalion-like fantasy. In Meyerhold's production, male-fetishized accessories—silk stockings and button boots—protrude from under

Stella's neutral, "apron-like *prozodezhda*," combining the old and the new in the female mannequin/gynoid.[39] Meyerhold's production of *Tarelkin*, with its largely male cast, featured cross-dressing. Stepanova's "constructivist machine," "something between a barred cage and a meatgrinder," underscored both the play's theme of the little man's emasculation and the designer's enthusiasm for the Taylorized movements of the Little Tramp, Charlie Chaplin.

In his 1926 production of Gogol's *The Inspector General*, Meyerhold fetishized his beautiful actress-wife Zinaida Raykh, apparently with her eager compliance (fig. 14). In his review of the production, entitled "Fifteen Portions of the Mayor's Wife," Viktor Shklovsky said of Raykh's frequent costume-changes and scene-stealing actions (both partially justified by the text), "The mayor's wife [Raykh] was on almost all the dishes offered to the audience." This "exhibitionist fascination with dress and style" is, as Gail Finney argues in reference to Frank Wedekind's Lulu, "crucial to [the character's] feminine function as an image of visual perfection, inviting the male gaze." In Meyerhold's precisely choreographed *mise en scène*, Raykh/the mayor's wife became a beautiful gynoid, whom the automatic liar and android Khlestakov seduced interchangeably with her daughter. In a quadrille, the two ladies were exchanged by Khlestakov and his double, the Meyerhold-invented Visiting Officer.[40]

Meyerhold's interpretation of Gogolian woman as a symbol of what Konstantin Rudnitsky calls "automatic sensuality" and "the mechanics of shamelessness" coincided with the advent of the "first machine age" in the Soviet Union and Western Europe in the 1920s. Anna Andreyevna's "tragic smile," which by the end of Meyerhold's production became a "tragic mask," can be read as a sign of the new Soviet order's oppression of type (woman as coquette) and class (woman as symbol of the creative intelligentsia). The state isolates its enemies by ascribing to them such socially marginalizing traits as vanity and coquetry, signifying antisocial individualism. Thus, some members of the Soviet critical intelligentsia read Raykh-Anna's grotesque materialism (*poshlost'*) as "Bovaryism" (after Flaubert's *Madame Bovary*), that is, as a romantic "dream of splendor and sophistication in grotesque surroundings" with which they could empathize. Anna's "frivolous" behavior might also be ascribed to the radical emotionalism unleashed by the (falsely) utopic revolutionary hope represented and engendered by Khlestakov. In this sense, the intelligentsia, as well as women, could interpret Meyerhold's 1926 production as a critique of the 1917 revolution and its aftermath.[41]

FIGURE 14
Meyerhold in front of a portrait of his wife, Zinaida Raykh, 1933.
Courtesy of Ardis, Ann Arbor.

Raykh has been portrayed by historians and by former Meyerhold associates as being a vain and destructive dilettante who compromised the work of her husband, which gave her artistic life. By her daughter (Meyerhold's stepdaughter) Tatyana Yesenina's account, Raykh was completely lacking in theatrical experience when she met and married Meyerhold in 1922. At that time, the former wife of poet Sergey Yesenin had recently been released from a psychiatric hospital. In the early 1920s, Raykh suffered from a neurasthenic condition which helped precipitate a series of physical ailments. Her psychological state was further shaken by Yesenin's suicide in 1925. Yesenina claims that Meyerhold promoted his wife's acting career as a possible cure for her condition—and because he saw manifest in that condition the instincts of a tragic actress.

Yesenina depicts her mother as an actress who demanded much of herself and her colleagues. Raykh was Meyerhold's soulmate and confidante and dreamed of becoming a director herself like the husband whom she considered to be a genius and theatrical "god." According to Yesenina, although Meyerhold doted on his wife at home, he treated her purely professionally at work, often ignoring her in favor of other actors. In her thirteen-year career, Raykh played nine or ten leading roles, beginning with Aksyusha in Ostrovsky's *The Forest* (*Les*, 1871; Meyerhold Theatre premiere 19 January 1924). Yesenina ascribes criticism of Raykh by her contemporaries to their envy of her physical beauty, which won her two artistic geniuses for husbands and leading lady status at a major theatre. There is probably some truth to this and to Yesenina's claim that the casting of Raykh in major roles at the Meyerhold Theatre, especially following the departure of Mariya Babanova prior to the 1928–1929 season, was justifiable given the lack of potential leading actresses in the company.[42]

However, there is also a sociopolitical way of understanding the charge of artistic vanity which Soviet critics of the 1920s and beyond applied to the Meyerhold-Raykh relationship. To her critics—and those of her husband—Raykh represented Meyerhold's forbidden prerevolutionary obsessions set in a postrevolutionary context. She personified woman as *objet d'art* and the artist's self-regarding intelligence. The artist's narcissism and the model's vanity together produced a double portrait, reminiscent of Aleksandr Golovin's painting of Meyerhold dressed as Pierrot (1917; see fig. 10), staring out at and yet excluding his imaginary audience. Golovin's Meyerhold-Pierrot constituted a visual reference both to the director's performance in *The Little Showbooth* and to the conjugal drama of the play's author and his wife, the symbolist Galatea, Lyubov Mendeleyeva.

In an admiring letter written to Zinaida Raykh by Michael Chekhov, whom she had impersonated indirectly in *A List of Blessings*, the actor enthused: "How rare it is to see on stage beauty which is fully realized! You make miraculous use of your beauty."[43] What

Chekhov here seemed to suggest was that the realization and the use of beauty are both two-sided. Raykh was the agent for and the artist of her beauty. Raykh's Galatea not only embodied but shaped Meyerhold's Pygmalion vision. Their socially engineered and consumed *demimondaine* Marguerite Gautier, in *La dame aux camélias* (Raykh's greatest stage triumph, premiere 19 March 1934), contrasted dramatically with the self-liberating bourgeois Emma Bovary in Tairov and Koonen's husband-wife collaboration, which was based upon Koonen's 1938 adaptation of Flaubert's novel (premiere 1941). In the masquerade ball which ended the first act of Meyerhold's production, there appeared fleetingly in the crowd of guests "a mask of Death—as though direct from *Masquerade* and *The Little Show-booth*—with a grinning face and a scythe in hand." This appearance foretold more than one death.

Raykh's husband Meyerhold was arrested and disappeared into the Soviet *gulag* (the national prison camp system) on 20 June 1939, where he was executed on 2 February 1940 for the crime of "formalism."[44] At the time that he was first charged with this "crime," Meyerhold was also criticized for giving his wife leading roles in his productions, which she presumably did not deserve on the basis of her talent alone. Thus, in the minds of the public and of Soviet historians thereafter, Raykh (Galatea) was associated with, even synonymous with and to some degree responsible for, Meyerhold's (Pygmalion's) formalism.

On 14 July 1939, Raykh, whom the press described as "one of the most beautiful women in Soviet Russia," returned to her Moscow apartment on Bryusovsky Street after a stay at her country house. Although a series of Moscow apartment break-ins made Raykh's daughter, Yesenina, anxious about leaving her mother alone, her own child fell ill, forcing her to return home. Yesenina knew that Raykh's apartment building had an armed guard and that if necessary her mother could call upon the young man who had recently been seen in her company. Yesenina later suspected that both the apartment's night watchman and the mysterious young man whose name she forgot might have been implicated in the gruesome proceedings of that fateful night.

At about 1 A.M., two intruders entered Raykh's apartment via the rear balcony. One wounded the housekeeper before she could reach the bedroom, where the second intruder viciously attacked Raykh in her bed. Raykh, who apparently screamed while resisting her attacker, had her throat cut and received eight knife wounds around the heart. Raykh's eyes, her most expressive physical feature, whose radiance could reach the back of a theatre auditorium, were gouged out. The two assailants escaped, never to be found or named. The two women were taken to the hospital where, from her bed, the housekeeper overheard Raykh tell the doctor not to bother treating her, because she was dying. A moment later, she expired from loss of blood.

The housekeeper was soon released from the hospital and after a brief respite was sent to Lubyanka prison for questioning. She remembered or at least said nothing and upon her release was sent away, presumably to a prison camp. "Someone in the know" later told Raykh's son Konstantin Yesenin that his mother was murdered by assassins employed by Stalin's henchman Lavrenty Beria. Immediately following Raykh's murder, Beria's secretary and chauffeur moved into Raykh's now subdivided apartment. Shortly thereafter, some disgruntled citizens tried to get them evicted, a move which MAT actor Ivan Moskvin, a deputy of the Supreme Soviet, tried to counter by (unsuccessfully) enlisting the support of Raykh's father. The press carried no news of Raykh's burial on 18 July at the Vagankovo Cemetery. The corpse was dressed in the black velvet gown the actress wore as Marguerite Gautier in her husband's production of *La dame aux camélias*. It was the last role she played at the Meyerhold Theatre before it closed on 7 January 1938. In retrospect, premature death illuminated the fated lives of the consumptive *demimondaine* and the neurasthenic actress who so convincingly played her. Yesenina regretted that in all the photographs of Raykh as Marguerite her eyes were downcast.[45]

Whether the murder of Zinaida Raykh was premeditated, as most believe, or to some degree accidental, there are certainly some messages encoded in the spectacular nature of her demise. Raykh's gouged-out eyes and slit throat rendered fatal beauty silent, antique, and sculpted. Her death evokes for us the pornographic fetishizing of both faux-classical and faux-romantic art. She resembles in death not only Galatea but Hoffmann's doll-eyed, soulless gynoid Olympia, whom Nathanael, the mad hero of the fable "The Sandman" (1816), wants to marry. Nathanael's narcissistic, Pygmalion-like longing for his fantasy woman, which brought Galatea to life, eventually destroys them both. In the story's climactic scene, the evil eyeglass salesman Coppelius/Coppola ("eyesocket" in Italian) steals Olympia, leaving behind *only her bloody eyes*, a cruel reminder of the wages of forbidden (self)-love.

This fable helps us to dramatize how Meyerhold, the self-styled "Doctor Dapertutto" (his theatrical pseudonym, borrowed from Hoffmann's "A New Year's Eve Adventure," 1816), became an invisible corpse, while Raykh's corpse was made even more visible by public desecration. Raykh's vanity concerning her formal beauty and Meyerhold's vanity regarding the formalist art he created from that beauty (and as an analogue to formal beauty) made Raykh into the simultaneously longed for and despised Olympian Eve. Not content simply to transform soulless beauty into art, Meyerhold insisted on hubristically "shaming" his audience by making Raykh his equal and forcing them to accept her as such. Even while a prisoner in a Soviet labor camp (where he apparently heard of his wife's death), Meyerhold petitioned the president of the Council of People's Commissars of the USSR under the name "Meyerhold-Raykh."[46] Meyerhold embedded the artist's self-love in the model's performative image, which replayed the forbidden drama of the prerevolutionary period. The state could not abide this and so, assuming the role of Coppelius, killed Olympia and stole her eyes—the windows to her soul and the symbol of the artist's vision that she modeled.

Raykh's murder warned Soviet artists and citizens alike of the methodical, irrationally excessive potential of Stalinist evil. Raykh's very public death advertised and foretold the death not only of Meyerhold but of thousands of invisible, anonymous corpses in the Great Terror. Her death was a horrifying monument to the future.

Traditionally, Russian male artists had symbolically purchased their freedom of personal expression at the cost of woman's life. Decadent Salomes and sphinxlike spiritual destroyers were fetishized as idealized feminine corpses, able only to articulate their male ventriloquists' voices and not their own. The revolution confirmed woman's death but also prescribed her anonymity. In Eisenstein's *October*, the director frames a dead Ophelia, victim of a revolutionary skirmish, between statues of Minerva and the sphinx. Her long hair is fetishized when the drawbridge on which her corpse is lying opens with horrifying slowness, returning this *rusalka* to the sea. The image may have reflected directorial prejudice, but it likewise reinforced the male party leadership's unease with woman. They considered both her and the creative intelligentsia to be frivolous, silently subversive, easily led and easily killed "lackeys of reaction" who were only masquerading as revolutionary subjects.[47]

By Stalin's time, the Soviet Galatea had at least nominally become an object of social rather than aesthetic beauty. Soviet art depicted her, together with her male counterpart, as an icon of restless striving, albeit paradoxically toward an already achieved end, thus re-encoding the officially discredited decadent theme of arrested movement and the fetishizing of objects and ends. The "new" act in the drama of the female icon, coinciding as it did with the new revolutionary order, began in an atmosphere of hope; but the state's romantic creation of the new Soviet man and woman disguised its co-optation of their active roles in the new culture. The highly publicized union of Soviet man and woman, communism's quasi-religious construct, was realized in the creation of an only nominally revolutionized Galatea, whose eyes, voice, and soul had already been stolen by the state.

CHAPTER 4

THE MASKING MACHINE

Revealing the souls of machines,

enthusing the worker with the lathe,

the peasant with the tractor,

the driver with the engine,

we bring creative joy to every mechanical labor,

we join men with machines,

we educate the new man.

—Dziga Vertov

Protest is inevitable, just like Charlie Chaplin's

mustache.

—Leonid Trauberg [1]

In 1921, the Civil War ended, the RSFSR became the USSR (that is, Russia became a republican part of a union), the New Economic Policy (NEP) was initiated, Aleksandr Blok died, and Maksim Gorky temporarily emigrated, ending the immediate postrevolutionary era. Many theatres lost their government subsidies and, as Katerina Clark has noted, "closed down virtually overnight." Russian society had just passed through the period of War Communism and was about to enter into an extended process of "Sovietization," whereby a new stabilized society was defined and implemented. The Russian population suffered tremendous attrition as a result of the Civil War (some two million deaths), and a terrible famine in 1921–1922 claimed more lives in the tens of thousands. Despite demographic shifts to and from the country, the population remained very largely rural. At a time when Meyerhold applied Taylorist industrial mechanics (biomechanics, beginning in 1921) and, with Tairov, a constructivist aesthetic to the stage, industrial production and the income that it generated were at an all time low. The precipitous decline was felt mainly in heavy industry. Illiteracy remained high, especially in the rural areas, and unemployment rose, especially in the cities.[2]

In 1926, the Soviet urban population accounted for 18 percent of the total national population. Workers and employees (*rabochie i sluzhashchie*) amounted to 10.8 million. A new Soviet intelligentsia of specialists, determined by education and occupation and controlled by the party through *nomenklatura* (government and economic administration appointments), was emerging ᴄo meet the needs of industrialization. The increase in numbers was most dramatic or at least most characteristically measured in the area of the technical intelligentsia and the *apparatchiki*, those who made the party and state apparatus work. The creative intelligentsia (*tvorcheskaya intelligentsiya*), along with the critical intelligentsia (*kriticheskaya intelligentsiya*), suffered most as the machinery of party and state was securely put in place. Since 1917, the disproportionate number of critical positions within the party occupied by *intelligenty* could not compensate for their only 10 percent membership in its ranks. Overall, the *embourgeoisement* of portions of the intelligentsia siphoned off part of its identity and prerevolutionary *raison d'être*.[3]

By the mid- to late 1920s, the creative intelligentsia had become self-critical of its role in the revolution and of the program of "historical materialism" which had devolved into mundane materialist obsession. The intelligentsia's self-delusion as regards class conflict, class consciousness, and class construction was parodied at decade's end in Mayakovsky's dystopic satire *The Bathhouse* (*Banya*, 1930). In it, a stage director cynically instructs three actresses in a revolutionary pageant, Miss Liberty (Svoboda), Miss Equality (Ravenstvo), and Miss Fraternity (Bratstvo), to "stir up the imaginary masses," referred to later in the play as "would-be workers," with an imaginary call to arms.[4]

The postrevolutionary period coincided with what, in West European culture, was called the [utopic] first machine age. Nineteenth-century Slavophiles had been inhospitable to the notion of Western mechanical (logical and artificial) culture, which they feared threatened Russia's "sacred traditions and moral unity." However, atheistic Soviet culture, which was seeking to redress the backwardness of Russian thought, felt that it could not afford to persist in these reservations and embraced the idea of a new cultural beginning. Hungarian

Bauhaus artist Laszlo Moholy-Nagy enthused: "There is no tradition in technology, no consciousness of class or standing." The machine, like the Russian revolution, represented what Thoreau called a socially "constructed fate." However, the machine advertised not only technical mastery over nature but freedom to become master of or slave to the technology which people had created.[5]

Theoretically, the machine shared a heroic anonymity with the common people and defined the heroic dynamism of the future nominally captured and harnessed by the revolutionary masses. In reality, the aspiration of the "new person" to achieve the perfect functionalism of the machine derived in part from the Marxist(-Leninist) dehumanizing process of economic development, in which people served only as an instrument. The machine helped create "the alienated labor" necessary for the new Marxist order to develop. Similarly, the machine realized Lenin's promise to reduce the nineteenth-century "superman of literature" to a "small cog and a small screw in the social-democratic mechanism . . . set in motion by the entire conscious vanguard of the whole working class." Later, Stalin would tell Soviet factory workers that the new person "would be as solid and as irreproachable as the most perfect screw they could produce."[6]

In the early 1920s, the state was satisfied with trying to create "Taylorism with a human face." This was pursued in collaboration with artists and scientists at the Central Institute for the Scientific Organization of Man (under the direction of Aleksey Gastev), at the Choreological Laboratory in the Russian Academy of Artistic Sciences (organized by Aleksandr Larionov and Aleksey Sidorov), and in society at large.[7] In the debate between humanist and antihumanist forces, emotive will was fused to the social mechanism of fate and expressed via nonobjective, cubist, and constructivist design. The symbolist puppet man was replaced by the technocratic machine-man, who nevertheless remained the object of a constructed fate.

In this new scenario, the intelligentsia translated the state's utopic mechanistic iconography of progressive arrival (trains, planes, rocketships, etc.) into a dystopic iconography of necessary but futile escape. Protagonists in the Fellow Traveler or formally experimental literature of this period, like their creators, were alternately obsessed with the future and fearful that they could not get out of its way. The hero of Mikhail Bulgakov's novella *Diaboliad* (1924), walled in by society's growing "fascination with elevators, skyscrapers and public transport," committed suicide by jumping off one of Moscow's tallest buildings. Yury Olesha said that H. G. Wells's stories and Charlie Chaplin's films (both of which he admired and emulated) presented "little English clerks in bowlers and narrow ties who run every which way to escape the marvel of an emerging futuristic technology or on the contrary, who run to look at it and perish." "Humanity['s] crusading in the pursuit of happiness" (the first title card in Chaplin's *Modern Times*, 1936) was, Olesha and the other Fellow Travelers maintained, blocked if not terminated by technology and technocracy.[8]

In 1926, Meyerhold transformed Gogol's anonymous cipher Khlestakov (in his production of *The Inspector General*) into an assembly-line bribery machine, "predicting" Chaplin's reassembly of a proletarian according to machine rhythms in *Modern Times*. Here as elsewhere in early Soviet culture (and in the conceptual strategy of this chapter), Chaplin appears to leap, like Blok's Harlequin, among different performance modes of being in space and time. His image mediates theatre and film through poetic intuition born of the postrevolutionary intelligentsia's individual and collective yearning. It was in fact the Fellow Travelers' untenable social and existential status which precipitated the apparent causality of an iconic drama in which Chaplin was cast but did not star. Like "woman" during the Silver Age, Chaplin became some other agent's performative mask (which I shall call "Charlie"), with the protagonistic options of hope and dread somewhat reconfigured.

Meyerhold claimed retrospectively to have appreciated Chaplin's "predilection for monumental subjects," as early as 1917, the year that American silent film comedies were first discussed in the Russian press and three years prior to the first Soviet premiere of a Chaplin film (*A Dog's Life*, American premiere, 1918). While Chaplin in the early years seemed to the Russian viewer to be an amusing clown, there was as yet nothing to distinguish him for this audience from his fellow American or European silent film *farceurs* (who would have been more familiar). Prerevolutionary Russian and, for that matter, European critics found Chaplin's early style of acting to be coarse and inelegant, that is, not very European. They took note of and were somewhat mystified by Chaplin's growing popularity in the United States. Much was later made of this prerevolutionary "critical blindness" by postrevolutionary Soviet critics, who, in retrospect, could appreciate Charlie's incipient proletarianism and acute deconstruction of familiar bourgeois types.[9]

In the battle between free will and determinism which accompanied world war, revolution, and civil war in Russia, the nineteenth century's romance with individualism expired and with it its larger-than-life heroes. Charlie's pantomimic automatism, now seen through a machine-age filter, could likewise be read by the intelligentsia as an absurd response to the crisis of modern times. In 1937, Viktor Shklovsky recalled the conclusion of a 1918 film, *Creation Can't Be Bought*, written by Mayakovsky (adapted from Edmond de Amicis's *The Workers' Teacher* and Jack London's *Martin Eden*) and directed by Nikandr Turkin, in which the poet, rejected by his beloved and himself rejecting suicide after considering the option, "goes out on the road, homeless and free, like Chaplin. . . ."[10]

"Charlie Chaplin" became for a segment of the Russian intelligentsia in the Soviet period a talismanic presence, the image of freedom, in baggy pants and size fourteen shoes, warding off co-optation by the absolutist state and the mechanical age. Mayakovsky, the machine-age futurist who ended as a suicide, fantasized in his work about breaking free. He and his fellow futurists believed that through a poetic and cultural shift (*sdvig*), the figurative apparati of liberated time (that is, time machines and radicalized "transrational" linguistics [*zaum*]), they could overtake and defeat old time and effect a new, utopian reality. But on the contrary, Prisypkin, the antihero of Mayakovsky's play *The Bedbug* (*Klop*, 1928), is caged by a sanitized future and futurian society. His vulgarity and sentimentality undercut the false heroism of the new age, while his sloppy romanticism struggles to break free of the play's futurist machine rhythms. Film director Lev Kuleshov spoke of Chaplin's ability to remain free, even of the burden of his own celebrity: "You have to be Chaplin to know how to carry the burden of real grandeur."[11] However, the gulf between iconic "proletarian heroism" and proletarian autonomy, between the fictional and the factual proletariat, was widening. State power and its propaganda machinery were by the 1920s making a concerted effort to render the proletariat even more inaccessible to the intelligentsia which had helped create it.

Possibly in an effort to retrieve the "real grandeur" of "the people" as a romantic construct, the intelligentsia partially dreamed "Charlie Chaplin" into being in a manner which purposely confused what Soviet society knew about him at a particular time and even what Chaplin knew about his own artistic aspirations by that same time. A case in point is the heroine of Olesha's play *A List of Blessings* (1931), the actress and would-be Hamlet Goncharova who is lured to Paris by the iconicity of Charlie as a decontextualized symbol of Western freedom. She first sights Charlie under a lamppost in Paris, seemingly replaying in his sleep the imaginative boot-eating scene in *The Gold Rush* (1925). Olesha's Charlie is being illuminated by a character who recalls the Lamplighter in Mayakovsky's play *Mystery-Bouffe* (*Misteriya-buff*, 1918–1921). Mayakovsky's Lamplighter appears in the Promised Land of the Socialist Workers' Commune, speaking of the electricity which will power and illuminate the bright new social order, as per Lenin's 1920 dictum: "Socialism equals Soviet power plus electrification." However, *The Gold Rush* had not played in the Soviet Union at this time, despite Chaplin's popularity among Soviet audiences in the 1920s. In fact, during the period of the Soviet cinema's conversion to sound and citing a hard currency shortage, the state banned *all* foreign films from Soviet screens (ca. 1930–1935). For his part, Chaplin refused to sell his films to the Soviet Union, Hollywood screenwriter Ivor Montagu recalls, because "the money they were offering was less than he would get for a film from one middling-size town in the United States." Montagu explained to him about the Five-Year Plan and Russia's cash shortage, to which Chaplin responded, "It is the principle of the thing. Pictures are worth something. They give Henry Ford valyuta for tractors and my pictures must be worth at least as much as several tractors."

While members of the intelligentsia may have managed to see certain of Chaplin's films during this period, we know only one person who saw them in the Soviet Union: Stalin apparently counted them, along with American westerns and musical comedies, among his favorites. Those Russian artists and intellectuals who had the opportunity to travel abroad during this period, such as Meyerhold, who was in France and Germany from spring to September 1930, first with his theatre company, then only with Zinaida Raykh, would certainly have been (over)exposed to Charlot's image and probably to his most recent films. On the evidence of his essay "Thoughts on Chaplin" (*Mysli o Chapline*, 1936), Olesha had either seen or else was familiar with specific story and scenic details of *The Kid* (American premiere 1921), *City Lights* (American premiere 1931), and *Modern Times* (American premiere 1936). By one account, *City Lights* and *Modern Times* were imported by the Soviet Union in the 1930s. Chaplin's maturation as an artist must have been particularly poignant for Olesha, who published almost no original work during the Stalin years.[12] Whether or not Olesha and others managed to see Chaplin's later films at home through unofficial channels, while traveling abroad, or only to hear about them from those who had seen them, they utilized that iconicity which was available to them. Like Goncharova, who is thrice marginalized as a woman, an actress, and an emigré, members of the intelligentsia projected on their mental screens their own dream, their own agony, their own image, which was ennobled by an evocative association with Charlie.

In 1931, the same year in which *A List of Blessings* was produced, Viktor Skhlovsky wrote an "open letter" to Chaplin. Like Goncharova's yearning, the letter encoded distance from an unrealizable object as well as an imaginatively forged intimacy. "The Soviet people," Shklovsky wrote to the letter's nominal, imaginary addressee, did not wish to see a Chaplin who does honest, hard work like themselves. No doubt speaking of and for the people's producers, the intelligentsia as much as for the people, Shklovsky wrote that "they" needed someone on whom to project their self-pity and desire for reciprocal empathic response. While seeming to criticize Western bourgeois society, which, he wrote, had already lost the possibility of achieving true empathy, Shklovsky's "letter" was a calculated attempt to reverse the balance of power between the intelligentsia, which communicated its inner thoughts in public (Aesopian) codes and in private correspondence, and the state, which historically and systematically sought to open both. As in Olesha's play, a mythical Charlie was not the object of but the medium for this communication of social and existential (non)being.

Charlie Chaplin first emerged in the USSR during the NEP period (1921–1928) as an ambiguous icon of intelligentsia-proletarian codependency in inadvertent collusion with the developing state ideology. The state sought to advertise the new cultural order by "taking films to the masses" across the country. The vast majority of venues frequented by peasants, proletarians, and even intellectuals were workers' clubs and "itinerant cinemas," in which the national dream of class and cultural unity was nominally realized.[13]

In fact, Soviet provincial audiences saw less of everything but especially of foreign films, which were best (but not exclusively) seen in well-appointed urban theatres, whose admission prices were unaffordable to many urban workers as well. Still, if we may use as exemplary data the sixty-seven-night run of *A Dog's Life* in sixty-seven different Siberian communities, we see that there were (and still are) cases in Soviet culture where a particular foreign work or image, like Chaplin's Tramp figure, could and did become commonly known. While the people's response to Charlie in the early postrevolutionary period, as to most other things, is unrecorded, they certainly might have seen in him their own concomitant glorification and humiliation as abstract revolutionary symbols and as real citizens of the new social order.

In a 1939 tribute to Chaplin on the occasion of his fiftieth birthday, Leonid Trauberg, a member of the creative intelligentsia which vested Chaplin's "common literacy" with Gogolian, Gorkyesque, and even Hamletian traits, alluded to or perhaps imagined a vast Soviet audience living "in remote districts, which in the past hardly ever received a newspaper." The pervasive force of Chaplin's charisma, like Lenin's, which one foreign observer imagined "penetrating into the cabins of the peasants in the remotest villages," embodied "the vividness of art made accessible at the cost of terrific struggles." This description not incidentally defined the intelligentsia's self-imaged scenario of its sociohistorical fate.

The anti-Taylorism of the Tramp, which would not fully emerge until *Modern Times*, was built into the Russian intelligentsia's construction of Charlie in the 1920s. On the evidence of this usage, the intelligentsia of the twenties saw in Chaplin a socially sanctioned syncretism of class, gender, education, geography, and time, of the humanistic, antisocialist past and the revolutionary future. Charlie personified not only the intelligentsia's sense of alienation from modern society but a mythically empathic social acceptance which, owing to the mask's proletarian coloring, the state could not reject out of hand. This was after all the decade during which the Proletkult or Proletarian Cultural-Educational Organizations Movement (Proletarskie Kul'turno-prosvetitel'nye Organizatsii, 1917–1932) nationally championed a working-class aesthetic in as many as three hundred chapters among some four thousand members. These organizations, which fought against incursion by the intelligentsia and high culture, were greatly influenced by intellectuals, whose skill and education enabled them to create romanticized low or popular culture theories and artifacts. Self-consciously iconic populism is invariably a pursuit of the intellectual class.

The emigration of skilled personnel and the shortage of equipment and film stock during the Civil War (celluloid was imported until 1922) resulted in a dearth of Soviet-made films in this period (only thirteen silent features, 1918–1921, as compared to 112 in 1928). Lenin, whose prescient regard for the cinema has been somewhat exaggerated, saw in American movies a useful testimonial to modernization, urbanization, and the disciplined labor of mass production. Film was to be a corrective to habitual Russian lassitude. Lenin realized that importing and screening popular American films, starring Douglas Fairbanks, Mary Pickford, Harold Lloyd, and Charlie Chaplin, could help sell homemade propaganda films to Soviet audiences. Wherever possible, the star quality of American films was advertised in the Russian translations of their titles. For example, Chaplin's *The Champion* (American premiere 1915) became *Charlie the Boxer*. The removal of American stars from the Soviet screen under Stalin signaled the wholesale transformation of 1920s cultural experimentalism into 1930s political retrenchment. This development paralleled Stalin's conversion of Soviet cinema into a "lifeless abstraction."[14]

With this in mind, Charlie's appearance on the Soviet *stage* in Meyerhold's production of Olesha's play (premiere 4 June 1931) was highly significant. The absurdist fate of the apolitical Goncharova, who dies after stepping into the path of a bullet intended for a political strike leader in Paris, not only characterized the fate of the intellectual Fellow Traveler but "predicted" that of Chaplin's Tramp, who came to represent her/him. In *Modern Times*, the Tramp emerges from a sanitorium onto a street, where he picks up a red flag dropped from a passing truck. As he waves the flag in an effort to get the truck to stop, striking workers fall in behind him, making it appear that he is leading a demonstration of which he has no knowledge. Similarly, the Russian intelligentsia and the people, each unsure of which led the other, were like Charlie blind-sided by noncontinuous perception and made into something more or other than what history and, in some cases, the state meant or wanted them to be. Goncharova's list of blessings and crimes (Chaplin called this "the age of crimes"), bequeathed by the state to its citizens after the revolution, represented what Konstantin Rudnitsky referred to as the state's naively dualistic reduction of the entire "mystery of the Russian intelligentsia."[15]

As his career developed abroad and his iconicity unfolded in Soviet society, Charlie spoke to both formalist "alogical" and socially "logical" Russian cultural traditions, which were updated to the machine age. In particular, the construction and critique of the clown in stage, film, and circus production illuminated the difficulty of reconciling formalism and social realism in Soviet art and culture. Certainly, as a formal(ist) sign, Charlie cross-coded diverse, even visibly contradictory meanings. He combined Bergsonian vitalism and mechanical automatism, humanist and materialist values (for example, *faktura*, the expressive life of materials *per se*), socially existential and historically determinist meanings, which, in different ways, served the needs of the self and the state. As a "montage of attractions" (composition of individual edits/association of stimuli) in human form, Charlie advertised the ultimate imperviousness of the body to mechanization and of the individual spirit and personality to regimentation.[16] He also seemed to the intelligentsia to embody a number of twenties avant-gardist concerns, including the viewing of art as technological craft and scientific process; the consideration of art's virtuosity (individualism) and utility (collectivism); and the application of a mechanistic metaphor to the discussion of the deautomatization of art and culture (via defamiliarization).

Constructivist artists Varvara Stepanova and (her husband) Aleksandr Rodchenko enthused over the spatial implications of Chaplin as "the geometricization of the human body." For the Russian formalists, influenced by their reading of Bergson, Chaplin's movement manifested the throwing off of received rhythms and the deadly parodying of their mechanical nature. He made the mechanical seem *more* mechanical and thus *less* relevant. Chaplin's functionalism was consistent with the constructivists' and with Meyerhold's antidecorative, proutilitarian approach to art in the 1920s. In Charlie's iconic image were conflated themes and elements devised and retrieved by the Soviet avant-garde, including popular performance art, "supergraphics" (public art on a large scale), multimedia, folk art neoprimitivism, and the reintegration of art and life.[17]

Stepanova's 1926 image of Charlie as fallen skater (fig. 15), inspired by his film *The Rink* (1916), showed the machine-man out of order, much as does farce. Its antithesis appeared one year later in the celebrated and ideologically charged image of Dziga Vertov's brother and cameraman Mikhail Kaufman, who appeared on the cover of *Soviet Cinema* (*Sovetskoe kino*, no. 1), with a camera at his eye (that is, a cine-eye) and with roller skates on his feet (fig. 16). "The perfect electric man" embodied and expressed "the poetry of the machine," Lenin's new electrical aesthetic.

Stepanova, who designed Meyerhold's "eccentric *balagan*" production of Aleksandr Sukhovo-Kobylin's *Tarelkin's Death* (*Smert' Tarelkina*, written 1869; staged 1922), completed in the same year a series of prints of Chaplin for the third issue of the Soviet film journal *Cinema-Photo* (*Kino-foto*, 1922), in which he performed somersaults and posed with such modern implements as an automobile, a tire, and a meat grinder. Stepanova's meat-grinder set design for Meyerhold's production of *Tarelkin's Death* borrowed from the mechanics of farce in general and from the imagery in Sukhovo-Kobylin's play in particular, rather than from Chaplin's early films. However, the similarities between the Tramp's, the play's, and the *mise en scène*'s eccentrism

FIGURE 15
Varvara Stepanova's cover for Charlie Chaplin, *1926, unpublished.*
Courtesy of the MIT Press, Cambridge.

are evocative. Rasplyuyev, Tarelkin's tormentor in the play, has devised a "mechanics," whereby a man may be broken down to his essential core, to the confession of his guilty, because imperfect, humanity. The Meyerhold-Stepanova *mise en scène* presented a double
critique of Russia's tsarist past (specifically its judicial and prison sys-

FIGURE 16

Cover for Soviet Cinema, *no. 1, 1927, featuring Dziga Vertov's cameraman Mikhail Kaufman. Courtesy of the MIT Press, Cambridge.*

tems), which victimized the play's author, and the West's capitalist present, which in the eyes of the Soviets rendered the individual passive as Marx had predicted.[18] The release of *Modern Times*, in which Chaplin like Tarelkin became a literal *apparatchik*, an apparatus-assembly line man fed into the social mechanism (which spits him out owing to his human "difference"), coincided not with the hopeful artistic and social experimentalism of the twenties in the Soviet Union but rather with Stalin's autocratic social engineering in the thirties and forties.

In this context, the modern *balagan* of Chaplin's brutalization by a machine and panoptic surveillance via television by a disembodied, amplified, and enlarged boss paralleled without perforce causally connecting with the Russian intelligentsia's perception and experiencing of Stalinism. In this film, Chaplin demonstrated the physical, spiritual, and moral resiliency under oppressive circumstances which the intelligentsia had already imagined for Charlie, even if the specific example of *Modern Times* was not immediately available to them. Actually, by the early 1930s, the Soviet state had also progressed from the Proletkult's optimistic belief (derived from Marx) in "the beneficence of technology" and the idealization of "the assembly-line automaton." As Katerina Clark explains, "the guidelines for socialist realism [loyalty to the party and its leaders, the legitimacy and historical inevitability of the revolution, heroic struggle] were thought out during a wave of reaction *against* [my emphasis] machine-age values."[19]

The formalist conception of the individual as a consistent "action-function," to borrow Vladimir Propp's term, rather than as a psychologically consistent character, was central to Meyerhold's biomechanics and constructivist stagings in the 1920s. Meyerhold, whose stage-montage helped precipitate Soviet film-montage (primarily through his former theatre student Sergey Eisenstein), believed that only by working from within a popular tradition—circus, music hall, pantomime, *commedia dell'arte*, fairground booth—toward a mirroring of timeless popular reality could great art be achieved. The people may not embody the truth, but their cultural tradition performs the "action of actuality."[20] Meyerhold originally favored the formally artificial, psychologically unconflicted silent film personae of Harold Lloyd, who "cried with vaseline," and Buster Keaton, whose *Our Hospitality* was, he said, "the best American film comedy [he] had seen." Meyerhold stated that for him the essential problem of the actor's play was "the creation of the comic effects of the mechanism," and no actor-director, in his opinion, was more exact or more tactful than Keaton in getting results. Meyerhold's enthusiasm for Keaton's formalist framing at first seemed to subsume any real appreciation of Chaplin's sentimental "realism," which the stage director had excised from his own artistic work.

Meyerhold's approval of Chaplin, whom he considered along with Mikhail Chekhov to be "the most brilliant" of contemporary actors, grew along with his recognition of Charlie's viability as a proletarian sign. Charlie's natural, concrete populist iconicity contrasted favorably with the abstract, schematic quality of political "poster art." His revolutionary romanticism preserved, as had Mayakovsky, the lyrical element in realistic art that for Meyerhold had disappeared under Stalin. In the 1930s, Meyerhold came to see Chaplin's work as the realization of his own vision for theatre and cinema, "to decide the great contemporary problems." "Through his caricature," his Kabuki-like formalist mask, Meyerhold asserted, "Chaplin seems to stress the monstrousness of the work [and the society] he is unmasking." Meyerhold apparently regarded Chaplin's affected populism as a respectful borrowing as opposed to Soviet culture's coercive appropriation.

Meyerhold's linkage of Chaplin with social realism, in a lecture delivered on 13 June 1936, speaks not only to the naturalness of Charlie's clowning but to the unnaturalness of Meyerhold's position at that time. As a suspected "formalist," his statements were monitored by the watchdogs of government-sponsored socialist realism. Meyerhold saw tremendous relevance in Chaplin's work to Russian theatrical traditions and to his own work in the theatre. Chaplin's brand of "laughter through tears" placed in the service of the oppressed was compared favorably to Gogol's work (for example, his short story "The Overcoat," *Shinel'*, 1842). Meyerhold's characterization of Chaplin as a citizen poet and defender of the weak borrowed from nineteenth-century Russian romanticism and social criticism. Chaplin's careful construction of "effects" reminded Meyerhold of Blok's *The Little Showbooth*, which he wished to re-stage as a "Chaplinade." Khris. Khersonsky, who worked with Meyerhold on his production of *The Magnanimous Cuckold* (1922), retrospectively saw stylistic similarities between it and Chaplin's film *A Woman of Paris* (1923).[21]

In his constructivist manifesto (1922), Aleksey Gan declared that "art is dead," effectively claiming a proletarian victory over aestheticism. Gan also attacked Chaplin, Meyerhold, Fernand Léger, who featured Chaplin's image in his *Ballet mécanique* (created with Dudley Murphy, 1923–1924), and other "music hall artists," for compromising constructivist principles in art by, among other things, making them (too) subjective. In an article entitled "The Industrialization of Gesture" (1922), Soviet critic Ippolit Sokolov stated that "on stage the actor must become an automaton, a mechanism, a machine, a master of industrialized gesture, that is, the gesture of labour, built on the principle of economy of effort . . . linear, a geometric order." Gan's criticism notwithstanding, Meyerhold greatly admired Chaplin's building of the stunt or gag, the artistic correlative to "industrialized gesture" and the near-relation of his own system of biomechanics (1921).[22]

Meyerhold was interested in the scientific organization of material, and biomechanics was, in one sense, organized according to the principle espoused by Meyerhold's student and future wife, Zinaida Raykh: "The body is a machine operated by a machinist." However, Meyerhold's biomechanics, like Chaplin's plastique, aimed at achieving for people machinelike economy and mastery of expression and realistic human expressiveness, not at emulating dehumanized machine rhythms or, worse still, a machinelike mind-set. In fact, the future film actors who were schooled in Meyerhold's system—N. I. Bogolyubov, E. P. Garin, N. P. Okhlopkov, and I. V. Ilyinsky—helped to develop Soviet film realism. Igor Ilyinsky, the Soviet cinema's most popular actor in the 1920s, was often compared to Chaplin. Walter Benjamin erroneously dismissed Ilyinsky as "an unscrupulous, inept imitator of Chaplin." More accurate was Viktor Shklovsky's assessment in 1962 that "given the right scenario, Ilyinsky would certainly join Chaplin's ranks." The theatre training which Meyerhold offered in "the culture of movement" and in such specific techniques as "preacting" (which he observed as well in Chaplin's "momentary pauses for aim") and "self-mirroring" proved to be helpful to actors making the transition from stage to film. While the filmmaker Lev Kuleshov called Chaplin "our first teacher," Soviet film directors S. I. Yutkevich, N. P. Okhlopkov, A. M. Room, and, of course, Eisenstein were first taught by Meyerhold.[23]

Chaplin and Meyerhold both critiqued spoken language via the aesthetic of movement. Chaplin proclaimed that all of his film work was based on pantomime. In the prerevolutionary "crisis in the theatre" period, Meyerhold first suggested that "pantomime is a good antidote against excessive misuse of words." Chaplin claimed that he did not talk in pictures sooner because the sound equipment had been too bulky to fit into his small studio. Once the equipment had been simplified (that is, prior to the filming of *The Great Dictator*, 1939–1940), he said, he was able and willing to use it. Chaplin's initial foray into speech was actually the French song which he coquettishly sang at the urging of the Gamin (Paulette Goddard) in *Modern Times*. The foreignness of the song, which he performed in his workplace (a restaurant), and the marginalized status of his female ally further contributed to Charlie's "otherness." Chaplin first identified his marginalized outsider status with the feminine other in his 1915 film *A Woman*. In a sequence which may have partially inspired Marcel Duchamp's female persona "Rrose Selavy" (*Eros c'est la vie*), Chaplin cross-dressed in order to visit his girlfriend in an all-female boarding house.[24] Olesha's appropriation of Charlie as a mirrored sign of Goncharova's socio-sexual otherness might certainly have found inspiration if not a direct source in Chaplin's early work.

What Viktor Shklovsky referred to as Chaplin's "dotted" movement, broken up and mechanical and ending in a pose, conformed to the episodic nature of film montage, its framing of noncontinuous perception, as well as to the new, episodic, "cinefied" stage which indirectly it and he helped to engender. Shklovsky called Chaplin the *first* film actor, because he embodied fully and exclusively the medium's means and its aesthetic. Eisenstein stated that "the lyrical effect of a whole series of Chaplin scenes was inseparable from the attractional quality of the specific mechanics of his movements." Chaplin's films, said Shklovsky, make us aware of "the stunt as such," "a series of 'constant movements' repeated with varying motivations from film to film." Chaplin's prolonged resistance to the use of sound in his films defined an "aesthetic of laconism." This laconism, which Chaplin and his films had in common with the machine and the new Soviet order, achieved as well "maximum economy of the expressive means." It also assured maximum intelligibility of Chaplin's cinematic image on the electrified world stage. As Meyerhold noted, "the Russian peasant refuses to understand Chaplin the Englishman. Chaplin was close to him and intelligible because he only mimed."[25] Another meaning can be extracted from a slight rephrasing of the end of this statement to read "because he had no voice."

Charlie presented an image of the machine "made strange," a mobile construction built from unequal parts—oversize shoes, undersized jacket and hat, slight cane, and truncated mustache. His gait was composed of a series of edits, which together demonstrated the destabilization of the mechanical by the human. Charlie's mismatched costume elements, action-edits, and syncretized male/femaleness created a montage text within a realistic societal context. His presence exposed the typicality of character, class, gender, education, and geography (city versus country/center versus periphery), the elements which marginalized large segments of humanity and certainly of the Soviet populace.

Both Meyerhold and Chaplin were influenced by the circus, and Eisenstein identified with circus clowns. Lenin likewise saw the value of the circus, which satirized bourgeois reality and institutions. Gorky professed to enjoy the circus because it resembled work more than play and dreamed, as did Olesha, of becoming a circus performer. Olesha viewed Chaplin as the personification of the new circus of modern urban life, where compassion and distrust maintained an uneasy equilibrium and often collided. During the 1920s, circus acts were frequently interpolated into the texts of plays for various special effects, "to propel the action" and "generate tension." Meyerhold actually declared the circus to be "nobler than the theatre." However, Shklovsky maintained that circus business was consciously employed in the theatre to conceal the deficiencies of the text and so compromised the role of language in literary performance. Furthermore, he argued, circus acts and the then popular mass spectacles which incorporated them did not represent the real tradition of popular performance but were "merely condescending imitations of genuine folk art."[26]

The double incursion of circus and film onto the Soviet stage in the 1920s, as an effort to reframe art in the broader, more popular culture, led in some cases to a confusion of new aesthetics, entertainment values, and agit-prop motives and techniques. Sergey Radlov's Theatre of Popular Comedy in Petrograd specialized in "circusized" stagings, while Eisenstein's *mise en scène* for Sergey Tretyakov's adaptation of Ostrovsky's *There's No Fool Like a Wise Fool* (*Na vsyakogo mudretsa dovol'no prostoty*, 1868) included the director's first short film, *Glumov's Diary*. At the Factory of the Eccentric Actor (Fabrika Ekstsentricheskogo Aktyora or FEKS) in Petrograd, future film directors Leonid Trauberg, Grigory Kozintsev, Georgy Kryzhitsky, and Sergey Yutkevich made Chaplin's tramp persona central to their experimental syntheses of theatre, circus, and film. Their call for "Charlie's ass" to take precedence in the theatre over "Eleonora Duse's hands," an apparent homage to Marinetti's "The Variety Theatre" Manifesto (*Il Teatro di Varieta*, 1913), aimed at "the rhythmic battering of nerves" and the electrification of the senses.

Alogical formalist experimentalism with popular forms in the Soviet theatre was not yet altogether "incorrect" in the early 1920s. Even Lenin while in exile had attended the music hall in London and the Folies Bergères in Paris. Meyerhold said that Sarah Bernhardt's performance as the melodramatic heroine Marguerite Gautier in *La dame aux camélias* made Lenin cry.[27] Melodrama, which was another

FEKS staple, had its revolutionary pedigree renewed in the twenties by, among others, the politically astute formalist Tairov, who viewed its "fundamental laws" as being "mockery and abuse of evil, philistinism and meanness of spirit, and affirmation of justice and truth." The *feksy*, who also included S. Gerasimov, Ya. Zheymo, A. Kostrichkin, E. Kuzmina, O. Zhakov, and P. Sobolevsky, may have seen in Charlie's persona what they saw in the popular genres (also including detective and science fiction) which they embraced: the romantic pathos of individualism falling out of rhythm with the mechanics of contemporary culture. Still, it was only the physically eccentric Chaplin they saw. While they might have sensed the inevitable reconciliation of "inner and outer eccentrism" into more full-bodied psychological characterizations which transpired in Chaplin's later films, these works had not yet been produced let alone released in the Soviet Union in the early 1920s. FEKS's Charlie, like Olesha/Goncharova's, was intuited and co-created.[28] The pairing of Charlie in giant poster form with two clowns named "Albert" and "Einstein" in FEKS's 25 September 1922 staging of Gogol's *Marriage* (*Zhenit'ba*, published 1841), the author's dramatic fantasy of paranoid entrapment and escape, parodied the catalytic energy of revolutionary culture using the techniques of revolutionary agit-prop art.[29]

Mock revolutionary clowning was closely shadowed by despotic clowning's "comic fear." In the Soviet circus of the 1930s, the clown Mikhail Rumyantsev's Chaplin mask Karandash ("Pencil" or "Crayon") performed Hitler parodies even prior to the release of Chaplin's *The Great Dictator* in the United States in 1940.[30] Soviet artists and critics extolled and analyzed the nature of Chaplin's opposition to cultural and political fascism, including in America Al Capone and William Randolph Hearst, and this opposition's links to clowning, capitalism, and machine-culture. Ilya Erenburg, who no doubt had seen Chaplin's work while living abroad, wrote to Chaplin in 1942 from Moscow (where he again lived from 1941): "All your life on the screen you have defended the little man against the malevolent and soulless machine. We are glad to see you taking a stand against Naziism. It isn't humans who've fallen upon us but ersatzmen, brutal, repulsive automatons."[31]

Sergey Eisenstein was befriended by Chaplin when he visited Hollywood in 1930 and had ample opportunities to view his films on his many trips outside of the Soviet Union. Eisenstein believed that Chaplin's fascination with the short-statured, terrifying child-clowns Napoleon and Hitler embodied the infantile dream (and popular Russian cultural theme) of escape from reality, the child's dream of "supreme egoism and absolute freedom from 'the fetters of morality.'" But this dream is shadowed by reality, "still taller, still more terrible, still stronger and still more ruthless," like the massive character actors Mack Swain, Eric Campbell, and Tom Murray, who pummel the diminutive Charlie in his films.[32]

In an eccentric pamphlet published in 1947, Parker Tyler conflated the images of Chaplin's two selves—the large adult and the small child—into one recognizable one: "Charlie is a little boy lost in the trousers of a huge man, the very man who is his classic enemy, the hoodlum from whom the little knight paradoxically flees." He is, Tyler wrote, "the daddy-envious presumptuous child who steals his father's pants." French aesthetician Elie Faure named this empowered child the "obstetrician to a new world." Chaplin performed "the two opposite poles of infantilism—the victor and the vanquished," its amoral cruelty and its appealing charm.

Eisenstein argued that Chaplin's growing-up process was a typical rite of passage for a Western capitalist. Anxiety over the striving for material success and social standing breeds infantilism, which in turn engenders the dream of escaping from reality to fairy tale. Communism's classlessness and distribution of wealth commensurate with self-determined labor productivity, Eisenstein contended, frees people from this anxiety, thus transforming reality into a fairy tale.[33] This reality-as-fairy-tale motif was espoused in the doctrine of socialist realism and was dutifully represented in a succession of drab plays with contrived, machinelike plots and heroes and with machines as central props. More interestingly, it recurs as a sad-ironic theme in plays by Bulgakov, Mayakovsky, Olesha, Erdman, and Yevgeny Shvarts, in which reality is measured against fairy tale and futurian promises and dreams.

Chaplin embodied the doubleness of the child/adult in his impersonations of Napoleon and Hitler, the two would-be conquerors of Russia and the Soviet Union. In Chaplin's unproduced idea for a screenplay, a "false Napoleon"—reminiscent of the False Dmitry in Pushkin's *Boris Godunov*—dies on the island of St. Helena, just as the real Napoleon is secretly gathering his forces to reconquer France. When Napoleon hears of his double's demise, which robs him of his reality in the eyes of the world, he proclaims, "The news of my death has killed me." One of Soviet film director Aleksandr Dovzhenko's earliest scripts, *Chaplin Lost*, placed Charlie on a desert isle, perhaps unintentionally alluding to the emperor's fate. While rehearsing his unrealized production of *Boris Godunov* in 1925–1926 and again in 1936, Meyerhold defined receiving blows as the common function of the tsar/historical protagonist (Boris) and the clown/theatrical protagonist. Meyerhold likewise linked the popular pretender Dmitry to Chaplin by calling him a "mysterious tramp."

In much the same way, Chaplin contested Hitler for his identity. The press of their day was intrigued by the notion of convergence, even doubleness between these two radically dissimilar men, born into poverty-bred anonymity a mere four days apart, who eventually became the two greatest actors of their day. Chaplin accused Hitler of having stolen his mustache. It was a legitimate theft in that Chaplin had intended his mustache "to be a gibe at all pomposity." Chaplin's successful impersonation of a parodic Hitler, called Hynkel in *The Great Dictator*, accomplished in part what the "false Napoleon" did at the expense of the real emperor—he made him seem simultaneously more threatening, less real, and more buffoonish, truer as a grotesque than as a man. "It is not too much to say," wrote a reviewer of Chaplin's film, "that no one but Chaplin, not even Adolf Hitler, could have taken this part."[34]

The film's protagonist, a ghetto-dwelling Jewish barber (the Charlie-Other), parodically realizes proletarian dictatorship.[35] Following a lengthy period of hospitalization after World War I, he remakes his identity in the process of rebuilding his memory and his semiotic reading of the world's social, moral, linguistic, and emblematic textual codes. He is essentially remade as a formal sign, the sum of the dictator Hynkel's "double cross" insignia and his gestural codes, without meaning or reality, since he is a pretender, a terrifying reminder of historical instability. In addressing a vast popular mass, depicted in documentary film footage taken at a Hitler rally, Chaplin-Hynkel, the actor-false Hitler, visually inscribed the spectatorial passivity of the people and the absorption of authenticity by charisma. These were all themes which the West read as attacking not only Hitler but Stalin.

Like the Soviet circus clowns who imitated him, Chaplin developed his persona from pantomimic eccentric to an urbanite with a social conscience, "not drenched in flour, humane, real, truthful and no longer humiliated." Charlie recouped his dignity as a human being by counter-objectifying the police and bosses, the despots who oppressed him. Chaplin boasted in 1941 that "ninety per cent of the public has often wondered just what the capitalist would do if he had his whiskers pulled, and now it is as plain as day." His image of the bloated capitalist in "whiskers, light trousers, spats, frock coat, and silk hat" recalled the straw men targeted for "red laughter" and extinction in the Soviet mass spectacles of the early 1920s.[36]

Chaplin was biographically attractive to the new Soviet state as a Gorky-like legendary tramp and autodidact, a self-made revolutionary populist, a former victim who now sought recompense not only for himself but for the poor, the ignorant, the inarticulate, and the oppressed. As regards self-education, Chaplin said: "I wanted to know not for the love of knowledge but as a defense against the world's contempt for the ignorant."

Chaplin was able to transform his unsentimental observations on life into sentimental art. He saw formalism, idealism, and entertainment abetting rather than undermining social realism. "I am protected by being a charlatan," he said. "I don't think in terms of common sense and to be honest, I don't search for truth. I search for effectiveness."[37] Chaplin was a nonliterary type whose roots in popular entertainment could make the Soviet people and especially the Bolsheviks, whom Lenin called "barbarians," feel themselves to be his equal. He showed himself in his films to be suppressed by bourgeois society and alienated from the meaningless jobs he was forced to take in order to survive. His rebellion was not so much against machines as against those who employ them to transform the worker into an object. This let machine-crazed early Soviet culture off the hook.

"The subject and object of mechanical reproduction," Chaplin "*was* mass culture," J. Hoberman wrote in a contemporary critical appreciation. Wearing the face of collective desire, "the original parody automaton" was a proletarian who resisted not only authority but work. He was both the culmination of a long tradition in popular culture and the invention of a new form, an event signaled, says Shklovsky, by his parodic nature. He simultaneously embodied the incursion of low into high culture and the attempt to extract more play, that is, greater leisure time, out of work. He aimed, as did the Soviet Central Institute of Labor in the early Soviet period, to dismantle the artificial boundaries between work and leisure, production and culture.[38] The Tramp as free man and agent provocateur lived an exemplary revolutionary life, with a ferocious grace bordering alternately on cruelty and heartbreak.

Charlie's heroism was earned in the workplace, a cornerstone of the the new Soviet order and the locale in which the new Soviet drama would be set. As he developed his social vision, the generic Tramp became the unemployed proletarian, a "social mask" of conflated realistic, grotesque, and mechanical elements, living in a specific socio-political context. Chaplin's naive internationalism intersected with both intellectual humanism and early Soviet state and intellectual uto-pianism. Chaplin had correctly identified the central theme of the modern era, this "time of crisis," as being the battle between capital and labor. He had even managed somewhat to overcome personal solipsism in his work. Like many Soviet orphans of the revolution, most notably Lenin (the revolutionary as common man) and Stalin, who lost their fathers at an early age, Charlie the fatherless child sought his identity in the great human family and in sociopolitical activism. His story, which generally originates and concludes on the road, inadvertently retraced the morphology of the Soviet socialist re-alist novel's master plot of questing, visionary orphans.[39]

Charlie was, like many Soviet workers, someone for whom work was of supreme value, but leisure the occupation of choice. One sees this attitude expressed in Gorky's *The Lower Depths*, which opens with the self-proclaimed "working man" Kleshch, a locksmith, fu-tilely attempting to get his fellow flophouse habitués interested in work. The most recalcitrant of the group is the unconscious proto-revolutionary Satin, who tells the highly unsympathetic character Kleshch, "make it so I like working and maybe I'll work" (114). Satin is, according to Soviet critics exercising divine hindsight, theoretically willing to work for a new order, in which labor controls the means of production and its own destiny. Satin, like Charlie (in Shklovsky's coinage), is a "perpetual failure" who embodies and envisions a fu-ture which will break/has broken the pattern of failure attached to a continuous (that is, prerevolutionary) past.[40]

Chaplin/Charlie achieved what the Soviet worker could not—a cri-tique of capital *and* labor, a defined morphology of comic subversion within the workplace and a romantic valorization of unemployment as the noblest profession of all. The formalists argued that artists engage in a revision and a critique of their medium. Chaplin offered a critique of work as a medium potentially expressive of an artistic aesthetic at a time, beginning in 1927 under Stalin's first Five-Year Plan, when the Soviet government began granting awards for "heroic labor."[41]

Charlie's heroic dwarfism, which was pitted against the heroic body of labor, the worker's physique, the massiveness of systems and insti-tutions, and the force of institutional history, inadvertently inverted the prescribed monolithic gigantism of Soviet culture (especially un-der Stalin), even as it subverted the hierarchically structured values and leaders of Western capitalism. Indeed, Chaplin partially revived the spindly figure of recalcitrant nineteenth-century Russian individualism. This represented both the intelligentsia and its construction of the people as the little man engaged in a slippery, ambiguous revenge against the society that rendered him and them superfluous and small. While the Tramp could escape the burden of productivity, however, he could not and to this day cannot avoid being forged into a symbol of production by the intelligentsia and the state.

CHAPTER 5

THE SLEEPING IDOL

Art is Free; Life is Paralyzed.

— *World of Art* (Mir iskusstva) [1]

In the 1920s and into the 1930s, the new Soviet order's much publicized revolutionary Prometheanism was contested by the representative iconography and iconoclasm of the state and the intelligentsia. The state finally "solved" the cultural problems of country, class, and self's measureless interior and exterior distance and difference in the embodied inertia and charismatic anonymity of living corpses, secret police, and machine-people (*apparatchiki*). As iconicity hardened into idolatry after 1917, an "opposition between the living statue and the vanishing man" emerged. Soviet artists and intellectuals of necessity struggled to identify, extract, and represent the emotional pathos at the heart of the heroic monumentalism being constructed by the state, to separate the expression of emotionalism from the condition of stasis and the silence that monumentalism encoded and produced. Even as a propagandistic culture of advertised outspokenness was being born in the New Economic Policy (NEP) on the one hand and in NEP satire on the other, an unspoken panoptic surveillance was being achieved, in which the Russian's talent for "holding his tongue" was exploited. [2]

This chapter treats the aforementioned character types and cultural themes in the order that I have just presented them. Proceeding from historical background on the Russian cultural habits of silence and stasis, I illustrate particular iconic instances of these themes in notable productions of *The Inspector General* and *Woe from Wit*, which have become almost talismanic for Western scholars of Russian theatre, but which have been treated mainly in their entirety as illuminated episodes in the theatrical *oeuvre* of Meyerhold rather than to argue a social thesis. I then discuss Tairov's slightly earlier staging of *Phèdre*, which successfully synthesized most of this chapter's stated concerns.   123

The shift in focus in this chapter to theatrical *mise en scène* (from literary texts in the first three chapters and a film actor in the fourth) may be explained by two factors, one historical and one interpretative. Historically speaking, the twenties saw an uneasy marriage between experimentalism and caution, as the evolving Soviet state sought to see and portray itself clearly in terms that it was in the process of defining for its citizenry. The theatre was a direct means of expressing the new society's advertised and covert spectacular nature and intentions.

While the new regime was eager to inscribe the eventfulness of revolutionary performance, reimagined in the mass spectacles of the late 1910s and early 1920s, it was less anxious to underscore the spectatorial condition which this attitude imposed upon the people, the so-called makers of the revolution and inheritors of its legacy. This relates to my interpretative point, which is one of the theses of this chapter. More than literary texts, theatrical *mise en scène* is protected by the relative invisibility of artistic direction and interpretation. Simply stated, fewer people know how to read the subtext of a theatrical performance than a literary work and to identify the direct source (dramatist, actor, director, designer) of a particular choice or intention. Furthermore, the speed of performance does not permit rereading: as a temporal document, the performance is both perishable and subject to change at a moment's notice temporarily to satisfy the demands of a particular spectator, such as a censor. While this chapter directly discusses artistic interpretation in the theatre, it is also concerned with theatrical spectatorship within a spectatorial culture, which in the twenties was negotiating between newly and partially achieved literacy and its oral and visual traditions.

Yury Lotman has remarked that "lack of understanding of words becomes [in Russia] the cultural sign of true understanding. . . . The word is an instrument of falsehood, a social sclerosis." Since the nineteenth century, Russian literature has regularly contrasted popular silence with the self-absorbed, self-serving loquaciousness of the intellectual "class." The "secret history" which the people's silence contained was interpreted by intellectuals with social reformist ideals as being opposed to manifest history and therefore revolutionary. Unsurprisingly, the Bolsheviks interpreted the famous silence of "the people" at the investiture of the new tsar, which concludes the 1831 published text of Pushkin's historical drama *Boris Godunov*, as representing a moral response to the linguistic perfidy practiced by history's makers—tsars, nobles, clergy, and historians.[3]

In *Boris Godunov*, the people's "protorevolutionary" silence is precipitated not by physical evidence, but by the *reported* death of the Tsarina and Tsarevich. "Three members of the tsar's special guard" (*troe strel'tsov*) announce to the people, "We saw the corpses." The play, which begins with a clerical scribe's false history of Tsarevich Dmitry's reincarnation, concludes with the state's reported history of Tsar Boris's wife and son's demise. Meyerhold, who planned two unrealized productions of *Boris*, one in 1925 for the Vakhtangov Theatre and another in 1936 for his 2,000-seat theatre on Moscow's Mayakovsky Square, felt that the stage direction "the people keep silent" (*narod bezmolvstvuet*) would require true genius to realize. Alluding to the fact that the people are *not* silent in the play's second and third scenes (nor at the conclusion of the 1825 manuscript edition of the play), Meyerhold directed them to shout bitterly, "Long live Tsar Dmitry Ivanovich!" (the pretender's name) at play's end as a prediction of future strife. The False Dmitry represents the recurrence of the people's fate, the wish fulfillment of co-conspiratorial, co-tyrannical pretendership and passivity in a play which had as a possible source Calderón de la Barca's *Life Is a Dream* (*La vida es sueño*, 1635).[4]

The 1920s saw the culmination of "demotheism" or worship of the people by a state enamored of its power to effect its own and others' iconicity. Charisma became a function of anonymity, the perfect sign of which was "the dead among the living," the idol which in sustaining its timeless authority casts idolaters in stone by encouraging them to pay obeisance to an already revealed and completed perfection. In a country whose Orthodox religious tradition had considered "human statues, even those of saints [to be] graven images," the proliferation of such tributes after the 1917 revolution signaled Russia's official conversion not only to official atheism but to the charismatic anonymity of "the people" and the ruler who governed by their authority and not God's. Richard Stites has characterized Soviet culture in the 1920s as undergoing an intense, albeit limited (by class, geography, Communist "deophobia") process of ritual building, based on Bolshevik myth rather than Orthodox religion and designed to distract the people from harsh economic realities. Communist rituals of the 1920s included antireligious pageants and "revolutionary countercelebrations"; Red weddings, which stressed equality between the sexes in civil ceremonies and settings, and Red funerals, which redemocratized death by substituting cremation for burials of unequal expense; and "Octobering" (Oktyabrina), which replaced Christening and saints' names with revolutionary coinages like "Spartak" (Spartacus), "Pravda" (Truth), and "Elektrifikatsiya" (Electrifica-

tion).[5] The secular ritualization of life in the 1920s (which recurred under Stalin and in the 1960s) was not a sudden, revolutionary development. It merely updated, recoded, and eventually intensified a long-standing Russian cultural tradition of immobile systematization in thought, expression, and deed. Soviet culture in the 1920s ended up reproducing and, to a certain extent, reinventing the irrational discourse of mechanical structure and inert form which the revolution was nominally staged in order to destroy.

In May 1922, Lenin suffered partial paralysis from the first of three strokes and temporarily lost his ability to speak. By March 1923, his political activity was effectively at an end, almost a full year before his death in January 1924. In his final year, the immobile Lenin was moved to his dacha outside of Moscow, the modern center of power he had helped create.[6] Lenin was now imprisoned within his mind, and his writing returned to the invisibility of his prerevolutionary exile from which secret missives and a "sealed" train had once delivered him. Like Ilya Ilyich Oblomov, who was for the Bolsheviks a detested literary symbol of prerevolutionary apolitical inertia, Vladimir Ilyich Lenin would soon be made permanently recumbent. Soon the living monument to Lenin (celebrity's ironic, iconic inversion of the Unknown Soldier's Tomb) would dematerialize his corpse, and the people whom he had activated and nominally empowered would joke about what percentage of the eternally living Lenin was actually made of wax.[7] Like the Russian nemesis, the pretender, who in *Boris Godunov* is rumored to be living in a reincarnated form, Lenin's preserved remains were a mythic erosion of history through the agency of timelessness.

Whereas Lenin had been stricken by fate, Tsar Peter I, once dubbed "Fate's Powerful Master," had anticipated a destiny of future immobility for himself. Peter the Great not only ordered his own posthumous mannequin, but helped Carlo Rastrelli design it. It was executed in 1725, the year of Peter's death. Peter, like Lenin, valued work and thrift and to that end himself purchased his mannequin's shoes at a market several months prior to his death. Peter, like Lenin, would be remembered as the bold deliverer of the future to his people. The tsar as visionary was immortalized in Ernest Falconet's statue of Peter on horseback (modeled after the statue of Marcus Aurelius in Rome) overlooking the Neva River and the city of St. Petersburg, which had been created from the tsar's Westernizing vision. Pushkin, who later became an adversary of Tsar Nikolay I, animated Falconet's statue in his poem "The Bronze Horseman" (*Medny vsadnik*, written 1833; published 1837), transforming the ruler into a fearful symbol of politically directed paralysis.[8] Peter's Westernizing political program, like Lenin's Bolshevik revolution, was essentially a European import imposed from above. And like Lenin—with whom his identity became fused in Russia's new/old capital of St. Petersburg/Leningrad—Peter's name encoded both animation and petrification. Peter's godless rationalism, his "evil genius," created the mechanical culture which Lenin and later Stalin fully realized.[9]

The 1917 revolution formally ended the system of social stasis and estatism (*soslovie*) which Peter had begun in 1722. The table of ranks (*chin*) was, like Westernism and like Petersburg itself, a manifestation of Peter's will. It effected a metalanguage for society, an "*écriture* of bureaucracy" translated into a fourteen-step pyramidic sociopolitical structure. The "table," which assigned faux-military ranks to civil service positions, nominally substituted a meritocratic for a hereditary hierarchy of power. In reality, it was a monument to hopelessness and what nineteenth-century social critic Aleksandr Herzen called a "living pyramid of crimes, abuses and extortions . . . soldered together by complicity . . . a world of governing cynicism. . . ." This system, likened by Herzen to a dysfunctional machine of noninteractive parts, prefigured the Communist Party apparatus (and *apparatchiki*), which lumbered into being in the 1920s.[10] Peter's unwieldy "table," with its cumbersome designations and modes of address ("Your Excellency" translated as *Vashe vysokoprevoskhoditel'stvo*), distinguished its constituency as functions, titles (*chiny*), offices (*dolzhnosti*), and ceremonial awards (*ordena*), rather than as individual people.

Stripped of significant being and so compelled to act upon its own evidence, the *chin* self learned to lie as a means of reinvention and in an effort to mask the terrible truth that it no longer existed as a viable social subject. Thus, Ivan Khlestakov, the protagonist of Gogol's dramatic *chin* satire, *The Inspector General* (1836), is both an anonymous cipher and a charismatic liar. He doubles himself, as Yury Lotman maintains, simultaneously concealing his real identity in exaggerated lies and revealing his real identity in his story of the "little rat of a copy clerk" whom he claims to order around in his St. Petersburg government department but who clearly represents himself.[11] Mikhail Chekhov, who played Khlestakov in 1921, described the character in Erast Garin's performance for Meyerhold in 1926 as a man "driven mad by his own falsehood, one who has lost the sense of time, who would seemingly lie *forever*." The lying Khlestakovs of Chekhov and Garin almost exactly framed the NEP period in the 1920s, in which slippery Soviet profiteers ("Nepmen") exploited the new society's provisional economic freedoms for personal gain.

Lying's infusion of history with timelessness offered self-protection against *chin*'s (and later the Soviet system's) opposition to self-promotion, self-definition, and self-expression, its prescribed social immobility and personal anonymity. Lying's inventive, transformative personal narrative countered *chin*-conditioned "niche-assignment thinking," whereby all ranks became virtually "inaccessible to rational discourse" and wholly resistant to change. The system's inertia and invisibility expressed the will and secret logic of the ruler. Public knowledge of the tsar's prerogative to abolish positions, sections, and departments, if and when he so chose, undermined not only job security but social and personal reality. This state of affairs preconditioned the people for Stalin's paranoid engineering of invisibility, his creation of "the dead among the living," the real and hypothetical "nonpersons" of the next century.[12]

Inertia and invisibility are bodied forth as well in the restriction of time, which constrains the individual's mutation and self-expression. Condensing and stopping time amid the historical chaos engendered by Lenin's paralysis and demise and Stalin's rise to power was a recurring motif in Meyerhold's stage work of the 1920s. Mute characters and pantomimic elements occurred in his productions of Cromelynck's *The Magnanimous Cuckold* (premiere 25 April 1922), Ostrovsky's *The Forest* (*Les*, premiere 19 January 1924), Aleksey Fayko's *Bubus the Teacher* (*Uchitel' Bubus*, premiere 29 January 1925), and Erdman's *The Mandate* (premiere 20 April 1925). These theatrical experiments culminated significantly in Meyerhold's production of *The Inspector General* (premiere 9 December 1926), which he co-adapted with M. Korenev and co-designed with V. P. Kiselev. Meyerhold's *mise en scène* for *The Inspector General* presented instances of spatiotemporal constraint, culminating in the full-scale paralysis of the mute scene ending Gogol's play. Altogether, this represented an "Aesopian" or secret coding of social oppression in the tsarist and Soviet eras.[13] Meyerhold's "montage of attractions" staging of Gogol's work, which he and Korenev adapted from six author's variants of the text along with elements from Gogol's play *The Gamblers* and his short stories, concerned Soviet critics. These critics believed that Meyerhold's episodic staging, largely on small tracking platforms,

FIGURE 17
The mute scene concluding Meyerhold's staging of The Inspector General,
1926. Courtesy of Ardis, Ann Arbor.

presented an atomized and miniaturized social vision rather than the
unified and monumental one being promulgated by the state.

   The cast of the original 1836 production of *The Inspector General*
resisted playing the final mute scene (*nemaya stsena*), and for nearly
a century thereafter Russian actors and directors struggled with the
question of how (and perhaps even why) to transform a *litso* (person)
into a *podstavnoe litso* (a false or substitute person, a dummy), as
Gogol had directed.[14] Two years after Stalin placed a waxen Lenin in
a public mausoleum and just prior to the advent of Stalinist terror,
which transformed Gogolian tableau into new historical representation, Meyerhold changed the final tableau of living actors into a life-
size, lifelike revolutionary waxworks (fig. 17). Meyerhold's scenic
solution recalled his removal of the Mystics' heads from their cardboard body façades in his prerevolutionary production of Blok's *The
Little Showbooth*. In both stagings, Meyerhold revealed how utopic-
apocalyptic fetishism and the impulse to fix fate retrospectively and
prospectively from the present results in the evacuation of humanity
from the historical mechanism and in the negative valorization of the
outer, spectatorial icon which constitutes idolatry's visual sign.

Only after members of Meyerhold's opening night audience approached the stage and the "real actors" (followed by Meyerhold) reentered from the wings was the "true identity" of the mannequins in the final tableau revealed. The purposeful subversion of "constructed presence" and the overdetermination of physicalized absence in Meyerhold's 1926 tableau, through the use of unreal but lifelike bodies, exposed the immobility of revolutionary fetishism, involving newly made abstract people and utopian presence.[15] The mute scene, which may have suggested to the amused Nikolay I the toy theatre models of his childhood, likewise affirmed the autocratic state forged from the revolutionary movement which toppled and killed Nikolay II. Meyerhold's mute scene and Lenin's mute corpse incarnated the revolution as rumor, historical event, and mythic/absurd remnant. Like Gogol's play, Meyerhold's and Stalin's waxworks destroyed the logical reality of historical chronology, casting suspicion on the authenticity of both early and late arrivals, on time, identity, and theatrical-cultural notations of the end.

The Inspector General depicts what Mihajlo Mihajlov has called the incursion of the irrationality of the external world into the internal world, which provokes and defines the grotesque. "The more incomprehensible and horrible the [external] world," Mihajlov notes, "the more petrified and dead the internal world. . . . Because fear of this outside world is irrational . . . it paralyzes time."[16] Gogol's "external" world is doubled, representing both a real place, St. Petersburg, and a parallel reality out of which "the damned incognito" Khlestakov, as a sign of charismatic anonymity, emerges.

Khlestakov, whom Gogol described as being "matchlike," empties the ignobly fattened townspeople, placing their reality "in parentheses," while filling them with a reality of his own. Thus, the Mayor's wife and daughter stand frozen at a window "for a whole hour" of their "real" time (substantially less in actual stage time), awaiting news of the inspector general's (actually Khlestakov's) arrival. Significantly, the two women are "unfrozen" at the window by the arrival of Dobchinsky, who along with his virtual twin Bobchinsky, seems to have consumed *chin*, where it sits protruding from his body in a "small paunch" (8) and in the middle of his surname.[17] The false durative time/actual stage time (act 2) which separates the women's two appearances at the window (at the end of act 1 and the beginning of act 3) is taken up with the Mayor's bribing and idolizing of the pretender Khlestakov, setting up the arrival of the "real" inspector general at play's end. The exposure of Khlestakov's ruse and the mute

scene which follows shortly after the Mayor's lines to the theatre audience—"What're you laughing for? You're laughing at yourselves"
(94)—impress the doubleness of the play's un/reality upon the society
of real people in the auditorium.

V. V. Gippius notes that, while mute scenes were found elsewhere
in Russian drama and fiction, they did not occur at the end of these
works. The primacy of the mute scene for Gogol was reflected in the
three sketches he executed of the final tableau after his own precise
verbal description, as well as in the extraordinary length of time given
over to this moment ("nearly a minute and a half," 96). Vladimir Nabokov theorized that the idea for the tableau may have occurred to
Gogol while he was visiting Lubeck, Germany, in summer 1829.
There he became fascinated with life-size, three-dimensional repre-
sentations of the twelve apostles in the cathedral clock, which at
twelve o'clock passed in procession, singing with heads bent before
"the statue of our Lord." Like the dumb show of the clock, Gogol's
final tableau clearly performed the action of moral authority (the inspector as tsar's and God's representative) and civil autocracy (the
tsarist system of *chin*) combining to reveal the immobility of the
human condition (mortality). This combined action likewise sought
to set the immobility of the human social condition (tyranny) in
measureless (divine/utopic-catastrophic) and measurable (historical/
theatrical) time.

Nabokov wrote that in Gogol's world "all reality is a mask," but
often the presence of this mask helps us to see through to a truer
reality.[18] On first hearing of the inspector's imminent and, by his
own description, fateful arrival, Gogol's Mayor calls for a town-wide
cover-up, as opposed to a purge, of all the corrupt civic institutions
under his jurisdiction. He orders the police chief to station the tallest
policeman atop the town bridge, "for the sake of town improvement
[that is, appearances]" (*dlya blagoustroystva*, 22). The police chief
Pugovitsyn represents little more than an official mask or uniform
(*pugovitsa* means "button" in Russian). Like the townspeople who
will compose the play's final tableau, he is a false or substitute person,
whose façadism both represents the town's masked reality, its performed orderliness, and reveals its unmasked reality, the fact that the
town is populated by puppets of *chin*-induced paranoia rather than
by people.[19]

A historical analogue to the futile civic façade constructed by Gogol's town officials can be found in Herzen's account of a provincial
governor, who, in preparation for the tsarevich's visit, "ordered the

fences of the towns to be painted and the sidewalks to be repaired."
When a widow in Orlov pleaded that she lacked personal funds sufficient to repair the wooden sidewalk outside her house, the governor
ordered that the floorboards in her house be taken up to replace it. A
wealthy merchant who threatened to tell the tsarevich of this was
placed under a doctor's care for the length of the royal visit. Herzen,
who was considered by the government to be a political trouble-
maker, was arrested during just such a visit.[20]

"The appearance of a police-officer in Russia," wrote Herzen, "is
as bad as a tile falling on one's head." In Russia, which de Custine
described in 1839 as being "more artful and better served with spies
than any other [country] in the world," despotism's "gendarme romance," the ubiquitous and seemingly omniscient presence of the
state police, created the secret police of paranoid self-surveillance
and its idolatrous theatrical display. During his employment as a provincial government councillor and department head, Herzen, who
had a record of arrests for antigovernment activities, was compelled
to countersign police surveillance reports on himself.[21] *The Inspector
General*'s final tableau, which exposes the futility of trying to mask
an already masked (or false) reality, is precipitated not by the government's "real" inspector who is announced but does not appear, but
by its gendarme, who does.

Gogol's comment that "the real inspector general" was "awakening
conscience" has been generally dismissed as a guilty self-corrective
issued by the author's divided soul.[22] It is, however, another instance
in which the truth is unmasked in the process of masking. Early in the
play the Postmaster tells the Mayor that his reading of other people's
correspondence has revealed to him the secret arrivals of inspectors
not from St. Petersburg, as one would expect, but from provincial
Saratov. In Khlestakov's letter to his writer friend Tryapichkin, which
is read aloud just prior to the gendarme's arrival and the final tableau,
it is revealed that the *flâneur* is now living in Saratov. Khlestakov's
already doubled identity as the "little rat of a copy clerk" and the false
inspector general is redoubled in the revelation that he might as easily
be everyone as no one he pretended to be. Khlestakov's true identity
is ultimately unknown because it is in a sense irrelevant. He embodies
only reported history and a rumored self.[23] The "incognito" represents the evacuation of humanity from the mechanism of reportage
and surveillance.

While coalescing the power of the state, lying and spying together
erode the cohesivenesss of self and society, resulting in fragmentation

and the mechanical performance of paranoid social rituals. Thus, the mechanical performance of Meyerhold's Gogolian montage seemed purposedly to rob the human performers of their self-determination. In the bribery episode, for example, a wall of fifteen doors seemed to spy upon an entranced, spiritually and emotionally dead Khlestakov as disembodied hands that were extended through these doors proffered bribes which he automatically accepted. The doors' mute stares were later replaced in the similarly configured mute scene by the dead presences of the disembodied souls who previously stood behind the doors. The mute scene is a testament to Khlestakov's and *chin*'s vampiric performance, their bloodletting of humanity, the replacement of people with machines and corpses.

Meyerhold's *mise en scène* exposed the empty ritual and the empty conscience of a soulless system, in which "the word of the emperor . . . [could] animate stones by destroying human beings" and unmask the puppet.[24] Meyerhold discovered in Gogol's dialogism of sound and silence, fluidity and stasis, lying and façade, an analogue to the contemporary struggle in the 1920s between romantic revolutionary iconoclasm and authoritarian tableauism, between laconism and suppression. Gogol's/Meyerhold's embodiment of reported and resolved history revealed and indicted the spectatorial state and its citizenry, who, like "the people" at the conclusion of *Boris Godunov*, lived in "a perfect state of expectation of commands." Lenin's commissar of enlightenment, Anatoly Lunacharsky, could applaud in Meyerhold's staging the exposure of tsardom's terrible "automatic essence," in which the intelligentsia perceived the motive of the new Soviet state. Meyerhold had coaxed into being the new "Soviet comedy of manners, one of laughter and indignation," called for by Trotsky. And he did so out of a Russian classic which the Bolsheviks had considered to be irrelevant and unworthy of revival.[25]

Meyerhold's staging of his favorite Russian play, Griboyedov's *Woe from Wit*, which he adapted with M. Korenev from the author's three dramatic variants under his original title *Woe to Wit* (*Gore umu*, premiere 12 March 1928), clearly distinguished between the two continually contentious orders in Soviet society—the alienated spiritual order and the self-protective social order. The spiritual order found its societal equivalent in Griboyedov's disempowered intellectual Aleksandr Chatsky. The dreamer-deliverer-disorderer Chatsky returns to Russia from a European sojourn of three years and unsuccessfully attempts to awaken sated, corrupt, and socially inbred Moscow society from its slumbers. Chatsky is expelled by members of the *dvoryanstvo* (gentry and nobility)—Pavel Famusov, his daughter Sofiya, their family and friends. Chatsky's aristocratic class of intellectual, observed Jean Bonamour, is, in Griboyedov's conception, as liberal and generous in word and thought as the *dvoryanstvo* is servile and miserly. The language of the social order is punctuated by phrases embodying "the social signification of menace," including exile, serfdom, hard labor, and the specter of Siberia (which also appears in *The Inspector General*).[26]

By 1821, three years prior to *Woe from Wit*'s composition, "Siberia had already become the place of exile in literary plots and the oral mythology of Russian culture."[27] Siberia became a cultural metonym for erasure/deauthentification and at the same time for *gulag* entrapment and petrification. Chatsky, who, like Khlestakov, suddenly crashes through the carefully defined and defended borders of the known world, just as suddenly vanishes into the speculative unknown (after being rejected by his former sweetheart Sofiya and Moscow society), which in the nineteenth century meant Western Europe but in the twentieth more likely meant Siberia.

A complete, uncensored text of *Woe from Wit* was not published in Russia until 1861, the year that serfdom was abolished. By that time, some forty thousand manuscript copies of the play had been circulated in Russia. The play had already been recited at private gatherings of cultured urbanites, as was then common practice. The controversial nature of the play had to do with its author's and its protagonist Chatsky's apparent association with the Decembrists, the radical republican branch (the Southern Society) of a coalition with constitutional monarchists (the Northern Society), formed in 1816 by young officers who had fought in the Napoleonic Wars. The evolution of a spiritual brotherhood after 1818 into a secret, violent revolutionary cell became a model for future historians and political organizations and a harbinger of the prerevolutionary liberal versus radical intelligentsia theme. The most extreme among the Decembrists, Pavel Pestel, was more of a pragmatist than a romantic, a Jacobin whose radicalism, specifically his humorless asceticism, authoritarianism (his call for a central revolutionary state), and willingness to use terror to achieve political ends separated him from other "champagne liberals." These same qualities linked him to future extremists among the Populists, the Socialist Revolutionaries, and the Bolsheviks (namely, Lenin). The ill-planned and ill-fated revolt, which began with a demonstration on Senate Square in St. Petersburg on 14 December, was in immediate response to the imminent succession to the throne of the conservative Nikolay I following the death of Aleksandr I, who had not fulfilled his earlier progressive promise.

Although Griboyedov was in fact arrested and briefly imprisoned in 1825 under suspicion of having had ties to the Decembrists, Simon Karlinsky argues that neither he nor Chatsky was actually of their number or persuasion. He offers as evidence of his position Chatsky's rejection of the Decembrist societies in act 4. Furthermore, as poetess Anna Akhmatova maintained and Karlinsky repeats, Griboyedov's successful diplomatic career after 1825 argued against such an association. The Decembrists' "aristocratic liberalism" actually prevented the Bolsheviks from forging a link between them through Chatsky. Karlinsky traces the formal connections among Chatsky, the Decembrists, and the Bolsheviks to Stalinist historian M. V. Nechkina's book *Griboyedov and the Decembrists* (*Griboedov i dekabristy*, 1951).

The specific model for Griboyedov's Chatsky was not a Decembrist but almost certainly the Westernizing philosopher Pyotr Chaadayev (1794–1856).[28] Like Chatsky, Chaadayev traveled abroad (serving in the Napoleonic Wars) and upon his return home sharply criticized Russia's cultural backwardness in his *Philosophical Letters* (*Filosoficheskie pis'ma*, 1829), as a result of which he was denied a diplomatic post. Chaadayev denounced Slavophilic utopianism, which, he believed, assured Russia only of an "empty" past and an "insufferable" present, without a viable future, that is, a destiny. Declared by the state to be "instantly insane" for his espousals, Chaadayev was ostracized by society and placed under house arrest.

Chaadayev's enforced silence—he was eventually freed on the condition that he no longer write—testified to what Herzen called "the power of the spoken word ["Slav" may derive from *slovo* or "word"] in a land . . . unaccustomed to free speech." Chaadayev, like the great tongueless Russian bell which tourists were taken to see in his day, was forged into "a hieroglyph," symbolic of Russian muteness. This muteness was especially pronounced in those (largely the gentry, nobility, and intelligentsia) with the education to perceive the contradiction between "the *words* they were taught" and "the *facts* of life around them."

Like Chatsky at the Famusovs' ball, Chaadayev projected a "hopeless pessimism" derived from the foregoing contradiction. Standing like Hamlet "with folded arms, by a column," he represented "an embodied veto, a living protest," gazing "at the vortex of faces senselessly whirling around him." Chatsky/Chaadayev had what Herzen called "that restless turbulence which cannot endure to be out of harmony with what surrounds it, and must either break it or be broken. . . ." The "embodied veto" was also a "working yeast." Chatsky/ Chaadayev's melancholy spectatorial otherness constituted the soul's active independent spying upon the self and the state. The "tragically emancipated" conscience expressed itself as "implacable negation," "bitter irony," "painful self-analysis," and "insane" but joyless laughter.[29] This defined the romantic revolutionary iconoclast, as opposed to the orthodox political revolutionary, both in the 1820s and in the 1920s.

The view of Chatsky as Decembrist/romantic iconoclast has been promulgated not only by official Soviet interpreters who co-opt his eccentric individualism in the name of ideological iconicity but by intellectuals who empathize with the quixotic nature of his eccentric resistance to social norms. The intelligentsia is attracted to both Chatsky and the Decembrists as characters in a play, who behave in an exclamatory, rhetorical manner, speaking in tirades and bookish quotations. In their "ballroom propaganda," these "characters" seemed to publicize the self-regarding intellectual's dissociation from state-conditioned and choreographed "social sclerosis."[30] Unlike the "superfluous" intellectuals, the Onegins of the same era who entered freely into social festivities as "drawing-room automata," the Decembrists (and Chatsky), Yury Lotman states, "went to balls *in order not to dance there.*" The Decembrists "replaced the prosaic accountability to authority with accountability to history and the fear of death with the poetry of honor and freedom."[31] They proudly made themselves available to fate by disowning society's silencing rituals and advertising their social isolation in public places. One of their number, Kondraty Ryleyev, who was hanged for his part in the rebellion, composed a poem entitled "Nalivayko's Confession," which proclaims, "Fate has already doomed me." Chatsky declaimed this poem, surrounded by his respectfully silent Decembrist allies, in the library episode (number thirteen) in Meyerhold's seventeen-part *mise en scène.* A Soviet critic compared Chatsky's final exit in this same production to Ryleyev's final march to the gallows.[32]

Meyerhold's Chatsky, whom the director called ardent but not prescient, owed more to romantic literature (for example, to Griboyedov's one-time roommate, author Wilhelm Küchelbecker/Kyukhelbeker) than to radical politics. Chatsky's love of music reflected Griboyedov's, while his taste in music coincided with Meyerhold's. Meyerhold told the Prague Theatre D-37 that he was from a musical family: he played piano as a child and later played violin. "My musical education," Meyerhold wrote, " is the basis of my directorial work." This statement was borne out by his precisely scored and notated "musical realist" *mise en scène* for *Woe to Wit*. Chatsky's "musical Decembrism," as one critic called it, was reminiscent of Blok's "musical Bolshevism," a sensory-spiritual metaphor for and expression of revolutionary romanticism, which Chatsky's loneliness reinforced. Meyerhold's Chatsky wrapped himself in romantic airs for solitary piano by Bach, Beethoven, Mozart, Gluck, and Schubert, which he played as lyrical counterpoint to the noisy conversations and orchestral and choral sounds which surrounded him.[33]

Meyerhold's Chatsky was closer to Hamlet than to Alceste (Griboyedov's two literary models), projecting an insularity that was more idealistic than cantankerous. His behavior and his countenance embodied his own tragic fate rather than a narrow-minded judgment of the worth of others. In the context of Griboyedov's world, Meyerhold's Chatsky is a proto- rather than a pre-Decembrist, a man who is ahead of his time and not merely arrived too early and in the wrong setting, as Pushkin thought, to do any good. As a result, he is melancholy, instead of merely foolish in his isolation. However, within the context of Meyerhold's world, Russia in the 1920s, Chatsky represents the old intelligentsia, not the new. His melancholy stems not from his lonely prescience but from his threatened obsolescence. Meyerhold's Chatsky must then be read through a double temporal filter, which renders him even more ambiguous than originally written. Certainly, in retrospect, Meyerhold's production invites the historian to read Chatsky more in terms of the director's fate than the author's intentions. Meyerhold, who in the 1920s dressed like a commissar but still thought like a formalist, was himself caught and eventually crushed in the time warp which saw the overlap of the old (prerevolutionary) intelligentsia and the new. In his 1973 production of Molière's *Don Juan*, another politically persecuted director, Anatoly Efros, parodied the hero's father, Don Luis/Louis, who spoke in the cadences of the Bolsheviks, the old intelligentsia of Efros's day.

Theoretically, the proto-Decembrist Chatsky lives inside the unadulterated truth, while Khlestakov, the grotesque issue of post-Decembrism, lives inside the unadulterated lie, each in response to the normative social and moral order of his day. Chatsky's truth-telling, which society perceives as "madness," and Khlestakov's lying, which society perceives as "truth," are, as exiled Soviet writer Andrey Sinyavsky has asserted, both strategies for encoding the doubleness of dream, rumor, mimicry (imposture), and tableau (mirage) in their play worlds and in the illusory real worlds to which these play worlds refer.[34] Both characters "move through life uniquely alive and uniquely alone" rather than settling for the coherent, reduced, and structured space of "a cell, a closet, a grave."[35] Their public performances imaginatively and creatively retrieved the privacy which society had co-opted from them.

Meyerhold's *Woe to Wit* shifted the focus from "the official boorishness" of Famusov's world to the loneliness of Chatsky's world. Chatsky, an intellectual who is out of step with the times, believes deeply in something but has not yet discovered what it is or how to serve it. This shift echoed Meyerhold's earlier approach to *The Inspector General*, which took its cue more from Khlestakov's otherness than from the Mayor's and the town's *poshlost'* or boorishness. In *Woe to Wit*, Meyerhold presented a self-satisfied world whose social ethos was embodied in social pastimes, for example, dancing and billiards, which advertised a false healthiness. Chatsky's wan romanticism seemed by contrast to be socially self-defeating but spiritually and morally self-affirming.[36]

Meyerhold-Griboyedov's celebrated dining room episode (number 14), performed to John Field's "Nocturne, No. 5 in B-flat," demonstrated society's definition of socially resistant, solipsistic romanticism as counterproductive "madness." This judgment coincided with the deepening prescription of a social code of "usefulness" in the 1920s. The new social ethics proclaimed that "usefulness," defined as that which is created directly by or for the proletariat, was the sole bestower of moral authority on a person, a class, an activity, or a thing. In a decade whose credo was "it makes no difference how durable you make a 'useless' thing," the sanctity of the self was considered to be not only socially anachronistic but counterrevolutionary.[37]

Meyerhold's staging of the dining room episode served up Chatsky as the living corpse of revolutionary romanticism to the voracious new social ethics. Thirty-two diners sat doll-like on the upstage side of a long table, positioned on and stretching across the forestage (fig. 18). Seated behind this dais, the diners appeared as though they were preparing to commence a testimonial dinner of the sort that was commonly held in the many workers' clubs (*rabochie kluby*) which had grown up in the Soviet Union in the 1920s. Only in Meyerhold-Griboyedov's version, the honored guest would be both dishonored and figuratively eaten. The diners sucked on animal bones, representing Chatsky's body, while passing his "madness," his Khlestakovian rumored and reported self, across the table. Their rhythmic, uniform

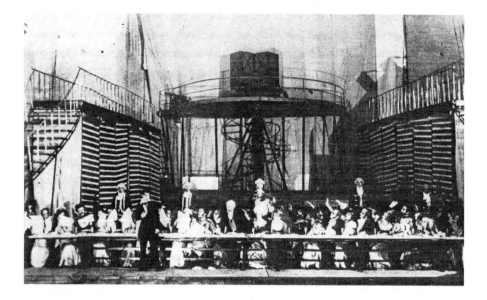

The Dining Room episode from Meyerhold's staging of Griboyedov's Woe
to Wit, *1928. Courtesy of Ardis, Ann Arbor.*

actions were reminiscent of those of the caricatured bourgeoisie and
counterrevolutionaries in Soviet mass spectacles of the early 1920s.
Chatsky's spatial isolation downstage of the long table recalled Pierrot's physical relationship to the Mystics in Meyerhold's staging of
The Little Showbooth. Chatsky's movement from stage right to stage
left along the table's downstage edge served as visual counterpoint to
the spreading of the rumor. At the same time, his movement between
stage proper and auditorium defined an interlinear spatial corridor
between Blokian ("I'm very sad. You think it's funny") and Gogolian
("What're you laughing for? You're laughing at yourselves") two-way
self-mirroring and public surveillance. Chatsky, like Blok's Pierrot
and Meyerhold as Pierrot in Golovin's 1917 portrait of the director,
was trapped in the "sad panopticon" of virtual reality which was
Russian and Soviet culture. Chatsky's romantic revolutionary iconoclasm, presented as a physically embodied spiritual abstraction (music, silence, solitude), was consumed by the charismatic anonymity of
the mass.

Meyerhold's staging and Viktor Shestakov's constructivist design,
which placed the long dining table between two industrial-looking
side ladders connected to fifteen-foot walkways and culminating in a
captain's bridge at the stage's rear wall, parodied the decade's drab   *139*

monumentalism. N. P. Ulyanov's rich costumes, drawn from several periods of French fashion and accented by Russian accessories, uneasily cohabited with the scenic design, echoing the peculiar marriage in the 1920s of classical imperial façades and Communist iconography on Soviet city streets. Meyerhold's presentational framing of the dining room episode "virtualized" reality as does a photographic set-up, flattening it and transforming the temporal condition of movement into the static construction of space.[38]

The undiplomatic Chatsky's symbolic dismemberment eerily foreshadowed the murder and tearing apart of the diplomat Griboyedov by an angry Teheran mob in 1829. Griboyedov died when the embassy in which he served was stormed by a group seeking to prevent the repatriation to Russia of a group of Georgian, Armenian, and German women who claimed to be Russian citizens captured and taken against their will into Persian harems during the Russo-Persian War.[39] The proto-Decembrist author and protagonist of a play which the Bolsheviks dubbed a "people's creation" and from which Lenin and Lunacharsky drew characterizations of the proletariat were ironically, and from the intelligentsia's perspective presciently, destroyed by a mass action.[40]

Meyerhold's 1935 production of Griboyedov's play was generally considered by Soviet critics and historians to be less ambitious and inspired than his earlier treatment and has been largely ignored by Western scholars. This thirteen-episode version was not only more compressed than its predecessor but more realistic and more narrowly satirical as well. Yet, in some ways, the later staging is even more revealing of a cultural progression in modern Russian history.

Meyerhold, who by 1935 had rejected Chatsky's Decembrism as "a contemporary vulgarization by the Soviet press," shifted the focus of the *mise en scène* from revolutionary romanticism to the charismatic anonymity of social compliance and surveillance. Chatsky's accuser Sofiya, Célimène to his Alceste, became more important to Meyerhold after he read a letter (dated 25 January 1825) in which Pushkin named her the key figure in the play. More significantly, Griboyedov's secret policeman and proto-*apparatchik* Molchalin (from *molchanie* or "silence" in Russian) also became more important to Meyerhold at a time of increased spying, social and moral hypocrisy, and externally and internally imposed personal restraints. Molchalin's silent surveillance, like that of Russia's "imperial actors," Herzen's term for the nation's "secret and open police," was aided by an understanding of other people's silence, of "words that were not uttered." Meyerhold

observed that among all of Griboyedov's second-rank Moscow bureaucrats, only the careerist Molchalin appears by reason of ambition
and temperament to be on track for a government appointment in St.
Petersburg. At the time that Griboyedov wrote his play, St. Petersburg, not Moscow, was the seat of national power—home to the tsar,
senate, synod, ministry, and secret police—and the locus of hope and
dread.[41] While Chatsky, as Sinyavsky argues, represents Griboyedov's
inspector general, in that he exposes the truth, Molchalin embodies
society's fear of exposure and the active dissembling it undertakes to
prevent the truth from being revealed.[42]

Molchalin is both Famusov's countenance-keeping secretary and
Famusov's daughter Sofiya's secret lover. He is not only Chatsky's
secret rival for Sofiya; he is, like Chatsky and like Chatsky's "madness," also the creation of Sofiya's fearful, sentimental imagination.
But while Chatsky performs the iconoclast's role, Molchalin is constructed, with society's active compliance, as an idol of sincerity imbued with ostentatious moral value. If Chatsky represents revolutionary romanticism, Molchalin is self-regarding spectacle, which "aims
at nothing, other than itself." Molchalin's masklike silence publicizes
conformity while concealing opportunism. This opportunism co-opts
the social will to which Molchalin is presumably subordinating himself. Molchalin's mute ethics, which Chatsky mourns (21) and society
rewards, was a metonym for "the dead pause of Russian state and
society in the years 1812–1825," when state censorship of theatre
(including *Woe from Wit*) and culture was reaffirmed.[43]

Molchalin's muteness is not only behavioral but professional. He is,
as secretary and historian, a scribe, who has "received three decora-
tions" (56) for his archival research at a time when, Chatsky notes,
"under pain of great penalty, / We're made to acknowledge any man /
A geographer or an historian" (20), that is, an expert on how the
known world is configured. The Russian historian's profession mirrors Molchalin's mute ethics. Russian history, in Griboyedov's and
Meyerhold's estimation, is conspiratorially co-created by scribes who
do not write the truth and a state-run society which has no desire to
read or know it. This theme is echoed by a deafness motif in the play.
The bribed and brokered history which results is essentially written in
advance. By way of illustration, in 1833, Count Arakcheyev deposited
a monetary reward in a Russian bank to be paid in the future to the
scribe who penned "the best," that is the most favorable, history of
the reign of Aleksandr I (Arakcheyev's tsar). "Our historians of literature," Meyerhold wrote, "pass through Pimen's monologue." Here

Meyerhold invoked the name of the clerical scribe in *Boris Godunov* whose "history" inspired a monk to become a tsar-pretender.[44]

Although the self-dramatizing Chatsky threatens to disrupt history, it is the ostensibly self-effacing Molchalin who finally subverts it by translating the spectacle of Promethean authorship into the spectacle of social consumption. By refocusing attention on Molchalin in 1935, Meyerhold expressed his belief that the Soviet *apparatchiki* had eroded the principles of the 1917 revolution and not the unreconstructed Russian intelligentsia, that is, the Fellow Travelers, who were being destroyed in the name of these principles. Molchalin is to Chatsky as Osric was to Hamlet, what Grigory Kozintsev called a new breed of "obsequious young men on the make," "a member of a generation which grew up with the notion that it is dangerous to think and pointless to feel." Molchalin/Osric is, as Kozintsev said of "The Unknown," Arbenin's "double" in Lermontov's *Masquerade*, "a sign of ruin and the approach of the end." Molchalin embodies the Elsinore (and Gogolian) trope of ready compliance. To illustrate the terrifying absurdity of such self-denial in Russian culture, Kozintsev cites the petty bureaucrat Zemlyanika's willingness to agree with Khlestakov's suggestion in *The Inspector General* that yesterday he indeed might not have been so tall.[45]

While Molchalin calls forth and reinforces an authoritarian history of pure appearance, Chatsky asserts a phenomenology of absolute truth ("I'm no diviner of dreams . . . I believe my own eyes," 23), linking him to his literary prototypes, Alceste and Hamlet. Meyerhold's recognition of the scribe's ascendancy over the true historian coincided with the Soviet government's renewed commitment to artistic censorship and to the administrative consolidation and homogenization of artistic agencies in the period 1932–1934.

Meyerhold based his Molchalin on Nikolay II's tough-minded, moderately reformist advisor Pyotr Stolypin (1862–1911), who was prime minister of turbulent Saratov province (a Gogolian resonance) in 1906–1911. Stolypin was assassinated, with the possible compliance of the secret police for whom he worked as an informer, while in the tsar's presence at a theatrical gala in Kiev (14 September 1911). Lenin viewed Stolypin as his counterrevolutionary double and adapted his tactical combination of police force, legislative manipulation, and economic and political reform.[46]

Revolutionary laconism's mirror image may already have been subtly invoked and grounded by Meyerhold in his 1928 staging of Molchalin in relation to Chatsky. In this earlier version, a disdainful and

more formidable Molchalin, one with a low voice rather than the traditional tenor, was cast as a more equal adversary to Chatsky in the
play's act 3, scene 3 "verbal duel" ("Episode 9: At the Door").[47] Meyerhold stood Chatsky and Molchalin at separate pedestals, framing
on either side Sofiya's cream-colored double doors (fig. 19). This staging suggested a well-known photograph, taken on 25 October 1917,
the day of the revolution, of two Latvian security guards standing outside Lenin's temporary headquarters in the former Smolny Institute
for the education of the daughters of the St. Petersburg aristocracy.
Until he knew for certain that Kerensky and his cabinet were under
Bolshevik arrest, Lenin on this day left his room only "incognito"—
that is, "bandaged, wigged and bespectacled." These behavioral habits of the exile proved to be largely unnecessary, since the Smolny
had already been surrounded and overrun by Bolshevik soldiers and
sympathizers. The photographic concordance between these Meyerholdian theatrical and Leninist historical moments signified the apparent revolutionary victory over bourgeois empowerment and surveillance.[48] However, the iconic completion of this revolutionary
trope in the corrupted, static, and silent bureaucratic aftermath signi-

fied by Molchalin (especially in 1935) suggested that the oppressiveness of the satiated world depicted in Griboyedov's play had merely been recoded and more severely reapplied in Soviet society.

Nationwide self-surveillance, the population's policing of itself, was posited by the Bolsheviks after 1917 as an idealistic rejection of the tsar's omniscient and omnipotent system of police monitoring. This method died as a humane ideal amid the disruptions caused by the Civil War, only to be immediately reborn as a cynical reality, rooted in a preexistent cultural imperative. Russian culture's attraction to surveillance is related to its dread of disclosure. Its "fear of things being understood" encodes the paranoid center-fixation of a culture which has no desire to exchange the inside and the outside, the known and the unknown. State surveillance makes every member of society nominally responsible for its maintenance and aware of the consequences of breaking secrecy and silence. The great incidence of lying and pretending in Russian cultural discourse expresses people's Aesopian breakage of this ethics of muteness. Not only "heinous chatter" but the "naked truth" or *istina* (feminine in Russian) has been felt by many in society to be culturally "unbecoming."[49] Unsurprisingly, during the unstable and contentious societal discourse which characterized the early postrevolutionary period, there was a revival of interest in Phèdre. Like other popular icons of the Russian stage (for example, Hamlet, Chatsky, and Khlestakov), Phèdre was designed by rumor, disordered by misperception, shadowed by (self-)surveillance, and impelled by a combination of inner and outer motives toward disclosure.

Racine's *Phèdre* (1667) dramatizes the irreconcilability of vision and understanding and the tenuous equilibrium between speech and sign, resulting in "the dynamic disorder of everything." In 1924, Stanislavsky described Mikhail Chekhov's Hamlet as "perishing in his frenzy," and Trotsky had already called revolution "the frenzy of history."[50] The Kamerny Theatre (Moscow) production of *Phèdre* (premiere 8 February 1922), directed by Aleksandr Tairov, designed by Aleksandr Vesnin, and starring Alisa Koonen in the title role, represented the disordering emotionalism of human motive and of historical moment, the attempted erasure of the boundaries between builders and materials, people and history, inside and outside, between subjective and objective histories, lodged in the human body as historian and historical sign. It presented fracture disclosed in multiplanarity and concealed by heroic monumentalism that is at once frankly acknowledged and strategically disavowed. In its design and execution, the Kamerny *Phèdre* bestrode the mythic, the avant-garde, and the socially "real"/heroically monumental worlds of Russia in the early 1920s.

In much the same way that Tairov's directorial work on *Phèdre* made no distinction between inner psychological experiencing and physical enactment/objectification, it discovered the heroic individual in both the classical and the contemporary type. A rational construction was built around an emotional core, and a secret was publicized through the formal mask of repressed sinfulness. Tairov, like Hamlet, viewed the individual as having intrinsic value, not as an instrument to be played upon, a principle which his staging of *Phèdre* made abundantly clear. Kamerny Theatre staff designer Georgy Yakulov saw in Tairov's *Phèdre* "a victory over the [romantic] grotesque with its sense of man being ruled by supernatural forces which turned him into a will-less marionette."[51] If a portion of Tairov's audience found this fate theme to be too distancing in its antique religious and metaphysical meaning, the social connotations of doubled surveillance by self and society struck much closer to home.

The classical revival in Russian arts and letters began during the Silver Age. Lev Bakst, the World of Art painter most attracted to the culture of ancient Greece, designed sets and costumes for productions of *Hippolytus* (in Dmitry Merezhkovsky's translation, 1902) and *Oedipus Rex* (1904). Aside from his neo-Hellenist/neo-Nietzschean dramatic theories, Vyacheslav Ivanov wrote two plays, *Tantalus* (1905) and *Prometheus* (1919), which imitated Aeschylus in terms of their archaic language, mythological subjects, and structure. Innokenty Annensky wrote four dramas based on Greek myths—*Melanippe, the Philosopher* (1901), *King Ixion* (1902), *Laodamia* (1906), and *Thamira, the Cither Player* (*Famira Kifared*, 1906). The Euripidean myth of Laodamia was also the source for Fyodor Sologub's play *The Gift of the Wise Bees* (1907) and Valery Bryusov's *Protesilaus Deceased* (1913). *Thamira*, like Racine's *Phèdre* based on Euripides' *Hippolytus*, compared the service of Thamira/Hippolytus to the goddess Artemis (to the exclusion of the goddess Aphrodite) to the artist's self-isolation from life in service to art. In the end, Thamira is blinded and stripped of his talent by the Muses to whom he had bragged of it. Staged by Tairov at the Kamerny Theatre (premiere 2 November 1916) with a cubist design by Aleksandra Ekster, *Thamira* was a prelude to his work on *Phèdre*.

Although Koonen remarked that Racine's *Phèdre* had largely been neglected by Russians since Pushkin's time, Racine's drama was a common point of reference and the character of Phèdre, like that of Salome (Kamerny Theatre production 1917), actually became quite popular in Russia in roughly the first quarter of the twentieth century. Soviet critic V. N. Solovyov commented upon the Racinian character of Anna Andreyevna's "leaving her senses" (that is, fainting) at the news of Khlestakov's imposture at the conclusion of Meyerhold's *Inspector General*. Meyerhold stated that he directed *Woe to Wit* not as a neoclassical French comedy, as was traditional on the Russian stage, but as a neoclassical French tragedy, "in the spirit of Racine and Corneille."[52] Marina Tsvetayeva's (1892–1941) incomplete dramatic trilogy *Aphrodite's Rage* included the verse plays *Theseus-Ariadne* (*Tezey-Ariadna*, 1927) and *Phaedra* (*Fedra*, 1928), the latter based on Gustav Schwab's nineteenth-century version of Greek mythology, *Die schönsten Sagen des klassischen Altertums*. Osip Mandelstam's (1891–1938) poem "Theseus, Hippolytus, and Phaedra" (*Tezey, Gippolit i Fedra*, 1916) suggested the idea of inexplicably fated personal and cultural performance, which seems both foreign and familiar. Mandelstam's pronouncements "I shall never see famed Phaedra" and "Phaedra is Russia" hung over the culture though the 1930s and 1940s, when both Mandelstam and Tsvetayeva fell victim to the Soviet state's redefinition of Russia's destructive maternal muse. Nadezhda Mandelstam, the poet's widow, observed bitterly after his death: "Our people loves its rulers, and the rulers love only themselves. The highest honor they can confer on a writer is to steal his body—as happened with Pushkin—or throw him in a mass grave."[53]

Perhaps with this grim legacy in mind, Tairov instructed Koonen to play Phèdre not as a tragic queen but as a real person whose loss of control conveys the overwhelming, heroic compulsion to affirm and express the self, the revolutionary agency of the human will. Koonen-Phèdre's disorderly "sincere emotionalism" aggravated the self-dispossession from the social order which her presentiment of death conditioned and the state helped fulfill. Her social predicament represented the "ethical phenomenon" of the individual who refused to subject herself to an externally determined fate in a period when the myth of "universal typage" encoded the fatalism of socialist (re)construction. Koonen's Phèdre in Tairov's *mise en scène* sought to distinguish tragedy's "emotionally algebraic formulas" from the state's, to separate heroism from (heroic) monumentalism, and to illustrate the social determination of human fate and its distinctiveness from the capriciousness of chance and the determinism of socialist rule.[54] Tairov's *mise en scène* sought to reconcile "the problem of plasticity on the stage" with "the deepest and most lyrical human feelings." Valery Bryusov's translation likewise broke up the monotonous regularity of Racine's alexandrine verse and moved the language of the play closer to Euripides' more emotional rhythms. In keeping with this historical shift, Bryusov's translation replaced the Latin names of the divinities with Greek names.[55]

Although, as Yury Golovashenko has noted, no one could agree on a definition of "realism" in the early Soviet theatre, all of the major Soviet directors, including Yevgeny Vakhtangov ("fantastic realism"), Meyerhold ("musical realism"), and Tairov ("synthetic realism") sought one which would properly balance their aesthetic concerns with the social necessities and historical forces then at work in their culture. In the process, each of these directors removed realism from the exclusive preserve of psychological experiencing (Stanislavsky's *perezhivanie*), while objectifying psychology scenographically. In its rejection of lightness, gentleness, and playfulness in favor of the strictures of straight lines, geometric shapes, and rigorous, multivalent poses, the Kamerny *Phèdre* differed from the prevailing tone of Vakhtangov's, Meyerhold's, and even some of Tairov's production work in the period 1917–1927.[56]

During this same period, artists like Vasily Kandinsky and Kazimir Malevich were using flattened geometric shapes to suggest spiritual construction, a synesthesia of the visual and the musical, aspiring to the abstract purity and immeasurable dimensions of inner being. Constructivist design, by contrast and at the same time, sought to depict "the logical structure of organized space" as a semiotic for "the control of morality and socialist happiness" in real, albeit ideologically elevated, life.[57]

While architect Aleksandr Vesnin's original model for the Kamerny *Phèdre* was "almost entirely naturalistic" (a number of Soviet architects turned to stage design in the 1920s due to a lack of money and materials with which to construct buildings), his second was "almost entirely stylized or schematic." Abram Efros wrote that in the first model, which stressed archaism, "Phèdre had no place to live." In the second, modernist and abstract model, "Phèdre had nothing to breathe." The third, finally realized model combined concreteness and abstraction in a dynamically shifting relationship of contemporary movement and antique architecturally static façade. Konstantin Derzhavin characterized Vesnin's final design for *Phèdre* as "stasis disturbed by dynamic linear and planar dislocations."[58]

Vesnin came to his *Phèdre* design straight from his work with

Lyubov Popova on the unrealized mass spectacle *Struggle and Victory of the Soviet*, commemorating the Third Komintern Congress and planned for Khodyuskoye Field. These cubist architectural designs, prepared for Meyerhold, earned Vesnin the director's enthusiastic support. Vesnin sought in his *Phèdre* design to solve the problems of pictorial space and spatial organization of fixed and mobile forms through an architectonics of scenic rupture. He accomplished this by combining a severely geometricized "real pictorial space," composed of a three-tiered stage floor, broken up and connected by stairs, with a "fictional" background of "irregular cloth," which moved and shifted color under light from red, to yellow, to black, to signify on stage changes in character and in mood. Jean Cocteau, who saw the production on its 1923 European tour, wrote that "the profound architecture" of actor and scenery (figure and ground) in Vesnin's design "abolishes facile picturesqueness." In this, Vesnin answered Efros's call in 1921 for a new Soviet theatrical design, which would offer the reality of sculpture, architecture, and materials in place of the aesthetic illusions of pictorial mimesis. The rapidly developing passion for objectness and materiality, for a sculpted, more real reality embodying the new cultural order, was likewise logically expressed in the wax effigies which Meyerhold substituted for mannequinlike people at the conclusion of his production of *The Inspector General*.

The *Phèdre* set's raked walls and platforms represented Hellenic/neoclassical architecture (and the old world view/old world order) as a listing ship, on which the seasick heroine awaited imminent shipwreck. Vesnin executed a series of precise sketches and cubist schematizations of ancient sailboats in preparation for constructing his scenic model.[59] The sensation of seasickness, which was aided by varying the intensity of the stage lighting, sought to capture the heroine's "restless rhythm." Vesnin's *Phèdre* set quoted Ekster's earlier design for *Salome*, in which "dynamic changes in the scenic atmosphere," which resembled both floating sails and "a suite of colorfully flowing planes" breathing with the play, were made in plain sight of the audience. The sense of scenery changing to reflect shifts in the dramatic situation demonstrated Tairov's belief that "realism" is perceptually determined and changes through time.[60]

Phèdre's set was "menacing" in its boldly articulated colors—cobalt, ocher, red lead (minium), and white lead (zinc white). The playing platforms resembled stone slabs, across which fell the long shadows cast by connecting cubes and columns struck by shafts of diagonal light. The costumes, which left the actors free only to move

FIGURE 20

A. G. Koonen (Phèdre) and N. M. Tseretelli (Hippolytus) in Tairov's Phèdre,
1922. Courtesy of Izdatel'stvo iskusstvo, Moscow.

their exposed arms and legs, and the helmets designed to resemble
statues of ancient Greek gods created a statuesque, visual concordance between actors and scenery (fig. 20).

Relative to this overall architectural monolithism/monumentalism,
not only movement and emotion but color suffusion functioned as
(semiotic) enjambment. Phèdre, who was attired in passion-red cloak,

flaming red wig, Amazonian gold helmet (gilded cardboard), and breastplate worn over a long black and white striped tunic and who balanced atop stylized cothurni, stood in visual resistance to and as a visual critique of the scenic architecture from which she was constructed (Cocteau compared Tairov's *Phèdre* actors to "blocks") and of which she was a part.

On the surface, Tairov's and Vesnin's neoclassical cubism defined a socialist baroque, pseudo-classic (*lozhnoklassik*) style for a culture seeking to reinvent the past via renewed orthodoxy.[61] In reality, Vesnin's set and costumes destabilized what it asserted. This subversive motive linked the design and *mise en scène* to such seemingly disparate *uslovnye* (stylized, conventional) theatrical experiments of the 1920s as Eisenstein's "circusization" and Nikolay Foregger's "music hallization" of the stage.

Phèdre's scenic plan sought to represent the struggle between concreteness and abstraction in the aftermath of the revolution and in the early period of socially materialist construction. While the Kamerny's production style veered away from the realistic toward the constructivist and the cubist, it embodied a laconism which was consistent with the new order's sense of the heroically monumental.[62] At the same time, the Kamerny's scenic aesthetic not only destroyed illusionism, but undermined the illusory solidity of stereometrically treated form and constructed space via the instability of movement and emotional shift. The social order of mechanical regularity, expressed in both concrete and abstract form, was subverted by the variable, unpredictable intensity of human will and desire. Stage space became not only the context for but the text of the decisive battle between internal (human) and external (social, mechanical) authority, between speech and silence. *Phèdre*'s concretely abstract *mise en scène* revealed that, as much as chaotic disordering (freedom through emotionalism), social ordering (the autocracy of emotional restraint) can devolve into nothingness.

Koonen relates that in his *mise en scène* for *Phèdre* Tairov sought to break free of both the classical French tradition and the classical staging traditions of the Russian imperial theatres. The "revolutionary communion," which postrevolutionary emotionalism sought to effect and coalesce, differed from the symbolists' call for communal action (*sobornost'*) by eschewing "generalized" (*obobshchyonye*) feelings for clear and concrete (social) content embodied in equally vivid form. Similarly, "gentle Racine" was necessarily replaced by a more sharply and rigorously emotional Racine. Phèdre's emotion was to be represented as no less than a heroic "cleansing storm" (*ochish-chayushchy uragan*), "virginal passion" perceptually corrupted by an unenlightened status quo.[63]

Despite retrospective and retroactive claims by Soviet theatre historians and political propagandists that the Kamerny *Phèdre* helped define monumentalism and forged a "theatrical-revolutionary path" (*teatral'no-revolyutsionnaya put'*) in its blending of style, theme, spirit, and form, Tairov's *mise en scène* actually reaffirmed the credo of prerevolutionary aestheticism by extolling purity of emotional expression. It eschewed the Cartesian abstract psychologizing of feelings which came into play under socialist realism in the 1930s, while equally avoiding the self-indulgent spiritualism which characterized certain segments of prerevolutionary culture. Tairov's *mise en scène* offered a critique, created from similar verbal and visual languages, of heroic monumentalism, excising strictly ideological content from aesthetically resonant theatrical form.[64]

The "[black] sun of guilt and doom," to which Osip Mandelstam first alluded in his "Phaedra" poem, linked the hope and dread at the heart of Russian culture. Guilt is a personal dystopia, the individual's sense of having dispossessed the national dream of cultural mission. "*Phèdre*," wrote Roland Barthes, "proposes an identification of intensity with guilt; in *Phèdre* things are not hidden because they are culpable . . . things are culpable from the very moment that they are hidden." Phèdre suffers more for her secret as a formal sign of transgression than for the particular substance or content of a transgression. She is fated to body forth the form of transgression as "artificially constructed" objective guilt (for example, adultery and incest).[65] This condition was readily recognizable in early Soviet society, which was evolving from the presumption of guilt as a basis for distinguishing the old culture and its sympathizers from the new. Under these circumstances, Russians discovered, as Terry Eagleton said of Lear's Cordelia, that "to speak or keep silent . . . is equally falsifying." The destructiveness of speech and the publicity of silence (censorship) represent a two-sided "falsification of time."[66]

Nikolay Volkov, who likened Koonen's Phèdre to "Cordelia taking Goneril's path," a radiant spirit plunged into the darkness of her inner chaos, credited the Kamerny *Phèdre* with "illustrating theatre's feminine origin as being aggressive and terrible rather than weak and defenseless." Koonen's Amazonian Phèdre, who typified nominal female agency in Soviet Russia of the 1920s, spoke in a deep voice. Koonen's regular leading man, Nikolay Tseretelli (Hippolytus), said that he had difficulty withstanding the power of her performances. Koonen's Phèdre, consumed by the fire of self-consciousness, could not be saved, even if Hippolytus loved her. Her extreme and absolute passion was incapable of being quenched.[67] Similarly, Phèdre's insatiable Schopenhaurian willing could never be fully mitigated, and her attendant guilt, relative to societal restraint of such willing (symbolized by the incest taboo), could never be adequately confessed.

"Phaedra is Russia," as Mandelstam asserted, because in both individual and social initiatives the self that wills and the society that orders are in eternal conflict. Racine's play illustrates this point in the relationship between Phèdre and her nurse, Oenone. Whereas Phèdre, like Chatsky, embodies romantic revolutionary iconoclasm, heroic resistance, and natural moral understanding, Oenone, like Molchalin, represents socialized speech and silence and moral compromise. Sent by the state both to censor and to inform upon Phèdre by ferreting out her secret guilt, Oenone represents the confidante as secret policewoman.

Tairov's Phèdre performed a visual semiotic of pain, a pain which Soviet dance critic Andrey Levinson described as being "a Russian trait." This "Russian trait," like fate or destiny in Racine's tragedies in Georges Poulet's definition, seemed "already long accomplished in idea before being accomplished in act."[68] This fatalist recipe applied as well to Soviet culture after 1917. Tairov's Phèdre managed to satisfy both the state's social project of theatrical typification/heroic monumentalism and the artist's personal project, "the enlargement of personality" (ukrupnenie lichnosti). Tairov's theatrical oeuvre demonstrated that it is far better to die standing than to live on one's knees. If Phèdre's sacrificing herself to the community suggested otherwise to a new order anxious for social confirmation, it no less affirmed the pathos of apparently untenable, clandestine, Aesopian social rebellion under the state's and the public's watchful eye.

At one point in Tairov's production, Koonen's Phèdre, stricken with pain and shame for loving her stepson, suddenly threw herself on the stage platform, bent down to the ground, and raised her arms to the sky. She called damnation down upon her head in a monologue in which, Pavel Markov observed, she "transformed her mournful cry into a sickly shout." This moment expressed what Tairov described as Phèdre's feeling that "she carries the weight of the world [upon her shoulders] and is bonded to the earth by gravity." Whether this weight and gravity and the chaos it both expressed and held in check were of internal or external origin was here a central issue.[69] Yet Koonen's

Phèdre was attractive to her public less for her bowed countenance than for her unbowed emotional resistance to the social order, which was literally and figuratively depicted in her theatrical world. The heroic pathos which monumental socialist art hoped to achieve was expressed, albeit with different motives, in Phèdre's public suffering.

In her moment of kneeling, Phèdre's wide red cloak, representing emotion incarnate, emotion monumentalized, was spread around her, giving her the appearance of a great wounded bird. She would, on her subsequent exit, drag this cloak behind her "like a bloody trail," her bare shoulders exposed in a gesture of continued vulnerability. As André Antoine observed, in her kneeling Koonen's Phèdre (despite her raised and outstretched arms) did not stress "the Christian motif of raising one's face to heaven" but seemed instead to be "appealing to the bowels of the earth." As she did so, Koonen recalls, two guards stood upstage, immobile like statues and implacable like fate, observing her heroic agony. The testimony of authoritarian presence, which silenced public expression at the conclusion of *Boris Godunov* and *The Inspector General*, here iconically legitimized without speaking the demonstrative staging of emotion as an idea. Similarly, the overall cubist design of the Kamerny *Phèdre* expressed the purer relation between form and idea through concrete abstraction called for by socialist realism, as opposed to the aesthetic and ideological blending practiced in conventional realism.[70]

Lunacharsky credited the Kamerny *Phèdre* with having discovered the theatrical style and method which expressed the Nietzschean sense of "the great ancient atmosphere of grandiose collective myth-creation" and captured the monumentally tragic theme of contemporaneity. Alisa Koonen recalls receiving a kiss from Lunacharsky after he saw her play Phèdre, a performance which he experienced as "a beautiful shock" (*krasivoe potryasenie*).[71] But in reality the "beautiful shock" of romantic revolutionary iconoclasm, embodied by Phèdre (Chatsky, and even somewhat by the liar Khlestakov), broke open the facade of beneficent, empowering iconicity to reveal the sleeping idol of totalitarianism.

CHAPTER 6

THE PROCRUSTEAN BED

Historical experience does not exist for us.

— *Pyotr Chaadayev*

The State in its idea is a lie.

— *Konstantin Aksakov*[1]

On his arrival at the Finland Station on 3 April 1917 to assume the leadership of the Russian revolution, Lenin told his colleagues: "It would be indeed a grave error if we tried now to fit the complex, urgent, rapidly-unfolding practical tasks of the revolution into the Procrustean bed of a narrowly conceived 'theory,' instead of regarding theory first of all and above all as a *guide to action*." By 1931, seven years after Lenin's death, the actress Goncharova in Olesha's *A List of Blessings* observed, "in Russia, cast iron is in vogue" (47).[2]

The Procrustean bed owed something to what Renato Poggioli calls the "pronounced tendency of the Russian critical spirit to translate artistic and cultural facts into religious or political myths." Concretely, the Procrustean bed misrepresented the revolutionary spartanism embodied by Rakhmetov (the self-disciplined revolutionary in Chernyshevsky's *What Is to Be Done?*), who slept upon a bed of nails. While Lenin lay upon his deathbed, Stalin, who ruthlessly demonstrated that "totalitarianism is . . . its *own* utopia," was already at work to make it Procrustean.[3]

Stalin initiated the "cult of Lenin" in April 1924, with the publication of *Foundations of Leninism*. Lenin's permanent marble mausoleum, designed by Aleksey Shchusev, was built in 1930. It replaced the second of two earlier temporary wooden structures, the first having been completed in 1924.[4] The placement of Lenin's tomb in Red Square proclaimed Moscow's identity in the 1920s as the new national center and as the locus of revolutionary "pastness" (history) and futurity (utopia). Lenin's mummified remains, constituting his eternal life, represented utopic engineering, the defeat of old time that Mayakovsky had predicted in his play *Mystery-Bouffe* (*Misteriyabuff*, 1918; revised 1921).

Revolutionary time in general and Lenin's tomb in particular resemble the court clock at Versailles, which, Herzen noted, "pointed to one hour, the hour at which the King died." Lenin's artificially preserved corpse embodied both cultural obstinacy and "rhetorical revolutionary chastity," the objectification of the faithful's denial of all doubt and self-analysis. It murdered reason at the center of the new, ostentatiously rationalist culture. Lenin's tomb and its inventor's *nom de guerre*, "Stalin" ("a one word précis of the new steel era"), not only linked the past with the future, but further inscribed the revolutionary fetish of permanency.[5] This transpired in the decade of the culturally experimental New Economic Policy, which tentatively ventured upon dissolution of such permanency.

In the postscript to his "secret testament" (4 January 1923), Lenin questioned Stalin's wisdom, commented on his brutality and lust for personal power, and declared Stalin to be an unworthy and dangerous successor. Lenin's tomb not only reverenced Lenin but effectively legitimized Stalin as the "reverencer" and constructor of Lenin's memory and as the living embodiment of his memory's continuance. Lenin's waxen corpse was what Slavoj Žižek called "a body redoubled in itself," simultaneously less than and more than its material self. Stalin extracted from this body its sublimity, its power—the aura of the leader—and appropriated it to himself. Lenin's entombment effectively transformed him into a holy relic and into the ironic realization of the religiosity which his atheistic political philosophy had condemned. "Every little god," Lenin wrote, "is the lying with a corpse." Stalin was the first Soviet leader to position himself atop the Kremlin Wall above Lenin's tomb, a symbolic arrangement which James H. Billington has likened to the Russian Orthodox cathedral's iconostasis rising "directly over the grave of a local saint."[6]

The mummification of Lenin "corrected" Stalin's sense of belatedness, of having not been Lenin's trusted advisor or, for that matter, not having been Lenin, the maker of the revolution. Although Stalin, returning from four years in Siberian exile, actually beat Lenin to Petrograd by three weeks (arriving on 12 March 1917), he found that the organizations necessary to administer the revolution were already in place. When Lenin arrived, Stalin was not among those who met his train. Since there was no contemporary newsreel footage of Lenin's arrival (his train arrived too late for the camera crew to film), Stalin instructed Soviet filmmakers to create "historical reconstructions" of the event, in which the dictator was featured prominently in Lenin's welcoming party. The purges of the 1930s were instituted by Stalin in part to eliminate the Old Bolsheviks, in particular historians, who "failed to remember" Stalin's role in 1917. Although footage from *October* (1927), Eisenstein's fictional cinematic restaging of the 1917 revolution, was appropriated by the state as the event's documentary record, the film as a whole was banned for not showing Stalin's leading role in it. John Reed's eyewitness written account, *Ten Days That Shook the World* (1919; also the variant title for *October*), suffered the same fate in the 1930s for a similar omission. Reed had by that time already been granted the extraordinary honor, especially for a foreigner, of burial in Red Square near the Kremlin Wall, that is, in Lenin's precinct.[7]

In order both to assert his presence and to avenge his former absence, Stalin maliciously redesigned methodological components of the revolutionary generation's mythic folklore as symbolic forms of retribution—for example, the Procrustean for the revolutionary bed. Similarly, Stalin's attempt to erase his personal belatedness transposed into a minor key Lenin's social program for combating Russia's cultural backwardness, "its low literacy and poor work habits." Yury Lotman and Boris Uspensky have traced back to the ecclesiastical reforms of the medieval Russian churchman Nikon the link not only between memory (early cultural development or the old ways) and ignorance (backwardness) but also between forgetting, the break with early cultural development (the new ways), and enlightenment.[8] The loss of cultural memory invariably valorizes the "presentness" of moral and social utilitarianism. The presumption of Russian cultural backwardness further enhanced the desire and the prerogative to distance and if possible to erase the past.

Commenting upon the peculiar Russian linkage of forgetfulness and utility, Blok wrote in "The Decline of Humanism" (*Krushenie gumanizma*, 1919), "Here they raised what for a European was the indecent question of which was more important: Shakespeare or a pair of shoes?" Kazimir Malevich later dubbed Stalin's program of socialist realism a "philosophy of shoemakers." Stalin's opportunistic reading for his society of the embarrassment of cultural backwardness allowed him (as philosopher Herman Baronov had earlier said of Gorky's and Lunacharsky's linkage of religion and economics) to put the "saddle of religion" on the "cow of science," that is, to render the spiritual and the aesthetic technocratic. As the title of Aleksandr Afinogenov's play *Fear*, written during Stalin's first Five-Year Plan (1928–1932), suggested, fear was the crank that turned the mechanism of the Procrustean bed. Stalin himself said that he trusted the people to be loyal out of fear, rather than conviction.[9] Characteristically, Afinogenov's play ended with a retraction of its thesis.

Stalinist Procrusteanism was at odds with the original conception of socialist realism, Stalinist society's official cultural doctrine. The term "socialist realism" first appeared in the 25 May 1932 issue of the *Literary Gazette* (*Literaturnaya gazeta*). It entered into the official lexicon as Gorky's coinage after Stalin used the term at a "secret meeting" with Soviet writers at Gorky's apartment on 26 October 1932. Stalin's cultural henchman Andrey Zhdanov wrote in *Literary Critic* (*Literaturny kritik*) in 1933 that socialist realism intended to offer a "historical presentation of concrete reality in its revolutionary development" via "a choice of forms, styles and various genres," manifesting the fullness of artistic initiative. Originally, the new policy was designed to offset the attempt by RAPP (the Russian Association of Proletarian Writers) to establish proletarian supremacy in Soviet culture in the 1920s. Nevertheless, Zhdanov's definition, formalized at the first Writers' Congress in Moscow in 1934, completed and codified the social initiative of nineteenth-century Russian literature and criticism. Lenin and his cultural commissar Lunacharsky had argued in the 1920s in behalf of artistic diversity and against "leveling" (*uravnilovka*), "the rule of the majority over the minority." Stalin likewise opposed leveling but for the purpose of systematically solidifying hierarchical authority in a pyramidal structure.[10]

While the new art and culture was to be "tendentious" (Mayakovsky had earlier called for "tendentious realism"), socialist realism's chief aim was to combat formalist atomization and alienation. Fragmented imagery transfers the authenticating power of integration from collective to individual consciousness. It was believed that harmony and vitality were related values, that this reintegration would redefine culture's organic base in labor. Specialization, seen by Soviet culture as representing professional fragmentation, was identified with capitalist societies.[11] Typification of character and circumstance, signifying an essential (temporal, class-based) reality, would counteract bourgeois realism's fixation on the irrationalism of the individual human psyche. Friedrich Engels had defined realism as "truthfulness of reproduction of typical characters in typical circumstances." Via "totality" and "typicity," socialist realism aimed to combine "the epic, heroic and legendary gesture with the verisimilar forms of realism and representation." The "impossibility" of this task was borne out by the sheer number (400) and contentiousness of Soviet articles written on the subject between 1932 and 1934.[12]

Ivan Gronsky, editor of the state-controlled newspaper *Izvestiya* and party supervisor of literature, claimed that Stalin designated the drama as the genre best suited to educating the masses. The Writers' Congress urged leading prose writers to become dramatists, and the government sponsored new play competitions with monetary awards. The primary point of contention in the discussion of the new dramaturgy was the relationship between romanticism and realism. Socialist realism rejected Sergey Tretyakov's call for a "factographic" literature and embraced Lenin's assertion of the necessity of collective dreaming, stripped of its bourgeois subjective, individualistic, and aesthetic tendencies. Romanticism was to be revolutionary rather than reactionary, an instrument for transforming reality rather than a means of escaping from it into illusion. The dream of the building of communism was synonymous with reality and truth in their essence. Gorky, following Marx's and Engels's view as to the necessity of "Shakespearizing" reality, championed the heroic proletarianism found in classical tragedy and romantic melodrama.[13] The three decades of official socialist realism (it persisted informally for a long time afterward) marked the low point of Russian literature. While *mise en scène*, as the previous chapter illustrated, can render artistic intention invisible, it can as easily manifest the full extent of political determination of artistic matters. This chapter demonstrates how a politically determined, artistic (choreographed and directed, homogeneous, and spectatorial) cultural *mise en scène* operated according to a megalomaniac metatext. The extraction of theatricality from the theatre and its attribution to life marked the recurrence and in many ways the culmination of cultural performance in modern Russian history.

Socialist realism represented the last and most formal inscription of "revolutionary eminence" to date, the theme of myth production as a cultural value in Soviet society. The nineteenth-century theme of redemption and the twentieth-century theme of legitimacy were forged by the revolutionary flame into the new value of "worthiness." This value was then written into the culture via the mechanism of ritual, whose qualities of iconicity and objectification transferred this value from the individual to the collective plane of experience.[14] In Soviet culture, as reflected in socialist realist drama, work (defined in both the economic and the ideological sense) makes men and women worthy of a true, productive love, which presumes comradeship and the loss of self-absorption, the state-perceived shortcoming of the intelligentsia.

Socialist realism came to constitute a "normative aesthetics," "a universal category of thought."[15] Its transformation of the result of historical process "from a criterion of historical truth into an instrument for constructing it" defined a virtual semiotics of closure.[16] By building the conclusion into the point of departure, socialist realism imparted the quality of predestination to historical development. The credo of Stalinist society—"Fairy tale has become reality"—was structurally true, if substantively false. Stalinist culture theoretically formalized with revolutionary consciousness the functionalist aesthetic and the irreversible sequencing of functions and adherence to character types, which Vladimir Propp ascribed to the folktale.[17] Fate becomes the metafunction of such cultural formalism, which is dependent upon heroic arrival and deliverance. By casting social deliverance in terms of the outside (a hero, fate, *deus ex machina*, that is, happy endings), socialist realism promotes the tyranny of self-disempowerment among the people whom the hero is called upon to save.

Russia's historical phantom rulers (tsar-deliverers and tsar-pretenders) and phantom ruling subjects ("the people" and the proletariat) are necessary functions of the conspiratorial desires of the intelligentsia's romance of thought and feeling and the state's romance of power and ideology. In the fairy tale that is Russian history, tsars may be pretenders and pretenders tsars (the frogs and princes scenario), heroes may be despots, and "once upon a time" and "happily ever after" are state myths designed to induce compliance with an authoritative and authoritarian vision. The optical trickery of Stalinist culture's monumental façadism is embodied by the protagonists of Yevgeny Shvarts's dramatic fables of the Stalin era, especially *The Shadow* (*Ten'*, 1940) and *The Dragon* (*Drakon*, 1944). Both of these plays were briefly realized in productions whimsically designed and directed by Nikolay Akimov at the Leningrad Theatre of Comedy, where they became repertory mainstays after Stalin's death. Typically, Shvarts's heroes are disoriented by the defamiliarized fairy-tale worlds in which they find themselves and are politically naive and shortsighted concerning the totalist myth and logic of fairy-tale rulers and rule. In the Stalinist looking-glass worlds which Shvarts portrays, the future is foretold and the past is falsified, so that the historian's profession, to which *The Shadow*'s hero belongs, is particularly perilous.

Shvarts employed the defamiliarizing aesthetic strategy of the fairy tale to encode deformation as a social mechanism for amoral reconstruction. This strategy undermines the "dream" solution of the socialist utopia by offering an alternative and more evocative definition of actual social reality. Defamiliarization both extends and spatializes perception, causing perspective to be not only produced but inhabited. The temporal profundity produced by formalist consciousness reveals the inertia of "social masks," the politically instructive socialist realist typification of character, theme, and situation. Shvarts's defamiliarization of utopian reality captures the moral opportunism of ideological posturing. Ministers of state, reduced to a Swiftian state of mind-body separation in *The Shadow*, must be carried around and set in physical poses meant to advertise the correctness of their political thought and expression to the seen and unseen (panoptic) audience. Conceptual vision (that is, prefigured and judgmental) rather than perceptual vision, Shvarts warns, is the self-victimizing component of human nature upon which the tyranny of spectacular culture depends. Written at the height of the Stalin "show trials," *The Shadow* revealed that real people and societies are not easily led into abstract evil as in fairy tales. Instead, seduced by the illusory performance of truth, they ascribe moral value to what they see (the state's preserve), rather than to what they think or feel (the intelligentsia's preserve). Stalinist culture was designed to be universally seen but not seen into or seen through. It was visibly iconic but opaque in the implications of its imagery. Space was divested of time, of extrarevolutionary historical consciousness and perspective. The irony of the Soviet utopia was that in evacuating time from space it likewise evacuated the hope that defined it.

The revolutionary solution to history was succinctly dramatized within Zamyatin's dystopic novel *We* in the tale of the savage who noticed that every time the barometer indicated rain, rain actually fell. Since he desired rain, the savage simply tinkered with the barometer until he had let out just enough quicksilver to bring it to the level of rain. Manipulating form did not necessarily produce the desired effect but created the illusion that the end, somehow implicit in the means, had already been achieved. This determinist image, which represented an extension of the trope of revolutionary determinacy and reduction, was *iconically* correct and therefore true. Leon Trotsky wrote that "if the symbol is a concentrated image, then the revolution is the supreme maker of symbols, since it presents all phenomena and relations in concentrated form." Stalinism was, in this sense, revolutionary symbolism's apotheosis.[18]

Socialist realism codified Stalin's cruel penchant for rhetorical questioning, the "truth" of which was predetermined by the asking and routinely reinforced by the already obviated response. Stalinist rhetorical iconism inverted the Bolshevik ideal of heroic assertiveness, exemplified by Pasternak's likening of Mayakovsky's manner of carrying himself to an irrevocable decision that has already been made. Rhetorical iconism, together with Stalin's tendency to transform "obstinate" facts into compliant theory, further subverted historical truth. The disappearance and reappearance of "stubborn" corpses (Herzen's term), like obstinate facts, recalibrated historical "truth" in and for Soviet society. Stalin's disdain for history and historians was evident in his statement that "paper will put up with anything that is written on it" and in his decision to write history as well as to make it. The official *History of the Communist Party of the Soviet Union*, which appeared anonymously in 1938, was added to Stalin's *Collected Works* in 1946.

Stalin's paranoid fear of being delegitimized by the past compelled him to render the past (and present) as unpredictable as the future. "The trouble is," a Soviet historian complained, "you never know what's going to happen yesterday."[19] Stalin's paranoid, improvisational history-writing rendered historical process mysterious and historical truth invisible. Thus, Stalin's fictional proxy, the dictator Varlam in the Soviet film *Repentance* (*Pokayanie*, made in 1984 by Georgian director Tenghiz Abuladze; released in 1986), spoke of being able to catch a black cat in a dark room, if he wished to, "even if there's no cat there."

Although Stalin's political cohort Karl Radek attacked modernism for stressing insignificance and fragmentariness, under Stalin even more than under Lenin Soviet society performed the modernist function of extricating art and culture from memory. A character in Gladkov's 1925 reconstruction novel *Cement* proclaimed that the revolution had inverted Euclidean geometry and dissolved the fetish of permanency. However, Stalin stubbornly reconstructed an absurdly immobile and abstract "Euclideanism," with Lenin's tomb as its chronotope, in defiance of the new space-time formulations of Einstein's physics and modernist art.

The reconfiguration of historical reality by Soviet authority represented a skewed "montage of attractions" approach to structural plotting. The radical speed of Stalinist cultural montage—each of Stalin's Five-Year Plans of the late 1920s, 1930s, and 1940s was to be completed in four years—was necessitated by the fact that the Soviet utopia, not yet a generation old, lacked a real history. The terrifying illogic of Stalin's five-in-four social construct was again paralleled by Varlam's statement in *Repentance* that "four out of every three persons is an enemy." The radical speed of the "great [social] mechanism" represented Stalin's social engineering of Lenin's revolutionary avant-gardism. The fast-forwarding of the past to meet the future and of the future to outdistance the past created a sense of temporal dislocation. A flummoxed bureaucrat in Mayakovsky's *The Bathhouse* complained of not knowing "where the beginning ends and where the end begins" (344).[20]

Temporal recurrence as a cultural trope was suggested by *The Inspector General*, which begins at the end and ends at the beginning (the two announcements of the inspector's arrival), with reality vacating the space in the middle. The delirium of historical erasure in Stalinist culture rendered beginnings and endings interchangeable and irrelevant, so that the present could regenerate the past anachronistically and eternally as an ideological icon, as in the case of Lenin's corpse. In the "collective dreaming" of the past historical truth became a performing corpse.

Soviet totalitarianism had to defeat time in order to assert its omnipotence, correctness, and perfection. In order to legitimize its revolutionary illegitimacy, Stalinist culture ascribed to time a final, universal value, effectively freezing it as in an eternal utopian and iconic present. "The paralysis of time" in Soviet culture "worked to advance the dynamism of the category of space." Stalin, who valued architecture above all arts, sought to render literature architectural and purposely mistook architecture for literature, making it speak with his voice and often in his words by way of inscriptions. With its urbanist, industrial, and architectural bias, Soviet culture came to be defined as the truth under construction, thus ascribing moral value exclusively to the present-future. However, the Potyomkin Village created by Stalin, after the *trompe l'oeil* façades originally executed by Catherine II's (the Great's) court favorite Count Potyomkin in the eighteenth century to placate the monarch with a false sense of national well-being, offered the insubstantiality and impermanence of the stage set. Façadism, Herzen had suggested in reference to the empress and her minister-lover, constituted the state's attempt to fool not only its citizens but itself.[21]

Stalinist culture's absurdist Procrusteanism (self-erasure) was the reverse of messianic Prometheanism (self-deliverance), promoting a state-engineered cultural spectacle nominally for but not by the people. Guy Debord identifies five principal features of "the society whose modernisation has reached the integrated spectacle," which correspond with Stalinist culture: "incessant technological renewal; integration of state and economy; generalized secrecy; unanswerable lies; an eternal present." "The society of the spectacle" appropriates the individual's right to contradict or even to question the state, which assumes these rights for itself in the form of arbitrariness (that is, self-contradiction) and rhetorical questioning. History is "outlawed" by the society of the spectacle (and by its dictatorial director), which equates memory with criminality and aims "to make us forget that [it has] *only* [that is, just] arrived." This enables spectacular society to legitimize its recent usurpation. This sham culture links its constituent elements, as do *Macbeth* and *Boris Godunov* (Pushkin's Russian *Macbeth*) and *The Inspector General*, "not by sequence, not by confrontation or causality, but by rumor." Thus, Caryl Emerson asserts, history is presented "as a series of manipulated secrets."[22] History no longer represents what may have happened, only what may be revealed and presently embraced.

Stalin's "social ambitiousness," like Macbeth's, came perilously close to eradicating "the frontiers between illusion and reality, madness and sanity, word and thing." In the Stalinist scenario of cultural inversion, in which the dead were alive (for example, Lenin) and the living dead (the "nonpersons" in physical and historical exile), even language, rendered "oxymoronic," was turned against its own logical meanings. Meyerhold compared the False Dmitry's (the pretender's) escape through a "real" window in Pushkin's play to Harlequin's leap through a frankly acknowledged prop window in Blok's *The Little Showbooth*, written in an earlier era of subverted reality which included the *fin de siècle* and the first Russian revolution of 1905. Katerina Clark has suggested that the prerevolutionary era's symbolism and early Bolshevism shared and often merged their "god-seeking," radical politics and neoplatonist binary of the real (*realia*) and the superreal or surreal (*realiora*). The "real" False Dmitry was said to have had his body shot out of a cannon across the Polish border, falling into nothingness like Harlequin and like Meyerhold, who failed to produce *Boris Godunov* twice prior to his permanent disappearance.

The real Boris Godunov began the tyrant's practice of banishing political enemies to Siberia, "predicting" Stalin's full-scale theatre of disappearance. Speaking of his nocturnal arrest during the tsar's visit to Moscow in 1834, Herzen wrote, "All these things are done in darkness to avoid disturbing the public." Explicit in this statement is the rationale of façadism. Implicit in this and in Shvarts's plays is a truth restated in the memoirs of Osip Mandelstam's widow, Nadezhda: the public's willingness to overlook corpses contributes to their invisibility.[23] Both Lenin's visible corpse and the invisible corpses of state enemies embodied Stalin's stage directions for his antihistorical cultural text.

The stage direction of stasis and silence, which concludes the published texts of *Boris Godunov* and *The Inspector General*, exposes the inauthenticity/artificiality of utopianism's temporal finiteness and inclusiveness.[24] Meyerhold's recasting of Gogol's characters as wax effigies in the final moment of his 1926 production at once underscored life's betrayal by death, which utopian society sought theoretically to reverse, and life's betrayal by theatre, the appearance of real life onstage and in society at large which masked petrified spectatorship. Meyerhold's Gogolian tableau not only appropriated and critiqued the utopia's Faustian motive of stopping time (see, for example, the stopped clocks at the conclusion of Eisenstein's *October*), but predicted the Great Terror's (1936–1939) invisible iconography of monumentalized death (between seventeen and sixty million dead), which realized the chronotope of temporal consumption. Meyerhold's wax figures, like those on permanent display as symbolic victims of oppression in faithfully preserved tsarist prisons, represented totalist cultural performance onstage and in the public at large. Stalin, who vengefully seized history, and Meyerhold, who was "seized by history," defined authenticity as effigy and as actuality.[25]

While photography, the most "realistic" artistic medium, and socialism were born in roughly the same historical moment, socialist realism was (only) a falsely photographic medium. It was, as W. J. T. Mitchell has said of the camera in relation to Marx's thought, "a model of false understanding, that is for ideology." Socialist realism incorporated what Mitchell calls "the magic of the fetish [which] depends on the projection of consciousness into the object, and then a forgetting of that act of projection." It constituted "an ideological projection," a spatial construction, a "made object" that is "irrationally reverenced."[26] Socialist realist art resembled medieval icon painting in its canonicity, its strict limitations as to subject and style of composition, its iconic certainty, its unified arrangement "as a dynamic model of the eternal world order," its static and obsessive fetishizing of coded orderliness, and its ritualistic reordering of reality. This motif was manifested in the show trials of the 1930s, with their uniform, performative pattern of confession, repentance, forgiveness, and nominal transubstantiation into new personhood.[27]

Since socialist realism originally represented creative mimesis, a means of structuring actions in order to construct rather than to reflect reality, it was imperative that its development should erase the formalist aesthetic, which performed the role of its grotesque, nonideological double, its petty demon. The attack on formalism, initiated by RAPP in 1925, was renewed with greater intensity in the mid- to late 1930s. "Real art must make sense"—that is, it must be accessible to the average spectator—the bureaucrat Pobedonosikov proclaimed in The Bathhouse (313). The revolution had, after all, regularized history. Unfortunately, logic and canonicity had already become one and the same thing.

In Zamyatin's We, a metallically immobile ruler called "the Benefactor" prefigured Stalin, whose powerful cult of personality, initiated on his fiftieth birthday, replaced the authority of the machine. Stalin's mask of beneficence, which he shared with the machine and machine-culture of this period, allowed him to disguise means which later resurfaced suddenly as necessary and inevitable ends. Leon Trotsky had dubbed this sort of formula the "ethical universal." This largely subterranean process, pioneered by the secretive but less paranoid Lenin, served to intensify the illusion and efficacy of Stalin's mysterious and superhuman power. Alex de Jonge writes that, like Dostoyevsky's "Grand Inquisitor," Stalin governed by the three principles of miracle, mystery, and authority. The relevant passage in The Brothers Karamazov reads: "for man seeks not so much God as the miraculous. And as man cannot bear to be without the miraculous, he will create new miracles of his own for himself, and will worship deeds of sorcery and witchcraft, though he might be a hundred times over a rebel, heretic and infidel." The Benefactor's culture, which embraced Frederick Taylor as a god and the Timetables of All the Railroads as its Bible, previewed the new Soviet state's mad race to outrun capitalist progress before economic necessity overran ideological choice. Zamyatin's Benefactor parodied Stalin, much as Stalin's "technism," "the reduction of nonmaterial values to the brute categories of the mechanical and technical," parodied the revolutionary plan initiated by Lenin's railway train and time.[28]

Pretendership involves the theme of false patriarchy, the pretender becoming tsar, the people's secular patriarch, only after murdering the true tsar's son and heir apparent. The False Dmitry became tsar after murdering Boris Godunov's children, as Boris had murdered Ivan the Terrible's son, the real Dmitry, before him. Soviet story, song, and iconography promulgated ruler myths and symbolic linkages with animals, natural elements, and titans, which legitimized Stalin both as the nation's utopic deliverer from tsarist despotism and as the politically enlightened redefinition of tsarist patriarchy. Stalin, the historical pretender as tsar-murderer (which was actually Lenin's role), became father to the new Soviet state and its people. Ironically, the paternity of Stalin's biological father may have been faked, so as to erase the taint of a possible tsarist association. The only extant photograph of Stalin's father, the cobbler Vissarion Djugashvili, which hangs in the dictator's childhood home, has been retouched to resemble closely his grown son. It is as if Stalin, the revolutionary orphan, gave birth to himself, in what is certainly the ultimate historical appropriation.[29]

Stalin's several public masks or invented identities appear in Shvarts's play *The Dragon*, in the form of the eponymous character's three heads, which allow him to be alternately punitive and conciliatory. The Dragon falls out of the sky without warning, a fierce parody of Stalin's "revolution from above" and of Stalin's self-assigned role as omniscient (and paranoid) executioner/*deus ex machina*. Shvarts combined the overt villainy of dragons, ubiquitous in Russian folktales, with the public semblance of heroism (pretendership). The Dragon's gigantism and cracked Olympian authoritarianism, like the Stalin-based Gargantua or "people eater" in Bakhtin's *Rabelais and His World* (*Tvorchestvo Fransua Rable*, written 1940; published 1965), consumed vestigial revolutionary proletarianism and presumed a Manichean hierarchy of totalist values.[30] Shvarts's play also offers an unflattering portrait of the people as being fickle, will-less, even desirous of the ruler's knout, a variation on one of the major themes in *Boris Godunov*. The people cannot imagine life without the Dragon, nor that he can be defeated, and in fact constitute the Dragon's body, as does Stalin its heads. This attitude foreshadowed the popular response to Stalin's death in 1953, which was generally one of shocked disbelief and near panic over the nation's future. What life/course remained for a body without its head(s)? In Shvarts's parables, if the people manifest a desire to be ruled, the heroes harbor moral weakness and tyrannical traits—a scholar who releases his power-hungry shadow in order to win the hand of a beautiful princess and,

in *The Dragon*, a knight-errant who after defeating the Dragon omi-
nously expresses a new paternalism.

When party leader Emelyan Yaroslavsky challenged the First Congress of Soviet Writers in 1934 with the rhetorical question "Have you
shown us Stalin in all his magnitude?" he received ideological ap-
plause. Throughout Soviet culture, Stalin's scale was equated with the
enormity of the task of building communism on a national stage. Four
of the first Stalin Prizes in the arts (later named Lenin Prizes), whose
nominees were judged by Stalin, were awarded in 1939 to works
which recreated Stalin as a national symbol. Khrushchev's possibly
apocryphal image of "Stalin strolling with maniacal delight among
his own statues" was recreated by Grigory Kozintsev, using the
pretender-king Claudius as Stalin's double, in his 1964 film *Hamlet*.
Only after Stalin's death, a time of expected hyperbolic tributes, was
there a break in the linkage between the ruler's personal history and
that of ongoing Communist construction. Stalin's birthday, which
was a significant holiday during his lifetime, ceased being publicly
celebrated in the period between Khrushchev's "secret speech" to the
Twentieth Party Congress (February 1956) and the appearance of a
Pravda birthday remembrance (21 December 1969). In the interven-
ing period, Stalin's body had been removed from the mausoleum,
where it had lain alongside Lenin's preserved corpse.[31] Fittingly, the
death of Stalinist forgetting was inscribed in a book of remembrance,
Khrushchev Remembers (1970), as the title of the former Soviet pre-
mier's memoirs was rendered in English.

Stalin's patriarchal omnipotence was imaged in carefully posed and
at times cobbled-together photographs of the dictator in the company
of the male party leadership, the occasional female worker, and, of
course, Lenin. These photographs were intended not only to project
an aura of ruler worship but the appearance of normalcy (Stalin as a
comrade) and legitimacy (Stalin as Lenin's successor). The doctored
version of the separate photographs that Lenin's sister Mariya Ulyanova took of Lenin and Stalin in the summer of 1922 were published
in the early 1930s as a single photograph of the two men together
(fig. 21). The deployment of people and places as stage props and sets
for the purpose of advertising Stalin's masks underscored his artificial
humanness and his nearly total, inhuman isolation. The message of
this isolation was Stalin's symbolic and personal inaccessibility to
popular comprehension—that is, the magnitude of Stalin's greatness
exceeds human standards of measurement.[32]

Stalinist culture proved Walter Benjamin's thesis that the corrup-

FIGURE 21

Doctored photo of Lenin and Stalin sitting together, from original photos taken by Lenin's sister Mariya Ulyanova in Gorky, summer 1922. Courtesy of Pergamon-Brassey's International Defense Publishers, McLean, Virginia.

tion of historical authenticity jeopardizes "the authority of the object" and shifts the basis of art from ritual to politics. Politics then reinvents ritual in its own image. Stalinist genre classification and repetition, mask and rehearsal, monument and ritual, the unholy relics of the dictator's training as a youthful seminarian (he was expelled from the Tiflis Seminary in May 1899 for political activism), consigned familiarity to obsolescence and quasi-deistic authority to Stalin. Stalin's national theatre of the scaffold combined the former seminarian's homiletic conceptions with the paranoid's baroque overstatement. Stalin's self-reinvention, nominally at the revolution's behest, recalled the deathbed ritual cleansing and tonsuring of Ivan the Terrible (whom Stalin "rehabilitated") so as to "become" a monk. Stalin's saturnine disposition and impassive public mask, parodied thoughtfulness, tranquillity, and Lenin's heroic laconism, which defined and expressed what Nadezhda Krupskaya called the "grand solemn beauty" of the revolution.[33]

Stalin the director recognized that, while actors were expendable, masks were not. Even as Trotsky slipped quietly out of Moscow on Stalin's assumption of power (the anti-Trotsky campaign began in 1924; Trotsky was expelled from the party in 1927), he was replaced by a Trotsky impersonator from film, who performed in public the mask of Trotsky in abject defeat. When Krupskaya objected to Stalin's corruption of her husband Lenin's ideas and ideals, Stalin threatened, "If you don't shut up, we'll make somebody else Lenin's widow."

The show trials of former Stalin chiefs Grigory Zinovyev, Karl Radek, Lev Kamenev, Nikolay Bukharin, and Genrikh Yagoda (August 1936, 23–30 January 1937, 2–13 March 1938) reduced former icons to rehumanized masks. These masks were rehearsed in their "sincere confessions" (Yevgenia Ginzburg's term), which represented the sole evidence of their guilt, and were performed as mock ritual cleansings on courtroom stage sets. Sir Fitzroy Maclean, a British embassy staffer of this period, reported that Stalin was an invisible spectator in a concealed private box behind darkened glass on these occasions, as he was at other more openly acknowledged theatrical events. The show trials, which were staged largely for *external* consumption, undermined the emotional apparatus of truth-telling, a variety of latter day "khlestakovism." The uniform text on which the accused were tried and convicted was "wrecking," retarding or stopping the Five-Year Plans. The show trials publicized the disposability of all authority and celebrity, that is, of all actors, save Stalin. In his memoirs, Khrushchev wrote that "the rapid turnover among the characters created by Stalin was very much part of Stalin's logic."[34]

Stalin's tyrant's mask objectified his desire to fix fate. In Stalin's pretendership, as in Boris Godunov's, self-nomination broke the continuum of historical narrative and initiated apocalyptic time in which myth and messianism reigned. A new drama, a fetishizing cult of personality (that is, of the mask), was created to sustain the pretender's magic and mystery. Several actors specialized in impersonating Stalin on stage and film, following the introduction of the Lenin and Stalin masks in Mikhail Romm's film *Lenin in October* (*Lenin v oktyabre*, 1937).[35] Stalin frequented only the Bolshoy, Maly, and Moscow Art theatres, since they alone possessed "special government boxes and bullet-proof walls, separate entrances from the street and direct phone wires." Breaking tradition with the tsars, Stalin's box did not face the stage from the center of the auditorium but was instead off to one side of the stage and veiled by a curtain. This arrangement recalled the dictator's show trial spectatorship. In paranoid isolation in his theatre box, the Oz-like Stalin consumed hard-boiled eggs and watched without being seen the frightened actor literally choking on his impersonation of him.[36] In the Stalinist court masque, the "eye of the duke" receded into a darkly inferential panoptic anonymity.

Belief in Marxist scientific determinism rendered Stalin's assumption of authority inevitable and that authority, along with his tastes, judgments, and opinions, infallible. Unlike Lenin, who seldom interfered in artistic matters, Stalin remade art according to his personal taste. His taste ran to pompous operetta and grand opera, Modest Mussorgsky's *Boris Godunov* being a notable favorite. The infallibility of Stalin's artistic taste led him to direct a famous conductor to play a musical score without any flats and to order Sergey Prokofyev and Dmitry Shostakovich to write orchestral music that could be hummed. Stalin and Zhdanov, who gave his name to the repressive shaping of Soviet art and culture (*zhdanovshchina*), redefined art as engineering. Actually, Stalin's designation of artists as "engineers of human souls" was borrowed from Meyerhold's theatrical collaborator Sergey Tretyakov, who first dubbed them "psycho-engineers" in 1924. Tretyakov later died in a Stalinist labor camp.[37]

Stalin's and Zhdanov's social engineering of theatre sought to typify stage and auditorium by purposely confusing performance and spectatorship. The May Day celebrations and other commemorative spectacles of the early postrevolutionary years had by 1930 grown to the point where there were no longer any spectators. These "perfectly planned and organized parades" announced "the victory of mechanization," "the perfectly functioning production process."[38] The street, and also the factory, became the curtainless stage for the theatrical experiments of Blue Blouse and Proletkult in the 1920s. Stalinism and socialist realism appropriated this model and plunged both the actor and the spectator into anonymity. The object of the closed system of authoritarianism was to guard against astonishment, the modernist imperative, and against nostalgia for the once lived-in reality of the past which the actor and the audience conspire to cocreate.

Meyerhold, who helped pioneer the curtainless stage *within* the Soviet theatre (a variation on symbolist and early Bolshevik communion), planned in his new theatre (ca. 1935) to merge the stage and auditorium with the street. "On holidays," he wrote, "when there are parades on the streets, the processions can be diverted, enter the theatre, march around the stage, waving their banners and singing, and then pass on toward Red Square." He envisioned that automobiles and other forms of transport would do the same. At the time, Meyerhold told H. W. L. Dana, an American who has left firsthand reminiscences of the Soviet theatre, that he was not afraid of destroying illusion, "because there is no illusion [left] to destroy." Meyerhold's theatre, designed by architect A. V. Shchusev (who had previously designed Lenin's tomb) on Moscow's Triumphal Square, was to be topped by a colossal statue of Mayakovsky, another of the intelligentsia's martyrs to the revolution. The building's façade was to contain bas-reliefs of striking scenes from the director's most famous productions, no doubt including *The Inspector General* tableau, which embodied astonishment's critique of authoritarianism.[39] This plan for the theatre was abandoned when Meyerhold was arrested in 1939.

Socialist realism reversed the course of modernist thought by largely invalidating psychic activity and filling the existential void perpetrated by nineteenth-century Russian culture with Soviet concrete(ness). Stalinist culture contrived art and people to be mechanically mass-produced, a logical by-product, according to Bergson and Benjamin, of a stopped-time scenario. The only astonishment that remained was again embodied in Meyerhold's wax effigies, "the silence and unanimity of the grave," "the spectacle of the many and disparate" become one. What Soviet novelist Vasily Grossman referred to as the state's "ecstatic wonder at [its] own superiority" was legitimized by state-created audiences and artistic genres.[40]

The curtainless stage theoretically derived from the opportunistically imagined and collectively constructed proletariat. It nominally extended pre- and postrevolutionary theatrical avant-gardists' (for example, Meyerhold, Yevreinov, and Nikolay Okhlopkov's) efforts to *unmake* the Procrustean bed of bourgeois-fed and mimetically encoded pictorial realism. Under Stalin, however, the absorption of the spectator and the audience *en masse* into performance, like the attack on formalism, was part of the larger program to eliminate difference. Socialist realist art redefined dramatic character as the blueprint for audience identity construction. At the same time, it appropriated and reassigned the modernist artists' imperative to translate themselves into art to the spectators. This was all supposedly done to effect "the Great Mimesis" of life's immense totality and to celebrate the heroic anonymity of revolutionary monumentalism. It likewise accomplished the dismantling of formalism as the Trojan Horse in which socialist realism first entered Soviet culture, the structurally tendentious prelude to formulaic art.[41]

Not all of the revolutionary masses wished to have their roles recast. The intellectual "montage of attractions" approach pioneered in the theatre (and film) by the formalists Eisenstein and Meyerhold was actually rejected by a significant portion of the audience surveyed at the Moscow Proletkult and Meyerhold Theatres in the 1920's. The flustered bureaucrat in *The Bathhouse* exclaimed in 1928, "Why do you want to turn us into some kind of characters in a play? We don't want to play active roles. We want to be—what do you call them—spectators" (317). This contradicted Gorky's optimistic assessment of 1919 that "the people no longer are passive figures living their lives according to the dictates of the classes which formerly controlled their will; the people have ceased to be spectators of events, they wish to be the actors and create new forms of social life."[42] In fact, the people's participation in their reconstruction following the revolution was only nominal. The mask of anonymity which Stalinism imposed upon them was not heroic but paralytic. Stalin's curtainless stage misappropriated the intelligentsia's long-sought-after popular theatrical tradition, misrepresenting it as hegemonic extratheatrical politics, a community of enforced popular belief, a mythic popular identity, and a formal sociopolitical aesthetic.

"Khlestakovism," the anonymous authority of the lie which impersonates the authenticity of the truth, is dependent upon forgetfulness and takes root in a vacuum. Yury Lotman has ascribed cultural memory loss to the precipitous substitution of quick "costume changes" for organic evolution—the theatricalization of life as performed most notably by the 1917 revolution. The resultant Bolshevik reworking of Oscar Wilde's critical formula of seeing the object "as it [really] was not" was authenticated by Stalinist Procrusteanism, under the rubric of "socialist realism."[43] In its belated rush to retrieve lost time, to correct the social and spiritual inertia of the previous century, Soviet culture succeeded in rendering itself inert and in exacerbating Russian culture's long-standing sense of inauthenticity. However, for the savage standing at the barometer, it still looked like rain.

CHAPTER 7

THE *HAMLET* GULAG

The cold prison of life surrounding Hamlet has made

him its prisoner, but the prisoner has become a rebel. . . .

— *Nikolay Okhlopkov*

The imagination and the spiritual strength of

Shakespeare's evildoers stopped short at a dozen corpses.

Because they had no ideology.

— *Aleksandr Solzhenitsyn* [1]

As early as 1775, Hamlet's "To be or not to be" was translated into Russian as "To live or not to live." The social question of
how one lives in an oppressive culture engendered in Russian and Soviet intellectuals the existential question of how one lives at all. The
late eighteenth century witnessed the rise of an "aristocratic suicide"
cult among Russia's intellectual class. It modeled itself after the Roman statesman-philosopher Cato (Marcus Portius Cato Uticensis,
95–46 B.C.) and Hamlet in proclaiming an unwillingness to serve ty-
rants and the tyranny of self-censorship.[2] The Decembrist M. S. Lunin, who later became a symbol of the intellectual's self-liberation
from these phantom tyrannies (in Edvard Radzinsky's 1977 play), visited the Hamlet castle at Elsinore in 1816, at the start of his European
education as a Russian revolutionary. Russian intellectual martyrology was formalized in the persons of those Decembrists whose execution, in Herzen's remembrance of his youth, represented the "murder" of sleep and "childish" dreams by "the inexorable Macbeth of
real life." Young Herzen not atypically associated the Decembrist revolt in his mind with a romantic drama, Friedrich Schiller's *The Rob-
bers* (*Die Räuber*, 1781).

174   The nineteenth-century conflict between Westernizers' self-con-

scious individualism and Slavophiles' culturally conscious anti-individualism was soon joined by historical determinists' forging of a collectively imagined revolutionary consciousness for the twentieth century. However, each revolution dramatized the intelligentsia's further social slippage, which in turn produced a new wave of aristocratic suicide as a form of unofficial "class" expression. The intelligentsia rejected the part of the European Hamlet that was a purely asocial compositional device but embraced his resolve to reconstruct history, in opposition to state-engineered forgetfulness, or at least to construct a counterhistory of performative fate.[3]

The Hamletian intellectual sought through a combination of suicidal openness and interiority (frankness and self-absorption) and irrationalism ("madness") to reject state logic and valueless existence (*byt*), in favor of a poeticized life and death. Boris Pasternak, quoting the mythical trope of "the kenotic Russian artist," proclaimed that life becomes readable as poetry only in the freely made decision to end it. At best, the intellectual might, as was said of Blok, perceive the "End" but not the "Way." At worst, by choosing timelessness over temporal reality, the Hamletian intellectual unintentionally fulfilled the state's desire to rid itself of all hostile witnesses to authentic history and to inauthentic myth-creation.

Hamlet incarnated the authentic secret history of "Holy Russia," the moral core of memory, which rejects the illusory historical life founded on political pretendership and embraces the ghost, the spiritual presence of the past. Hamlet represents a true rather than an engineered utopic fate. Furthermore, the romantic self-imprisonment of reasoning consciousness and self-martyring sensitivity combined in the intellectual a Christ *mise en scène* and a "*Hamlet* gulag." Blok expressed his doubt in 1907 that many of the self-dramatizing/self-victimizing "aristocratic intellectuals" of his generation, already weakened by mystical religion and "free aesthetics," that is, by disempowering performative consciousness, would or could endure Siberian torture.[4] The intellectuals' identification with Christ and Hamlet invited their silencing by the state and deepened their pathos of exclusion even among representatives of their own class. Their profound sense that thought invariably leads to suffering ("woe from wit") quickly and easily devolved into the Pierrot-like love of suffering. This complemented their feeling that action is inevitably meaningless, which resulted in "oblomovist" inertia and in the superfluity described in Pushkin's, Turgenev's, and Chekhov's work. Progressive revolutions rendered "Hamletism" ever more morbidly and fatally retrograde in its self-advertisement's opposition to anonymous collective publicity. Still, as Hamlet's inner world "seized on the phantom" of his father to achieve personal and social definition, so have Soviet artists and audiences grasped at the Prince's lessons in conscience, in reading their times, and in the tenuous, untenable nature of all realities.[5]

While Russians today generally consider Hamlet always to have been one of their own, he was, in fact, slow to learn their language. *Hamlet* was first performed in Russia in 1748, in what has been called a "garbled translation" by the neoclassical man of letters A. P. Sumarokov. Sumarokov, who called Shakespeare "a boor," reduced *Hamlet*'s varied language to a succession of uniformly stately rhymed couplets. He likewise "corrected" the plot, making Polonius rather than Claudius King Hamlet's murderer and ending the play happily by marrying Hamlet to Ophelia. Sumarokov admitted that his *Hamlet* bore "very little resemblance to Shakespeare's tragedy." Russia was first exposed to a more accurate *Hamlet* in the German translation by A. W. Schlegel and Ludwig Tieck (ca. 1795). Mikhail Vronchenko published the first Russian translation (as opposed to adaptation) of *Hamlet* in 1828, but it was workmanlike and unstageable. It was followed by Nikolay Polevoy's free and abridged translation, which was performed by "the Russian Kean," Pavel Mochalov, in an epochal production at Moscow's Maly Theatre in 1837 and continued to be used into the twentieth century. The nineteenth century also saw translations of *Hamlet* which combined Polevoy's and Andrey Kroneberg's (1849) poetic versions with Nikolay Ketcher's prose rendering. The first modern Russian translation was by the Grand Duke Konstantin Nikolayevich, the tsar's cousin and a poet, who performed his *Hamlet* in 1902 at the Hermitage Theatre, St. Petersburg, with a company of military officers, for an invited audience. In the twentieth century, there have been professional performances of *Hamlet* in Russian translations by Mikhail Lozinsky and by Anna Radlova, the wife of Soviet stage director Sergey Radlov.

It was not, however, until Boris Pasternak's highly idiomatic free translation of *Hamlet* premiered in Vera Redlikh's 1939 production at the Red Torch Theatre of Novosibirsk that the Danish Prince was heard to speak fluent Russian. Russians familiar with the English text were startled at how well Pasternak had captured the essence and nuances of even the minor characters' speech. Professor Mikhail Morozov, who completed a literal translation himself, remarked: "We have never been so intimately acquainted with the real persons of great tragedy. We had not even known that it was possible to be so closely acquainted with them."

Pasternak reworked his *Hamlet* translation twelve times, first for his theatrical idol Meyerhold (commissioned for the Pushkin Theatre, January 1939) and then for the Moscow Art Theatre (winter 1939–1940), but neither produced it. Pasternak's *Hamlet* translation was first published in 1940 in the journal *Young Guard* (*Molodaya gvardiya*) and later that year by the State Publishing House. A 50,000-copy printing of this translation was published by the Children's State Publishing House for secondary school students in 1942. Pasternak's translation was later employed by Grigory Kozintsev on the stage, at the Bolshoy Dramatic Theatre in Leningrad (spring 1954), and on film (1964). Although Pasternak also translated *Romeo and Juliet, Othello, Antony and Cleopatra, Henry IV, Parts 1 and 2*, and *King Lear* for the Soviet stage, it was *Hamlet* which best captured his own celebrated social and moral dilemmas.[6]

The efforts by Russian artists to reconcile the performative struggles of Hamlet's and the Russian intellectual's lives evolved alongside the recreation of *Hamlet* as a performable Russian text. The two most celebrated productions of *Hamlet* in Russia prior to the formal imposition of socialist realism in the theatre in 1934 were Gordon Craig's much written about monodramatic staging at the Moscow Art Theatre in 1912 and Mikhail Chekhov's mystical version at the Moscow Art Theatre 2 in 1924. Chekhov's production relied mainly upon Kroneberg's nineteenth-century translation, with elements inserted from earlier versions by Polevoy and Nikolay Gnedich, the Russian translator of *The Iliad* (1829). Chekhov's anthroposophic Hamlet was inspired by the Ghost (a "pure shaft of light" symbolizing "the unalloyed voice of revolutionary conscience") to infiltrate and dissolve Elsinore's medieval darkness. Illumination, in Chekhov's interpretation, revealed Elsinore's "world of the dead," its "soulless automata," who, as in Gogol's world, impersonate living human beings. Elsinore as a necropolis in Russian and Soviet society, beginning in the Silver Age, represented more than moral decay. It signaled the cultural shift from the "dying" Egyptianate city of St. Petersburg, overseen by the stone ghost/stone guest of Peter the Great, "the ironclad herald of history," to the new bureaucratic center of Moscow, concentrated behind the fortress walls of the Kremlin, which the Marquis de Custine had called the horrible architectural dream of a superhuman but malevolent tyrant.

The Ghost, states Vladislav Ivanov, gave Hamlet a place to be (the stage) and a role to play (the actor). Hamlet's staging of the truth in a world of empty appearances affirmed the truth of his being. He went out to meet his fate rather than passively await its arrival. Chekhov's *Hamlet* validated the inner man in an era of social masking. Chekhov's interpretation of the Prince, Ivanov maintains, previewed Pasternak's construction of the Hamlet-Christ. Chekhov conceived the Ghost as a signal to Hamlet that there existed a higher spiritual life beyond Elsinore's living death. Hamlet "received his cross," his fate from the Ghost, as did Chekhov from Hamlet.[7] Olesha captured this actor-role symbiosis in *A List of Blessings*, which was said to have been partially inspired by Chekhov and his *Hamlet*.

Nikolay Akimov's eccentric formalist *Hamlet* (Lozinsky translation, Vakhtangov Theatre, 1932) sought to remove the "tombstone of mysticism" fashioned for the play by Chekhov and, earlier, Craig. Akimov's paunchy, "bourgeoisfied" Hamlet (played by the comedian Anatoly Goryunov), victimized equally by his feudally "conditioned reflexes about the loss of his throne and the decaying action initiated by his humanist education," balanced unsteadily on the brink of socialist realism. In Akimov's parodic production (which Yevreinov claimed was partially derived from his conception), the "mad" Ophelia drowned while intoxicated, and the "mad" Hamlet pondered only whether to kill the king while getting drunk in a bar. Akimov's Hamlet was not so much a philosopher as "a political intriguer," whose actions became comprehensible to an unsophisticated audience. In this interpretation, the Ghost was a political ploy perpetrated by Hamlet, effected by shouting into a clay pot. The production's composer Dmitry Shostakovich used Hamlet's recorder speech to ridicule proletarian musical hacks. Akimov's lavish sets reversed the severe constructivist experiments of the 1920s. Akimov, who was accused of demonstrating a "flagrantly nihilistic attitude toward the classics," cut most of the graveyard scene.[8]

Sergey Radlov's 1938 production at his own theatre (Anna Radlova translation) announced socialist realism's arrival in a *mise en scène* which meaningfully deployed individuals in relation to groups. The production's monumental character portraits, which threatened to crush Hamlet from above, prefigured Kozintsev's multiple iconic references to Claudius's (that is, Stalin's) "revolution from above" and the resultant "cult of personality" in his film version (1964). It also underscored Russia's historical paranoia, in particular Stalinism's "introverted insularity," itself a cruel parody of Hamletian interiority, which was served by spying, conspiracy, and informing. These were time-honored national practices. Significantly, Soviet productions of *Hamlet* in the 1930s were not updated but were set in the Renaissance, thereby discouraging audiences from drawing parallels with contemporary figures and situations. At a banquet in spring 1941, Stalin, the Soviet Macbeth, labeled *Hamlet* "decadent." Throughout the 1930s and 1940s, scholars and artists were discouraged from probing the play's mysteries and profundities, which were facilely reduced and concretely resolved in production. The play was read as a straightforward depiction of the struggle for power. Read through the lens of atheistic Soviet culture, in which Christian sin had been devalued, the self-created social engineer Claudius became a potentially more attractive revolutionary personality than the morbidly nostalgic and self-absorbed Hamlet.[9]

Nikolay Okhlopkov's 1954 production at the Mayakovsky Theatre had, as its commanding scenic image, a pivoting and tracking iconostasis, which, when it opened, resembled a beehive and directly recalled the Elsinore as prison simile (fig. 22). Okhlopkov's *Hamlet* depicted humanism's victory over tyranny, the spiritual rebirth of Mother Russia embodied in an activist but nonideological Prince. This was a *Hamlet* of the Soviet people's "own sufferings," of their "immature soul." In 1947, Okhlopkov had discussed a revolutionary Hamlet, cleansed of indecision in his commitment to complete his plan and, metaphorically, Stalin's Five-Year Plan. Stalin's "new Soviet intelligentsia" had dismissed Hamlet as "a symbol of the brooding [indolent] and indecisive old intelligentsia." In *Repentance*, the Stalinist dictator Varlam's statement to his grandson—"it was a question of to be or not to be"—asserted totalitarianism's justifiable necessity rather than intellectualism's equivocal desire. The healthy vacillation of Okhlopkov's 1954 Hamlet symbolized the director's abandonment of the prescribed certainty of socialist realism, his learning to balance, in the post-Stalin "Thaw," his newfound freedom with the living memory of his historical imprisonment.

The Soviet Hamlet at the beginning of the Thaw period was, according to Aleksey Bartoshevich, a generally unphilosophical "rosy youth, whose sudden discovery of the cruel truth of the world [especially in the Stalin years], cracked his child-like faith."[10] In reclaiming the Prince's philosophical questions and existential motives, the Hamlet of the 1960s rid himself of vestigial, internalized social automatism. Theatricalist stagings of *Hamlet* announced the artist's escape from the void of dehumanized absolutism that had presented itself as stage realism. Hamlet's "tragedy" became nonideologically optimis-

FIGURE 22

The Hamlet *iconostasis or beehive designed by Vadim Ryndin for Nikolay Okhlopkov's 1954 production. Courtesy of Izdatel'stvo sovetsky khudozhnik, Moscow.*

tic as it was rehumanized. Yury Lyubimov's *Hamlet* (29 November 1971–13 July 1980), which was the most important post-Thaw interpretation, arrived during the Brezhnev "years of stagnation." This production stood in a sort of historical no-man's-land, in which Hamlet's choices were clear but the state's response to and tolerance of these choices were not. In order to understand Lyubimov's intentions and the intellectual tradition within which his *Hamlet* operated, it is first necessary to examine its link to Pasternak, who was not only its translator but its inspiration. It was at this historic juncture that *Hamlet* realized its full potential as the primary dramatic, behavioral, and performative text of the Russian intelligentsia.

Pasternak viewed Hamlet not as a weak, vacillating figure but as someone who acts out of a sense of "duty and self-abnegation." "Hamlet," he stated, "is chosen as the judge of his own time and the servant of a more distant time." *Hamlet* is a drama of "entrusted destiny," in which the poet both becomes fate's avenger and realizes his personal integrity. Pasternak likened both Hamlet and his original creation Yury Zhivago to the Christ at Gethsemane, who confronts his solitary fate with "resigned but dignified acceptance." This "passive sufferer," kinsman to Michael Chekhov's Prince of the 1920s, was offered by Pasternak as a positive alternative to the programmed, unconflicted action of the new Soviet person.[11]

Pasternak's poem "Hamlet," ostensibly written by the eponymous hero of his novel *Doctor Zhivago*, was still banned at the time of Pasternak's death on 30 May 1960 and was recited illegally by the mourners at his funeral. The poem speaks of the poet's isolation and of the difficulty of life, two prevailing themes in Russian and Soviet culture, which became more pronounced during Stalin's engineering of individual and collective fate:

> And yet, the order of the acts has been schemed and plotted
> And nothing can avert the final curtain's fall.
> I stand alone. All else is swamped by Pharisaism.
> To live life to the end is not a childish task.

When asked upon what principles the Taganka Theatre was based, Lyubimov quoted Pasternak's "Hamlet"'s opening lines:

> The stir is over. I step forth on the boards.
> Leaning against an upright at the entrance,
> I strain to make the far-off echo yield
> A cue to the events that may come in my day.[12]

Lyubimov, who had visited Pasternak in 1958 in internal exile at his home in Peredelkino, was saddened and angered by the humiliation that the poet had endured. He was confused by the two letters of self-criticism which Pasternak wrote, expressing culpability for having written the banned novel *Doctor Zhivago*. The book had won Pasternak the Nobel Prize for Literature in 1958, but he was forced by the Soviet government to turn it down.

Pasternak wrote that life is spent "in a struggle with one's self. . . ." Renato Poggioli has remarked that Pasternak regarded "the self as an object rather than subject," a receptive vehicle for egoless action in behalf of humankind, an entity to be valued for its sacrifice. Pasternak's heroic struggle in this direction led to courageous as well as compromised action. His prototype in this regard was the actor, and he clearly regarded both Hamlet and himself as such. This reaffirmation of the actor's role, which countered its negative depiction in nineteenth- and twentieth-century Russian literature by Gogol and Gorky, was furthered in the Taganka Theatre's production of the Pasternak _Hamlet_. The actor's brave act of self-nomination in "the spotlight's cold flame" (Anna Akhmatova), his search for the complete truth of being in selfhood and otherness, exploded the purposeful misrepresentations which produced moral failure in Soviet life.[13] By 1971, the Moscow Theatre of Drama and Comedy on Taganka Square, which Lyubimov took over in 1964, had become a social and moral emblem for the Soviet avant-garde and for the Soviet theatre-going public, which fought to gain admission to its productions. It _was_ Hamlet, a theatrical savior doubling as a social rebel.

Following a two-year imbroglio over his proposed production of an adaptation which conflated several of Shakespeare's history plays into a single evening, Lyubimov turned to Pasternak's translation of _Hamlet_. In the beginning, many Taganka actors and its leading actress, Alla Demidova, had clamored to play Hamlet. Lyubimov selected Vladimir Vysotsky, he said, because he believed that as a poet Vysotsky could best understand the poet Hamlet (via Shakespeare and Pasternak) and as a singer he could discover the musical subtext in Hamlet's speech. In his career, Vysotsky wrote nine hundred songs and poems, which, in Lyubimov's words, offered "an irreplaceable chronicle of daily life in the Soviet Union of the past twenty years" (ca. 1960–1980). Demidova, who played Gertrude, recalled that the role of Hamlet came with difficulty to Vysotsky. It was too close to his own celebrated persona, which he did not want simply to replicate as "an icon of himself." Naturally, his interpretation of the role evolved over the course of ten years, but throughout Vysotsky's was a somewhat mature, thoughtful, even mournful Hamlet. He recognized that in this life of struggle the prisoner is punished for acting independently and for speaking his thoughts aloud.

By design and historical circumstance, the Taganka-Lyubimov-Vysotsky Hamlet perilously advertised individually and collectively iconic celebrity and contemporaneity. Lyubimov had earlier investigated the "talent's crown of thorns" theme in his stagings of plays featuring independent thinkers at war with authority, such as Brecht/Galileo (_Life of Galileo_, starring Vysotsky, 1966), Mayakovsky (_Listen! [Poslushayte!]_, 1967), and Molière (_Tartuffe_, 1968). Like the suicide Mayakovsky, the democratic voice of his generation and a prince in the new Soviet society of the early 1920s, Vysotsky manifested Hamletian disgust with the social mechanism and artistically critiqued it. The Taganka Hamlet shared the courage of Vysotsky's convictions. His antipathy to "stupidity, mediocrity, vileness" and "double-dealing," as well as his reputation for "singing hooliganism," opting for "honest death" over "tortured life," inverted the Turge- nevian model of the Russian intellectual's passivity, self-pity, and superfluity. Vysotsky's poem "My Hamlet" (*Moy Gamlet*), written several years after the Taganka premiere, suggested his identification with and appropriation of the role.

Like Molière, a symbol of suppressed genius for Soviet artists, who collapsed while playing Argan in *The Imaginary Invalid*, Vysotsky played Hamlet, his favorite role, at the edge of his life. In his 217th and final performance of the role, on 13 July 1980 (he had rehearsed it for about two years prior to performing it for ten), Vysotsky was ill. He periodically forgot his lines and had to rush offstage to secure medication. During this performance, the heavy curtain which constituted the production's major scenic device accidentally landed upon a coffin on which Gertrude was sitting and revealed to her the ghost of Hamlet's father, who had been hidden behind it. In retrospect, this moment seems prophetic of an actual death and reappearance. Twelve days after the curtain fell on the coffin, Vysotsky was dead. With him died the production, since, by the time of his death, Vysotsky *was* Hamlet for the Taganka company and its audience. But like King Hamlet's ghost at Elsinore, Vysotsky's restless spirit would again walk the Taganka stage.[14]

When parts and props from this *Hamlet* were recycled in the Taganka's commemorative production *The Poet Vladimir Vysotsky* (1981), the conflation of actor and character into cultural icon was complete. Both *Hamlet* and *Vladimir Vysotsky* marked the appearance of a ghost and the disappearance of a man, the experiencing of an absence—Hamlet's, Vysotsky's, and the Taganka's historical moment of truth and actuality. The "silence" which concluded *Hamlet* was extended into life and given a voice in *Vladimir Vysotsky*, as cast members took up their Hamlet's familiar stage position, seated on the floor, their backs against the theatre's back wall. In September 1988, the Soviet journal *Teatr* reprinted two paintings of Meyerhold (1986) and Pasternak (1987) by scenic designer Pyotr Belov which seemed to evoke and extend this artist-wall fusion (figs. 23 and 24). Meyerhold's head, produced from what looks like his Communist Party identification card, was superimposed upon a naked and emaciated *zek*'s (from *zaklyuchyoenny*, prison slang for "prisoner") body and stood against a spartan (perhaps cell) wall. Pasternak's body was walled in, save for his head and his right hand, outstretched with palm up and

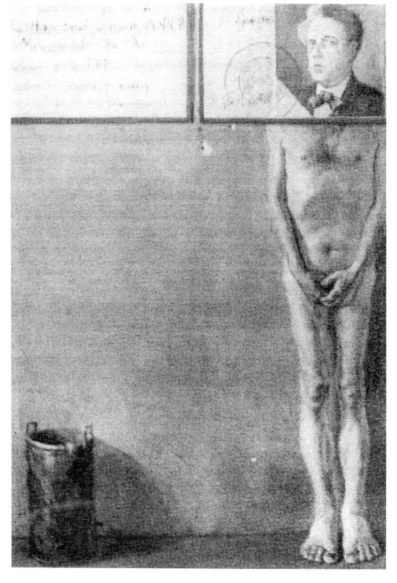

FIGURE 23
Pyotr Belov, Meyerhold, *1986. Courtesy of* Teatr, *Moscow.*

index finger extended to suggest Christ's stigmata and pointing to
a discarded copy of the state newspaper *Pravda* (*Truth*). Buckets
were pictured at the feet of both artists, evoking the *zek*'s cell. Pasternak's bucket was filled with the plaster with which his wall
was constructed, perhaps signifying the theme of Hamletian self-
imprisonment.

FIGURE 24
Pyotr Belov, Pasternak, *1987. Courtesy of* Teatr, *Moscow.*

In response to a journalist's question of how he would stage Hamlet's most famous monologue, Meyerhold answered, "Radically. I would cut it [entirely]." Meyerhold, who proposed casting a self-doubting Hamlet and a decisive Hamlet together in a single production, understood that familiarity breeds contempt but also that in his day, and especially in his voice, the question "To be or not to be" could not be asked. The prescribed, mythologized rationalism of a tyrannical world, Denmark or the Soviet Union, obviates the posing of rational questions, except, perhaps, in an irrational voice. Hamlet must be mad, which Russian culture suspected from the beginning, and the means by which his story is told must likewise be alogical and absurd.[15] The Taganka production freed the play and the player from the imprisonment of the Soviet *Hamlet*'s theatrical tradition. The Taganka reconciled the easy oppositions of power/powerlessness, will/will-lessness, activity/passivity, superman/common man projected upon *Hamlet* by Soviet criticism and engendered by the aura of "putrescent Hamletism," which decades earlier the director Akimov had said the play creates. At the same time, the Taganka production directly addressed the Hamletian life condition of the Russian creative intelligentsia, exemplified by Pasternak, who was silenced, and Meyerhold, whose picture hangs in the theatre's foyer and who was imprisoned and murdered in the Soviet *gulag*.

"A modern Elsinore would have no objection to closing the barbed wire of concentration camps around humanity like a crown of thorns," Kozintsev wrote in a conflation of the *Hamlet* gulag and the Christ *mise en scène*. A modern *Hamlet*, Kozintsev maintained, must make it seem to every person "that a number had been burnt into his own arm." Like the "spiritually dead people" who emerged from Stalin's prison camps, the mad, haunted Prince, especially in the Taganka production, appears at Elsinore as "a corpse among the living, pretending to be alive and full of feeling." "But why pretend," asks camp survivor Yevgenia Ginzburg quoting Blok, "To be accepted by society, / One needs only to conceal the rattling of one's bones." Hamlet the prisoner, like these survivors, is, wrote Pasternak, "ennobled and purified" by his prison and by "the climate of apparitions" it engenders. His suffering, not his vengeance, reveals and frames his most human qualities.

The advent of apocalyptic time, signaled by the arrival of his father's ghost, "stopped the clock" of Hamlet's life. This paralleled the camp inmate's experience of arrest and imprisonment. The prisoner's spiritual inner emigration laid bare the surreality of the material world outside. Hamlet's madness bears witness to his times rather than conspiring with them, revealing the horror of prison life, via the prisoner's Aesopian code, a "secret language," to a public still largely imprisoned. The madness resurfaced in Solzhenitsyn's accounts of the Soviet gulag in the 1960s and 1970s. These reports extended and deepened Khrushchev's "secret speech" exposure of the real madness, the Soviet state's crimes against its own people. The prisoner's tale reinstates the individual's and society's human dignity. The story's theme, as Pasternak told Stalin in his telephone defense of imprisoned poet Osip Mandelstam (July 1937), is "life and death." Stalin hung up on Pasternak, and Mandelstam died in a labor camp. The Taganka *Hamlet* stressed the post-Stalin era's life theme, survival and salvation, rather than the Stalin era's death theme, revenge. Hamlet's action lost him his "seat near the columns," the privileges attendant to his noble birthright, but gained him a noble rebirth. The once solitary actor, now reabsorbed into the ensemble, humanity, history, and the life of society, buried the Stalinist charge of cultish individualism in an open grave.[16]

Hamlet seeks to dissolve the social (and Russian cultural) habit of lying, which, Kozintsev maintained, had precipitated "the loss of natural feelings" and turned the world to stone. Vysotsky's protest-singing Hamlet addressed the culpability of fathers, such as Stalin, who had yet to confess their guilt. Hamlet's mousetrap play and the testimony of his overall action addressed the shadowy absence of a trial—that of Claudius for his brother's murder. His testimony of conscience sought to balance the "sincere confessions" which Stalinist forces coerced from prisoners and the rehearsed show trials which displaced guilt from its rightful source and made a mockery of contrition.

While the court at Elsinore, which was no longer in mourning, dressed in bright colors, Hamlet as per stage tradition wore black, mourning the absence of light, honor, and beauty and, like a cultural avant-gardist, flaunting social custom. Hamlet's "blackness" in Soviet culture announced an intensified otherness and alluded to the collapsed energy, the black hole at the center of a falsely demonstrative, active, and healthy universe, a scenario which Meyerhold likewise discovered in *Woe from Wit*. Michael Chekhov's Hamlet, the aesthetic and ethical man, had worn a white shirt in the final scene of the play, in which he extracted redemption from the corpse of tormented guilt and (self-)murder. The Taganka Hamlet also was the sole mourner of the ghost of Russian humanism whose epitaph, penned by

Pasternak, read: "And here art ends; here breathe the soil and fate." It befell this Hamlet to resist the shadow life of neurasthenic nonresistance to evil, the retreat into "the bliss of penal servitude," that "kind sleep that makes the prisoner king."[17] It was incumbent upon this Hamlet to escape Claudius's mousetrap, the Soviet imprisonment, and to spring a trap of his own.

Like *Woe from Wit* and the other great Russian dream play *The Inspector General*, *Hamlet* bodies forth a nighttime state of mind. It evokes historical context while obscuring and distorting historical boundaries to capture the timelessness of human consciousness. Accordingly, the Taganka *Hamlet* presented a historical drama of ideas in the performative mode of the universal play of consciousness. The nighttime Prince is disoriented by two phantom fathers, one a ghost (King Hamlet) and the other a pretender (King Claudius), and by two somnambulent, sexed, but will-less women, two "living corpses" (Queen Gertrude and Ophelia as male constructions). Hamlet is also confused by a court, peopled with anonymous, shadowy machine/ ersatz men such as Rosencrantz and Guildenstern, like those envisioned by Gogol, Chaplin, and Shvarts. The Taganka *Hamlet* sought to identify a real, "dirty" world of experience, to eschew style in favor of memory, thereby evoking a meaningful link between Elsinore and Soviet "chimerical culture."

Vysotsky's Hamlet understood and accepted the existence and persistence of evil in the world. He did not seek to prove Claudius's villainy but rather to disprove it so as to break free from the tyranny of violence. This indirectly recalled the aftermath of the Russian revolution, in which the party leadership debated and approved the moral and social efficacy of prolonged violence to counter lingering resistance. The danger of adopting the tyrant's means to overthrow him and by so doing becoming the tyrant had been the message of Shvarts's fairy-tale plays of the Stalin era. Lyubimov believed that *Hamlet* called forth "a universe of unequaled violence" in Shakespeare's work but also offered the most direct and pervasive reference to the Divine Presence. This spiritual orientation recalled the prerevolutionary symbolist aesthetic toward which Pasternak was likewise sympathetically disposed.

From the beginning, the Taganka Hamlet knew that he was a man alone, whose mission it was to teach people what troubled their souls, to help them to transcend mundane reality. Shakespeare has been the Russian intelligentsia's spiritual nurturer, and Pasternak's Hamlet was a sort of neo-symbolist God-seeker. Hamlet was infected with something of the spirit of the Thaw (post-Stalin) generation of the 1960s, which encouraged boundaryless art, with its boundless enthusiasm for life, its reckless openness, its belief in its power to help people to see and experience the world anew and to aspire to spiritual perfection via questioning and agitation. The ghost that haunted this Hamlet was not his father's but his brother's. His was a generational voice. "We see in his eyes," wrote Sergey Yutkevich, "the eyes of our contemporary." Soviet audiences saw in Vysotsky's Hamlet, the sacrifice of youth, "caught in the mousetrap."

Vysotsky's Hamlet was impatient with the "external obstacles" which mitigated his freedom to act. He moved through his "To be or not to be" soliloquy without pause, "resisting delusion," as he believed Russian and Soviet culture had charged him to do. He whipped himself into the action, moving quickly, like the production's cinematic *mise en scène*, from moment to moment. As the years progressed, Hamlet's sense of urgency was intensified by Vysotsky's and his generation's sense that time was running out. Vysotsky, who began as a romantic rationalist believing in the possibilities of this uncompromised life rather than in the possibly vain promises of the next, eventually came to be imbued with the play's mystical irrationalism. He became more aware of life as an unanswerable proposition. In ten years, the audience's social conscience had grown, in some measure as a result of Vysotsky's influence. They had been brought to the point where they understood the questions of human value, of justice and violence, and could be asked once again, after a long, enforced respite, to confront and question the "imponderables." The social and philosophical implications of self-willed and externally enforced death, and of a spiritually deprived living death, which had fallen into programmed disuse as subjects for theatrical discourse, were revived. Once again, "To be or not to be" *was* the question, in a meaningful and not merely a conventional sense.[18]

Beginning with his fourth production at the Taganka, an adaptation of John Reed's *Ten Days That Shook the World* (*Desyat' dney, kotorye potryasli mir*, Taganka premiere 2 April 1965), Lyubimov employed Meyerholdian machines for acting and Rembrandt chiaroscuro lighting effects. These devices exploded the theatrical framing of time and space into a prismatic extrapolation of historical, novelistic, and poetic essences. As Blok had demonstrated in *The Little Showbooth*, the torn-up stage, which defamiliarizes its own reality and conventions, allows for rapid and frequent tonal shifts, back and forth between tragedy and farce, reminiscent of Shakespearean technique.

Vysotsky's uncompromising Hamlet was brilliantly served by Lyubimov's metaphorical "poor theatre" production. Lyubimov presented *Hamlet* "in a torn cloak," as a "rough-draft tragedy," a theatre of the poet and of the street, in accord with the troubadour tradition of his ensemble. Nikolay Erdman called Lyubimov, who staged "twenty-three adaptations from novels, poetry and popular song" at his theatre, the Taganka's only resident playwright. His production of *Hamlet* embodied something of the "montage of attractions" approach pioneered by Meyerhold and his student Eisenstein in the 1920s and 1930s. Lyubimov attributed his rediscovery of their principles of construction to his work with Shakespeare and to the latter's conception of time and space. Lyubimov's montage, the breaking down of the text into a series of brief episodes, constructed around a strong scenic metaphor, was designed to "shock" or "alienate" the audience and the text. It subverted reality via self-consciously advertised theatrical devices.

Lyubimov's production was constructed via an editing process which captured the discontinuity of the modern Soviet Hamlet's experience, while honoring Shakespeare's own subversive tactics. In performances of this production, Lyubimov began his notorious practice of signaling his actors with colored flashlight beams to indicate: (red) the performance is going badly; (green) all is well; (white) something in particular is off—the tempo-rhythm of the movement; the audibility of the voices; the naturalness of the acting. Similarly aggravating to the actors but important to the production was Lyubimov's habit of cutting scenes short at their emotional peaks, in order to effect what he considered to be a cinematic rhythm. Likewise, Lyubimov rehearsed numerous scenic variants, in order to achieve a cinematic multifacetedness of perspective. He rehearsed, for example, seventeen scenic variants of the scene between Hamlet and the Ghost.

In the climactic duel scene between Hamlet and Laertes, Lyubimov opted for "real" sound over choreographed fury. By striking their own rapiers and daggers together at opposite sides of the stage rather than engaging one another directly with their weapons, the duelists fully engaged the audience's imagination. The sudden outbursts of unrestrained flurries were unmitigated by the audience's and actors' normal fear for the performers' personal safety. This recalled an earlier Polish stage production of Dostoyevsky's *Crime and Punishment,* in which Raskolnikov and the pawnbroker together stylized the horror of her axe murder in spatial separation accentuated by light. Perhaps too, Lyubimov remembered a near tragic dueling incident from his own acting career. Pasternak came to see Lyubimov, a famous romantic actor in his day, perform in his translation of *Romeo and Juliet* at the Vakhtangov Theatre. During a staged duel, Lyubimov's rapier broke and hurtled into the audience, just missing the head of Pasternak, who was seated in the orchestra. Pasternak joked that Lyubimov had evidently failed to kill him.[19]

The Hamlet-Laertes duel represented a series of movements, rhythmically interrupted by alternating spurts of sound and silence, action and inaction, stitched together by an act of viewer montage. The viewer/listeners not only held the overall action of the play together in their minds, and by so doing co-created the performance, but grounded the isolated figure of Hamlet in the larger frame of the court at Elsinore, from which the Prince was alienated. Lyubimov retrieved for the spectators the real danger of Hamlet's predicament from the staginess of his tradition. At the same time, he created a surreality, via the audience's direct participation in Hamlet's inner process and condition.

David Borovsky's set for Lyubimov's *Hamlet* began upstage with the exposed, whitewashed wall of the theatre. Against this leaned crudely made metal swords and gauntlets, implements for revenge and torture. Hung from this wall was a large, rough-hewn wooden cross, which, in a sense, mediated Hamlet's action. The set ended downstage in an open grave, in which the gravediggers dug real dirt. Likewise, a real skull was used for "poor Yorick." Lyubimov told Hedrick Smith: "We used skulls in several different scenes to make people think of the moment of death. Maybe if you think more about that, maybe you will be more decent in your life."[20]

Stalinist prison camp inmates were intimately acquainted with the lessons and publicity of the grave. Failure to complete work successfully was announced to the community by the appearance of a coffin bearing the prisoner's name. Prisoners were regularly crowded into Black Marias (prison transports) and into prison cells "only as big as two good-sized graves" and held in descriptively named "kennels" and "standing cells," in which it was physically impossible to sit down. They were isolated and silenced, essentially buried alive. Stalin, "the gravedigger of the Revolution," buried millions of his "children" secretly. Meanwhile, Stalin entombed Lenin, the spiritual brother who disowned him (King Hamlet to his Claudius), publicly at the base of the Kremlin ("fortress"/Elsinore's) wall. Hamlet witnessed the Ghost's extraordinary appearance; the Soviet people witnessed the "technological miracle" which preserved Lenin's mortal remains.[21]

The Taganka *Hamlet* began at the open dirt grave, at cock crow, the point of both death and renewal. There Vysotsky's Hamlet declaimed, to the accompaniment of his guitar, Pasternak's once forbidden poem "Hamlet" over the dead king and the dead poet. This action signified not so much a call to arms as a spiritual victory already won. Sometimes the actors, hidden in the wings, sang with Hamlet, improvising a musical dialogue on the theme of freedom. "The silence of the grave" and the "unanimity of belief" which blanketed Soviet culture for decades were broken. The prisoner's unspoken vow to "suffer in silence," a recognition of the fatality of "careless talk" and Pasternak's enforced creative silence during his lifetime, were evoked and laid to rest. The Taganka *Hamlet* immediately proclaimed its intention to tear down the wall of silence, which separated social classes, contemporaries, and artists from their audience.

The Elsinore trope, which includes walls of silent repression and surveillance, was, according to Kozintsev, "a speculative concept." Huge in scale, the metaphor had at least partially resisted the forfeit of its mystery in Craig's and Ryndin's plastic forms. Ryndin's biographer, V. Berezkin, stated that his design "re-established the right of a stage setting to be metaphoric" in the post-Stalin Soviet theatre. Critic Aleksandr Anikst suggested that the monumental presence of the prison metaphor in Okhlopkov's *mise en scène* was intended to invoke its absence or obsolescence in the new free life of the Soviet artist. However, this intention was overwhelmed by the visual weight and ponderous tempo of the Okhlopkov-Ryndin *mise en scène*.[22]

The Lyubimov-Borovsky scenic solution stressed lightness (and speed). Their work on this production was influenced by Peter Brook's minimalist *Hamlet*, which premiered in Moscow in 1955 on the first English company tour of the Soviet Union since the revolution. The bare gray set which Georges Wakhevitch designed for Brook, allowing for rapid and "ingenious" scene changes, contrasted sharply with Okhlopkov's and Ryndin's maximalist plan, with its overbearing iron gates and catacombs. The Taganka design, which utilized a giant woven hemp curtain, was even closer to Kozintsev's characterization of Elsinore as "a stone sack," in which the mind and soul of Hamlet were imprisoned (fig. 25). Activated by an expensive aluminum track system, the *Hamlet* curtain, which moved in all directions except straight up and down, followed the Prince every-

FIGURE 25

Vladimir Vysotsky (center) in front of the Taganka Theatre's Hamlet *curtain. Courtesy of Alma Law Archive.*

where. The curtain policed the stage with the hyperbolic power of the state, fate, and death, pushing Hamlet toward the ordinary reality (*byt*) of the grave, where the guilty and the just meet and where *Hamlet* figuratively begins. The grave, like the curtain, is a speculative presence, a metonym of the state's massively scaled and empowered capacity for destroying and burying bodies, secrets, history, and memory. The public graves of mythically living heroes in and at the Kremlin Wall and the Siberian "Tomb of [actually] living men," which de Custine in the eighteenth century called "only an exaggeration of Russia," inscribed death at the center and the periphery of Russian and Soviet culture.

Ushered in by Yury Butsko's choral music, set to the accompaniment of piano, clarinet, violin, accordion, and contrabass, the curtain (and the grave), which appeared at first to represent the Soviet Hamlet's anonymous doom, was revealed in the end to be his theatrical salvation.[23] Pasternak wrote that artists use metaphor as a spiritual shorthand measuring the distance "between man's short life and the immense and long-term tasks he sets himself." The curtain and the grave are custom-made metaphors, offering theatre and life a perfect fit. Lyubimov's and Borovsky's treatment of these two scenic metaphors subverted death's mystery and mastery over the Soviet imagination by reversing the theatre audience's anticipation of closure. As in Shakespeare's writing, which "makes vulgar mediocrity snort and rush in on the funereal solemnity of his finales," these metaphors, in their open-endedness, suggested to Pasternak (and to Lyubimov) that "no situation as seen by the artist or the thinker is final; every position is the last but one."

Lyubimov's theatricalist *mise en scène* questioned "reality" and represented theatrical androgyny, the doubleness of convention (*uslovnost'*)—theatre's impersonation of but resistance to closure. Theatrical voyeurism's surveillance was exposed like Polonius, "the informer or 'secret collaborator' (*seksot*)," who is stabbed through a curtain. This Polonius metaphor was extended by Lyubimov, who directed actors to thrust swords through the curtain from behind as armrests for the members of Claudius's court, while exposing them as spies to the surveillance of the theatre audience. An "eyeless monster," perhaps representing the Stalinist corruption of what Trotsky called Lenin's "revolutionary gaze," the curtain's surveillance seemed limitless and ubiquitous to the paranoid citizenry which it encompassed. The *Hamlet* curtain not only revealed people, places, and scenes, it dramatized the appearing/disappearing action of theatre itself. In playing upon audience expectations and spectatorial identity, the curtain re-discovered and reinvented them. Viktor Shklovsky wrote: "Art develops according to the technical possibilities of the time. The technique of the novel created the stock character. Hamlet was created by stage techniques."[24] In its symbolic and (stage) managerial functions, the *Hamlet* curtain not only unfolded the play but, to an extent, (re)created it. Theatre embodies the "Hamlet question." It transpires and quickly expires within the womb of time, occupying the stage between the matrices of a curtain, which functions as a veil of mystery and illusion, and a stage and auditorium, which delimit (im)mortality. Russian and Soviet history in particular has eavesdropped at the curtain and at the grave.

The old Taganka Theatre, at which *Hamlet* was performed, did not normally make use of a stage curtain. Beginning with his 1969 production of *Mother* (*Mat'*), adapted from Gorky's novel, Lyubimov made periodic use of a curtain of light, projected from instruments recessed in the stage floor and aimed at a thirty-degree angle toward the audience. So, for the Taganka, the idea of a material curtain represented the invocation of an absent tradition. At the same time, the *Hamlet* curtain inverted the Elizabethan public playhouse's and the Taganka's conception of an absent presence, a convention which the audience creates, even though it does not appear.[25] The *Hamlet* curtain was conceived to provide an Elizabethan-like continuous flow across an empty stage (Borovsky's idea) and to impersonate objects and locales, which would otherwise have to be built and shifted—solid walls and tapestries, a shawl and swing. Metaphorically, it suggested the state's giant snare, Hamlet's "mousetrap" and Hamlet's ensnared, intricately weblike mental and emotional condition. The latter function recalled the mobile, giant screens in Craig's monodramatic *Hamlet*. The cinematic split-screen performance/visual montage of parallel actions on either side of the *Hamlet* curtain suggested the beehive effect produced in Okhlopkov's *Hamlet* by exposing a cross-section of the inner workings of Elsinore Castle to the spectators' gaze.

The *Hamlet* curtain captured the statuesque silence of the state's "unswerving power." The curtain was the wind against which the Prince bent his fragile figure and the cloak which protected him from it. It evoked the memory of the cloak with which the Prince shielded his father's ghost in Meyerhold's unrealized plan for staging the play. It invoked the spirit of the Ghost himself as a present absence—as death and the renewal of life, as the millennium and the renaissance.

It was Winston Churchill's "iron curtain" and the great storms of history and revolution that were blowing it away. It was God and Hamlet's and his world's fate, defined in and by time, space, and nature, as well as the veil of silence drawn before irrational truth, deathless mystery, and the Gogolian spatial abyss which silence represents. It was Prospero's magic cloak, theatrical illusion as succor for and salvation from the tyranny of illusory reality and ineffable meaning. It was the funeral shroud in which Hamlet's corpse and that of his alter ego, Vysotsky, were wrapped (the latter in his commemorative production). And it was the image of their unconquered spirits, which had flown away.

The curtain captured Hamlet's stitched-together life as dramatist and actor, son and lover, student and avenger, prince and rebel. It also suggested Gogol's capacious and ubiquitous overcoat, stitched together from Slavic traditions, superstitions, and conventions, out of which French critic Melchior de Vögué claimed modern Russian literature had tumbled. Gogol's overcoat, which Lyubimov figuratively stitched together and used as a curtain in a later production (*The Inspector's Recounting* [*Revizskaya skazka*], Taganka premiere 1978), doubled Prospero's cloak as the symbolic mantle of the poet and the language of poetry. By becoming an agent in the action, the curtain ceded its conventional neutrality. It revealed an invisible historical "pastness" and a visible theatrical "presentness," the counterclaims of testimony and tradition, which Hamlet felt compelled to serve and to save.

While the movement of the curtain was meant to evoke "the breathing of unsolved mysteries," the breathing quickly became labored. The curtain represented another of Lyubimov's and his designer's habitual attempts to create actor-sensitive decor (following from Meyerhold and Vakhtangov), compliant with and expressive of the actors'/characters' wills. However, to the company members it seemed that the curtain had a will of its own, which it sought to impose upon them. The sound emitted by the tracking aluminum mechanism drowned out the actors' voices. The rhythm of the curtain's movement dictated the rhythm of the production, usurping an important part of the actors' role. The curtain even received a curtain call.

Once, while the actors rehearsed Ophelia's burial scene, the aluminum mechanism collapsed, dropping the curtain over the entire stage in an eerie reenactment of Craig's falling screen fiasco in the dress rehearsal for his *Hamlet*. While Lyubimov's actors escaped with minor injuries, the mechanism and the curtain did not, necessitating the closing of the production for six months. It was while nursing the tyrant back to health that the actors first came to forge a personal relationship with it as a fellow performer and to recognize it as a boon to the production. Inadvertently and ironically, the ensemble's rapprochement with and reconstitution of the phantom tyrant (Soviet critics referred repeatedly to "the Curtain") realized one of Soviet history's most tragic themes.

In the Taganka *Hamlet*, the curtain lost its tradition of architectural permanence and in its movement (and the ghostly memory of its permanence) underscored the impermanence of its realm, the stage. We theorize that the Elizabethan stage ended in a stationary scenic façade, anchored by a cosmic canopy. All of this was enfolded by a building whose shape was numerologically determined to reinforce the consistent code of permanence and order.[26] The disordered and disorderly Hamlet could be vicariously embraced by the Elizabethan audience as a hero of their collective imagining, even as the nightmare of irrationalism which he enacted was diminished by the orderly architectural semiotic which contained him.

In *Hamlet*, the Taganka performed the nightmare of Soviet imprisonment and historical erasure, of chaos masquerading as cultural order. The corpses of the dead, of the "superfluous," "former," and "nonpeople," which have littered Russian and Soviet history, were swept from the stage by the giant curtain in the production's final image. But their ghosts had already taken flight in the theatre's enactment of tragic loss and heroic retrieval.

EPILOGUE

In the late 1970s and early 1980s, prior to being stripped of his artistic position at the Taganka Theatre and his Soviet citizenship in 1984, Lyubimov periodically spoke on record to the Western press. In one such calculated scene in the prolonged drama of the artist contesting the state for control of his personal fate, Lyubimov proclaimed that Lenin and communism were European imports alien to Russian history and consciousness.[1] While he did not directly say so, he implied that these foreign viruses had paralyzed and partially erased cultural memory. Lyubimov, a theatricalist without peer, understood in life and artistic practice, as did Lotman in theory and Hamlet in fiction, that while cultural interruption may not in itself always constitute a moral problem, it nearly always has moral consequences.

In the middle of *Hamlet*'s run, Lyubimov staged *The Exchange* (*Obmen*, Taganka premiere June 1976), which he co-adapted with Yury Trifonov from the latter's novella of the same name. The story centers on a man and his wife who cynically attempt to manipulate his dying mother into ceding them her soon-to-be vacant apartment. Upon her death this inheritance can be packaged with the couple's (and their daughter's) room in a Moscow communal apartment in an exchange for more spacious living quarters. The *mise en scène* by Lyubimov and his designer David Borovsky did more than merely equate the physical and moral (in)conveniences of modern Soviet life. It translated the paradox of communism's utopian dream into a small space that is too crowded (blighted inner life metamorphized into the reality of communal living) and a large space that is too empty (the vastness of provincial Russia/the unreality of a communal ideal which has voided the self).

The family members sat inside a makeshift scenae frons of material possessions that extended far downstage toward the audience. Dispossessed among their possessions, distanced from their dream and alienated from the social order, the characters resembled Ranevskaya and company in the final act of *The Cherry Orchard*. However, the audience for Trifonov's play in Lyubimov's *mise en scène* understood from their own lives the essential social condition being portrayed in a way that the spectators at the MAT production of *The Cherry Orchard* could not. In the nearly three-quarters of a century separating the two plays' premieres, history had not only naturally evolved but been artificially remade in a revolutionary and postrevolutionary mode. The theatre program distributed to the audience took the form of an application for an apartment exchange. The application named Lyubimov and the Taganka staff as the relevant parties in what has been an ongoing and to the intelligentsia who frequent the theatre well-known exchange or negotiation with bureaucratic authority for space, that is, artistic freedom. This extratheatrical device, characteristic of Lyubimov's productions at the Taganka, positioned the theatre and its director inside the drama of both the play and the larger history of the creative intelligentsia that was still in the making. Chekhov, who died just as Russian symbolism was establishing its coterie theatre, could only dream of such a convergence of creators and an audience so intensely focused upon intellectual "class" interests.[2]

In the opening moments of Lyubimov's production, the protagonist, seated downstage of the wall of furnishings, watched the performance of Soviet iceskaters on television. The skaters' routine, the perfect union of (sports) science and art according to the propagandistic model constructed by the state, was enacted for the theatre audience upstage of the wall by two dancers dressed in the red and gold colors of the Soviet flag. The freedom of movement of the "skaters" within an unencumbered space and the dreamlike waving of the patriotic colors which it produced seemed to transpire at an unreachable distance from the stationary figures, the "living corpses" or "dead souls," stuck in the despirited and despiritualized tableau of their quotidian existence.

The two spaces, representing two realities, merged in the consciousness of the two viewers, the dramatic protagonist and the audience member. The staging of idealized proximity and actual distance in contiguous spaces summoned up for both viewers the twice-lived-in utopia that had been promised then theatricalized in the iconography of spectacular culture as if it had already been fulfilled. The Soviet viewer understood that these two physical/moral spaces, though contiguous, were in reality irreconcilable.[3] The hyperbolized dream of the cultural center, a metonymic national soul, and the hope and comfort it contained receded farther into a distance that these contemporary, downsized Prozorovs were unlikely ever to reach.[4] The audience saw represented what they already knew—the spiritual absence and the vacancy of truth at the geopolitical and ideological center of what for nearly the entire twentieth century had passed for cultural memory.

NOTES

INTRODUCTION

1. Lewis H. Siegelbaum discusses the *oblik/mentalité* approach to Russian history in *Soviet State and Society: Between Revolutions, 1918–1929* (New York: Cambridge University Press, 1992), 26, 31, 115. See also Sheila Fitzpatrick, "The Bolsheviks' Dilemma: Class, Culture, and Politics in the Early Soviet Years," *Slavic Review* 47 (1988): 599–613. On "revolutionary dreaming" in Russian culture, see Richard Stites, *Revolutionary Dreams: Utopian Vision and Experimental Life in the Russian Revolution* (New York: Oxford University Press, 1989).

2. Yuri M. Lotman, *Universe of the Mind: A Semiotic Theory of Culture* (Bloomington and Indianapolis: Indiana University Press, 1990), 60 ("translation-code"). Lotman's interest in theatre is primarily theoretical. He has considered the principle of theatricality within the context of theatre in "Yazyk teatra," *Teatr* 3 (March 1989): 101–103. He has also discussed the semiotics of the stage in "Semiotika stseny," *Teatr* 1 (January 1981): 89–99.

3. Boris Gasparov, "Introduction," in *The Semiotics of Russian Cultural History*, ed. Alexander D. Nakhimovsky and Alice Stone Nakhimovsky (Ithaca: Cornell University Press, 1985), 20–21 (quotes); Iurii M. Lotman, "Concerning Khlestakov" (1975), trans. Louisa Vinton, in the same collection, 153, 165, 183–184 ("completely"), 187. Nikolay Berdyaev has suggested that "interruption" is characteristic of and even programmed by "a people of revelation and inspiration," who are accustomed to "facing infinitude" (Nikolay Berdyaev, *The Russian Idea*, trans. R. M. French [Hudson, N.Y.: Lindisfarne Press, 1992], 20).

4. Iurii M. Lotman and Boris A. Uspenskii, "Binary Models in the Dynamics of Russian Culture (to the End of the Eighteenth Century)," in *The Semiotics of Russian Cultural History*, ed. Nakhimovsky and Nakhimovsky, 31 ("binary nature"); Priscilla R. Roosevelt, "Emerald Thrones and Living Statues: Theater and Theatricality on the Russian Estate," 2–3 (quotes), Laurence Senelick, "The Erotic Bondage of Serf Theatre," 24–34, and Richard Wortman, "Theatricality, Myth and Authority," 48–49, all in *Russian Review* 50 (January 1991). "Sacral semantics" is Wortman's translation of a coinage in N. M. Zhivov and B. A. Uspensky, "Tsar' i Bog: Semioticheskie aspekty sakralizatsii monarkha v Rossii," in

B. A. Uspensky, ed., *Yazyki kul'tury i problemy perevodimosti* (Moscow: n.p., 1987), 72, 121–122.

5. "Utopian apocalypse" is Martin Buber's term, quoted in Krishan Kumar, *Utopia and Anti-Utopia in Modern Times* (Cambridge: Basil Blackwell, 1991), 54. "To make the extraordinary repeatable" was a goal of the surrealists, according to Peter Bürger in *Theory of the Avant-Garde*, trans. Michael Shaw (Minneapolis: University of Minnesota Press, 1984), 65.

6. Alexander Vucinich, *Science in Russian Culture, 1861–1917* (Stanford: Stanford University Press, 1970), 243–244, 246, 337, 354 (paraphrase of Lev Tolstoy).

7. Dwight MacDonald, "Preface," in Herzen, *My Past and Thoughts*, xiii (quote). While in exile in England (1852–1858), Herzen wrote (in reference to Robert Owen's philosophy): "It is only by depriving history of every predestined course that man and history become something earnest, effective and filled with profound interest. If events are stacked in advance, if the whole of history is the unfolding of some anti-historic *plot*, if the result of it all is one performance, one *mise en scène*, then at least let us too take up wooden swords and tin shields. Are we to shed real blood and real tears for the performance of a charade by providence? If there *is* a pre-ordained plan, history is reduced to an insertion of figures in an algebraical formula, and the future is mortgaged before its birth" (*My Past and Thoughts*, 520).

8. Guy Debord, *Society of the Spectacle* (Detroit: Black and Red, 1983), 219.

9. Berdyaev, *The Russian Idea*, 31–32.

10. Friedrich Nietzsche, *The Gay Science*, trans. and ed. Walter Kaufmann (New York: Vintage/Random House, 1974), 273, 273 n. 71. Michel Haar relates Nietzsche's concept of *amor fati* to such "metaphysical contradictions" ("Nietzsche and Metaphysical Language," in *The New Nietzsche: Contemporary Styles of Interpretation*, ed. David B. Allison [Cambridge, Mass.: MIT Press, 1986], 32–33). Nietzsche's discussion of fate as "the greatest weight" (*Das grosste Schwergewicht*) in *The Gay Science* (*Die fröhliche Wissenschaft*, 1882) helped introduce the notion of eternal recurrence, which became the basis of *Thus Spake Zarathustra* (*Also sprach Zarathustra*, 1891). See chapter 1 of the present study for a discussion of Nietzsche's influence upon *fin de siècle* Russian culture.

11. Isaiah Berlin, "Introduction," in Herzen, *My Past and Thoughts*, xxxii–xxxiii; Sheila Fitzpatrick, *The Cultural Front: Power and Culture in Revolutionary Russia* (Ithaca and London: Cornell University Press, 1992), 14–15.

12. Joseph Brodsky, "Less Than One," in *Less Than One: Selected Essays* (New York: Farrar, Straus and Giroux, 1988), 31.

13. Pyotr Chaadayev, "First Philosophical Letter" (1836), quoted in *Russian Philosophy*, vol. 1, *The Beginnings of Russian Philosophy: The Slavophiles, The Westernizers*, ed. James M. Edie, James P. Scanlan, and Mary-Barbara Zeldin (Knoxville: University of Tennessee Press, 1984), 105, 109 (quote), 111, 112 (quotes).

14. Jeffrey Brooks, *When Russia Learned to Read: Literacy and Popular Literature, 1861–1917* (Princeton: Princeton University Press, 1985), xiii.

15. Lotman, *Universe of the Mind*, 231–232, 234, 238–239, 246–247 (quote).

16. Vladimir Nahirny, *The Russian Intelligentsia: From Torment to Silence* (New Brunswick: Transaction Books, 1983), 1 (quotes); Berdyaev, *The Russian Idea*, 20 ("immensity"); Katerina Clark, "The 'Quiet Revolution' in Soviet Intellectual Life," in *Russia in the Era of NEP: Explorations in Soviet Society and Culture*, ed. Sheila Fitzpatrick, Alexander Rabinowitch, and Richard Stites (Bloomington and Indianapolis: Indiana University Press, 1991), 222; Karl Mannheim, *Ideology and Utopia: An Introduction to the Sociology of Knowledge*, trans. Louis Wirth and Edward Shils (New York: Harcourt, Brace and Company, 1936), 9; Vucinich, *Science in Russian Culture*, 446; James H. Billington, *Fire in the Minds of Men: Origins of the Revolutionary Faith* (New York: Basic Books, 1980), 451.

17. Lotman, *Universe of the Mind*, 238.

18. Joanna Hubbs, *Mother Russia: The Feminine Myth in Russian Culture* (Bloomington and Indianapolis: Indiana University Press, 1988), 185, 187, 201; Michael Cherniavsky, *Tsar and People: Studies in Russian Myths* (New York: Random House, 1969), 101, 104–106, 112 (quotes), 116; Boris Kagarlitsky, *The Thinking Reed: Intellectuals and the Soviet State from 1917 to the Present*, trans. Brian Pearce (New York: Verso, 1988), 10; "Preface," in *Russian Philosophy*, vol. 3, *Pre-Revolutionary Philosophy and Theology, Philosophers in Exile, Marxists and Communists*, ed. James M. Edie and Mary-Barbara Zeldin, with George L. Kline (Knoxville: University of Tennessee Press, 1976), ix; Lydia Ginsburg, "'The Human Document' and the Formation of Character," trans. R. Judson Rosengrant, in *The Semiotics of Russian Cultural History*, ed. Nakhimovsky and Nakhimovsky, 217. The concept of Holy Russia was popularized in the latter half of the seventeenth century in the writings of Prince Kurbsky, who opposed Tsar Ivan IV's subjugation of the family, the church, and the ruling class (the *boyarstvo*) to the will of the state. The term "Holy Russia" seems to have appeared first in a poem by Prince Pyotr Vyazemsky, circa 1848.

19. Nahirny, *The Russian Intelligentsia*, 1, 4–7, 9, 150. V. G. Belinsky (1811–1848) is generally called "the father of the Russian intelligentsia." A. I. Herzen (1812–1870) is credited with having defined the intelligentsia as a class in terms of sociopolitical marginality. Populist theorist N. K. Mikhaylovsky's 1868 essay "Letters on the Russian Intelligentsia" gave the class its name. For relevant discussions of the interrelated concepts of Holy Russia and the Russian intelligentsia, see James H. Billington, *The Icon and the Axe: An Interpretive History of Russian Culture* (New York: Vintage/Random House, 1970), 388–390; Aleksandr Blok, *Rossiya i intelligentsiya (1907–1918)* (Petersburg: Alkonost', 1919), 26; E. F. F. Hill, "Introduction," in Alexander Blok, *The Spirit of Music*, trans. I. Freiman (London: Lindsay Drummond Limited, 1946), 2; Aleksander

Blok, "Narod i intelligentsiya" (1908), in *Sobranie sochineny v vos'mi tomakh*, ed. V. N. Orlov, A. A. Surkov, K. I. Chukovsky, vol. 5, *Proza 1903–1917*, ed. A. Bikhter (Moscow-Leningrad: Gosudarstvennoe izdatel'stvo khudozhestvennoy literatury, 1962), 318, 322; Jeffrey Brooks, "Popular Philistinism and the Course of Russian Modernism," in *Literature and History: Theoretical Problems and Russian Case Studies*, ed. Gary Saul Morson (Stanford: Stanford University Press, 1986), 90; Richard Pipes, ed., *The Russian Intelligentsia* (New York: Columbia University Press, 1961), 56, 66; Cherniavsky, *Tsar and People*, 125. From the vast literature on the origins and evolution of the Russian intelligentsia, see also R. Ivanov-Razumnik, *Istoriya russkoy obshchestvennoy mysli* (St. Petersburg: n.p., 1914); D. N. Ovsyaniko-Kulikovsky, *Istoriya russkoy intelligentsii*, in *Sobranie sochineny* (St. Petersburg: n.p., 1910); Vyacheslav Polonsky, *Ukhodyashchaya Rus': Stat'i ob intelligentsii 1920–1924* (Moscow: n.p., 1924); M. P. Kim, *Sovetskaya intelligentsiya: Istoriya formirovaniya i rosta 1917–1965 gg.* (Moscow: n.p., 1968); S. A. Fedyukin, *Veliky oktyabr' i intelligentsiya* (Moscow: n.p., 1972); St. R. Tomkins, *The Russian Intelligentsia: Makers of the Revolutionary State* (Norman: Oklahoma University Press, 1957); Marc Raeff, ed., *Russian Intellectual History: An Anthology* (New York: Harcourt, Brace and World, 1964); Marc Raeff, *Origins of Nobility* (New York: Harbinger Books, 1966); and Charles Rougle, "The Intelligentsia Debate in Russia 1917–1918," in *Art, Society, Revolution: Russia 1917–1921*, ed. Nils Åke Nilsson (Stockholm: Almqvist and Wiksell International, 1979), 54–105.

20. Cherniavsky, *Tsar and People*, 117 (quote). See Sheila Fitzpatrick, "The Problem of Class Identity in NEP Society," in *Russia in the Era of NEP: Explorations in Soviet Society and Culture*, 12–33; Clark, "The 'Quiet Revolution' in Soviet Intellectual Life," 210–230.

21. For a good discussion of how the various philosophical factions of the prerevolutionary intelligentsia developed, see George F. Putnam, *Russian Alternatives to Marxism: Christian Socialism and Idealistic Liberalism in Twentieth-Century Russia* (Knoxville: University of Tennessee Press, 1977). The political elements among the intelligentsia are treated in many books in English, including, most recently, Richard Pipes, *The Russian Revolution* (New York: Vintage/Random House, 1990). Brian Boyd discusses V. D. Nabokov in *Vladimir Nabokov: The Russian Years* (Princeton: Princeton University Press, 1990). The specific circumstances surrounding his murder are recreated on pages 189–190. For a useful overview of movements in Russian literature of the period, see Renato Poggioli, *The Poets of Russia 1890–1930* (Cambridge: Harvard University Press, 1960).

22. For a highly intelligent overview of Russian symbolism, see James West, *Russian Symbolism: A Study of Vyacheslav Ivanov and the Russian Symbolist Aesthetic* (London: Methuen, 1970). In particular, see pages 66, 70 ("pathos"), 72–73, 78 (other quotes), for a discussion of Ivanov's Dionysianism. I have also benefited from a discussion with Laurence Senelick

on this theme. West discusses symbolist incomprehensibility and issues related to symbolist drama on pages 108, 111, 141, 151, 160. His sources are Valery Bryusov, *O iskusstve* (Moscow, n.p., 1899), 18; and "Ellis," "Chto takoe teatr?" in *Vesy* 4 (1908): 89–90. Bryusov suggested the impossibility of achieving "general comprehensibility or accessibility" based upon the reality of individual difference. "Ellis" (L. L. Kobylinsky) defined symbolist art in terms of "aristocratic exclusivity and . . . absolute insuitability for any kind of social experiment." "It is no accident," he wrote, "that the outstanding symbolist poets of our age have been bad dramatists, and the greatest of them have not been dramatists at all." On symbolist "liturgical" theatre, see Fyodor Sologub, "Teatr odnoy voli," in *"Teatr," kniga o novom teatre: Sbornik statey A. Lunacharskogo, E. Anichkova, A. Gornfel'da, Aleksandra Benua, Vs. Meyerkhol'da, Fyodora Sologuba, Georgiya Chulkova, S. Rafalovicha, Valeriya Bryusova i Andreya Belogo* (St. Petersburg: Shipovnik, 1908), 180, 182. For a brief overview of symbolist drama, see George Kalbouss, *The Plays of the Russian Symbolists* (East Lansing: Russian Language Journal, 1982). On Russian scythianism, see Stefani Hoffmann, "Scythian Theory and Literature, 1917–1924," in *Art, Society, Revolution 1917–1921*, 138–164, specifically, 146–147, 150–153 ("lost" on 152; "mythic" on 153).

23. Lars Kleberg, "'People's Theater' and the Revolution: On the History of a Concept before and after 1917," in *Art, Society, Revolution: Russia 1917–1921*, 183–184. Pushkin expresses his sentiments on popular drama in his essay "O narodnoy drame i drame 'Marfa Posadnitsa'" (written 1830; published 1841–1842), in *Pushkin i teatr: Dramaticheskie proizvedeniya, stat'i, i zametki, dnevniki, pis'ma* (Moscow: Iskusstvo, 1953), 392–393. He put these ideas into practice in his play *Boris Godunov* (written 1825; produced 1870). In relation to Lunacharsky's appropriation of Ivanov's communal ideal, Nikolay Berdyayev wrote in the 1920s, "I have abandoned Marxian pseudo-*sobornost'* and decadent romantic individualism for the *sobornost'* of mystical neo-Christianity" (Vucinich, *Science in Russian Culture*, 241).

24. Andrey Bely, "Teatr i sovremennaya drama," in *"Teatr," kniga o novom teatre*, 264–265.

25. Nahirny, *The Russian Intelligentsia*, 139, 150; Rougle, "The Intelligentsia Debate in Russia," 70; Herzen, *My Past and Thoughts*, 649–650. Caryl Emerson made the point about Russian culture's inability to define the self in a public lecture at Brown University, 9 February 1993.

I. ARRIVALS AND DEPARTURES

1. Velimir Khlebnikov, *Proza: Sobranie proizvedeny*, ed. N. Stepanov and Yu. Tynyanov, 5 vols. (Leningrad: Izdatel'stvo pisateley, 1928–1933), vol. 4, 312–313, quoted in Vyacheslav V. Ivanov, "The Category of Time in Twentieth-Century Art and Culture," *Semiotica* 8 (The Hague: Mouton, 1973), 2.

2. The Russians' comfort with time over space is explained in part by Chaa-dayev's assertion that "we ourselves make time," despite the Western sense that modern Russia has largely "made space" as well in the periodic redefinition of its national borders ("Philosophical Letter III," in *Russian Philosophy*, vol. 1, 130, 131). The term *oprichnina* (from *oprich* or "apart, beside"), which came into being in February 1565 during the reign of Tsar Ivan IV (the Terrible, reigned 1533–1584), had two mean-ings. It referred to a special territorial subdivision in the Muscovite state managed by the tsar through a separate administration which reported directly to him and also to the *oprichniki*, the tsar's political police. Their ranks, which swelled from one thousand to six thousand, dressed in black, rode black horses, and destroyed "those whom the tsar considered to be his enemies" (Nicholas V. Riasanovsky, *A History of Russia*, 4th ed. [New York: Oxford University Press, 1984], 150–151).

3. Marquis de Custine, *Empire of the Czar: A Journey through Eternal Rus-sia* (New York: Anchor/Doubleday, 1989), 508.

4. B. A. Uspenskij, "Tsar and Pretender: *Samozvančestvo* or Royal Im-posture in Russia as a Cultural-Historical Phenomenon," trans. David Budgen, in *The Semiotics of Russian Culture*, ed. Ann Shukman (Ann Arbor: Michigan Slavic Contributions, 1984), 283 n. 65, 272, 288 n. 87; Jan Kott, "The Eating of 'The Government Inspector,'" *Theatre Quar-terly* 17 (March–May 1975): 25. In the opening of Gogol's novel *Dead Souls* (*Myortvye dushi*, 1842), two muzhiks speculate on whether a wheel that is rolling by them will reach Moscow or even Kazan. Vladimir Na-bokov notes that "what fascinates them is solely the ideal problem of fix-ing the imaginary instability of a wheel in terms of imaginary distances" (*Nikolai Gogol* [New York: New Directions, 1944], 76; Boyd cites this incident in *Vladimir Nabokov*, 465).

5. Quoted in Susan Ray, "Afterword: Nietzsche's View of Russia and the Russians," in *Nietzsche in Russia*, ed. Bernice Glatzer Rosenthal (Prince-ton: Princeton University Press, 1986), 393; Stephen Kern, *The Culture of Time and Space 1880–1918* (Cambridge, Mass.: Harvard University Press, 1983), 255.

6. A. P. Chekhov, *Vishnyovy sad*, in *Polnoe sobranie sochineny i pisem v tridtsati tomakh*, vols. 12–13, *P'esy 1889–1891*, ed. N. F. Bel'chikov (Moscow: Nauka, 1978), 216 (all textual references to Chekhov's major plays are to this edition).

7. Konstantin Mochulsky, *Andrei Bely: His Life and Works*, trans. Nora Szalavitz (Ann Arbor: Ardis, 1977), 212.

8. Ray, "Afterword," 393, 397. In some passages relevant to this discus-sion of the self's negotiation with internal and external space and time, W. J. T. Mitchell writes that "space is the body of time. . . . Time is the soul of space" and "the most complex and vividly imagined spatial form in literature is finally the labyrinth of ourselves" ("Spatial Form in Literature: Toward a General Theory," in *The Language of Images*, ed. W. J. T. Mitchell [Chicago: University of Chicago Press, 1980], 276–277 [quote], 294).

9. The introduction of the railway, along with the telephone and telegraph, helped the police state to coalesce, to monitor its citizenry better, and so to produce more political exiles like Lenin. While political prisoners still constituted a small percentage of Siberia's population of nearly 300,000 in 1898, their number steadily increased. In 1901, there were 4,113 political exiles in all of Russia, of which 3,838 were under "overt police surveillance." See Richard Pipes, *Russia under the Old Regime* (New York: Macmillan/Collier, 1992), 295, 310–311; J. N. Westwood, *A History of Russian Railways* (London: George Allen and Unwin, 1964), 120, 138.

10. Max Weber, *Theory of Social and Economic Organization*, trans. A. M. Henderson and Talcott Parsons (New York: Oxford University Press, 1947), 358 ("repudiates"); Robert C. Tucker, "The Theory of Charismatic Leadership," *Daedalus* 97 (Summer 1968), 737, 743 ("distress," "acute"), 745; Robert C. Tucker, "Introduction," in *The Lenin Anthology*, ed. Robert C. Tucker (New York: W. W. Norton and Company, 1975), xlvii (Max Eastman quote), xlviii, xlix, l ("proved").

11. Quoted in Stites, *Revolutionary Dreams*, 41, 262n.9.

12. A. P. Chekhov, *Chayka*, in *Polnoe sobranie sochineny i pisem v tridtsati tomakh*, vols. 12–13, 5.

13. Remarks by Laurence Senelick at the annual conference of the American Society for Theatre Research, Seattle, Washington, November 1991; Chekhov, *Chayka*, 60.

14. A. P. Chekhov, *Dyadya Vanya* and *Tri sestry*, in *Polnoe sobranie sochineny i pisem v tridtsati tomakh*, vols. 12–13, 63, 243. Konstantin Rudnitsky has noted how often characters in Chekhov's plays state their age and count money. Remembering and counting demarcate time transpiring or being doled out in empty lives. See B. Zingerman, "Vremya v p'esakh Chekhova," discussed in Konstantin Rudnitsky, "Krasota v p'esakh Chekhova," *Teatr* 6 (June 1981): 73–74.

15. Chekhov, *Vishnyovy sad*, 199; Richard Peace, *Chekhov: A Study of the Four Major Plays* (New Haven: Yale University Press, 1983), 123.

16. Vladimir Nabokov, "Leo Tolstoy," in *Lectures on Russian Literature*, ed. Fredson Bowers (New York: Harcourt Brace Jovanovich, 1981), 228–229; Apollinaire quoted in Frederick R. Karl, *Modern and Modernism: The Sovereignty of the Artist 1885–1925* (New York: Atheneum, 1985), 300.

17. Vucinich, *Science in Russian Culture*, 7, 13 (quote), 14, 27; Patrick Gardiner, "Henry Thomas Buckle," in *The Encyclopedia of Philosophy*, ed. Paul Edwards, 8 vols. (New York: Macmillan and Free Press, 1967), vol. 1, 414–415.

18. Einstein quoted in Wim Mertens, *American Minimal Music* (New York: Alexander Brounde, 1983), 81; *Lenin o kul'ture i iskusstve: Sbornik* (Moscow: n.p., 1956), 250; Nicolas Berdyaev, *The Origin of Russian Communism*, trans. R. M. French (Ann Arbor: University of Michigan Press, 1960), 114, 118, 129; Robert Motherwell, ed., *The Dada Painters and Poets: An Anthology* (Cambridge: Harvard University Press, 1981),

xxiv; Vucinich, *Science in Russian Culture*, 266–268; Karl, *Modern and Modernism*, 268 n.; Kern, *The Culture of Time and Space*, 134; Vladimir Lenin, "Materialism and Empirio-Criticism," in *Russian Philosophy*, vol. 3, 420–421, 425; Nikolaj Erdman, *Mandat*, ed. V. Kazak (Munich: Verlag Otto Sagner in Kommission, 1971), 54–55. The railroad became in *fin de siècle* Russia as elsewhere a modern symbol of individual and cultural disaffection and agency, depending upon who was riding/writing it. In 1897, Lenin wrote home from his Siberian exile that the farther he traveled on the Trans-Siberian Railroad, the more slowly time seemed to pass. However, in *Materialism and Empirio-Criticism* (*Materializm i empiriokrititsizm: Kriticheskie zametki ob odnoy reaktsionnoy filosofii*, 1909), Lenin rejected the Kantian notion that spatiotemporal perception is a function of human experience, since it undermined the objective, materialist reality upon which Marxism was dependent. Lenin argued that time and space have objective reality, that is, exist outside the human mind. A character in Fellow Traveler Nikolay Erdman's play *The Mandate* (*Mandat*, 1924), written one year after Lenin's death, when asked her opinion of Einstein's theory, mistook it for a plotless movie that had played at her local theatre. Her response linked relativity to the "anti-Bolshevik" formalist poetics of the 1920s, which preferred *syuzhet* (subject, patterned theme) over *fabula* (plot, story).

19. Giles Deleuze, *Bergsonism*, trans. Hugh Tomlinson and Barbara Habberjam (New York: Zone Books, 1991), 79.

20. Peter M. Bitsilli, *Chekhov's Art: A Stylistic Analysis*, trans. Toby W. Clyman and Edwina Jannie Cruise (Ann Arbor: Ardis, 1983), 181; Karl, *Modern and Modernism*, 268 n.; Linda Dalrymple Henderson, *The Fourth Dimension and Non-Euclidean Geometry in Modern Art* (Princeton: Princeton University Press, 1983), 4, 241, 244, 250; Uspensky quoted in Marjorie Perloff, *The Futurist Moment: Avant-Garde, Avant Guerre, and the Language of Rupture* (Chicago: University of Chicago Press, 1986), 128; Vladimir Alexandrov, "Nabokov's Metaphysics of Artifice: Uspenskij's 'Fourth Dimension' and Evreinov's 'Theatrarch,'" in *Rossija/Russia* 6, nos. 1 and 2 (1988), ed. Vittorio Strada et al. (Venice: Marsilio Editori, 1989): 136–137; Debord, *Society of the Spectacle*, 126–127.

21. Proust likens memory to a train which speeds up and slows down to pick up passengers at succeeding stations (*Remembrance of Things Past*, trans. C. K. Scott Moncrieff and Terence Kilmartin, 3 vols. [New York: Random House, 1981], vol. 1, 693–694, and vol. 2, 118); Rudnitsky, "Krasota v p'esakh Chekhova," 78; Roger Shattuck, *Marcel Proust* (Princeton: Princeton University Press, 1974), 122; Vsevolod Meyerkhol'd, "Teatr (K istorii i tekhnike): Naturalistichesky teatr i teatr nastroeny," in *"Teatr," kniga o novom teatre*, 143–144; Henderson, *The Fourth Dimension*, 255 (Uspensky quote). Chekhov first had characters offer practical explanations for a strange sound (later employed in reference to the breaking string) in his short story "Happiness" (*Schast'e*, 1887).

22. Joseph Brodsky calls the *fin de siècle* a "chronological non-event" in "Catastrophes in the Air," in *Less Than One*, 285.

23. Kenneth N. Brostrom, "Andrei Bely," in *Handbook of Russian Litera-ture*, ed. Victor Terras (New Haven and London: Yale University Press, 1985), 45; Maria Szewcow, "Anatolij Efros Directs Chekhov's *The Cherry Orchard* and Gogol's *The Marriage*," *Theatre Quarterly* 26 (Summer 1977): 34 (on whiteness as abstraction and in Kandinsky); Mo-chulsky, *Andrei Bely*, 35; Mihajlo Mihajlov, *Russian Themes* (New York: Noonday, 1968), 271; Berdyaev, *The Origin of Russian Communism*, 92, 130–132; Andrey Bely, "*Vishnyovy sad*," in *Arabeski: Kniga statey* (Moscow: Musaget', 1911), 404. The next decade saw the revolutioniz-ing of sound and color symbolism. In Bely's novel *Petersburg*, which demonizes and politicizes foreign space from the perspectives of its con-servative (father) and radical (son) antagonists, the air itself sings "the October song of the year nineteen hundred and five." The attempt to identify a logical source of this sound as being "a factory whistle: a strike somewhere" gave a particular political cast to Chekhov's apolitical but revolutionary sound of the breaking string. That abstract sound, Lopa-khin theorized, was produced by a bucket falling down a distant mine-shaft. Bely's pseudonymous surname (his real name was Boris Bugayev), suggested to him by Vladimir Solovyov's younger brother Mikhail, means "white" in Russian. Mikhail Solovyov mockingly transformed Bely's original choice for a pseudonym, "Boris Burevoy," into "Bori-voy," "the wailing of Borya" (Borya is a familiar form of Boris). Bely claims to have chosen the pseudonym by which we know him for its sound value rather than for any possible symbolic meaning. See Georgette Donchin, "Introduction," in Andrey Bely, *Na rubezhe dvukh stolety* (Chicago: Russian Language Specialties/Bradda Books, 1966), 1–2; and Bely, *Pe-tersburg*, 486–487. Kazimir Malevich's painting *White on White* (1917), which depicted a tilted white square upon a white background, exposed the exhaustion or failure of history, predicted at the *fin de siècle*.

24. Deleuze, *Bergsonism*, 15–16, 24–25, 28–29, 35, 96 (Proust quote).

25. Vladimir Nabokov, "Ivan Turgenev," in *Lectures on Russian Literature*, 65–66; Konstantin Mochulsky, *Aleksandr Blok*, trans. Doris V. John-son (Detroit: Wayne State University Press, 1983), 24. In *Journey from St. Petersburg to Moscow* (*Puteshestvie iz Peterburga v Moskvu*, 1790; trans. Leo Weiner, ed. Roderick Page Thaler [Cambridge, Mass.: Harvard University Press, 1958], 41), which is often cited as the beginning of lib-eral reformist literature in Russia, A. N. Radishchev wrote: "Blessed is he who sometimes lives in the future, blessed is he who lives in dreams." Radishchev's promised sequel, *Journey from Moscow to St. Petersburg*, failed to materialize after Catherine the Great exiled the author to Siberia for the antimonarchical sentiments expressed in his original work.

26. Pipes, *Russia under the Old Regime*, 173, 189, 254.

27. Senelick, written communication, 8 January 1993; Herbert Blau, *Take Up the Bodies: Theater at the Vanishing Point* (Urbana: University of Il-linois Press, 1982), 81; David M. Bethea, *The Shape of Apocalypse in Modern Russian Fiction* (Princeton: Princeton University Press, 1989), 41; Terry Eagleton, "Bakhtin, Schopenhauer, Kundera," in *Bakhtin and Cultural Theory*, ed. Ken Hirschkop and David Shepherd (Manchester

and New York: Manchester University Press, 1989), 183. Konstantin Rudnitsky maintains that the "wandering symbol" of the Passerby does not represent anything but rather provokes a demonstration by Ranevskaya of her "careless generosity" ("Krasota v p'esakh Chekhova," 73). The Passerby requests thirty kopecks of her, but she gives him a gold piece. Caryl Emerson expressly linked Chekhov to Russian literature's antimessianic tradition in a public lecture at Brown University, 9 February 1993.

28. Dobrolyubov's coinage derives from his critical essay "What Is Oblomovism?" (*Chto takoe oblomovshchina?* 1859). The opening and closing scenes in *The Cherry Orchard* also parody actual ritualized landowner arrivals and departures through the filter of literary interpretations of these events that antedated Chekhov. Roosevelt writes: "Early accessible elements of court ritual such as celebratory fanfares, processions and parades served to theatricalize ordinary events such as trips to and from country estates. Witness the opening scenes of Turgenev's 'A Poor Gentleman,' in which an estate steward bustles around, freshening up the servants' livery and summoning the estate musicians to welcome an absentee owner. . . ." The memoirs of a Russian landowner named Gerakov, whom Roosevelt cites, depict a manor house and its immediate environs: a group of ecstatically happy peasants brought the traditional offering of bread and salt to the *barin* on his arrival and "ran alongside [the travelers'] carriage for twelve versts, singing and dancing 'as if it were a festival'" when the guests departed two days later ("Emerald Thrones and Living Statues," 13–14). In relation to the theme of oversleeping, Rudnitsky notes that in Chekhov's plays no one hurries to get anywhere, because no matter how quickly or slowly his characters move, they cannot change anything ("Krasota v p'esakh Chekhova," 77). Rudnitsky cites not only lateness but procrastination as illustrations of this theme. The doctors Dorn and Chebutykin are slow to relay news of Treplyov's and Tuzenbach's deaths in *The Seagull* and *Three Sisters*.

29. Lotman, *Universe of the Mind*, 185; Nahirny, *The Russian Intelligentsia*, 169; Henri Bergson, *Oeuvres* (Paris: PUF, 1970), xxiii, quoted in Ilya Prigogine and Serge Pahaut, "Rediscovering Time," in *Art and Time*, ed. Michel Baudson (London: Barbican Art Gallery, 1986), 14; Edith W. Clowes, "Social Discourse in the Moscow Art Theater," in *Between Tsar and People: Educated Society and the Quest for Public Identity in Late Imperial Russia*, ed. Edith W. Clowes, Samuel D. Kassow, and James L. West (Princeton: Princeton University Press, 1991), 278–279; Ju. M. Lotman and B. A. Uspenskij, "Myth—Name—Culture," in *Soviet Semiotics: An Anthology*, ed. and trans. Daniel P. Lucid (Baltimore: Johns Hopkins University Press, 1977), 237, 249 n. 11. "Dualism," writes Deleuze (after Bergson), "is . . . only a moment, which must lead to the reformation of a monism." Deleuze goes on to speak in terms that are consistent with the central image of this chapter, arrivals and departures framing the journey into fully integrated consciousness: "After we have followed the lines of divergence *beyond the turn* [in experience], these

ones must intersect again, not at the point from which we started, but rather at a virtual point, at a virtual image of the point of departure, which is itself located beyond the turn in experience; and which finally gives us the sufficient reason of the thing, the sufficient reason of the composite, the sufficient reason of the point of departure" (*Bergsonism*, 15–16, 24–25, 28–29, 35).

30. Robert Louis Jackson, "Chekhov's Cold Cave," in *Chekhov: A Collection of Critical Essays*, ed. Robert Louis Jackson (Englewood Cliffs: Prentice-Hall, 1967), 105.

31. *Letters of Anton Chekhov*, trans. Michael Henry Heim in collaboration with Simon Karlinsky (New York: Harper and Row, 1973), 375 (Tolstoy quote in n. 2); George L. Kline, "Foreword," in *Nietzsche in Russia*, ed. Rosenthal, xvi; Edith W. Clowes, "Friedrich Nietzsche and Russian Censorship," *Germano-Slavica* 4 (Spring 1983): 136–137.

32. Bert O. States, *Great Reckonings in Little Rooms: On the Phenomenology of Theater* (Berkeley and Los Angeles: University of California Press, 1985), 78; Kandinsky quoted in Leo Marx, *The Machine in the Garden: Technology and the Pastoral Ideal* (New York: Oxford University Press, 1964), 23.

33. The term "myth-historical design" comes from Richard Slotkin, *The Fatal Environment: The Myth of the Frontier in the Age of Industrialization 1800–1890* (New York: Atheneum, 1985), 20; Marx, *The Machine in the Garden*, 23, 71, 150, 159, 220–221.

34. The Russian text of the play which we now call *Platonov* after its protagonist has come down to us missing its original title page. See K. L. Rudnitsky, *Russkoe rezhissyorskoe iskusstvo 1898–1907* (Moscow: Nauka, 1989), 235, 238–239; Chekhov's letters to Olga Knipper and to Stanislavsky (23 November 1903) on the train matter appear in translation in Jean Benedetti, ed. and trans., *The Moscow Art Theatre Letters* (New York: Routledge, 1991), 185–186.

35. Bunin suggested that the intense beauty and proximity of the cherry orchard, Lopakhin's great rush to fell it, and the actual sound of the axe upon the trees at play's end were designed by Chekhov to be unbearable to his audience ("O Chekhove," in *Sobranie sochineny v devyati tomakh*, ed. A. S. Myasnikov, B. S. Ryurikov, A. T. Tvardovsky, 9 vols. [Moscow: Khudozhestvennaya literatura, 1967], vol. 9, 237–239). Together these effects help constitute the illusion that there was a precise moment in which change and loss were experienced on Russia's provincial estates. Bunin, who, as Rudnitsky suggests, probably knew more about country estates than Chekhov, was unsympathetic toward his aesthetes and aristocrats; Stanislavsky realized that the orchard symbolized the vanishing beauty, "the flowering white poetry of former gentry life" (Rudnitsky, "Krasota v p'esakh Chekhova," 72–73). Chekhov spoke the words "cherry orchard" to him like an invocation of something wondrous.

36. Laurence Senelick, *Anton Chekhov* (London: Macmillan, 1985), 127; the term "middle landscape" and its definition come from Marx, *The Machine in the Garden*, 23.

37. Hans Rogger, *Russia in the Age of Modernisation and Revolution 1881–1917* (New York: Longman, 1988), 95.

38. Nahirny, *The Russian Intelligentsia*, 157–158, 169; Rogger, *Russia in the Age of Modernisation and Revolution*, 91 (quote); Bethea, *The Shape of Apocalypse*, 58.

39. Nabokov employed the "moving skeleton" image in reference to *Anna Karenina*, in "Leo Tolstoy," 198; Filippo Tomasso Marinetti, "Technical Manifesto of Futurist Literature" (1912), in *Marinetti: Selected Writings*, ed. R. W. Flint (New York: n.p., 1971), 84–85; Boris Pasternak, *Doctor Zhivago*, quoted in Roger B. Anderson, "The Railroad in *Doctor Zhivago*," *Slavic and East European Journal* 31 (Winter 1987): 516.

40. Rogger, *Russia in the Age of Modernisation and Revolution*, 103.

41. Westwood, *History of Russian Railways*, 120, 138.

42. Ibid., 133; J. N. Westwood, with Holland Hunter, P. J. Ambler, A. Heywood, and F. M. Page, "The Railways," in *From Tsarism to the New Economic Policy*, ed. R. W. Davies (Ithaca: Cornell University Press, 1991), 176; Bethea, *The Shape of Apocalypse*, 276.

43. Brooks, *When Russia Learned to Read*, 15, 59.

44. Stites, *Revolutionary Dreams*, 146, 157, 162 ("mechanization"), 163; Erwin Panofsky, quoted in Marx, *The Machine in the Garden*, 26n. ("perfection"), also 205–206.

45. Simon Karlinsky, *Russian Drama from Its Beginnings to the Age of Pushkin* (Berkeley and Los Angeles: University of California Press), 286; de Custine, *Empire of the Czar*, 219; Aleksandr Ostrovsky, *Groza*, in *Polnoe sobranie sochineny*, ed. I. S. Grakov, 12 vols. (Moscow: Iskusstvo, 1973–1980), vol. 2, 236; Brooks, *When Russia Learned to Read*, 14–15; Gary R. Jahn, "The Image of the Railroad in *Anna Karenina*," *Slavic and East European Journal* 25 (Summer 1981): 1 (quote). Dying on the road, which possesses magical properties in a country so vast that even roads to somewhere seem to lead nowhere, is a romantic theme in Russian literary culture. Poetic eulogies over the corpses of Russia's martyred literary giants borne along the road home include Aleksandr Pushkin's *A Journey to Arzum* (*Puteshestvie v Arzume*, 1836) on Aleksandr Griboyedov and Mikhail Lermontov's *Death of Pushkin* (*Smert' Pushkina*, 1837).

46. Stephen L. Baehr, "The Troika and the Train: Dialogues between Tradition and Technology in Nineteenth-Century Russian Literature," in *Issues in Russian Literature before 1917: Proceedings from the III International Congress on Soviet and East European Studies*, ed. Douglas Clayton (Columbus: Slavica, forthcoming); Suzanne Massie, *Land of the Firebird* (New York: Simon and Schuster, 1980), 174, 376. Stites mentions Konstantin Leontyev's prerevolutionary "parable of a long black train blocking a religious procession," which became "a metaphor for modern evil" among the peasantry (*Revolutionary Dreams*, 108). Bethea notes that "in order to calm the fears of those who felt that this mechanical intrusion would destroy faith, Russian railway officials were compelled to hang icons in terminals, to build railroad lines to or near mon-

asteries, and, in the case of the Trans-Siberian Railway, to include a church car with bells and a cross on top" (*The Shape of Apocalypse*, 76 n. 33; see also 58, 76).

47. A. P. Chekhov, *Tri sestry*, in *Polnoe sobranie sochineny i pisem v tridtsati tomakh*, vols. 12–13, 128.

48. W. H. Bruford briefly discusses a number of short stories by Chekhov (in addition to "My Life"), in which the railroad appears or is mentioned, including "The Post," "Lights," "The New Villa," "The Cattle Dealers," "A Happy Ending," "Champagne," and "The Beauties" (*Chekhov and His Russia: A Sociological Study* [Hamden, Conn.: Archon Books, 1971; orig. pub. 1948 in Great Britain], 176–177). Bruford quotes a line from "Lights" (*Ogni*, 1888) in connection with the opening of the railway in Russia—"Things are beginning to move"—that recalls Chekhov's precursor in writing about coach and railway travel, Nikolay Leskov. Leskov's short stories "The Robber" (*Razboynik*, 1862) and "In a Coach" (*V tarantase*, 1862) followed the same group of travelers on the road, conveying the sense of movement on the journey. His short story "A Journey with a Nihilist" (*Puteshestvie s nigilistom*, originally entitled "Christmas Night in a Railway Carriage," *Rozhdestvenskaya noch' v vagone*, 1882) depicted a group of nervous travelers one year after the assassination of Tsar Aleksander II, who mistook a stubborn and unconventional figure on their train for a terrorist. He turned out to be a public prosecutor of terrorists. See Hugh McLean, *Nikolai Leskov: The Man and His Art* (Cambridge, Mass.: Harvard University Press, 1977), 101–103, 382–383.

49. *Letters of Anton Chekhov*, 328, 330 n. 3, 457 n. 9, 459; Laurence Senelick, "The Department of Missing Plays, Chekhov Division," *Theater* (Spring 1991): 33–38. As a boy in provincial Taganrog, Chekhov dreamed of travel. His adult journeys took him across Siberia (in prerailroad days) to the remote island of Sakhalin in 1890 to study and treat illness among the Russian (mostly convict) and native populations. Chekhov spoke of going to the Far East in a medical capacity, and his last unrealized play was set in the Far North. He died in Badenweiler, Germany.

50. Catriona Kelly, *Petrushka: The Russian Carnival Puppet Theatre* (New York: Cambridge University Press, 1990), 43; Bethea, *The Shape of Apocalypse*, 75.

51. Westwood, *History of Russian Railways*, 120, 138; Stites, *Revolutionary Dreams*, 49; Alexander Solzhenitsyn, *Lenin in Zurich*, trans. H. T. Willetts (New York: Farrar, Straus and Giroux, 1976), 31–32, 233; Joseph Brodsky, "A Guide to a Renamed City," in *Less Than One*, 87. Lenin secretly visited St. Petersburg for three months in 1905. In 1905, the year that Einstein published the Special Theory of Relativity and Japan defeated Russia in the battles of Mukden and the Trushima Straits, the Bolsheviks first infiltrated the recently formed All-Russian Railway Union (founded April 1905), leading to a general railway strike (October 1905) in support of the first Russian revolution.

52. The character Nils in Gorky's first play, *The Petty Bourgeoisie* (*Mesh-chane*, 1902), is a railway worker. My thanks to Laurence Senelick for reminding me of this fact. Among the many images of heroic trains and railroad workers as well as revolutionary heroes conveyed in and martyrs born on trains in later Russian fiction (see, for example, Vsevolod Ivanov's play *Armored Train 14-69, Bronepoezd 14-69*, 1922), N. Nikitin's story "Night" (*Noch'*, 1923) stands out for its symbolic depiction of Russia's divided national character. In this tale, James H. Billington notes, "the Civil War is portrayed as a nocturnal collision between two armored trains, red and white, moving from East and West to a fated collision in the heart of Russia" (*The Icon and the Axe*, 507).

53. Bruford, *Chekhov and His Russia*, 177–178; Vladimir Propp, *Morphology of the Folktale*, trans. Laurence Scott, ed. Louis A. Wagner (Austin: University of Texas Press, 1986), 57, 60; Laurence Senelick, verbal communication regarding Nina in *The Seagull*. In his short stories (and in his one-act play *On the Main Road*), Chekhov paid careful attention to the sort of temporary lodgings taken by travelers. For example, he noted that, given the often unsanitary conditions of these places, it was customary for Russian travelers to carry their own bedding with them. As we shall see in chapter 5 of this study, sudden and anonymous arrivals of characters, prefigured but visibly changed in dream or premonition, occur in Griboyedov's stage comedy *Woe from Wit* (*Gore ot uma*, 1824) and in Gogol's *The Inspector General*. The protagonists in these plays depart just as precipitously via horse-drawn carriage or troika. The practice of traveling incognito, which Lenin accomplished through the use of falsified documents and doctored photographs, was reversed by Stalin, who inscribed himself over the semieffaced image of Lenin beginning in the early 1920s.

54. Ivan Turgenev, *Fathers and Sons*, trans. George Reavey (New York: New American Library, 1961), 206–207.

55. I am grateful to Joseph Donohue for providing me with documentary material on *Bradshaw's Guide*; Proust, *Remembrance of Things Past*, vol. 2, 853.

56. Stites, *Revolutionary Dreams*, 246; the Pasternak quotes are from the title poem of *My Sister, Life* (*Sestra moya zhizn'*, 1922), quoted in Bethea, *The Shape of Apocalypse*, 236 ("crisis"), 237, 246 ("grander").

57. Chekhov, *Vishnyovy sad*, in *Polnoe sobranie sochineny i pisem*, vols. 12–13, 312; Stites, *Revolutionary Dreams*, 157 (on Taylor), 163 (on *seychas*). Taylor conducted time-motion efficiency studies of American industrial workers in the 1910s. Waiting is a particularly significant temporal condition in Russian history, variously signifying messianic hope, exile, and imprisonment. Curiously, waiting has often encouraged productivity in Russia. Chernyshevsky wrote the revolutionary primer *What Is to Be Done?* (*Chto delat'?* 1863) in prison, and Lenin wrote his revolutionary manifesto *What Is to Be Done?* (1902), titled in homage to Chernyshevsky's work, in exile. While Chernyshevsky's novel was conceived in a condition of enforced waiting, the title *What Is to Be Done?*

dispels the Hamletism of the Russian intelligentsia, its waiting to act, and its equivocation. The title in Russian is active, meaning literally *What to Do?* It asks not whether to act (that is, "To be or not to be") but how.

58. Rudnitsky writes that Lopakhin and Ranevskaya speak in different languages, with no interpreter to translate for them. Lopakhin is concerned with practicality, Ranevskaya with beauty and *poshlost'* ("Krasota v p'esakh Chekhova," 75). Rudnitsky argues that Chekhov affirms aesthetic criteria—that is, those of Ranevskaya and Gayev—as moral values.

59. Iurii M. Lotman, "The Decembrist in Daily Life (Everyday Behavior as a Historical-Psychological Category)," trans. Andrea Beesing, in *The Semiotics of Russian Cultural History*, ed. Nakhimovsky and Nakhimovsky, 110 (the quote concerning acts "accomplished in intent" originally described General Ivolgin in Dostoyevsky's novel *The Idiot* [*Idiot*, 1868]); Peace, *Chekhov*, 86 (on the Prozorov surname and on "fate"); V. V. Gippius, *Gogol*, ed. and trans. Robert A. Maguire (Durham: Duke University Press, 1989), 85 (Gippius orignally characterized the central action of Gogol's work as "the removal of the desired object to a great distance"; I find that this works just as well as a description of Chekhov's method); Renato Poggioli, *The Theory of the Avant-Garde*, trans. Gerald Fitzgerald (Cambridge, Mass.: Harvard University Press), 188.

60. Bethea, *The Shape of Apocalypse*, 58 ("ensemble" and "cut off"); Jonathan Kalb, *Beckett in Performance* (Cambridge: Cambridge University Press, 1989), 262n.24 ("coercive"). Richard Pipes has dispelled the myth that Lenin's train, provided him by the German general staff, was "sealed," that is, subject to neither search nor inspection (*The Russian Revolution*, 392). On directional time, see A. S. Eddington, *The Nature of the Physical World* (London: Macmillan, 1955), 86.

61. Apollinaire ("Absolute") quoted in Karl, *Modern and Modernism*, 300; Peace, *Chekhov*, 156; Bethea, *The Shape of Apocalypse*, 36 ("culture").

62. Billington, *Fire in the Minds of Men*, 450, 460; Simon Dreyden, *V zritel'nom zale — Vladimir Il'ich*, 2 vols. (Moscow: Iskusstvo, 1986), vol. 1, 64, 69 ("truth"), 70, 229 ("*poshlost'*"), 236, 241, 257; Jean Benedetti, *Stanislavski: A Biography* (New York: Routledge, 1988), 230; Senelick, written communication, 8 January 1993. For additional information on the opinions of Lenin the audience member/government leader on the theatre and drama of his day, see *Lenin i teatr: Bibliografiya* (bibliography of approximately 330 books and articles from journals and newspapers, 1933–1969), ed. Z. I. Zernitskaya, G. Kh. Dzasokhova, B. S. Meshcheryakova, N. D. Samoylova, and N. V. Shashkova (Moscow: n.p., 1969); *Lenin, Revolyutsiya, teatr: Dokumenty i vospominaniya* (about 100 items drawn from books, articles, and archival materials, 1919–1969), ed. A. Yufit (Leningrad: Iskusstvo, 1970); *V. I. Lenin i A. V. Lunacharsky: Perepiska, doklady, dokumenty* (about 100 archival documents and newspaper articles, 1919–1921), ed. V. D. Zel'dovich and R. A. Lavrov (Moscow: Nauka, 1971); B. Yakovlev, *Lenin i dramaturgiya* (about 70 pieces by Lenin on dramaturgy) (Moscow: Teatr, 1959); B. Yakovlev, *Lenin i sovetsky teatr* (about 20 of Lenin's little-known pronouncements on

art, theatre, and drama) (Moscow: Teatr, 1960); B. Yakovlev, *Lenin chitaet . . . Knigi po dramaturgii i teatru v lichnoy biblioteke Il'icha* (a bibliographic survey of the holdings on Soviet, Russian, and foreign drama, Soviet theatre, and theatre criticism, 1918–1922, in Lenin's personal library) (Moscow: Teatr, 1962).

63. Blok quoted in Stites, *Revolutionary Dreams*, 73.

64. Aleksandr Blok, "On the Railway" (*Na zheleznoy doroge*, n.d.), quoted in Avril Pyman, "Introduction," in *Alexander Blok: Selected Poems*, ed. Avril Pyman (New York: Pergamon Press, 1972), 43. Brian Boyd writes that Nabokov's first novel, *Mary* (*Mashen'ka*, MS. 1925, English translation 1970), treats exile as if it "were a railroad, a mere locus of movement, or at best a station where people only kill time between a place they remember coming from and a destination they do not know" (*Vladimir Nabokov*, 246).

65. Brodsky, "A Guide to a Renamed City," 84–85; Solzhenitsyn, *Lenin in Zurich*, 7, 19, 64; Billington, *Fire in the Minds of Men*, 444, 459. While *put'* is "footpath" and *doroga* a road for transport in Russian, *put'* was also used by the Bolsheviks to designate their ideological path to the future. It is in this sense that I am using the word.

66. Billington, *The Icon and the Axe*, 383; Westwood, *History of Russian Railways*, 7 (Lenin quote), 57, 175; Edmund Wilson, *To the Finland Station: A Study in the Writing and Acting of History* (New York: Farrar, Straus and Giroux, 1973), 537.

67. Brodsky, "A Guide to a Renamed City," 69, 85; David M. Bethea, "Remarks on the Horse as a Space-Time Image," in *Cultural Mythologies of Russian Modernism: From the Golden Age to the Silver Age*, ed. Boris Gasparov, Robert P. Hughes, and Irina Paperno (Berkeley and Los Angeles: University of California Press, 1992), 17–18, 123–124 n. 12.

2. ARTISTS AND MODELS

1. Blok quoted in Viktor Zhirmunsky, "Excerpts from *The Poetry of Alexander Blok*" (1921), in *Blok: An Anthology of Essays and Memoirs*, ed. and trans. Lucy Vogel (Ann Arbor: Ardis, 1982), 148; Michael Chekhov quoted in Vladislav Ivanov, "MKhAT vtoroy v rabote nad 'Gamletom': Gamlet—Mikhail Chekhov," in *Shekspirovskie chteniya*, ed. A. Anikst (Moscow: Nauka, 1987), 234.

2. Bely, *Petersburg* 292 (quote); Hill, "Introduction," in Blok, *The Spirit of Music*, 5; Irina Paperno, "Pushkin v zhizni cheloveka Serebryanogo veka," in *Cultural Mythologies of Russian Modernism*, ed. Gasparov, Hughes, and Paperno, 48 n. 53. In his essay "The Nineteenth Century," Mandelstam wrote that "in the veins of our century flows the heavy blood of extremely distant monumental cultures, perhaps Egyptian and Assyrian" (O. E. Mandel'stam, *Sobranie sochineny*, 2nd ed., 3 vols. [New York: Inter-Language Literary Associates, 1971], vol. 2, 9–10, 283). The statement is quoted in Leslie O'Bell, *Pushkin's Egyptian Nights: The Biography of a Work* (Ann Arbor: Ardis, 1984), 126. For further compari-

sons between Egypt, specifically Alexandria, and St. Petersburg, see
Vyacheslav Ivanov, *Po zvyozdam: Stat'i i aforizmy* (St. Petersburg:
Izdatel'stvo Ory, 1909), 238; Andrey Bely, *Simvolizm* (Moscow: Musaget', 1910), 50; and the works of Mikhail Kuzmin. For more data
concerning attempts by academics and intellectuals to channel antique
languages and scholarship directly into modern Russian cultural consciousness, see Marinus A. Wes, *Classics in Russia: Between Two Bronze
Horsemen*, trans. Anthony P. Runia (Leiden: E. J. Brill, 1993).

3. Mandelstam's allusion to the Petersburg sphinxes as a meeting place is
from his story "The Egyptian Stamp," in Mandel'stam, *Sobranie sochineny*, vol. 2, 9–10, 283, cited in O'Bell, *Pushkin's Egyptian Nights*,
126. Sphinx references in Russian symbolist literature include Vyacheslav Ivanov, "Sphinxes over the Neva" (*Sfinksy nad Nevoy*, 1911) and
Blok's "The Scythians" (*Skify*, 1918). For another treatment of the period's Apollonian-Dionysian cultural theme, see Fyodor Sologub's novel
The Petty Demon (*Melky bes*, 1907), which deals specifically with murder, madness, mysticism, and female eroticism in a provincial Russian
town. See also Clowes, "Friedrich Nietzsche and Russian Censorship,"
136–137; and *Nietzsche in Russia*, ed. Rosenthal.

4. Bely's statement regarding the "meeting of Greece and Christ" is quoted
(from an uncredited source) in Paperno, "Pushkin," 39–40. Ivanov's
"The Hellenic Religion of the Suffering God" is discussed in West, *Russian Symbolism*, 76–78, 87; and in Olga Matich, "Androgyny and the
Russian Silver Age," *Pacific Coast Philology* 14 (October 1979): 43.

5. The sphinx's lion body and human head was male in ancient Egypt and
female in ancient Greece. The sphinx's command was used by Villiers de
l'Isle-Adam as an epigraph to the chapter "Ambiguous Pleasantries"
(book 2) in his novel *Tomorrow's Eve* (*L'Eve future*, 1886), trans. Robert
Martin Adams (Urbana: University of Illinois Press, 1982), 78. Adams
calls the statement a "mythological commonplace" (220).

6. Aleksandr Blok, "Dnevnik 1901–1902 goda" (entry for 27 December
1901), in Aleksandr Blok, *Sobranie sochineny v vos'mi tomakh*, vol. 7,
Avtobiografiya 1915, Dnevniki 1901–1921, ed. V. N. Orlov, A. A. Surkov, and K. I. Chukovsky (Moscow-Leningrad: Gosudarstvennoe izdatel'stvo khudozhestvennoy literatury, 1963), 19. Blok's reference to the
"two-facedness" of his soul is from a poem that he wrote in 1902, quoted
in L. M. Kipnis, "O liricheskom geroe dramaticheskoy trilogi Aleksandra
Bloka," in *Russky teatr i dramaturgiya nachala XX veka: Sbornik nauchnykh trudov*, ed. A. Ya. Al'tshuller, V. V. Smirnov, A. A. Ninov, and
Yu. A. Smirnov-Nesvitsky (Leningrad: LGITMiK, 1984), 52. Blok referred to himself as "a corpse . . . among people" in a poem from his third
book of verse, quoted in Kornei Chukovsky, "Excerpts from *A. A. Blok:
The Man*," in *Blok: Essays and Memoirs*, ed. Vogel, 188 n. 13. Blok
quoted Heine in his essay "Ironiya," in *Sobranie sochineny v vos'mi tomakh*, vol. 5, *Proza 1903–1917*, ed. V. N. Orlov, A. A. Surkov, and K. I.
Chukovsky (Moscow-Leningrad: Gosudarstvennoe izdatel'stvo khudozhestvennoy literatury, 1962), 349.

7. Kipnis, "O liricheskom geroe," 45–46 (Blok quote); Harold Shukman,

Notes
to Pages
38–39

ed., *The Blackwell Encyclopedia of the Russian Revolution* (New York: Basil Blackwell, 1988), 104 (quotes). For added information on the 1905 revolution, see Pipes, *The Russian Revolution*, 3–51; and Riasanovsky, *A History of Russia*, 404–421. Riasanovsky characterized Father Gapon as an "adventurer" (407).

8. Fortunetellers advertising in Petersburg newspapers at this time lured prospective customers with the invitation "Learn your fate!" (Konstantin Rudnitsky, *Meyerhold the Director*, trans. George Petrov, ed. Sydney Schultze [Ann Arbor: Ardis, 1981, 235]).

9. Aleksandr Blok, "Dramatichesky teatr V. F. Kommissarzhevskoy (Pis'mo iz Peterburga)" (1906), in *Sobranie sochineny v vos'mi tomakh*, vol. 5, 98 (quote).

10. For discussions in English of Solovyov and the Divine Sophia, see, for example, Mochulsky, *Aleksandr Blok*, 43–44 (quotes), 166; Billington, *The Icon and the Axe*, 465–468; Samuel D. Cioran, "Vladimir Solovyov and the Divine Feminine," *Russian Literature Triquarterly* 4 (Fall 1972): 218–239; *Russian Philosophy*, ed. Edie, Scanlan, and Zeldin, vol. 3, 55, 58–60; Mochulsky, *Andrei Bely*, 29, 35; Kipnis, "O liricheskom geroe," 45–46, 48–49; Hoffmann, "Scythian Theory and Literature," 152–153; Matich, "Androgyny and the Russian Silver Age," 42–50; Olga Matich, "Androgyny and the Russian Religious Renaissance," in *Western Philosophical Systems in Russian Literature: A Collection of Critical Studies*, ed. Anthony M. Mlikotin (Los Angeles: University of Southern California Press, 1979), 165, 167–170, 173. Dionysus quote in Charlotte Rosenthal and Helene Foley, "Symbolic Patterning in Sologub's *The Petty Demon*," in Fyodor Sologub, *The Petty Demon*, trans. S. D. Cioran, ed. Murl Barker (Ann Arbor: Ardis, 1983), 326, 331 n. 23. On Solovyov's humanism, see also Berdyaev, *The Russian Idea*, 109.

11. Blok, "The Scythians," in *The Twelve and Other Poems*, trans. Jon Stallworthy and Peter France (New York: Oxford University Press, 1970), 162. In *Ashes* (1909), Bely personified (provincial) Russia as "a monstrous feminine figure, miserable and wicked, with 'yellow eyes' made by the lamps of her 'crazy taverns.'" In a statement echoing the theme of chapter 1 of the present study, Bely tells the Russian people: "Enough, don't wait, don't hope . . . disappear into space, disappear." In this same period, Blok likened Gogol to pregnant Mother Russia giving birth to "modern spiritual monstrosity," only to be ensnared by his/her creation (Poggioli, *The Poets of Russia*, 60, 155 [Bely quote], 190; Aleksandr Blok, "Ditya Gogolya," in *Sobranie sochineny v vos'mi tomakh*, ed. V. N. Orlov, A. A. Surkov, and K. I. Chukovsky, vol. 6, *Proza 1918–1921*, ed. D. Maksimov and G. Shabel'skaya [Moscow-Leningrad: Gosudarstvennoe izdatel'stvo khudozhestvennoy literatury, 1962], 377–379; Billington, *The Icon and the Axe*, 32). Barbara Heldt recently stated that "motherhood has overwhelmingly been used in modern Russian literature to generate images of patriarchal value, or as an icon to symbolize Russia" ("Motherhood in a Cold Climate: The Poetry and Career of Mariia Shkapskaia," *Russian Review* 51 [April 1992], 160–161). She calls for

a more meaningful construction of "a theory of Russian motherhood and female sexuality itself" to offset the "timelessly static" image of the Mother in Russian writing. This issue will perhaps be addressed in the forthcoming *Sexuality and the Body in Russian Culture*, ed. Jane Costlow, Stephanie Sandler, and Judith Vowles (Stanford University Press, forthcoming). On a related subject, see Barbara Heldt, "Men Who Give Birth: A Feminist Perspective on Russian Literature," in *Discontinuous Discourse in Modern Russian Literature*, ed. Catriona Kelly, Michael Makin, and David Shepherd (New York: St. Martin's Press, 1989), 157–168.

12. "Zhizn' i tvorchestvo," in M. Yu. Lermontov, *Izbrannye proizvedeniya*, ed. N. A. Chechulina (Leningrad: Lenizdat, 1968), 6; D. J. Richards, "Introduction," in M. Yu. Lermontov, *Geroy nashego vremeni* (Letchwirth, U.K.: Bradda, 1973), 5; Aleksandr Pushkin, epigraph to "The Queen of Spades" (*Pikovaya dama*, 1833), quoted in O'Bell, *Pushkin's Egyptian Nights*, 59; Bram Dijkstra, *Idols of Perversity: Fantasies of Feminine Evil in Fin-de-siècle Culture* (New York: Oxford University Press, 1986), 53 ("identity"); Barbara Heldt, *Terrible Perfection: Women and Russian Literature* (Bloomington and Indianapolis: Indiana University Press, 1987), 36 ("silent"). Lermontov's demonic protagonist and authorial double Arbenin murders his wife Nina with poisoned ice cream not for her sin, which is imaginary, but for his own sin of misplaced idealism, which is real. Prior to her death, Nina's reputation is impugned by the Baroness, whose aggressive male sensibility, Lermontov suggests, does not quite conceal her awareness of female self-victimization. The Baroness's destruction of another woman's good name and indirectly of the woman herself from behind the safety of a mask at a costume ball is a clandestine murder of her own feminine identity, which she despises for its social and moral vulnerability. This scenario reflects Lermontov's attraction to the romantic themes of tragic male weakness, compensatory female self-loathing, and perfidious feminine complicity in the social order. In addition to *Othello* and perhaps the example of Pushkin's fate at the hands of what the poet called Russian high society's "secret ill-will" (*taynaya nedobrozhelatel'nost'*), Lermontov borrowed aspects of the plot and theme of his play from two sources. In *Hamlet*, Ophelia is guilty by association in the Prince's mind with her father Polonius, the state spy. In *The Misanthrope*, Célimène's compliance with social norms and courting of social favor are to Alceste evidence of her moral ambiguity and disloyalty to him. Lermontov, who was educated in Greek, Latin, English, French, and German, would have read Shakespeare in English and Molière in French. He could also read Molière's play through the creative filter of Griboyedov's classic comedy *Woe from Wit*, which adapted *The Misanthrope* to a Russian setting.

13. Laura Engelstein, *The Keys to Happiness: Sex and the Search for Modernity in Fin-de-Siècle Russia* (Ithaca: Cornell University Press, 1992), 392 n. 75; Richard Ellmann, *Oscar Wilde* (New York: Alfred A. Knopf, 1988), 429 ("fantasized"). In her diary *Contes d'amour*, Zinaida Gip-

pius, a leading Silver Age poet and androgyne, who sometimes wore male attire, wrote, "In my thoughts, in my desires, my spirit—I am more a man; in my body—I am more a woman" (Temira Pachmuss, *Zinaida Hippius: An Intellectual Profile* [Carbondale: Southern Illinois University Press, 1971], 92).

14. Bernice Glatzer Rosenthal, "Introduction," in *Nietzsche in Russia*, 25–26, 41 ("perfect"); O'Bell, *Pushkin's Egyptian Nights*, 34.

15. O'Bell, *Pushkin's Egyptian Nights*, 3, 33, 56, 67 n. 9, 100, 102, 128 (Blok quotes), 129, 133 n.28 (Dostoyevsky quote); Paperno, "Pushkin," 25–26, 36–39 (Bryusov quote on 37); Matich, "Dialectics of Cultural Return: Zinaida Gippius' Personal Myth," in *Cultural Mythologies of Russian Modernism*, ed. Gasparov, Hughes, and Paperno, 53–54, 56, 67–68 n. 9; Aleksandr Blok, "O sovremennom sostoyanii russkogo simvolizma," in *Sobranie sochineny v vos'mi tomakh*, vol. 5, 425–436; West, *Russian Symbolism*, 132–133, 142.

16. For the Pandora interpretation of *Terror Antiquas*, see Christine Lahti, "Mayakovsky's Dithyrambs" (Ph.D. diss., Yale University, December 1991), 193. For the Aphrodite interpretation of the same painting, see John E. Bowlt, *The Silver Age: Russian Art of the Early Twentieth Century and the "World of Art" Group* (Newtonville: Oriental Research Partners, 1982), 229.

17. Poggioli links the decadent theme in Silver Age Russian literature to a series of paradoxes: decay and rebirth, civilization and barbarism, old and new, love and sin, the sacred and the profane, allegiance to God and to Satan. More specific to my discussion of male self-victimization through the female other is Poggioli's remark that "the Decadent Eros is primarily the Eros of senility; its sensuality, vicarious and vicious, constantly wavers between perversion and impotence, or between sadism and masochism." He adds that "the Eros of Decadence is also an Eros of exhaustion and fatigue, a fever of the brain leading to a spiritualized kind of sensualism" (*The Poets of Russia*, 80–86 [quotes on 86]). Decadent literary works of the period in which love triangles and other unsatisfactory sexual relationships ended in murder or suicide included *Sanin*, Zinovyeva-Annibal's lesbian sketch "Thirty-Three Abominations" (*Tridtsat'-tri uroda*, 1907) and Anastasiya Verbitskaya's six-volume romantic novel *Keys to Happiness* (*Klyuchi schast'ya*, 1908–1913), which Laura Engelstein discusses in her recent book of the same name. Engelstein lists sample offerings of St. Petersburg popular theatres in 1911 that highlighted sexual themes, including dramatizations of Lev Tolstoy's novella *The Kreutzer Sonata* (originally published in 1891) and Artsybashev's *Sanin* (retitled *How to Live*), as well as such provocative titles as *The Free Love League, Sinful Night, The Bacchante — Vampire of Love*, and *Living Goods*, which had white slavery as its subject (*The Keys to Happiness*, 372–376, 383, 392, 398, 418). On Verbitskaya's novels, see Brooks, *When Russia Learned to Read*, 153–154. See also Temira Pachmuss, "Women Writers in Russian Decadence," in *Journal of Contemporary History* 17 (1982): 110–112, 117, 121, 126.

18. Charles S. Mayer, "Ida Rubinstein: A Twentieth-Century Cleopatra,"

Dance Research Journal (Russian Issue) 20/2 (Winter 1989): 33 (Jean Cocteau quoted on Rubinstein's eyes, cheeks, and mouth), 36 ("lips").

19. Herod quote from Nikolay Yevreinov, *Pro Scena Sua* (Petrograd: Prometey, 1914) in *Kalmakoff: L'Ange de l'Abîme 1873–1955 et les peintres du Mir Iskousstva*, ed. Jean-Hugues Piettre (Paris: Musée-galerie de la Seita, 1986), 23.

20. Yevreinov's *The Spanish Dancer* (*Plyashushchaya ispanka*), inscribed by the artist, was originally published in the journal *Town and Country* (*Stolitsa i usad'ba*) 59 (1 June 1916). For a discussion of mythic female deities in Russian folklore, including the *rozhanitsy* or "goddesses of fate," see Hubbs, *Mother Russia*, 15–16, 18, 27, 30, 32–33; the Pushkin "Rusalka" reference is from Senelick, *Anton Chekhov*, 86; Linda J. Ivanits, "The Grotesque in Fyodor Sologub's Novel *The Petty Demon*," in Sologub, *The Petty Demon*, 316 ("unclean").

21. Georges Martin du Nord, "Kalmakoff, décorateur de théâtre," in *Kalmakoff*, 19; Laurence Senelick, "Salome in Russia," *Nineteenth Century Theatre Research* 12 (1984): 93–94; Sheila Stowell, "Re[pre]senting Eroticism: The Tyranny of Fashion in Feminist Plays of the Edwardian Age," *Theatre History Studies* 11 (1991), 53; Dijkstra, *Idols of Perversity*, 243–249; Spencer Golub, *Evreinov: The Theatre of Paradox and Transformation* (Ann Arbor: UMI Research Press, 1984), 9; Oscar Wilde, "The Sphinx," in *Complete Works of Oscar Wilde* (London and Glasgow: Collins, 1973), 841 (all quotes from Wilde's works are from this edition). Kalmakov's painting *Salomé Sphinge* is reproduced in *Kalmakoff*, 53. For a discussion of woman as the reflected image of male self-mirroring, see Luce Irigaray, *Speculum of the Other Woman* (Ithaca: Cornell University Press, 1985), 22.

22. For other references to "silent, framed and immobile" feminine beauty, associated with moon, mirror, and reflecting pool imagery, see Gail Finney, *Women in Modern Drama: Freud, Feminism and European Theater at the Turn of the Century* (Ithaca: Cornell University Press, 1989), 87–95. In her elegy on the death of Blok (August 1921), Anna Akhmatova called her fellow poet "our sun" but pictured him in a clearly lunar "silver coffin," returning him to his feminine source. This image and the moon's linkage to the Russian Silver Age are taken from Paperno, "Pushkin," 40.

23. Moreau's *Salome* paintings are reproduced and discussed in Dijkstra, *Idols of Perversity*, 381–382; J.-K. Huysmans, *Against Nature*, trans. Robert Baldick (New York: Penguin Books, 1959), 68 (quotes).

24. Daniel Gerould, "Russian Symbolist Drama and the Visual Arts," in *Newsnotes on Soviet and East European Drama and Theater* 1 (March 1984): 15; Merezhkovsky quoted in Kalbouss, *The Plays of the Russian Symbolists*, 7.

25. Dijkstra, *Idols of Perversity*, 384; Konstantin Bal'mont, "O lyubvi" (1908), in *Russky Eros, ili filosofiya lyubvi v Rossii*, ed. V. P. Shestakov (Moscow: Progress, 1991), 99.

26. Mayer, "Ida Rubinstein," 34–35 ("curveless," "disturbed"), 37, 39 ("slender," "long"), 47 ("body"). On the fetishized female corpse of Na-

stasya Filippovna in Dostoyevsky's *The Idiot,* see Heldt, *Terrible Perfection,* 36. Brooks's *Le Trajet* is reproduced and discussed in Dijkstra, *Idols of Perversity,* 52–53. Kalmakov's *Autoportrait en Adonis* is in *Kalmakoff,* 26. Radakov's matchstick Rubinstein is reproduced in Bowlt, *The Silver Age,* 115.

27. K. S. Stanislavsky, *Sobranie sochineny v vos'mi tomakh,* ed. M. N. Kedrov, 8 vols. (Moscow: Iskusstvo, 1954), vol. 1, 444–445, quoted in Rudnitsky, *Meyerhold the Director,* 196. On the subject of Salome and especially the theme of veiling and unveiling, see Elaine Showalter, *Sexual Anarchy: Gender and Culture at the Fin de Siècle* (New York: Penguin Books, 1990), 159–161. Katherine Worth suggests that Salome's unveiling might symbolize the revelation not only of the naked body but of "the soul or innermost being," especially that of the artist (*Oscar Wilde* [New York: Grove Press, 1983], 66, quoted by Showalter, 151). Ida Rubinstein appeared as the following androgynes and *neznakomki* in theatrical productions: St. Sébastien (in d'Annunzio's *Le martyr de St. Sébastien,* Paris, 22 May 1911, which decadently fetishized the actress's boyishly thin bare legs—Proust thought them "sublime"); the slave girl Pisanella (in d'Annunzio's *La Pisanelle, ou La mort parfumée,* Paris, 1913); Salome (in *The Dance of the Seven Veils,* St. Petersburg, 3 November and 20 December 1908, and in *La tragédie de Salomé,* Paris, 13 June 1912); Zobeida (in *Schéhérazade,* Paris, 4 June 1910); Helen of Troy (in Emile Verhaeren's *Hélène de Sparte,* Paris, 4 May 1912); Cleopatra (in the Ballets Russes's *Cléopâtre,* Paris, 2 June 1909). For a good overview of Rubinstein's stage work, see Mayer, "Ida Rubinstein," 33–51. See also Alexander Schowaloff, *Leon Bakst: The Theatre Art* (London: Sotheby's Publications, 1991), 57, 149, 161, 166, 192, 225. The most complete study in English of Rubinstein's life and work is Michael de Cossart, *Ida Rubinstein (1885–1960): A Theatrical Life* (Liverpool: Liverpool University Press, 1987). For information on the cult of "living statuary," see Roosevelt, "Emerald Thrones and Living Statues," 14; Senelick, "The Erotic Bondage of Serf Theatre," 30; Lahti, "Mayakovsky's Dithyrambs," 164–165, 172; Viktor Shklovsky, "O Mayakovskom," in *Sobranie sochineny* (Moscow: Khudozhestvennaya literatura, 1974), vol. 3, 41–42; Golub, *Evreinov,* 227–235.

28. Mayer, "Ida Rubinstein," 34.

29. Aleksandr Blok, "Vera Fyodorovna Kommissarzhevskaya" (11 February 1910), and "Pamyati V. F. Kommissarzhevskoy" (March 1910), in *Sobranie sochineny,* vol. 5, *Proza 1903–1917,* 415, 418, 419–420.

30. Ivanits, "The Grotesque in Fyodor Sologub's Novel *The Petty Demon,*" 316. The Tonya Zhivago reference is adapted from Heldt, *Terrible Perfection,* 148.

31. The staging of Nina as passive object was corrected in Aleksandr Tairov's 1944 production of *The Seagull*: Nina, played by the director's wife Alisa Koonen, appeared as a self-confident, talented actress and a natural woman, who harmonized matter and spirit and whose strength signified a new era of idealized positive heroes and heroines. Nina was freed by Tairov from the "bourgeois optics" of Treplyov's and the Moscow Art

Theatre's pictorial space into a nonpictorial staged concert (*spektakl'-kontsert*) format. Nina's "I have faith" proclamation in her penultimate speech was addressed not only to Treplyov but to the auditorium, which she directly approached in an attitude that one critic compared (ironically) to that of a Rodin sculpture. See K. L. Rudnitsky, "Tvorchesky put' Tairova," in *Rezhissyorskoe iskusstvo A. Ya. Tairova (K 100-letiyu dnya rozhdeniya)*, ed. K. L. Rudnitsky, (Moscow: Vserossyskoe teatral'noe obshchestvo, 1987), 38–39; Yury Golovashenko, *Rezhissyorskoe iskusstvo Tairova* (Moscow: Iskusstvo, 1970), 52, 89.

32. Rudnitsky, *Russkoe rezhissyorskoe iskusstvo*, 285–288 ("dictatorship"), 334 (on Hedda Gabler); A. Blok, "Dramatichesky teatr V. F. Kommissarzhevskoy (Pis'mo iz Peterburga)," in *Sobranie sochineny*, vol. 5, 415, 418; Robert Leach, *Vsevolod Meyerhold* (New York: Cambridge University Press, 1989), 57, 142.

33. Rudnitsky, *Russkoe rehissyorskoe iskusstvo*, 149, 285–288, 292, 297, 300, 331–334; K. Rudnitsky, "V teatre na ofitserskoy," in *Tvorcheskoe nasledie V. E. Meyerkhol'da*, ed. L. D. Vendrovskaya and A. V. Fevral'sky (Moscow: VTO, 1978), 146, 174 ("abode"); M. V. Alpatov and E. A. Gunst, *Nikolay Nikolayevich Sapunov* (Moscow: Iskusstvo, 1965), 23; Osip Mandelstam, "Shum vremeni," in *Vremya* (Leningrad: n.p., 1925), 70. The "beastliness" of the bourgeois was in part defined by their stubborn refusal or inability to see themselves as being a problem. The absurdly discordant polka which Meyerhold added to the ball scene in his 1907 staging of Leonid Andreyev's *The Life of Man (Zhizn' cheloveka*, 1906), for example, was turned into a popular standard by the play's bourgeois audiences.

34. On Hoffmann in Russia, see Norman W. Ingham, *E. T. A. Hoffmann's Reception in Russia* (Würzburg: Jul-Verlag, 1974); and Charles E. Passage, *The Russian Hoffmannists* (The Hague: Mouton, 1963). The caricatures of Kommissarzhevskaya and Meyerhold from 1907 to which I allude, executed by Aleksandr Lyubimov, Micco, Moisey Slepyan, and Re-mi, are reprinted and discussed in Yevgeny Binevich, "Rasskaz v karikaturakh o V. E. Meyerkhol'da, rezhissyore Teatra V. F. Komissarzhevskoy," in *Tvorcheskoe nasledie V. E. Meyerkhol'da*, 211–235; See A. V. Bogdanov-Orlova, "Meyerkhol'd repetiruet 'Noru,'" in *Tvorcheskoe nasledie V. E. Meyerkhol'da*, 252–262; Rudnitsky, *Russkoe rezhissyorskoe iskusstvo*, 292, 339–342. In recently published correspondence, Meyerhold's stepdaughter Tatyana Yesenina recounts a conversation in which her mother, actress Zinaida Raykh, suggested to Meyerhold that Kommissarzhevskaya might have been in love with him, even at the time of his firing from her theatre. Yesenina remembers Meyerhold saying to Raykh that, given Kommissarzhevskaya's independent, assertive nature (he did not mention her history of romantic affairs), it might have been true ("O V. E. Meyerkhol'de i Z. N. Raykh: Pis'ma K. L. Rudnitskomu [letter of 14 February 1983], *Teatr* 2 [February 1993]: 101).

35. Alexandre Benois, *Memoirs*, trans. Moura Budberg (London: Columbus Books, 1960), 125.

36. Z. G. Mints, "V 'khudozhestvennom pole' *Balaganchika*," in *Semi-*

otics and the History of Culture, ed. Morris Halle, Elena Semeka-Pankratov, Krystyna Pomorska, and Boris Uspensky (Columbus: Slavica, 1988), 401.

37. Aleksandr Blok, "Genrikh Ibsen" and "Pamyati Avgusta Strindberga," in Sobranie sochineny, vol. 5, 316 ("demons"), 467 (on the suffering soul). On the theme of marriage in relation to the self and egoism, see the following essays in Shestakov's Russky Eros: Vyacheslav Shestakov, "Vstupitel'naya stat'ya," 8 (Rozanov quote) and 9; Dmitry Merezhkovsky, "Lyubov' u Tolstogo i Dostoevskogo" (1903), 151–166, and "Zhizn' Dante" (1939), 167–173; Vasily Rozanov, "Sem'ya kak religiya" (1901), 126; Zinaida Gippius, "Vlyublyonnost'" (1908), 178, and "O zhenakh" (1925), 215–220; Vasily Rozanov, "Kontsy i nachala: 'Bozhestvennoe' i 'demonicheskoe': Bogi i demony (Po povodu glavnogo syuzheta Lermontova)" (1901), 106–119; Nikolay Berdyaev, "Lyubov' u Dostoevskogo" (1923), 273–283; and Vladimir Solovyov, "Smysl lyubvi" (1903), 35.

38. Aline Isdebsky-Pritchard, The Art of Mikhail Vrubel (1856–1910) (Ann Arbor: UMI Research Press, 1982), 63–64 ("perception" and "human"); Aline Isdebsky-Pritchard, "Art for Philosophy's Sake: Vrubel against 'the Herd,'" in Nietzsche in Russia, ed. Rosenthal, 230; Herzen quoted in Grigori Kozintsev, Shakespeare: Time and Conscience, trans. Joyce Vining (New York: Hill and Wang, 1966), 122. Vrubel's Demon cycle of paintings is discussed in Masters of World Painting: Mikhail Vrubel (Leningrad: Aurora Art Publishers, 1988), 5–6. After Bely departed for Europe, Mendeleyeva left Petersburg to pursue her acting career. She returned in 1908, pregnant by a man whom she called only "the page Dagobert," a name reminiscent of her husband Blok's enthusiasm for medieval romances (Evelyn Bristol, "Blok between Nietzsche and Soloviev," in Nietzsche in Russia, ed. Rosenthal, 154).

39. Valery Bryusov, "Alexander Blok," in Blok: Essays and Memoirs, ed. Vogel, 106 (quote). Blok played both Hamlet and Claudius at the primitive theatre at Bolblovo, which for him captured the essence of theatrical illusion. He also played Chatsky to Mendeleyeva's Sofiya in Woe from Wit. Blok acted on the St. Petersburg stage but without great success. In 1900, he began his career shift from actor to poet (T. Kudryavtseva, "Aleksandr Blok—Aktyor," Teatr 3 [March 1967]: 77–78). For information on the relationship between Blok and his wife and references to Lyubov Mendeleyeva as Ophelia, see Aleksandr Blok, "Ya—Gamlet. Kholodeet krov' . . ." (poem, 6 February 1914), in Sobranie sochineny v vos'mi tomakh, ed. V. N. Orlov, A. A. Surkov, and K. I. Chukovsky, vol. 3, Stikhotvoreniya i poemy 1907–1921, ed. Vl. Orlov (Moscow-Leningrad: Gosudarstvennoe izdatel'stvo khudozhestvennoy literatury, 1960), 91; A. Blok, "Pis'ma k zhene," in Literaturnoe nasledstvo 89 (Moscow: n.p., 1978), 156; Lucy Vogel, "The Poet's Wife: Lyubov' Dmitrievna Mendeleeva," in Aleksandr Blok Centennial Conference, ed. Walter N. Vickery (Columbus: Slavica, 1984), 382; Lyubov Mendeleeva-Blok, "Facts and Myths about Blok and Myself," in Blok: Essays and Memoirs, ed. Vogel, 16–18, 182n.14; Kipnis, "O liricheskom geroe,"

48–49; Chukovsky, "*A. A. Blok: The Man* (Excerpts)," in *Blok: Essays and Memoirs*, ed. Vogel, 66; and Mochulsky, *Aleksandr Blok*, 85–90. The Harlequin-Christ (*Khristos-Arlekin*) was the original title of Yevreinov's play *The Chief Thing* (*Samoe glavnoe*, 1921). See Golub, *Evreinov*, 65.

40. Another possible symbolist explanation can be surmised from Valery Bryusov's statement in his poem "To the Women" (in *Urbi et Orbi*, 1903), paraphrased by Joan Delaney Grossman, that "individually [women's] love was not enough. Private bliss is a paltry enticement compared to the real goal of entry into the extrarational sphere" (*Valery Bryusov and the Riddle of Russian Decadence* [Berkeley: University of California Press, 1985], 237).

41. Mendeleeva-Blok, "Facts and Myths," 185 n. 64; Mochulsky, *Aleksandr Blok*, 60–61 (Blok quotes); N. V. Gogol', *Vybrannye mesta iz perepiska s druzyami*, in *Polnoe sobranie sochineny*, 8 vols. (Leningrad: Izdatel'stvo Akademii nauk SSSR, 1952), vol. 8, 143–147 (quotes on 146), 224, 309; Billington, *The Icon and the Axe*, 349; Erast Garin, *S Meyerkhol'dom (Vospominaniya)* (Moscow: Iskusstvo, 1974), 124; David Magarshack, *Gogol: A Life* (New York: Grove Press, 1969), 78–80.

42. Shestakov, "Vstupitel'naya stat'ya," 9–10, and Vladimir Solovyov, "Zhiznennaya drama Platona," 91, both in *Russky Eros*, ed. Shestakov.

43. A. Pankratova, "Teatral'nye motivy zhivopisi Nikolaya Sapunova," in *Russky teatr i dramaturgiya nachala XX veka: Sbornik nauchnykh trudov*, ed. A. A. Ninov (Leningrad: LGITMiK, 1984), 114; K. Rudnitsky, "V teatre na ofitserskoy," 146, 149; T. M. Rodina, *Aleksandr Blok i russky teatr nachala XX veka* (Moscow: Nauk, 1977), 136; Alpatov and Gunst, *Sapunov*, 25–26; A. B. Rubtsov, *Dramaturgiya Aleksandra Bloka* (Minsk: Vysheyshaya shkola, 1968), 41–42 ("abstract"); Rudnitsky, *Russkoe rezhissyorskoe iskusstvo*, 339 ("window"); Boris Eikhenbaum, "Blok's Fate" (1921), in *Blok: Essays and Memoirs*, ed. Vogel, 136 ("unity").

44. Aleksandr Blok, "Dusha pisatelya (Zametki sovremennika)" (February 1909), in *Sobranie sochineny v vos'mi tomakh*, vol. 5, 367 ("bigger")–368, 370–371; Aleksandr Blok, "Ironiya" (1908), in *Sobranie sochineny v vos'mi tomakh*, vol. 5, 341, 349; Blok, "Dramatichesky teatr V. F. Kommissarzhevskoy," 95.

45. Bowlt, *The Silver Age*, 408. Blok's "lifelessness" in Somov's portrait was noted by Georgy Chulkov in *Gody stranstvy* (Moscow: n.p., 1930), 125, cited in Bowlt, *The Silver Age*, 210.

46. Natalya Sokolova, *Mir iskusstva* (Moscow-Leningrad: n.p., 1934), 13; Aleksandr Blok, *Balaganchik*, in *Sobranie sochineny v vos'mi tomakh*, vol. 4, *Teatr*, ed. V. N. Orlov, A. A. Surkov, and K. I. Chukovsky (Moscow-Leningrad: Gosudarstvennoe izdatel'stvo khudozhestvennoy literatury, 1961; all references and citations are to this edition). The Campo Santo reference is cited in Gerould, "Russian Symbolist Drama and the Visual Arts," 16–17. The fresco depicts in part Death as a dark cloaked woman who descends upon young lovers. Some scholars have attributed

it to Pietro and/or Ambrogio Lorenzetti. See Abel Letalle, *Les fresques du Campo Santo de Pise* (Paris: Bibliothèque Internationale d'édition E. Sansot, 1914), 25–35.

47. Matich, "Dialectics of Cultural Return," 69–70n.25. Zinaida Gippius sometimes wrote under the masculine pseudonym "Anton Krayny." The surname, appropriately, means "extreme" and derives from the word for "edge," "brink," or "border" (*kray*).

48. Matich, "Androgyny and the Russian Religious Renaissance," 170. Laura Engelstein notes that Weininger's book was "issued in thousands of copies and numerous editions by 1914" (*Keys to Happiness*, 301 [quote], 302, 317–318). For a balanced assessment of Weininger's contributions and limitations by a Russian writer of this period, see Andrey Bely, "Veyninger o pole i kharaktere" (1911), in *Russky Eros*, ed. Shestakov, 100–105.

49. Matich, "Androgyny and the Russian Silver Age," 45 ("mystery" and Rozanov quote); Pyotr Uspensky, "Iskusstvo i lyubov'" (fragment, 1911), 221, 226 ("harmonized"), 229, Gippius, "Vlyublyonnost'" (1908), 174, 183, and "O lyubvi" (1925), 191, Solovyov, "Smysl lyubvi," 49 ("Godmanhood"), and Shestakov, "Vstupitel'naya stat'ya," 7–9, 15 (Bulgakov quote), all in *Russky Eros*, ed. Shestakov. Anna Lisa Crone, "Nietzschean, All Too Nietzschean? Rozanov's Anti-Christian Critique," in *Nietzsche in Russia*, ed. Rosenthal, 98–99, calls Rozanov "the Russian Nietzsche."

50. Pavel Medvedev, *Drama i poemy A. A. Bloka: Istoriya ikh rozhdeniya* (Leningrad: Izdatel'stvo pisateley, 1928), 19, 23n.2; Rodina, *Aleksandr Blok*, 43; A. V. Fedorov, *Teatr A. Bloka i dramaturgiya ego vremeni* (Leningrad: Izdatel'stvo Leningradskogo universiteta, 1972), 43; Roger B. Anderson, "The Railroad in *Doctor Zhivago*," in *Slavic and East European Journal* 31 (Winter 1987): 513 ("ultimate").

51. Mochulsky, *Aleksandr Blok*, 124; Fedorov, *Teatr A. Bloka*, 50–51.

52. *Aleksandr Blok v vospominaniyakh sovremennikov v dvukh tomakh*, 2 vols. (Moscow: Khudozhestvennaya literatura, 1980), vol. 1, 424; Barbara Fass, *La Belle Dame sans Merci and the Aesthetics of Romanticism* (Detroit: Wayne State University Press, 1974), 17 and 168 (Baudelaire on Wagner), 22 ("perfection"), 28, 160; Shestakov, "Vstupitel'naya stat'ya," 15, and Sergey Bulgakov, "Vladimir Solovyov i Anna Shmidt" (1911–1915), 315–319, both in *Russky Eros*, ed. Shestakov.

53. Poggioli, *The Poets of Russia*, 203–204. A. L. Porfir'eva, "Meyerkhol'd i Vagner," in *Russky teatr i dramaturgiya nachala XX veka*, 126, 129, 136–137, 140–141, 143n.2; Blok, "Iskusstvo i revolyutsiya (Po povodu tvoreniya Rikharda Vagnera)" (1918), and "Krushenie gumanizma" (1919), in *Sobranie sochineny v vos'mi tomakh*, vol. 6, 21–22, 23–24, 29 ("directed"), 60 ("unity"), 105–106; Aleksandr Blok, "O naznachenii poeta," in *Sobranie sochineny v vos'mi tomakh*, vol. 6, 163; "K voprosi o tvorcheskom metode Bloka," in *Literaturnoe nasledstvo*, vol. 92, book 1 (Moscow: n.p., 1980), 73; Bely quoted in "Simvolistichesky teatr: K gastrolyam Kommisarzhevskoy," *Utro Rossii* (September 1907); Richard Wagner, "Über die Benennung Musikdrama," vol. 9,

18–19, in Rabochaya kartoteka Meyerkhol'da, TsGALI SSSR (fond no. 988, opis' no. 1, ed. khr. no. 842); Rodina, *Aleksandr Blok*, 141. Blok's dancers and the general flow of characters and action in *The Little Showbooth* embody part of the "dances of death"/death-in-life theme which runs through his poetry. His inspiration for this was no doubt Gogol's "dead souls"—living puppets/living corpses—as well as Baudelaire's *Danse macabre*. John E. Bowlt has written that in the work of Blok's portraitist Somov, "in the Columbines and Harlequins at play, in the 'cripples and lilliputs' making love beneath arabesques, in the flowers and butterflies of elegant bosquets, we see a magnificent dance of death" ("Through the Glass Darkly: Images of Decadence in Early Twentieth-Century Russian Art," *Journal of Contemporary History* 17 [1982]: 100; the "cripples and lilliputs" quote is from I. Repin, "Po adresu 'Mira iskusstva,'" in *Mir Iskusstva* 10 [1899]: 3).

54. Boris Zingerman, "Na repetitsiyakhu Meyerkhol'da (1925–1938)," *Teatr* 1 (January 1992): 113. "Terrifying marionetteness" is a partial paraphrase of Andrey Bely's statement: "The marionette-like character of the substance of Blokian symbolism in *The Puppet Show*—this is what is terrifying" (quoted in Mochulsky, *Andrei Bely*, 85).

55. Rodina, *Aleksandr Blok*, 131–132, 133 (Blok quote), 134, 136–137, 139; Kozintsev, *Shakespeare*, 122–123, 125, 231 ("callousness"), 242, 244 ("unities").

56. Sergey Makovsky, *Na Parnase "Serebryanogo veka"* (Munich: Izdatel'stvo Tsentral'nogo Ob'edineniya Politicheskikh Emigrantov iz SSSR, 1962), 149; Aleksandr Blok, "Bezvremen'e," in *Sobranie sochineny v vos'mi tomakh*, vol. 5, 71; Berdyaev, *The Russian Idea*, 245 ("integrality," "boundaries"); Nikolay Volkov, *Meyerkhol'd*, 2 vols. (Leningrad: Academia, 1929), vol. 1, 280–281. For information on the Evening of the Paper Ladies (*Vecher bumazhnykh dam*), see V. P. Verigina, *Vospominaniya* (Leningrad: Iskusstvo, 1974), 98, 107, 142, 205. Verigina played the female half of the second pair of lovers in Meyerhold's 1906 production of *The Little Showbooth*. The relationship between the theatricality and inescapability of a scene was a feature of the Versailles paintings (ca. 1897–1906) executed by Benois at the same time that Blok was writing *The Little Showbooth*. On the theme of inescapability in the Versailles paintings, see John E. Bowlt, *Russian Stage Design: Scenic Innovation, 1900–1930, from the Collection of Mr. and Mrs. Nikita D. Lobanov-Rostovsky* (Jackson: Mississippi Museum of Art, 1982), 23. Mikhail Bulgakov fastened on the death of Molière in order to express the same feeling of existential entrapment under Stalin that Blok wrote about prior to the revolution. In his play *The Cabal of Hypocrites (Kabal svyatosh,* or *Molière,* 1929), Molière, who is a stand-in for Bulgakov and who is being hounded by a state- and church-hired assassin, discovers that only self-imposed exile to the stage can save him from certain death. Taking liberties with a history he knew well (having written a biography of Molière), Bulgakov has Molière die onstage, strangled, as it were, by the rhetoric and the condition of theatrical performance. Like Chatsky, Hamlet, and other romantic intellectuals, Molière-Bulgakov performs the

role of the socially alienated and politically disempowered individual whose improvisatory mode of being in performance demonstrates both his marginalized condition and his opposition to the state's attempted scientific organization of human destiny. He ends by performing his own suffering. The play originally ended with La Grange, the "Registre" of Molière's company, remarking on Molière's death: "The cause was fate." (*Prichinoy etogo yavilas' sud'ba.*) This ending is quoted in Ellendea Proffer, *Bulgakov: Life and Works* (Ann Arbor: Ardis, 1984), 444, 628n.29. This ending is originally cited in M. Chudakova, "Arkhiv M. A. Bulgakova," *Zapiski Otdela rukopisey*, no. 37 (Moscow: n.p., 1976), 92. The published ending was changed to read: "The cause of this was the disfavor of the king and the Black Cabal! . . . And so it will be recorded!" (Mikhail Bulgakov, *Kabala svyatosh*, in *Kabala svyatosh: Roman, p'esy, libretti*, ed. M. I. Vostryshev, V. I. Losev, and V. V. Petelin [Moscow: Sovremennik, 1991], 86–87). For background information on variant versions of Bulgakov's dramatic texts, see Lesley Milne, "Mikhail Bulgakov: The Status of the Dramatist and the Status of the Text," in *Russian Theatre in the Age of Modernism*, ed. Robert Russell and Andrew Barratt (London: Macmillan, 1990), 236–259.

57. Blok, "Ditya Gogolya," 50–51; Benois, *Memoirs*, 125–126. Mints, "V 'khudozhestvennom pole,'" 402, 406n.4; Zingerman, "Na repetitsiyakh u Meyerkhol'da," 113 ("punch"); the soul's "police department" is from Blok, *Sobranie sochineny v vos'mi tomakh*, vol. 7, 13, quoted in Rudnitsky, *Meyerhold the Director*, 104; Blok, "Dramatichesky teatr V. F. Kommissarzhevskoy," 96–97. Laurence Senelick describes one of the "Western-style pantos" which Blok would probably have seen performed on the Field of Mars: in *The Mill for Women*, "crones were dumped in one end of the machine and came out comely lasses at the other" (written communication, 8 January 1993).

58. Dorothy Pam, "*Murderer the Women's Hope*," *Drama Review* 3 (September 1975): 11 (Kokoschka quote); Verigina quoted in Rudnitsky, *Russkoe rezhissyorskoe iskusstvo*, 341.

59. Alisa Koonen, *Stranitsy zhizni* (Moscow: Iskusstvo, 1975), 241; Oliver M. Sayler, *The Russian Theatre* (New York: Brentano's, 1922), 161 (quotes), 162. Finney writes that Wilde's is the only literary version of the Salome legend in which Herod has her killed (*Women in Modern Drama*, 66). See chapter 3 of the present study for a discussion of the state's murder of Zinaida Raykh as an example of the killing of Salome theme. Wilde's *Salome* ran simultaneously in three Moscow theatres and one Petrograd theatre during the 1917–1918 season; the new order had not yet been firmly established (Nils Åke Nilsson, "Spring 1918: The Arts and the Commissars," in *Art, Society, Revolution*, 25).

3. REVOLUTIONIZING GALATEA

1. Sologub, "Sergei Turgenev and Sharik Fragments," in *The Petty Demon*, 303.

2. V. I. Lenin, "Dialogue with Clara Zelkin," in *The Lenin Anthology*, ed. Robert C. Tucker (New York: W. W. Norton, 1975), 695. For a discussion of Marxism, family, and the "woman question" in the nineteenth century, see chapters 5 and 6 in Rosalind Coward, *Patriarchal Precedents: Sexuality and Social Relations* (London: Routledge and Kegan Paul, 1983). See also Alexandra Kollontai, "The Social Basis of the Woman Question" (1909), excerpted in Alexandra Kollontai, *Selected Writings* (London: Allison and Busby, 1977), 58–80, in which a leading Russian female revolutionary tied the resolution of the woman question to socialist victory and defended the commitment of Social Democratic Party leaders to women's issues. It was Kollontay who called Bebel's book the "woman's bible." Bebel is discussed in Alfred G. Meyer, "Marxism and the Women's Movement," in *Women in Russia*, ed. Dorothy Atkinson, Alexander Dallin, and Gail Warshofsky Lapidus (Stanford: Stanford University Press, 1977), 99 ("economic").

3. Temira Pachmuss, trans. and ed., *Between Paris and St. Petersburg: Selected Diaries of Zinaida Hippius* (Urbana: University of Illinois Press, 1975), 14–16 ("duality"); Sandra M. Gilbert and Susan Gubar, "Sexual Linguistics: Gender, Language, Sexuality," *New Literary History* 3 (Spring 1985): 516 ("feminine"); Richard Stites, "Iconoclastic Currents in the Russian Revolution: Destroying and Preserving the Past," in *Bolshevik Culture: Experiment and Order in the Russian Revolution*, ed. Abbott Gleason, Peter Kenez, and Richard Stites (Bloomington: Indiana University Press, 1985), 18 ("grim"). See also Katerina Clark, *The Soviet Novel: History as Ritual* (Chicago: University of Chicago Press, 1985), 15–24.

4. Steven A. Mansbach, *Visions of Totality: Laszlo Moholy-Nagy, Theo Van Doesburg, and El Lissitzky* (Ann Arbor: UMI Research Press, 1980), 31; Sheila Rowbotham, *Women, Resistance and Revolution* (1972; rpt. New York: Vintage/Random House, 1974), 149–150 ("capriciousness"), quoted in Judith Mayne, "Soviet Film Montage and the Woman Question," *Camera Obscura: A Journal of Feminism and Film* 19 (January 1989): 26.

5. *Pobeda nad solntsem*, opera by Aleksey Kruchenykh, prologue by Velimir Khlebnikov, music by Mikhail Matyushin, sets by Kazimir Malevich, ed. V. Marcade and J.-C. Marcade (Lausanne: L'Age d'Homme, 1976), 18; Igor Golomstock, *Totalitarian Art: In the Soviet Union, the Third Reich, Fascist Italy and the People's Republic of China*, trans. Robert Chandler (New York: IconEditions/Harper Collins, 1990), 191; David Elliott, *New Worlds: Russian Art and Society 1900–1937* (London: Thames and Hudson, 1986), 151; Gail Harrison Roman, *When All the World Was a Stage: Russian Constructivist Theatre Design* (exhibition catalogue; Louisville: J. B. Speed Art Museum, 1989), 8–10 ("dynamic"); Kern, *The Culture of Time and Space*, 142; Mayne, "Soviet Film Montage," 48.

6. Judith Mayne, *Kino and the Woman Question: Feminism and Soviet Silent Film* (Columbus: Ohio State University Press, 1989), 131 ("difficulty"), 133, 135, 140 ("presupposed"); G. A. Tokaev, *Betrayal of an Ideal* (Bloomington: Indiana University Press, 1955), 160 ("herrings"),

quoted in Alex de Jonge, *Stalin and the Shaping of the Soviet Union* (New York: William Morrow, 1986), 136; Adam B. Ullam, *Stalin: The Man and His Era* (Boston: Beacon Press, 1989), 25; Anne Eliot Griesse and Richard Stites, "Russia: Revolution and War," in *Female Soldiers — Combatants or Noncombatants/Historical and Contemporary Perspectives*, ed. Nancy Goldman (Westport: Greenwood Press, 1982), 63. Sheila Fitzpatrick notes that "communists were warned against marrying bourgeois women, and the 'degeneration' of revolutionary cadres was often attributed to the corrupting influence of their wives" (*The Cultural Front*, 237). In the early years of his rule, Stalin partially concealed his misogyny for the purposes of political expediency. On International Women's Day (1925), he proclaimed that "the victory or defeat of proletarian power depends on whether or not the reserve of women will be for or against the working class." He called for female workers and peasants to be educated politically and organized "beneath the banner of the proletariat" (Stalin, "International Women's Day, 1925," quoted in *The Woman Question: Selected Writings of Marx, Engels, Lenin and Stalin* [n.p.: International Publishers, 1951], 47).

7. Richard Stites, *The Women's Liberation Movement in Russia: Feminism, Nihilism, and Bolshevism 1860–1930* (Princeton: Princeton University Press, 1978), 320–321, 326; V. I. Lenin, "Report to the Second All-Russian Congress of Political Education Departments," in *Collected Works*, 4th ed., 45 vols. (Moscow: Foreign Languages Publishing House, 1960–1975), vol. 33, 78, quoted in Gail Warshofsky Lapidus, "Sexual Equality in Soviet Policy: A Developmental Perspective," in *Women in Russia*, ed. Atkinson, Dallin, and Lapidus, 120; Xenia Gasiorowska, *Women in Soviet Fiction 1917–1964* (Madison: University of Wisconsin Press, 1968), 133; Pipes, *The Russian Revolution*, 384 ("daughter").

8. Solzhenitsyn, *Lenin in Zurich*, 21, 24–29 (Lenin quote on 26), 271; Nadezhda K. Krupskaya, *Memories of Lenin*, 2 vols. (New York: International Publishers, 1933), vol. 2; Wilson, *To the Finland Station*, 535; Louise Bryant, *Six Red Months in Russia: An Observer's Account of Russia before and during the Proletarian Dictatorship* (London: William Heinemann, 1918), 164, 166, 169 ("temperament"); Barbara Evans Clements, "The Birth of the New Soviet Woman," in *Bolshevik Culture*, ed. Gleason, Kenez, and Stites, 233.

9. Chernyshevsky, *What Is to Be Done?* 293; Billington, *Fire in the Minds of Men*, 493–495.

10. V. I. Lenin, "On the Emancipation of Women," in *The Lenin Anthology*, ed. Tucker, 679–699; Billington, *Fire in the Minds of Men*, 494 (quote); Alexander Bogdanov, *Red Star: The First Bolshevik Utopia*, ed. Loren R. Graham and Richard Stites, trans. Charles Rougle (Bloomington: Indiana University Press, 1984), 44, 48, 68, 77, 93, 104–105, 113–116, 119 ("unity"); Stites, *The Women's Liberation Movement in Russia*, 321, 323–324, 326–327, 332, 341, 345; Gasiorowska, *Women in Soviet Fiction*, 177; Lapidus, "Sexual Equality in Soviet Policy," 120, 122.

11. V. I. Lenin, "Soviet Power and the Status of Women," in *Collected Works*,

vol. 30, *September 1919–April 1920*, trans. and ed. George Hanna, 122, quoted in Lapidus, "Sexual Equality in Soviet Policy," 119; Rose L. Glickman, "The Russian Factory Woman, 1880–1914," in *Women in Russia*, ed. Atkinson, Dallin, and Lapidus, 79–80, 82 ("appendage").

12. Fyodor Vasilievich Gladkov, *Cement*, trans. A. S. Arthur and C. Ashleigh (New York: Frederick Ungar, 1980), 237, 239, 240; Stites, *The Women's Liberation Movement in Russia*, 324, 333, 359–360; Gasiorowska, *Women in Soviet Fiction*, 115, 119, 123, 126; Louise Bryant, *Mirrors of Moscow* (New York: Thomas Seltzer, 1923), 111, 114–115.

13. Wilson, *To the Finland Station*, 538; Pipes, *The Russian Revolution*, 491; Berdyaev, *The Russian Idea*, 211; Alexander Gershkovich, *The Theater of Yuri Lyubimov: Art and Politics at the Taganka Theater in Moscow*, trans. Michael Yurieff (New York: Paragon House, 1989), 63. Material on *The Storming of the Winter Palace* was drawn from written breakdowns of the scenario for the spectacle in the Manuscript Division of the Leningrad State Theatrical Museum, Leningrad, USSR.

14. Wilson, *To the Finland Station*, 449, 543–544 (quotes); Chernyshevsky, *What Is to Be Done?* 229, 231, 236–237; see Gasiorowska, *Women in Soviet Fiction*, 134–139. While Lev Tolstoy and his followers practiced asceticism in real life at this time, theirs was more a Christian philosophical than an atheistic political choice.

15. Yuri Olesha, "Human Material," in *Envy and Other Works*, trans. Andrew R. MacAndrew (Garden City: Anchor/Doubleday, 1967), 199–200; Evgeny Zamyatin, *We*, in *An Anthology of Russian Literature in the Soviet Period from Gorki to Pasternak*, ed. and trans. Bernard Guilbert Guerney (New York: Vintage/Random House, 1960; all references are to this edition), 173 ("nobody").

16. Stites, "Women and the Russian Intelligentsia: Three Perspectives," in *Women in Russia*, ed. Atkinson, Dallin, and Lapidus, 56; Gasiorowska, *Women in Soviet Fiction*, 133 ("freak"); Mayne, "Soviet Film Montage," 43.

17. Julie Wheelwright, *Amazons and Military Maids: Women Who Dressed as Men in Pursuit of Life, Liberty and Happiness* (London: Pandora/Unwin Hyman, 1989), 29–31, 73 ("sexual," "maternal"), 74–75, 125–130; Bryant, *Six Red Months in Russia*, 212–213 ("ordered"). For further information on Mariya Bochkarova and the Women's Death Battalions, see Isaac Don Levine, *Yashka: My Life as Peasant Officer and Exile* (New York: Frederick A. Stokes, 1939). See René Fülöp-Miller, *The Mind and Face of Bolshevism: An Examination of Cultural Life in Soviet Russia*, trans. F. S. Flint and D. F. Tait (1927; rpt. New York: Harper and Row, 1965), 203; Griesse and Stites, "Russia: Revolution and War," 65; Cathy Porter, *Alexandra Kollontai: A Biography* (London: Virago, 1980), 265. Recently, much has been made by Russianists and feminists of Nadezhda Durova, who cross-dressed as a male cavalry officer in order to fight for the tsar in the Napoleonic Wars and wrote a memoir documenting her experience. Unlike the members of Kerensky's Women's Battalion, Durova consistently played the male role in and out of uniform.

Mary Fleming Zirin links Durova to the legendary Amazon of the southern steppes whose adventures are recounted in epic Russian folksongs (*byliny*) and tales. Some of these "fierce maidens" recalled the Women's Battalion in eventually submitting to male power, reverting to female meekness and dutiful service ("Translator's Introduction," in Nadezhda Durova, *The Cavalry Maiden: Journal of a Female Russian Officer in the Napoleonic Wars*, trans. Mary Fleming Zirin [London: Paladin, 1990], xvii).

18. Griesse and Stites, "Russia: Revolution and War," 64, 66–67.

19. Alla Mikhailova, "Nine Plays Out of Many" (introduction), in *Classic Soviet Plays* (Moscow: Progress Publishers, 1979), 12; Stites, *The Women's Liberation Movement in Russia*, 319; Koonen, *Stranitsy zhizni*, 355; Nadezhda Mandelstam, *Hope against Hope: A Memoir*, trans. Max Hayward (New York: Atheneum, 1980), 108–112; Vsevolod Vishnevsky, *Optimicheskaya tragediya*, in *Sobranie sochineny v pyati tomakh*, vol. 1, *P'esy 1929–1950* (Moscow: Gosudarstvennoe izdatel'stvo khudozhestvennoy literatury, 1954), 237 (quotes). For the positive or "mythic" view of Reysner, see Cathy Porter, *Larissa Reisner* (London: Virago, 1988), especially 67–68, 80. The negative or "realistic" view is expressed in Alla Zeide, "Larisa Reisner: Myth as Justification for Life," *Russian Review* 51 (April 1992), 172 ("Pallas," "woman"), 173–174, 178–179. For additional information on Reysner, see Vsevolod Vishnevsky, "Ostalas' v pamyati na vsyu zhizn' . . ." (1932), in *Larisa Reysner: V vospominaniyakh sovremennikov*, ed. A. I. Naumova (Moscow: Sovetsky pisatel', 1969), 103–104; Leon Trotsky, *My Life* (New York: Universal Library, 1960), 409; Halina Stephan, "Larisa Reisner: Revolution in Life and Art," in *Selected Proceedings of the Kentucky Foreign Language Conferences: Slavic Section* 5 (1987–1988), 36; and E. Solovey, *Larisa Reysner: Ocherk zhizni i tvorchestva* (Moscow: Sovetsky pisatel', 1985). Reysner's own writings have been collected in two volumes— *Sobranie sochineny v dvukh tomakh* (Moscow-Leningrad: Gosizdat, 1928)—and have been published in two editions of selected works, *Izbrannye proizvedeniya* (Moscow: Goslitizdat, 1958) and *Izbrannoe* (Moscow: Izdatel'stvo khudozhestvennaya literatura, 1965).

20. Camille Paglia, *Sexual Personae: Art and Decadence from Nefertiti to Emily Dickinson* (New Haven: Yale University Press, 1990), 7, 50 (quotes). Vadim Ryndin's set for Vishnevsky's play, which consisted of concentric circular platforms, manifested what Nick Worrall calls the centrifugal forces of Bolshevik or revolutionary integration in conflict with the centripetal forces of anti-Bolshevik or counterrevolutionary disintegration (*Modernism to Realism on the Soviet Stage: Tairov — Vakhtangov — Okhlopkov* [New York: Cambridge University Press, 1989], 60). Ryndin's set visually embodied the description of Russia as a "soul in the whirlwind," in which a metaphor for fate is discovered. The equation of woman/a woman with the eye of the storm was first realized at the Kamerny Theatre in Alisa Koonen's portrayal of Wilde's Salome in 1917.

21. Gasiorowska, *Women in Soviet Fiction*, 95; Alix Holt, "Marxism and

Women's Oppression: Bolshevik Theory and Practice in the 1920's," in *Women in Eastern Europe and the Soviet Union*, ed. Tova Yedlin (New York: Praeger, 1980), 89; Berdyaev, *The Russian Idea*, 267.

22. Solzhenitsyn, *Lenin in Zurich*, 23; Lapidus, "Sexual Equality in Soviet Policy," 121–122 (on Trotsky), 125; Stites, *The Women's Liberation Movement in Russia*, 339, 341–342, 344–345; Fülöp-Miller, *Bolshevism*, 202.

23. Gasiorowska, *Women in Soviet Fiction*, 96; Billington, *Fire in the Minds of Men*, 648 n. 100; Alison Hilton, "The Revolutionary Theme in Russian Realism," in *Art and Architecture in the Service of Politics*, ed. Henry A. Millon and Linda Nochlin (Cambridge, Mass.: MIT Press, 1978), 110, 112, 115, 119.

24. A. Kollontay, *Sem'ya i kommunisticheskoe gosudarstvo* (Moscow: n.p., 1918), 23, quoted in Gasiorowska, *Women in Soviet Fiction*, 186; Mayne, *Kino and the Woman Question*, 85–87, 111–116, 126–129.

25. Anatoly Glebov, *Inga*, trans. Charles Malamuth, in *Six Soviet Plays*, ed. Eugene Lyons (Boston and New York: Houghton Mifflin, 1934; all references are to this edition of the play).

26. Natalia Adaskina, "Constructivist Fabrics and Dress Design," *Journal of Decorative and Propaganda Arts* 5 (Summer 1987): 144–159; Alexander Lavrentiev, *Varvara Stepanova: The Complete Work*, ed. John E. Bowlt (Cambridge: MIT Press, 1988), 7, 104; Benedikt Livshits, *The One and a Half-Eyed Archer*, trans. John E. Bowlt (Newtonville: Oriental Research Partners, 1977), 128 (quotes), 129; Alexander Lavrentiev, "Experimental Furniture Design," *Journal of Decorative and Propaganda Arts* 11 (Winter 1989): 157.

27. Parts 1 and 2 of the "Code of Laws on Marriage and Divorce, the Family and Guardianship," cited in R. Schlesinger, *Changing Attitudes in Soviet Russia: The Family in the USSR* (London: Routledge and Kegan Paul, 1949), 156; Holt, "Marxism," 89, 93, 107; Beatrice Brodsky Farnsworth, "Bolshevik Alternatives and the Soviet Family: The 1926 Marriage Law Debate," in *Women in Russia*, ed. Atkinson, Dallin, and Lapidus, 140–141, 250.

28. Mikhail Bulgakov, *Zoykina kvartira*, in *P'esy 1920-kh godov* (Leningrad: Iskusstvo, 1989), 184–185 (the three-act version which premiered in 1926), 230 (the four-act "tragic farce" version, revised between 1926 and 1935); Kollontay quoted in Bryant, *Mirrors of Moscow*, 125.

29. Lavrentiev, *Varvara Stepanova*, 79. See chapter 6 of the present study for a discussion of what forcing of perspective and distortion of scale produced under Stalin.

30. Nikolay Erdman, *Samoubytsa*, in *P'esy, intermedii, pis'ma, dokumenty, vospominaniya sovremennikov* (Moscow: Iskusstvo, 1990), 113–114.

31. Yury Olesha, *Spisok blagodeyany* (Moscow: Federatsiya, 1931; all references are to this edition of the play).

32. See Gasiorowska, *Women in Soviet Fiction*, 134.

33. Elizabeth Klosty Beaujour, *The Invisible Land: A Study of the Artistic Imagination of Iurii Olesha* (New York: Columbia University Press,

1970), 89–90; Mel Gordon, "Michael Chekhov's Life and Work: A Descriptive Chronology," *Drama Review* 3 (Fall 1983): 13; Lendley C. Black, *Mikhail Chekhov as Actor, Director and Teacher* (Ann Arbor: UMI Research Press, 1984), 21–22.

34. Aleksandr Afinogenov, *Strakh*, in *P'esy* (Moscow: Sovetsky pisatel', 1956), 96 (all references to the play are to this edition, except for the character description of Yelena Makarova and the description of her apartment, which appear only in the English-language translation by Charles Malamuth, in *Six Soviet Plays*, ed. Lyons, 407).

35. Aleksey Arbuzov, *Tanya*, in *P'esy sovetskikh pisateley*, ed. Z. M. Pekharskaya, 8 vols. (Moscow: Iskusstvo, 1954), vol. 5, 419.

36. Andreas Huyssen, *After the Great Divide: Modernism, Mass Culture, Postmodernism* (Bloomington and Indianapolis: Indiana University Press, 1986), 73.

37. Yury Olesha, *The Conspiracy of Feelings*, in *Yury Olesha: The Complete Plays*, ed. and trans. Michael Green and Jerome Katsell (Ann Arbor: Ardis, 1983), 32 (quote). The observation concerning the aggressive nature of the android versus the passive nature of the "gynoid" (Laurence Senelick's euphonious coinage), metallic echoes of the male and female sphinx, was offered to me in conversation with Professor William Crossgrove of the German Department, Brown University. The gynoid as iconic representation of an emasculated, romantic prerevolutionary spirit also occurs in Yevreinov's emigré play *Radio-Kiss, or The Robot of Love* (*Radio-potseluy, ili Robot lyubvi*, 1925). This play is discussed in Spencer Golub, "A Kiss Is Not a Kiss: Evreinov and the Illusion of Desire," in *Wandering Stars: Russian Emigré Theatre, 1905–1940*, ed. Laurence Senelick (Iowa City: University of Iowa Press, 1992), 171–195.

38. Vladimir Mayakovsky, *Banya*, in *Polnoe sobranie sochineny v trinadtsati tomakh*, ed. A. V. Fevral'sky, vol. 11, *Kinostsenarii i p'esy 1926–1930*, ed. B. Rostotsky (Moscow: Gosudarstvennoe izdatel'stvo khudozhestvennoy literatury, 1958), 321 (all references are to this edition of the play; the Phosphorescent Woman appears in act 4); Olesha, *The Conspiracy of Feelings*, 32; Beaujour, *The Invisible Land*, 62, 69–71, 84; MacAndrew, "Introduction," in *Envy and Other Works*, xii; Olesha, *Envy*, 77; Sergey Yutkevich, "Gamlet s Taganskoy ploshchadi," in *Shekspirovskie chteniya 1978*, ed. A. Anikst (Moscow: Nauka, 1981), 87 ("marionette," "puppet"); Elizabeth Wright, *Postmodern Brecht: A Re-Presentation* (London and New York: Routledge, 1989), 132. For an insightful discussion of the gynoid theme in *Metropolis*, see Andreas Huyssen, "The Vamp and the Machine: Fritz Lang's *Metropolis*," in *After the Great Divide*, 65–81 ("machine-vamp" is his term).

39. Gladkov, *Cement*, 115 ("yearning"); Nick Worrall, "Meyerhold's 'The Magnificent Cuckold,'" *Drama Review* 1 (March 1973): 30.

40. Rudnitsky, *Meyerhold the Director*, 310 ("machine"), 311, 394, 404; Viktor Shklovsky, *Krasnaya gazeta* (22 December 1926); Finney, *Women in Modern Drama*, 90; Gordon McVay, *Esenin: A Life* (New York: Paragon House, 1988), 88–89, 102. Raykh's daughter Yesenina rejected the

impression promulgated in the twenties press and "folklore" that her mother was inordinately fond of appearing in a variety of costumes in a single stage production. Yesenina argues that these transformations represented what Raykh felt to be the characters' choices. Raykh carefully prepared for each role, working closely with her costume designers to capture a character's taste and style. She exhibited the same meticulous attention in selecting her own and Meyerhold's clothing, a trait which may be described as fastidiousness rather than vanity. It was while playing the role of Anna Andreyevna in *The Inspector General*, the performance in which her clothes-consciousness was most roundly criticized, that Raykh felt herself become a real actress. Many reviewers, especially in the foreign press, concurred. Raykh clearly relished playing the role of what her son called a real "sex bomb." Anna Andreyevna possessed feminine sexual allure, which Raykh defined for her daughter as the ability to attract at least three men out of every ten (Yesenina, letter to K. L. Rudnitsky, 14 February 1983, 103–105, 108–109, 111).

41. Rudnitsky, *Meyerhold the Director*, 415 ("automatic," "mechanics"); V. N. Solovyov, "Zamechaniya po povodu 'Revizora' v postanovke Meyerkhol'da," in *"Revizor" v teatre imeni Vs. Meyerkhol'da: Sbornik statey* (Leningrad: Academia, 1927), 61 ("tragic"); A. A. Gvozdev, "Reviziya 'Revizora,'" in *"Revizor" v teatre imeni Vs. Meyerkhol'da*, 33–34; Leonid Grossman, "Tragediya-Buff: 'Revizor' u Meyerkhol'da," in *Gogol' i Meyerkhol'd: Sbornik literaturno-issledovatel'skoy assotsiatsii*, ed. E. F. Nikitinaya (Moscow: Nikitinskie subbotniki, 1927), 43 ("Bovaryism," "dream"); Pyotr Zaytsev, "'Revizor' u Meyerkhol'da," in *Gogol' i Meyerkhol'd*, 67.

42. Although there have been several viable contenders, Yesenina's hope that a woman (who would presumably pay more attention to spiritual essence than to physical beauty) would write a book about Raykh has thus far not been realized (Yesenina, letters to K. L. Rudnitsky, 18 March 1970, 25 April 1982, 26 May 1982, and 14 February 1983, 74–75, 77, 79, 84–85, 93–97, 100). Rudnitsky, whose work Yesenina admired and to whom she ceded much valuable information, died in 1988, before completing a projected study of undetermined length on Raykh. Yesenina died in 1992. For an example of the sort of criticism to which Yesenina alludes, see Yury Elagin, *Tyomny geny (Vsevolod Meyerkhol'd)* (London: Overseas Publications Interchange, 1982, reprint from 1955), 306–307.

43. Lyubov' Rudneva, "Zinaida Raykh," *Teatr* 1 (January 1989): 110–129 (Chekhov quoted on 117).

44. A. S., "Actress Dramatizes *Madame Bovary* for Production by Kamerny Theatre" (newspaper title unknown; press clipping, Harvard Theatre Collection), 13 April 1938; Rudnitsky, *Meyerhold the Director*, 509 (quote). Edward Braun lists 2 February 1940 as Meyerhold's execution date, based upon information received from recently opened KGB files. As of 1982, Meyerhold's stepdaughter believed he died on or around 14 March 1942, a date which she acknowledges may have been invented by Soviet officials simply to discourage further inquiries. In 1952, an em-

ployee at Moscow's Bakhrushin State Central Theatre Museum discouraged Yesenina from examining the archives of the former Meyerhold Theatre "for her children's sake," an oddly Soviet amalgam of warning and concern (Yesenina, letter to K. L. Rudnitsky, 28 October 1982, 92).

45. This account of Raykh's murder was compiled from an unsigned article, "Meyerhold's Wife Killed in Moscow," *New York Times*, 18 July 1939, clipping in H. W. L. Dana collection, Harvard Theatre Collection; Yesenina's letters to K. L. Rudnitsky, 25 April and 26 May 1982 and 14 February 1983, 81, 84–87, 93, 98; and Edward Braun, "Meyerhold: The Final Act," in *New Theatre Quarterly* 33 (February 1993): 11. Braun's Russian (Moscow) sources are *Teatral'naya zhizn'* 5 (1989) and 2 (1990), *Ogonyok* 15 (1989), *Teatr* 1 (1990), *Vechernyaya Moskva* (14 June 1991) and *Mir iskusstv: Almanakh* (1991). Yesenina suggests a spiritual connection between Raykh and Marguerite Gautier in her letter to K. L. Rudnitsky (14 February 1983, 101–103).

46. Meyerhold's labor-camp petition appears in "Pages from the Past," *Soviet and East European Performance* (Summer 1989): 19.

47. Catriona Kelly describes the role played by female characters in postrevolutionary street theatre as being passive, inarticulate, subject to physical abuse, easily manipulated, socially ostracized, culturally backward, and politically reactionary (*Petrushka*, 203–204 (quote); Mayne, "Soviet Film Montage," 40.

4. THE MASKING MACHINE

1. Vertov quoted in Richard Taylor, *The Politics of the Soviet Cinema, 1917–1929* (Cambridge: Cambridge University Press, 1979), 125; Leonid Trauberg, "Cinema in the Role of Accuser" (originally published in *Ekstsentrism: Sbornik statey* [Petrograd: n.p., 1922]), in *The Film Factory: Russian and Soviet Cinema in Documents*, ed. Richard Taylor and Ian Christie, trans. Richard Taylor (Cambridge: Harvard University Press, 1988), 62.

2. Clark, "The 'Quiet Revolution' in Soviet Intellectual Life," 213; Rosenberg, "Introduction: NEP Russia as a 'Transitional' Society," 4–6.

3. Pipes, *The Russian Intelligentsia*, 72, 75–76; Siegelbaum, *Soviet State and Society*, 60. Sheila Fitzpatrick argues that members of the old (prerevolutionary) intelligentsia fared better in the 1930s than even they expected. While individuals suffered, she notes, they were as a whole spared mass arrests (like the clergy) and mass deportation (like the peasants). They were not removed from the capitals, conscripted into labor, or denied employment as a group (*The Cultural Front*, 146).

4. Mayakovsky, *Banya*, 312.

5. Nahirny, *The Russian Intelligentsia*, 99 ("sacred"); Moholy-Nagy quoted in Mansbach, *Visions of Totality*, 36; Thoreau quoted in Marx, *The Machine in the Garden*, 354.

6. Berdyaev, *The Origin of Russian Communism*, 182 ("alienated"), 183;

Stalin quoted in Youri Lioubimov, *Le feu sacré: Souvenirs d'une vie de théâtre* (Paris: Fayard, 1985), 104.

7. Nicoletta Misler, "Designing Gestures in the Laboratory of Dance," in *Theatre in Revolution: Russian Avant-Garde Stage Design 1913–1935*, ed. Nancy Van Norman Baer (New York: Thames and Hudson, 1991), 157 (quote), 158–159.

8. Victor Terras, ed., *Handbook of Russian Literature* (New Haven and London: Yale University Press, 1985), 135; Proffer, *Bulgakov*, 106 ("fascination"), 107–108; Yuri Olesha, *No Day without a Line*, trans. and ed. Judson Rosengrant (Ann Arbor: Ardis, 1979), 235 (quotes); Beaujour, *The Invisible Land*, 42, 56–58, 84, 104, 159. Trotsky's term "Fellow Travelers" described disparate artists and groups of artists who were willing to work within the socialist system toward the realization of revolutionary ideals. The term was most consistently employed between 1923 and 1932, when the newly created Union of Soviet Writers sought a rapprochement between proletarian and nonproletarian writers.

9. Vsevolod Meyerhold, "Chaplin and Chaplinism," in *Meyerhold on Theatre*, 312 ("predilection"); Jay Leyda, *Kino: A History of the Russian and Soviet Film* (New York: Collier/Macmillan, 1973), 145 n.; S. Ginzburg, *Kinematografiya dorevolyutsionnoy Rossii* (Moscow: Iskusstvo, 1963), 260–265. In 1912, Meyerhold rejected the viability of cinema as an art form, a position he reversed in 1915. Precise information on the viewing of Chaplin's films in the USSR is difficult to obtain. Recently, Richard Stites included Chaplin's films among those of other American silent screen stars, such as Mary Pickford and Douglas Fairbanks, who were popular in the Soviet Union between 1917 and 1927. Stites asserts that in the period 1914–1917 the enthusiasm of Soviet audiences for "the suave Frenchman Max Linder who inspired a number of Russian imitators . . . partly immunized [them] to the cruder art of Charlie Chaplin" (*Russian Popular Culture: Entertainment and Society since 1900* [New York: Cambridge University Press, 1992], 31 [quote], 56).

10. Leyda, *Kino*, 129, 130 (quote). Shklovsky spent 1922–1923 in Berlin, where he wrote his influential study *Literature and Cinematography* (*Literatura i kinematograf*, 1923).

11. Vladimir Mayakovsky, *Klop*, in *Polnoe sobranie sochineny*, vol. 11 (Prisypkin is propelled into the future in scene 5, which begins on 244); Roman Jakobson, "On a Generation That Squandered Its Poets," in Roman Jakobson, *Language in Literature* (Cambridge: Harvard University Press, 1987), 288; Luda Schnitzer and Jean Schnitzer and Marcel Martin, eds., *Cinema in Revolution: The Heroic Era of the Soviet Film* (London: Secker and Warburg, 1973), 76 (Kuleshov quote); Ginzburg, *Kinematografiya dorevolyutsionnoy Rossii*, 263–265.

12. Vladimir Mayakovsky, *Misteriya-buff: Geroicheskoe, epicheskoe i satiricheskoe izobrazhenie nashey epokhi* (2nd version), in *Polnoe sobranie sochineny v trinadtsati tomakh*, vol. 2, *1917–1921*, ed. N. V. Reformatsky (Moscow: Gosudarstvennoe izdatel'stvo khudozhestvennoy literatury, 1956), 344–345. Ivor Montagu, *With Eisenstein in Hollywood: A*

Chapter of Autobiography, Including the Scenarios of "Sutter's Gold" and "An American Tragedy" (New York: International Publishers, 1967), 96–97 (quotes); Yury Olesha, *Mysli o Chapline* (1936), in *Izbrannye sochineniya* (Moscow: Gosudarstvennoe izdatel'stvo khudozhestvennoy literatury, 1956), 436–437; Edward Braun, *The Theatre of Meyerhold: Revolution on the Modern Stage* (New York: Drama Book Specialists, 1979), 342–343; Denise J. Youngblood, *Soviet Cinema in the Silent Era, 1918–1935* (Ann Arbor: UMI Research Press, 1985), 3, 42, 115; Vance Kepley, Jr., and Betty Kepley, "Foreign Films on Soviet Screens 1922–1931," *Quarterly Review of Film Studies* 4 (Fall 1979): 436–439. See also Steven P. Hill, "A Quantitative View of Soviet Cinema," *Cinema Journal* 2 (Spring 1972): 18–25; G. M. Boltiansky, ed., *Lenin i kino* (Moscow: n.p., 1925), 16–17. Peter Kenez, citing *Kino i vremya* (1960), states that *The Gold Rush* never played in the Soviet Union (*Cinema and Soviet Society 1917–1953* [New York: Cambridge University Press, 1992], 74). Maya Turovskaya mentions in passing that *City Lights* and *Modern Times* were imported by the Soviet Union in the 1930s ("The Tastes of Soviet Moviegoers during the 1930s," in *Late Soviet Culture: From Perestroika to Novostroika*, ed. Thomas Lahusen with Gene Kuperman [Durham: Duke University Press, 1993], 101). During rehearsals for *A List of Blessings*, Meyerhold and Raykh became friends with Olesha and his wife, who were practically their neighbors. Olesha wrote in a book he gave to Raykh that she had made a substantial difference in his life (Yesenina, letter to K. L. Rudnitsky, 14 February 1983, 107).

13. Viktor Shklovsky, "Pis'mo Charli Chaplinu" (1931), in *Za sorok let: Stat'i o kino* (Moscow: Iskusstvo, 1965), 119–121. The Civil War took its toll on film distribution and exhibition. Louis Siegelbaum writes that "none of the 143 theatres operating in Moscow before the world war showed films by the fall of 1921" (*Soviet State and Society*, 56).

14. Youngblood, *Soviet Cinema*, 3, 42, 115; Kepley and Kepley, "Foreign Films," 436–439; Hill, "Soviet Cinema," 18–25; Boltiansky, *Lenin i kino*, 16–17; Brooks, *When Russia Learned to Read*, xiii ("literacy"), 317–319; Leonid Trauberg quoted in the *Daily Worker*, 19 April 1939 ("remote," "penetrating," "vividness"); Denise J. Youngblood, "The Fate of Soviet Popular Cinema during the Stalin Revolution," *Russian Review* 50 (April 1991): 148 ("lifeless"). Lynn Mally's *Culture of the Future: The Proletkult Movement in Revolutionary Russia* (Berkeley and Los Angeles: University of California Press, 1990) offers the most detailed analysis in English of the Proletkult, especially in its peak years, 1917–1922 (xviii–xix, xxiv–xxv, xxvii–xxviii). Richard Stites breaks down the numbers differently than Mally (*Russian Popular Culture*, 55–56), setting Proletkult's membership in 1920 at 84,000 but its following at 500,000.

15. Chaplin quoted in Olesha, *No Day without a Line*, 217; Rudnitsky, *Meyerhold the Director*, 491.

16. Steven A. Nash, "East Meets West: Russian Stage Design and the European Avant-Garde," in *Theatre in Revolution*, ed. Baer, 100. See Eisenstein's 1924 explication of the "montage of attractions" in Jay Leyda and

Zina Voynow, eds., *Eisenstein at Work* (New York: Pantheon/Museum of Modern Art, 1982), 17.

17. Lavrentiev, *Varvara Stepanova*, 104 (quote); James M. Curtis, "Bergson and Russian Formalism," *Comparative Literature* 28 (1976): 112. Professor Audrey Ushenko identified the theories and elements devised and retrieved by Russian avant-garde artists of the 1920s in her remarks for a panel discussion on "Russian Politics and Culture, 1900–1930," Bellarmine College (Louisville, Ky.), 26 September 1989.

18. Dziga Vertov, "We: A Version of a Manifesto," in *The Film Factory*, ed. Taylor and Christie, 71 ("perfect"); the Lenin quote from "VII s'ezd partii, rech' Lenina," *Pravda*, 24 December 1920, 2; Khris. Khersonsky, "'Na vsyakogo mudretsa dovol'no prostoty': Pervy rabochy teatr proletkulta 1923," in *A. N. Ostrovsky na stsene*, ed. E. G. Kholodov (Moscow: Iskusstvo, 1974), 22 ("eccentric"); Lavrentiev, *Varvara Stepanova*, 105, 107, 129; Aleksandr Sukhovo-Kobylin, *Smert' Tarelkina*, in *Trilogiya: "Svad'ba Krechinskogo," "Delo," "Smert' Tarelkina,"* ed. R. Sofronov and I. D. Glikman (Moscow: Gosudarstvennoe izdatel'stvo khudozhestvennoy literatury, 1955), 248 (all references are to this edition of the play); E. Dobin, *Kozintsev i Trauberg* (Moscow: Iskusstvo, 1963), 28.

19. Loren R. Graham, "Introduction," 4 ("beneficence"), and Katerina Clark, "The Changing Image of Science and Technology in Soviet Literature," 266 ("automaton"), both in *Science and the Social Order*, ed. Loren R. Graham (Cambridge, Mass.: Harvard University Press, 1990); Clark, *The Soviet Novel*, 98–99 ("guidelines").

20. Propp, *Morphology of the Folktale*, 20–21. Vladimir Mayakovsky, a Chaplin admirer and early proponent of the cinema, saw the relationship between the dynamic actor and his changing background in film as representing "the action of actuality" ("Theatre, Cinema, Futurism," trans. Helen Segall, *Russian Literature Triquarterly* 12 [Spring 1975]: 182 [quote]).

21. A. Fevral'sky, *Puti k sintezu: Meyerkhol'd i kino* (Moscow: Iskusstvo, 1978), 170–175 (Meyerhold quotes on 170, 173, 174, from *Izvestiya*, 21 February 1926; Khersonsky quote on 172); Youngblood, "The Fate of Soviet Popular Cinema during the Stalin Revolution," 151; Vendrovskaya and Fevral'sky, *Tvorcheskoe nasledie V. E. Meyerkhol'da*, 81 ("poster art"); Meyerhold, "Chaplin and Chaplinism," 319 ("caricature").

22. Aleksey Gan quoted in John E. Bowlt, "Modern Russian Stage Design," in *Russian Stage Design*, 34–35; Ippolit Sokolov, "The Industrialization of Gesture," originally published in *Ermitazh* 6 (1922): 9, quoted in Konstantin Rudnitsky, *Russian and Soviet Theater 1905–1932*, ed. Lesley Milne, trans. Roxane Permar (New York: Harry N. Abrams, 1988), 93.

23. Fevral'sky, "Puti k sintezu," 170–175, 195 (Kuleshov quote), 197 (Raykh quote); Meyerhold, "The New Theatre Foreshadowed in Literature," and "The Fairground Booth," in *Meyerhold on Theatre*, trans. and ed. Edward Braun (New York: Hill and Wang, 1969), 37, 124, 142; Leach, *Vsevolod Meyerhold*, 65; Walter Benjamin, *Moscow Diary*, ed.

Gary Smith, trans. Richard Sieburth (Cambridge, Mass.: Harvard University Press, 1986), 53–54; Viktor Shklovsky, "The Clown, Comedy and Tragedy," in *The Soviet Circus* (Moscow: Progress Publishers, 1967), 37–38.

24. Shklovsky, "Literature and Cinema (Extracts)," in *The Film Factory*, ed. Taylor and Christie, 98–99; Meyerhold, "The Fairground Booth," 124; Thierry De Duve, ed., *The Definitively Unfinished Marcel Duchamp* (Cambridge: MIT Press, 1991), 43, 65 n. 6; Huyssen, *After the Great Divide*, 50–51.

25. Shklovsky, "Literature and Cinema (Extracts)," 98–99 (quotes); Meyerhold, "The Fairground Booth" (Eisenstein quote), 124. See Adrian Piotrovsky, "The Cinefication of Theatre—Some General Points," 178–180, and Vsevolod Meyerhold, "The Cinefication of Theatre," 271–275 (quote on 272), both in *The Film Factory*, ed. Taylor and Christie.

26. A. Lebedeva, "Maxim Gorky's Impressions of the Circus" (1958), in *The Soviet Circus*, 205, 208–209; Yury Olesha, *V tsirke* (1928), in *Izbrannye sochineniya*, 365; Harry M. Geduld and Richard C. Gottesman, eds., *Sergei Eisenstein and Upton Sinclair: The Making and Unmaking of Qué Viva Mexico* (Bloomington and Indianapolis: Indiana University Press, 1970), 3; Viktor Shklovsky, "Kruzhevennoe varenie," in *Khod konya* (Moscow and Berlin: n.p., 1923), 50, quoted in Richard Robert Sheldon, "Viktor Borisovich Shklovsky: Literary Theory and Practice, 1914–1930" (Ph.D. diss., University of Michigan, 1966), 237 ("propel," "generate"), 238; A. Lunacharsky, *Teatr segodnya* (Moscow-Leningrad: n.p., 1928), 107 (Meyerhold quote); Schnitzer, Schnitzer, and Martin, *Cinema in Revolution*, 16 (quote).

27. Khersonsky, "'Na vsyakogo mudretsa dovol'no prostoty,'" 24–25; Dobin, *Kozintsev i Trauberg*, 10 (quote), 11, 25, 30, 44; Ronald W. Clark, *Lenin: A Biography* (New York: Harper and Row, 1988), 106. Yesenina cites the memoirs of M. Lyadov, the title and other bibliographic information for which she cannot recall, as the source of the Lenin-Bernhardt anecdote Meyerhold liked to repeat (letter to K. L. Rudnitsky, 14 February 1983, 103).

28. Dobin, *Kozintsev i Trauberg*, 12–13 (quote), 14–16, 21, 24 (quote), 27–29, 34, 47–48, 53; Daniel Gerould and Julia Przyboś, "Melodrama in the Soviet Theater 1917–1928: An Annotated Chronology," in *Melodrama*, ed. Daniel Gerould and Julia Przyboś (New York: New York Literary Forum, 1980), 88 (Tairov quote).

29. Rudnitsky, *Russian and Soviet Theater 1905–1932*, 94, 124.

30. For a brief discussion of Soviet parodies of Hitler and anti-Nazi satire on stage, in poster art, and on film, see Stites, *Russian Popular Culture*, 111–113; Viktor Erlich, *Russian Formalism*, 3rd ed. (New Haven: Yale University Press, 1981), 76; Ilya Fink, "Karandash," in *The Soviet Circus*, 65–66, 68–69; "Karandash," in *Nad chyom smeyotsya kloun* (Moscow: Iskusstvo, 1987), 22; Shklovsky, "The Clown, Comedy and Tragedy," 37 (quote); Ginzburg, *Kinematografiya*, 263–265.

31. Erenburg quoted in Charles J. Maland, *Chaplin and American Culture:*

The Evolution of a Star Image (Princeton: Princeton University Press, 1989), 193; David Platt, "Chaplin: Master of Film Satire—His Genius Grew Out of Love for the Common Man," *Daily Worker*, 10 April 1941.

32. Leyda and Voynow, *Eisenstein at Work*, 43; Sergei Eisenstein, "Charlie the Kid," in *Notes of a Film Director* (Moscow: Foreign Languages Publishing House, 1958), 179–180, 183 ("taller"), 185, 193 ("supreme"), 195; originally published in the collection *Charles Spencer Chaplin* (Moscow: n.p., 1945), 137–158. Eisenstein was in Hollywood in 1930 with his cameramen Edward Tisse (pseudonym of Nikolaitis) and Grigory Aleksandrov (pseudonym of Mormonenko) to develop a scenario based on Theodore Dreiser's novel *An American Tragedy*. While there he tried unsuccessfully to interest Paramount Studios in a number of projects. At this time he also conducted a lecture tour across America. Eisenstein also traveled widely around the world.

33. Parker Tyler, *A Little Boy Lost: Marcel Proust and Charlie Chaplin* (New York: Prospero Pamphlets no. 2, 1947), 6–7; Faure's remarks are quoted in John Willett, *Art and Politics in the Weimar Period: The New Sobriety 1907–1933* (New York: Pantheon Books, 1978), 65; Olesha, *Mysli o Chapline*, 438–439.

34. Eisenstein, "Charlie the Kid," 191, 194 ("news"), 195; Laurence Senelick, written communication, 24 December 1989, regarding the Dovzhenko film; Vendrovskaya and Fevral'sky, *Tvorcheskoe nasledie V. E. Meyerkhol'da*, 195 ("mysterious"), 451; Gerald McDonald, *The Picture History of Charlie Chaplin* (Franklin Square: Nostalgia Press, 1965), 47; "'Dictator' Box-Office Gross Passed GWTW," *Daily Worker*, 27 October 1940; Ella Winter, "Charlie Chaplin and 'The Great Dictator': He Lampoons Stuffed Shirts, Tyranny and Suppression," *Friday Magazine* (New York): 22, 23 ("gibe"); Daniel Todd, "Chaplin's Greatest Picture," *New Masses*, 29 October 1940, 30 ("no one").

35. "Film" entry in *A Concise Encyclopedia of Russia*, ed. S. V. Utechin (London: E. P. Dutton, 1964), 110–111. Stalin tried to discredit Chaplin by labeling him a Jew, which he was not. The dictator's target was not Chaplin but his numerous Jewish supporters in the Soviet film industry, who were charged with the crime of "cosmopolitanism," which essentially meant being Jewish.

36. Shklovsky, "The Clown, Comedy and Tragedy," 37 ("drenched"); Ginzburg, *Kinematografiya*, 263–265; David Platt, "Chaplin, Master of Film Satire," *Daily Worker*, 10 April 1941 ("ninety," "whiskers"); Stites, *Revolutionary Dreams*, 99 ("red"). In contrast, the Russian variety stage tradition at home and in emigration (for example, Arkady Raykin, as well as Arkady Boytler's character "Arkasha") remained more or less fixed on the physical eccentrism of Chaplin's Tramp persona.

37. Maland, *Chaplin*, 63 ("wanted"); I. V. Sokolov, *Charli Chaplin: Zhizn' i tvorchestvo: Ocherk po istorii amerikanskogo kino*, ed. N. P. Abramov (Moscow: Goskinoizdat, 1938), 99–102, 106–111; Robert van Gelder, "Chaplin Draws a Keen," *New York Times Magazine* (8 September 1940): 22; "Film" entry in *A Concise Encyclopedia of Russia*, 110–

111 ("protected"); Sender Garlin, "Those Peculiar Reviews of Chaplin's Films," *Daily Worker*, 19 October 1940, 7.

38. Billington, *Fire in the Minds of Men*, 451; J. Hoberman, "After the Gold Rush: Chaplin at 100, A Radical for Modern Times," *Village Voice*, 18 April 1989, 31–32 (quotes); Viktor Shklovsky, *Literatura i kinematograf* (Berlin: n.p., 1923) quoted in Sheldon, "Viktor Borisovich Shklovsky," 251; Charles Chaplin, *My Autobiography* (New York: Simon and Schuster, 1964), 274.

39. Clark, *The Soviet Novel*, 134–135.

40. Maksim Gor'ky, *Na dne*, in *Sobranie sochineny v tridtsati tomakh*, Akademiya nauk SSSR, Institut mirovoy literatury imeni A. M. Gor'kogo, vol. 6, *P'esy 1901–1906* (Moscow: Gosudarstvennoe izdatel'stvo khudozhestvennoy literatury, 1950), 114 (all references are to this edition of the play); Shklovsky, "The Clown, Comedy and Tragedy," 37–38.

41. Christel Lane, *The Rites of Rulers: Ritual in Industrial Society — the Soviet Case* (New York: Cambridge University Press, 1981), 209 ("heroic").

5. THE SLEEPING IDOL

1. The motto "Svobodno iskusstvo, skovana zhizn'" appeared on some "World of Art" publications (Bowlt, *The Silver Age*, 54).

2. Roman Jakobson, *Puškin and His Sculptural Myth*, trans. and ed. John Burbank (The Hague/Paris: Mouton, 1975), 39 ("opposition"); Herzen, *My Past and Thoughts*, 280 ("holding").

3. Lotman, "Problems in the Typology of Culture," 219; Berdyaev, *The Origin of Russian Communism*, 17, 26–27; the term "secret history" appears in Jules Barbey D'Aurevilly, *Dandyism*, trans. Douglas Ainslie (New York: PAJ Publications, 1988), 38.

4. Aleksandr Pushkin, *Boris Godunov*, in *Polnoe sobranie sochineny v desyati tomakh*, ed. B. V. Tomashevsky, vol. 5, *Yevgeny Onegin, Dramaticheskie proizvedeniya* (Leningrad: Nauka, Leningradskoe otdelenie, 1978), 280; Gershkovich, *The Theater of Yuri Lyubimov*, 143; N. V. Gogol', *Revizor*, in *Sobranie sochineny v shesti tomakh*, ed. S. I. Mashinsky, A. L. Slonimsky, and N. L. Stepanov, vol. 4, *Dramaticheskie proizvedeniya*, ed. A. L. Slonimsky (Moscow: Gosudarstvennoe izdatel'stvo khudozhestvennoy literatury, 1959), 5, 95; Paul Schmidt, ed. and trans., *Meyerhold at Work*, trans. Ilya Levin and Vern McGee (Austin: University of Texas Press, 1980), 82; V. Gronov, "Zamysel postanovki," 353, 390, and Lyubov' Rudneva, " Poiski i otkrytiya," 403, 430, both in *Tvorcheskoe nasledie V. E. Meyerkhol'da*, ed. Vendrovskaya and Fevral'sky. In his 1982 Taganka Theatre production of *Boris Godunov*, Yury Lyubimov extracted from the play's final silence a question and an invocation addressed to the public: "Why do you keep silent? Scream: long, live . . ." At this point, a puppetlike choir directed a mute scream at the audience from the edge of the stage. This combined action alluded to the traditional Russian self-indictment that was expressed in the folk epigraph to

The Inspector General, "Don't blame the mirror for your own ugly mug" (*Na zerkalo necha penyat', / Koli rozha kriva*) and in the Mayor's rhetorical exclamation, "What're you laughing for? You're laughing at yourselves!" directed at the audience near the end of the play. It also referred to the revolutionary insurgency which was captured in Chernyshevsky's and Lenin's leading question, "What is to be done?"

5. Mochulsky, *Aleksandr Blok*, 313 ("dead"); Xenia Gasiorowska, *The Image of Peter the Great in Russian Fiction* (Madison: University of Wisconsin Press, 1979), 67 ("human"); Richard Stites, "Bolshevik Ritual Building in the 1920s," in *Russia in the Era of NEP*, ed. Fitzpatrick, Rabinowitch, and Stites, 295–309 ("revolutionary" on 297).

6. Kagarlitsky, *The Thinking Reed*, 71; Rosenberg, "Introduction: NEP Russia as a 'Transitional' Society," 2; Tucker, *The Lenin Anthology*, xxii–xxiii.

7. Jakobson, *Puškin*, 39.

8. Gasiorowska, *Peter the Great*, 65–70 ("Fate's"), 235. Blok's poem "The Steps of the Commander" (*Shagi Komandora*, 1910–1912), which shifted the focus of the Don Juan legend from the hero to his stone nemesis, underscored the tyranny of paralysis earlier imaged in Pushkin's "Bronze Horseman" and in his Don Juan play *The Stone Guest* (*Kamenny gost'*, written 1830; published 1839). Blok's romantic iconoclast shouts at the idol, "Fate, old Fate, come out and fight!" (*The Twelve and Other Poems*, 105). Katerina Clark has recently noted the highly selective view among Russia's liberal Silver Age intellectuals of Peter the Great as a visionary reformer, "a sort of honorary founder of the Russian intelligentsia." ("Changing Historical Paradigms in Soviet Culture," in *Late Soviet Culture*, ed. Lahusen with Kuperman, 291).

9. Berdyaev, *The Russian Idea*, 32; Peter the Great was characterized as an "evil genius" by symbolist writers Valery Bryusov and Dmitry Merezhkovsky (in his novel *Pyotr i Aleksey*, 1904).

10. Herzen, *My Past and Thoughts*, 24 n. 2, 651–652; Kott, "The Eating of 'The Government Inspector,'" 23 ("*écriture*"). Herzen's description of tsarist Russia as a gigantic "machine [which] spun around in meaningless circles" is quoted in I. Ulitsky, *Logika upravleniya* (Kiev: Kievskoe knizhnoe izdatel'stvo, 1924), 4. The quotation appears in translation in Stephen Sternheimer, "Running Soviet Cities: Bureaucratic Degeneration, Bureaucratic Politics, or Urban Management?" in *Public Policy and Administration in the Soviet Union*, ed. Gordon B. Smith (New York: Praeger, 1980), 79.

11. Berdyaev, *The Russian Idea*, 147, 168, 257; Helju Aulik Bennett, "*Chiny, Ordena,* and Officialdom," in *Russian Officialdom: The Bureaucratization of Russian Society from the Seventeenth to the Twentieth Century*, ed. Walter McKenzie Pintner and Don Karl Rowney (Chapel Hill: University of North Carolina Press, 1980), 162, 165–166, 169–170, 187–188; Rudnitsky, *Russkoe rezhissyorskoe iskusstvo*, 310–311; Lotman, "Concerning Khlestakov," 162–163. Even the moral absolutist Lev Tolstoy spoke of the "pragmatism of falsehood," the useful lie which makes

life livable, at least to a Russian. Tolstoy's drama *The Power of Darkness* (*Vlast' t'my*, 1887) demonstrated the equally potent cultural impulse toward self-exposure. The maximalist character of Russian culture has made it vulnerable to and celebratory of the "exalted lie" which when it is not theatrically exposed becomes theatrically ensconced as "false objectivism," collectivist ideological certainty. The Russian demonology of lying, as of evil, takes the form of "peredonovism," referring to the tyrannical and cowardly protagonist of Sologub's *The Petty Demon*, who was externally mirrored by a grotesque double representing his madness and moral bankruptcy. Nabokov cites Khlestakov as an example of the *vral'*, "a trivial liar, a leasing-monger, a twaddle, a fribbling rogue . . . a boastful driveler, an irresponsible fool" ("Commentary," in Aleksandr Pushkin, *Eugene Onegin* [Princeton: Princeton University Press, 1981], vol. 2, part 1, 426). The lie is on one level an (overly) articulate protest lodged in what Herzen (in Siberian exile in 1837) called a "land of silence and dumbness" (*My Life and Thoughts*, 221).

12. Rudnitsky, *Meyerhold the Director*, 393 ("driven"); Bennett, "*Chiny*," 162, 165–166, 169–170, 187 ("inaccessible"), 188 ("niche-assignment"); Mochulsky, *Aleksandr Blok*, 313 ("dead").

13. Abram Terts, *V teni Gogolya* (London: Overseas Publications, 1975), 152 n.; Wallace Fowlie, *Jean Cocteau: The History of a Poet's Age* (Bloomington and Indianapolis: Indiana University Press, 1966), 119; Eugenio Barba and Nicola Savarese, *The Dictionary of Theatre Anthropology: The Secret Art of the Performer* (New York: Routledge, 1991), 90–91. My discussion of Meyerhold's staging of Gogol's dumb show owes much to *"Revizor" v teatre imeni Vs. Meyerkhol'da*, specifically the following essays included therein: A. L. Slonitsky, "Novoe istolkovanie 'Revizora'" (1926), 12, 14, 16; A. A. Gvozdev, "Reviziya 'Revizora,'" 24, 26–30, 34, 37, 41; V. N. Solovyov, "Zamechaniya po povodu 'Revizora' v postanovke Meyerkhol'da," 60–61; and E. I. Kaplan, "Neshchestvennoe oformlenie 'Revizora' v postanovke Vs. Meyerkhol'da," 71.

14. Rudnitsky, *Meyerhold the Director*, 388–389, 418; Nina Gourfinkel, *Nicolas Gogol: Dramaturge* (Paris: L'Arche, éditeur, 1956), 98; Raymond Williams, *The Politics of Modernism: Against the New Conformists* (New York: Verso, 1989), 103; Helju A. Bennett, "Evolution of the Meaning of *Chin*: An Introduction to the Russian Institution of Rank Ordering and Niche Assignment from the Time of Peter the Great's Table of Ranks to the Bolshevik Revolution," *California Slavic Studies* 10 (1977): 43.

15. Garin, *S Meyerkhol'dom*, 176 ("true"); Barba and Savarese, *The Dictionary of Theatre Anthropology*, 146 ("constructed").

16. Mihajlov, *Russian Themes*, 272.

17. N. V. Gogol', *Polnoe sobranie sochineny*, vol. 4, *Revizor* (Leningrad: Akademiya nauk SSSR, 1951; all references are to this edition). In his review of Meyerhold's 1926 production of Gogol's play, A. A. Gvozdev drew the connection between the disempowerment of the two women and that of the town's petty officials ("Reviziya 'Revizora,'" 33–34). In a

sense, the play's final tableau consigns men and women alike to the social paralysis of figurative window dressing.

18. Gippius, Gogol, 196n.28; B. V. Varneke, *History of the Russian Theatre: Seventeenth through Nineteenth Century*, trans. Boris Brasol, rev. and ed. Belle Martin (New York: Hafner Publishing Company, 1971), 342; Vladimir Nabokov, *Nikolai Gogol* (New York: New Directions, 1961), 25, 148 (quote).

19. In his commentary on Pushkin's *Eugene Onegin*, which depicts the same period as Gogol's play, Nabokov wrote that "the old [Russian] word for statue (now *statuya*) [was] *kumir* ('idol') and the old word for statuette (now *statuetka*) [was] *kukla* ('puppet')" ("Commentary," in *Eugene Onegin*, vol. 2, part 2, 85–86).

20. Herzen, *My Life and Thoughts*, 210–212.

21. Herzen, *My Life and Thoughts*, 271, 312, 313 (quote), 321; de Custine, *Empire of the Czar*, 72. The failure of the 1991 coup precipitated the revelation that there were six million "citizen spies" or secret policemen in the USSR. A mid-1970s production of *The Government Inspector* (*The Inspector General*) at the Citizens Theatre (Glasgow, Scotland), which set the play in 1917, featured a Khlestakov so paranoid about surveillance that he enclosed "a living flea" in his correspondence to surprise those who opened his mail (manuscript copy of *The Government Inspector*, p. 78, translated and adapted by Robert David Macdonald, who directed its Citizens Theatre production in the 1974–1975 season). I am grateful to Laurence Senelick for lending me his copy of this text.

22. Gogol's notorious mystical-moral apologia for his play, written in the form of a dialogue entitled "The Denouement of *The Inspector General*," was widely criticized by his friends, including the actor Mikhail Shchepkin, who had played the Mayor in 1836 at Moscow's Maly Theatre. The second "denouement," written after Gogol received Shchepkin's letter of complaint, seemed like an apologia for the first denouement. As regards the play's meaning, Gogol's spokesperson, the comic actor Mikhal Mikhalch, claimed that "the author didn't give me the key" (Nikolay Gogol', "Razvyazka 'Revizora,'" written 1846; published 1856; and "Vtoraya redaktsiya okonchaniya "Razvyazki 'Revizora,'" published 1896, in *Dramaticheskie proizvedeniya*, ed. E. Zhezlova, 7 vols. [Moscow: Gosudarstvennoe izdatel'stvo khudozhestvennoy literatury, 1967], vol. 4, 411–412, 490n.6 and n.7).

23. Intercepted correspondence has revealed significant functions throughout Russian history. Exiled Russian poet Joseph Brodsky tells of having worked in an agricultural machinery factory which was given the code name "Post Office Box 671" for security reasons. The factory was part of a Gogolian complex of identical buildings, which, as in *The Inspector General*, included a hospital and a prison. When Brodsky moved from the factory to work at the hospital, he sometimes collected the letters which prisoners, who were exercising in the courtyard, managed to throw over the prison wall. Playing the role of secret postman, Brodsky then mailed these letters (Brodsky, "Catastrophes in the Air," 14, 17–18). A

second example of intercepted correspondence reveals secret authorship, as well as secret delivery. For the Taganka Theatre's 1973 production of L. Tselikovsky's *Comrade, Believe!* (*Tovarishch, ver'!*), adapted from Pushkin's correspondence with his persecutor, Tsar Nikolay I, the audience of which I was a part received programs in the form of a letter in an envelope whose seal (the Taganka Theatre's official and immediately recognizable emblem, a red square) had already been broken. Presumably, state surveillance had intercepted the letter and the program, the playbill and the production, before they reached their intended audience. Authoritarian surveillance was then complicit in the play, which, in a sense, performed authority's power.

24. de Custine, *Empire of the Czar*, 81, 95 (quote), 102. The vampirism, hunger and thirst, and living corpse motifs in *The Inspector General* (and also in Gogol's short story *Vy*, in his collection *Mirgorod*, 1836) were extended by Aleksandr Sukhovo-Kobylin in *Tarelkin's Death* (*Smert' Tarelkina*, 1869), the last part of a dramatic trilogy attacking the corruption of the tsarist judicial system. Tarelkin and his colleagues in officialdom are a soulless pack of wolves, who prey upon the innocent and upon each other. Tarelkin steals another official's correspondence, lives under the identity of a dead man, and, in a punishment suited to a vampire, is denied all liquids by his torturers after he is captured. At the end of the play, Tarelkin turns the artificial mask which is his face (the inhuman face of logically positivist, scientific progress/spiritual regress) to the audience and asks them/us for a job. By co-opting the assumption of empathy implicit in the convention of direct audience address, Tarelkin attempts the ultimate act of theatrical vampirism—sucking the not so innocent blood of those who have been living vicariously through his theatrical actions (Sukhovo-Kobylin, *Smert' Tarelkina*, 257–258).

25. Elias Canetti, *Crowds and Power*, trans. Carol Stewart (New York: Viking, 1963), 315–316 ("perfect"); Rudnitsky, *Meyerhold the Director*, 418 (Lunacharsky quote); Leon Trotsky, *Literature and Revolution* (New York: Russell and Russell, 1955; orig. pub. 1924), 238 ("Soviet"). Katerina Clark has noted how in the late 1920s "non-party [creative] intellectuals" (newly split from the Soviet intelligentsia in the early 1920s) became interested in the Nikolayevan eras of the 1830s and 1840s, the repressive aftermath of the Decembrist uprising of 1825. This renewed interest precipitated many theatrical productions of Gogol's work during the 1920s (Clark, "Changing Historical Paradigms in Soviet Culture," 297).

26. Jean Bonamour, *A. S. Griboedov et la vie littéraire de son temps* (Paris: Presses Universitaires de France, 1965), 274 ("social"); Aleksandr Gladkov, "'Gore umu' i Chatsky-Garin," in Garin, *S Meyerkhol'dom*, 185, 187; M. Netchkina, *Griboedov i dekabristy* (Moscow: n.p., 1947), 303. A caricature by M. Babichenko, published at the time of the 1928 production depicting the director as the autocratic usurper of Griboyedov's text (the director as artistic pretender), recalled those which characterized Meyerhold as the usurper of Kommissarzhevskaya's performances at her

theatre. Babichenko's caricature showed a determined and humorless Meyerhold dragging an unwilling Griboyedov by his tail coat behind him, suggesting as well the fate of the Author in *The Little Showbooth*, which the director staged at Kommissarzhevskaya's theatre. Meyerhold has in his pocket a small ladder, a reference to one of *Woe to Wit*'s scenic elements, and holds in his hand a large club with the word *Postanovka* (*Mise en scène*) inscribed on it. Griboyedov, holding in his hand a large edition of *Woe from Wit* (the "authentic" text, minus the dramatic variants which Meyerhold included) shouts, "Unhand me, unhand me!" as an ambulance waits nearby. The Babichenko caricature of Meyerhold appears in a press clipping from an unnamed source in the Harvard Theatre Collection. For useful interpretive discussions of the production's themes, see S. D. Mstislavsky, "Odinoky: K diskussii o 'Gore umu,'" *Zhizn' iskusstva*, 17 April 1928, reprinted in *"Gore ot uma" na russkoy i sovetskoy stsene*, ed. O. M. Fel'dman (Moscow: Iskusstvo, 1987), 271.

27. Lotman, "The Decembrist in Daily Life," 111.
28. Karlinsky, *Russian Drama*, 308–310 (citing Nechkina). Dmitry Merezhkovsky linked Chatsky with Chaadayev in "Revolution and Religion (1907), which appears in English translation in *A Revolution of the Spirit: Crisis of Value in Russia, 1890–1924*, ed. Bernice Glatzer Rosenthal and Martha Bonachevsky-Chomiak (New York: Fordham University Press, 1990), 204.
29. George L. Kline, "Pyotr Yakovlevich Chaadaev," in *Handbook of Russian Literature*, ed. Terras, 76 ("instantly"), 77; Herzen, *My Life and Thoughts*, 41n., 84n., 248 ("*words,*" "*facts*"), 293 ("power"), 294 ("empty," "insufferable"), 295, 299 ("hieroglyph," "hopeless"), 300 (on *slovo*), 636 (quotes beginning "folded"), 653 (quotes beginning "tragically").
30. D. P. Costello, "Introduction," *Gore ot uma* (London: Oxford University Press, 1970), xvii; Herzen, *My Life and Thoughts*, 84n.; Lotman, "The Decembrist in Daily Life," 136 ("ballroom"); Jurij M. Lotman, "Problems in the Typology of Culture," in *Soviet Semiotics: An Anthology*, ed. Lucid, 219 ("sclerosis"). For a brief history of the Decembrists, see Billington, *The Icon and the Axe*, 264–268, and *Fire in the Minds of Men*, 140–143.
31. Vladimir Nabokov, "Introduction," in Aleksandr Pushkin, *Eugene Onegin*, vol. 1, part 1, 22; Lotman, "The Decembrist in Daily Life," 136 (quotes); Lotman, *Universe of the Mind*, 149.
32. Herzen, *My Life and Thoughts*, 42–43 n. 8; A. L. Slonimsky, "Stsenicheskaya poema o Chatskom-dekabriste," *Zhizn' iskusstva*, 10 April 1928, reprinted in *"Gore ot uma" na russkoy i sovetskoy stsene*, 270; Alma H. Law, "Meyerhold's *Woe to Wit* (1928)," *Drama Review* 3 (September 1974): 103 (quote), 104. Aside from Ryleyev, the Decembrist rebels who were hanged included P. I. Pestel, M. F. Orlov, N. I. Turgenev, Kakhovsky, A. A. Bestuzhev-Ryumin, and M. I. Muravyov-Apostol. Others were exiled and/or killed in other ways.
33. L. Varpakhovsky, "O teatral'nosti muzyki i o muzykal'nosti teatra," in

Tvorcheskoe nasledie V. E. Meyerkhol'da, 301–302 (Meyerhold quote); Gladkov, "'Gore umu' i Chatsky-Garin," 192–194, 197, 199, 201, 206; A. A. Gvozdev, "'Gore umu,'" *Zhizn' iskusstva*, 20 March 1928, reprinted in *"Gore ot uma" na russkoy i sovetskoy stsene*, 264 ("musical"); Slonimsky, "Stsenicheskaya poema," 269.

34. Mstislavsky, "Odinoky," 270–271; P. A. Markov, "Ocherki teatral'noy zhizni: K voprosy teatral'noy zhizni prochtenii klassikov," in *Novy mir*, ed. O. M. Fel'dman (Moscow: Iskusstvo, 1987), 275; Terts (Sinyavsky), *V teni Gogolya*, 152n. Alma Law pointed out to me the particular old Bolshevik nuance in Don Louis's/Luis's speech. For information on Efros's production of *Don Juan*, see Spencer Golub, "Acting on the Run: Efros and the Contemporary Soviet Theatre," in *Theatre Quarterly* 26 (Summer 1977): 22–24.

35. Brodsky, "In a Room and a Half," 452.

36. Mstislavsky, "Odinoky," 270–271; Markov, "Ocherki," 275; Brodsky, "In a Room and a Half," 452 ("official").

37. Sergey Radlov, *Desyat' let v teatre* (Leningrad: Priboy, 1929), 238; Alma H. Law cites George Grosz's work in general and in particular a Diego Rivera painting which depicts a group of bourgeois gorging themselves at dinner as possible models for Meyerhold's staging of the dining room episode in *Woe to Wit* ("Meyerhold's *Woe to Wit*," 104–105).

38. Law, "Meyerhold's *Woe to Wit*," 104–105; Stites, *Revolutionary Dreams*, 65; O. Litovsky, press clipping in Harvard Theatre Collection (20 November 1935, "sad").

39. For a detailed account and reassessment of the circumstances surrounding Griboyedov's death, see Evelyn J. Harden, *The Murder of Griboedov—New Materials*, Birmingham Slavonic Monographs no. 6 (Birmingham: Department of Russian Languages and Literatures, University of Birmingham, 1979); Karlinsky, *Russian Drama*, 285.

40. Mstislavsky, "Odinoky," 270–271; Markov, "Ocherki," 275.

41. V. E. Meyerkhol'd, "O vtoroy stsenicheskoy redaktsii 'Gore umu': Iz lektsii dlya sotrudnikov 'Inturista' 23 aprelya 1936 goda," in *Tvorcheskoe nasledie V. E. Meyerkhol'da*, 101–102; Riasanovsky, *A History of Russia*, 325–327; Dwight MacDonald, "Preface," in Herzen, *My Life and Thoughts*, vi ("imperial," "secret"), also 241 ("words").

42. Terts (Sinyavsky), *V teni Gogolya*, 109. In his brief assessment of Meyerhold's 1935 staging, Rudnitsky observes generally that "the image of Molchalin was brought to the foreground partly because the interpretation of the role was more active. Michurin played a substantial and self-assured careerist knowing his own worth and in no way blinded by the magnificence of his patron." Rudnitsky cites D. S. Mirsky's characterization of this Molchalin as "the synthesized image of the entire Russian bureaucracy" (*Meyerhold the Director*, 434; D. S. Mirsky, "Gore umu," *Literaturnaya gazeta* [24 November 1935]).

43. Debord, *Society of the Spectacle*, 14 ("aims"); Yury Tynyanov, *Literaturnoe nasledstvo*, vols. 47–48 (n.p., 1946), 185 ("dead"); Laurence Senelick, ed., *National Theatre in Northern and Eastern Europe 1746–1900* (New York: Cambridge University Press, 1991), 326.

44. Herzen, *My Life and Thoughts*, 278 n.; Lyubov' Rudneva, "Poisk i otkry-tiya," in *Tvorcheskoe nasledie V. E. Meyerkhol'da*, 424 (Meyerhold quote), 425. While in Paris in 1816–1817, the marginally implicated Decembrist conspirator M. S. Lunin wrote a novel about the False Dmitry. In historian-playwright Edvard Radzinsky's imaginative dramatic reconstruction of the final days of Lunin's life, *I, Mikhail Sergeyevich Lunin* (1977), the protagonist awaits his executioners, while in the adjoining prison cell the scribe who will record the official history of his demise has sex with the charwoman who will wash Lunin's blood away. See Alma H. Law, "Introduction" to her translation of Edvard Radzinsky, *I, Mikhail Sergeevich Lunin* (New York: Institute for Contemporary East European Drama and Theatre of the Center for Advanced Study in Theatre Arts, CUNY, 1980), 2.

45. Kozintsev, *Shakespeare*, 171 (quote), 172, 219–220.

46. Bertram C. Wolfe, *Three Who Made the Revolution: A Biographical History* (New York: Dell, 1964), 352, 359, 361–363; Pipes, *The Russian Revolution*, 165–166, 168, 187–190.

47. L. Varpakhovsky, "O teatral'nosti i o muzykal'nosti teatra," in *Tvorcheskoe nasledie V. E. Meyerkhol'da*, 341; Gladkov, "'Gore umu,'" 204.

48. According to Richard Pipes, Lenin trusted the Latvians more than Russian guards (*The Russian Revolution*, 493 [quote], 530, 611); Robert V. Daniels, *Red October: The Bolshevik Revolution of 1917* (Boston: Beacon Press, 1967), 173, 175, 178 (photo follows).

49. de Custine, *Empire of the Czar*, 52, 345 ("fear"); Lotman, "The Decembrist in Daily Life," 100 ("heinous"); Nahirny, *The Russian Intelligentsia*, 45, 149 ("naked," "unbecoming").

50. Debord, *Society of the Spectacle*, 189 ("dynamic"); Alma H. Law, "Chekhov's Russian *Hamlet*," *Drama Review* 3 (Fall 1983: Michael Chekhov Issue): 45 ("perishing").

51. Konstantin Derzhavin, *Kniga o Kamernom teatre, 1914–1934* (Leningrad: Khudozhestvennaya literatura, 1934), 112–113; Golovashenko, *Rezhissyorskoe iskusstvo*, 54; K. L. Rudnitsky, "Tvorchesky put' Tairova," 16; Yakulov quoted in Vladislav Ivanov, "Razmyshlyaya o 'Fedre,'" in *Rezhissyorskoe iskusstvo A. Ya. Tairova*, 101.

52. Koonen, *Stranitsy zhizni*, 270; V. N. Solovyov, "Zamechaniya po povodu 'Revizora' v postanovke Meyerkhol'da," in *"Revizor" v teatre imeni Vs. Meyerkhol'da*, 59; Meyerkhol'd, "O vtoroy stsenicheskoy redaktsii 'Gore umu,'" 99 (quote); Bowlt, *The Silver Age*, 227; Worrall, *Modernism to Realism*, 27; Vladislav Ivanov, "Polunochnoe solntse," *Novy mir* 3 (1989): 235–237.

53. "Phaedra," in *Tristia* (Petersburg/Berlin: n.p., 1922); Janet M. King, "Marina Ivanovna Tsvetaeva," in *Handbook of Russian Literature*, ed. Terras, 485–487; Roberta Reeder, "Program Notes" for the production of Tsvetayeva's *Phaedra*, directed by Roman Viktyuk at the American Repertory Theatre, Cambridge, Massachusetts, 17–23 June 1990; Nadezhda Mandelstam, *Hope Abandoned*, trans. Max Hayward (New York: Atheneum), 108 (quote), 109, 346–347; Rudnitsky, *Tvorchesky put' Tairova*, 21. Osip Mandelstam actually did see the Kamerny Thea-

tre's production of *Phèdre* but later died in one of Stalin's labor camps on 27 December 1938. Marina Tsvetayeva hung herself in 1941 and was buried in an unmarked grave.

54. Golovashenko, *Rezhissyorskoe iskusstvo*, 43, 54, 56; Koonen, *Stranitsy zhizni*, 238, 272; Vladislav Ivanov, "Polunochnoe solntse," *Novy mir* 3 (1989): 236 ("ethical"); Rudnitsky, *Russian and Soviet Theater 1905–1932*, 106; K. L. Rudnitsky, ed., *Istoriya sovetskogo dramaticheskogo teatra*, vol. 2, *1921–1925* (Moscow: Nauka, 1966), 142–146 ("universal"); Derzhavin, *Kniga*, 56 ("emotionally"); Ivanov, "Razmyshlyaya o 'Fedre,'" 98. The great realistic actress and tragedienne Mariya Yermolova, who played Phèdre (in a translation by M. P. Sadovsky) in 1889–1890 at Moscow's Maly Theatre, was the role's chief Russian stage interpreter prior to Koonen. Yermolova excelled at playing strong, complex, and sometimes heroic women. Her great performances included the roles of Joan of Arc, Maria Stuart, Sappho, Lady Macbeth, Kate in *Taming of the Shrew*, and Laurencia in *Fuenteovejuna*. Yermolova became associated with progressive and later revolutionary politics, which audiences saw reflected in her performances. Her interpretation of Phèdre was praised by Russian critics for capturing the intense emotional suffering not of a queen but of a woman in love. Some wanted Yermolova to replicate the neoclassical style captured in the Phèdre of the great French actress Rachel (1843). However, Yermolova's service to the character's inner life was deemed by others to be more successful than Sarah Bernhardt's artificial and idiosyncratic display of actor's mannerisms and techniques in the role (1877) (S. N. Durylin, *Mariya Nikolayevna Yermolova 1853–1928: Ocherk zhizny i tvorchestva* [Moscow: Akademiya nauk, 1953], 304–305, 598–599). For references to Phèdre in Yermolova's correspondence, see *Mariya Nikolayevna Yermolova: Pis'ma, iz literaturnogo naslediya, vospominaniya sovremennikov*, ed. S. N. Durylin (Moscow: Iskusstvo, 1955), 63, 64, 66, 69, 71. See also *Pis'ma M. N. Yermolovy*, ed. S. N. Durylin (Moscow-Leningrad: Iv. Fyodorov, 1939); A. Brodsky, ed., *Sbornik M. N. Yermolova* (Leningrad: Academia, 1925); and Boris Alpers, *Aktyorskoe iskusstvo v Rossii* (Moscow: Iskusstvo, 1945).

55. Golovashenko, *Rezhissyorskoe iskusstvo*, 54–56; Nash, "East Meets West," 111; Aleksandr Tairov, *O teatre: Zapiski rezhissyora, stat'i, besedy, rechi, pis'ma* (Moscow: Vserossyskoe teatral'noe obshchestvo, 1970), 543 ("problem"); Derzhavin, *Kniga*, 104–105; Rudnitsky, *Tvorchesky put' Tairova*, 24; Selim Omarovich Khan-Magomedov, *Alexandr Vesnin and Russian Constructivism* (New York: Rizzoli, 1986), 79. Tairov was first drawn to the idea of staging Racine's *Phèdre* while directing Eugene Scribe's and Ernest Legouvé's play *Adrienne Lecouvreur* (1849) at the Kamerny Theatre (premiere 25 November 1919). The character of Adrienne, who is based on the famous French tragedienne (1692–1730), recites monologues by the heroines of *Le Cid*, *The Winter's Tale*, and *Phèdre*. *Adrienne* helped prepare Alisa Koonen for her later work on Phèdre. Koonen's most successful roles depicted constructive/destructive

female emotionalism, which she was adept at playing. Her notable roles included Salome (1917); Phèdre (1922); Abbie in Eugene O'Neill's *Desire under the Elms*, which offers *Phèdre* in a contemporary mode (premiere 11 November 1926); Ella in O'Neill's *All God's Chillun Got Wings* (premiere 21 February 1929); Cleopatra in the dramatic compilation—from G. B. Shaw, Pushkin, and Shakespeare—*Egyptian Nights* (premiere 14 December 1934); Emma in Koonen's own adaptation of Flaubert's *Madame Bovary* (Far East premiere 2 April 1940; Moscow premiere October 1940); and Nina Zarechnaya in *The Seagull* (premiere 20 July 1944). Koonen used the theme of the woman in love to demonstrate the struggle for unattainable beauty inevitably lost to the pressures exerted by social reality. Critic Pavel Markov considered Koonen's performances of the 1920s to have grown "from the seed of the symbolist theatre," especially from Blok's Eternal Feminine (quoted in Ivanov, "Polunochnoe solntse," 240). Koonen's characters all equated the willfulness of love with freedom of will, and freedom with pride. Koonen's performances as Shaw's Saint Joan (*Saint Joan*, premiere 21 October 1924), Walter Hasenclever's Antigone (*Antigone*, premiere 1 October 1927), and Vishnevsky's Commissar in *An Optimistic Tragedy* (premiere 18 December 1933) translated romantic personal love into love for a romantic social ideal.

56. Derzhavin, *Kniga*, 59; Golovashenko, *Rezhissyorskoe iskusstvo*, 63, 76–77; Rudnitsky, *Tvorchesky put' Tairova*, 21.

57. Mikhail Grobman, "About Malevich," in *The Avant-Garde in Russia, 1910–1930: New Perspectives*, ed. Stephanie Baron and Maurice Tuchman (Los Angeles: Los Angeles County Museum of Art, 1980), 27.

58. Golovashenko, *Rezhissyorskoe iskusstvo*, 188 ("almost"); Leach, *Vsevolod Meyerhold*, 102; A. Efros, *Kamerny teatr i ego khudozhniki, 1914–1934* (Moscow: VTO, 1934), xxxiv; Derzhavin, *Kniga*, 89–90, 107; Khan-Magomedov, *Alexander Vesnin*, 64–65, 74. Vesnin's first work for Tairov, his cubist design for Claudel's "monumental" play *The Tidings Brought to Mary* (*Blagoveshchenie*; Kamerny Theatre premiere 16 November 1920), anticipated the "metrical abstraction" (*metricheskaya abstraktnost'*) of his *Phèdre* design. Tairov unexpectedly rejected Vesnin's 1921 "baroque cubist" set and costume designs for *Romeo and Juliet* late in the production process in favor of Aleksandra Ekster's more aesthetic plan.

59. Khan-Magomedov, *Alexander Vesnin*, 72, 74 ("irregular"), 76–78 ("real"), 80–81 (Cocteau quote); Abram Efros, "Khudozhnik i stsena," in *Kul'tura teatra* 1 (1921): 11–12; "Beseda A. Ya. Tairova s truppoy Kamernogo teatra o *Fedre*," 20 March 1946, TsGALI SSSR (fond. no. 2328, opis' no. 1, ed. khr. no. 392), quoted in Golovashenko, *Rezhissyorskoe iskusstvo*, 202 ("fictional").

60. Efros, *Kamerny teatr i ego khudozhniki*, xxxiv; Golovashenko, *Rezhissyorskoe iskusstvo*, 64, 188 ("suite"; from "Lektsiya A. Ya. Tairova truppe Kamernogo teatra," 2 January 1931, TsGALI SSSR [fond. no. 238, opis' no. 1, ed. khr. no. 69]), 189 ("dynamic"), 191–192 ("restless"), 246; Derzhavin, *Kniga*, 107. While preparing a later production

of *Phèdre* (Kamerny Theatre premiere, 20 March 1946), Tairov again impressed upon his company the need to imbue their plastique with "the rhythms of the epoch." Similarly, Konstantin Rudnitsky asserts that the unexpected rhythmic alternations of sound and silence, movement and stasis, in Meyerhold's 1920s stagings captured the "strange riddles of the times," which the director could not necessarily solve (*Meyerhold the Director*, 387).

61. Rudnitsky, "Tvorchesky put' Tairova," 21; N. Berkovsky, *Literatura i teatr* (Moscow: n.p., 1969), Gabriel Boissy, "Phèdre au Théâtre de chambre," *Comoedia*, 12 March 1923, and Jean Cocteau, *Les nouvelles*, 17 March 1923, all quoted in Khan-Magomedov, *Alexander Vesnin*, 74, 80, 81; Golovashenko, *Rezhissyorskoe iskusstvo*, 29.

62. Koonen, *Stranitsy zhizni*, 29; Golovashenko, *Rezhissyorskoe iskusstvo*, 76.

63. Derzhavin, *Kniga*, 49–50, 56, 81, 109; Golovashenko, *Rezhissyorskoe iskusstvo*, 27 ("revolutionary"), 28–29 ("generalized"), 31 ("gentle"), 57 ("cleansing"); Koonen, *Stranitsy zhizni*, 271.

64. Ivanov, "Razmyshlyaya o 'Fedre,'" 93; A. V. Lunacharsky, "'Fedre' v Kamernom teatre," *Izvestiya*, 11 February 1922, cited in Golovashenko, *Rezhissyorskoe iskusstvo*, 5, 12, 26, 34; Derzhavin, *Kniga*, 59, 62–63, 108, 110.

65. Mandelstam, *Hope Abandoned*, 109; Roland Barthes, *On Racine*, trans. Richard Howard (New York: PAJ Publications, 1983), 117.

66. Terry Eagleton, *William Shakespeare* (Oxford: Basil Blackwell, 1986), 28; Brodsky, "Catastrophes in the Air," 293.

67. Volkov quoted in Ivanov, *Rezhissyorskoe iskusstvo Tairova*, 99; Ivanov, "Razmyshlyaya o 'Fedre,'" 99–100; Ivanov, "Polunochnoe solntse," 242; Poggioli, *The Poets of Russia*, 66; Khan-Magomedov, *Alexander Vesnin*, 78; *Teatr i muzyka* 34 (1923): 1111. Cocteau compared Koonen-Phèdre's disordering passion to illness, and Gabriel Boissy, who saw her perform on the same Kamerny Theatre tour of Europe, declared the emotional spectacle to be "a barbarous sight"; these critical responses likewise reflected French anxiety over what André Antoine called "barbarously Asiatic" Russians "crushing heavily underfoot" a national dramatic treasure (Golovashenko, *Rezhissyorskoe iskusstvo*, 31). The 1924 European tour was advertised by the emblematic icon of Koonen as Phèdre, "which had already become something of a symbol of the theatre's work" (Mikhail Anikst, ed., *Soviet Commercial Design of the Twenties*, trans. and ed. Catherine Cooke [New York: Abbeville Press, 1987], 124).

68. A. Ya. Levinson, "Russkaya Fedre" (selection), in *Russky sovetsky teatr 1921–1926*, ed. A. Ya. Trabsky (Leningrad: Iskusstvo, 1975), 249; Georges Poulet, *The Interior Distance*, trans. Elliott Coleman (Baltimore: Johns Hopkins University Press, 1959), 125.

69. Golovashenko, *Rezhissyorskoe iskusstvo*, 57, 77; Markov and Tairov quoted in Ivanov, "Razmyshlyaya o 'Fedre,'" 99–100.

70. Antoine quoted in Leonid Grossman, *Alisa Koonen* (Moscow: Aca-

demia, 1930), 61; A. Koonen, "Iz vospominany o Tairove," *Teatral'naya zhizn'* 12 (1961): 24–25; Golovashenko, *Rezhissyorskoe iskusstvo*, 28 ("bloody"), 212, 224; Derzhavin, *Kniga*, 112–113, 115.

71. Golovashenko, *Rezhissyorskoe iskusstvo*, 29–30 (Lunacharsky quote), 75–76; Derzhavin, *Kniga*, 108–109, 111; Koonen, *Stranitsy zhizni*, 275.

6. THE PROCRUSTEAN BED

1. Chaadayev, *Philosophical Letters*, in *Russian Philosophy*, vol. 1, 115–116; Aksakov quoted in Berdyaev, *The Russian Idea*, 162. Konstantin Aksakov was a Slavophile journalist and ideologue. Slavophilism, which began in the 1830s, was "anti-rationalistic, anti-positivistic, and anti-materialistic"; Slavophiles favored a native culture grounded in the Orthodox church and the village-commune (*obshchina*) over the alien, urban-centered, bureaucratic state brought to Russia from Western Europe by Peter the Great (*Russian Philosophy*, vol. 1, 161–163).

2. Lenin quoted in Wilson, *To the Finland Station*, 547.

3. Poggioli, *The Theory of the Avant-Garde*, 6; Stalin quoted in Lars Erik Blomqvist, "Some Utopian Elements in Stalinist Art," *Russian History* 11 (Summer–Fall 1984): 298. For an informed treatment of the history and tradition of Russian revolutionary utopianism, see Stites, *Revolutionary Dreams*, in particular, 225–253, for his discussion of how Stalin, in his first decade of power (1928–1938), curtailed the openness and individualism of revolutionary utopianism in favor of a single utopian vision imposed from above.

4. For a detailed account of the construction of Lenin's tomb, see Nina Tumarkin, *Lenin Lives! The Lenin Cult in Soviet Russia* (Cambridge, Mass.: Harvard University Press, 1983).

5. Katerina Clark, "Political History and Literary Chronotope: Some Soviet Case Studies," in *Literature and History: Theoretical Problems and Russian Case Studies*, ed. Gary Saul Morson (Stanford: Stanford University Press, 1986), 233–234, 236; Golomstock, *Totalitarian Art*, 228; Herzen, *My Past and Thoughts*, 416 ("rhetorical"), 421, 449 ("pointed"), 501; Andrei Sinyavsky, *Soviet Civilization: A Cultural History*, trans. Joanne Turnbull (New York: Arcade/Little, Brown, 1990), xii ("précis").

6. Clark, *Lenin: A Biography*, 474; Slavoj Žižek, *For They Know Not What They Do: Enjoyment as a Political Factor* (New York: Verso, 1991), 260, 262; Lenin quote in Berdyaev, *The Origin of Russian Communism*, 161; Billington, *The Icon and the Axe*, 36–37.

7. Robert M. Slusser, *Stalin in October: The Man Who Missed the Revolution* (Baltimore: Johns Hopkins University Press, 1990), 50–51, 123–124, 255; Alain Jaubert, *Making People Disappear: An Amazing Chronicle of Photographic Deception*, trans. International Translation Center (McLean, Va.: Pergamon-Brassey's International Defense Publishers, 1989), 44, 47; Alan Wood, *Stalin and Stalinism* (New York: Routledge, 1990), 18.

8. Mally, *Culture of the Future*, 199 (quote); Lotman and Uspenskii, "Binary Models in the Dynamic of Russian Culture," 50; Berdyaev, *The Russian Idea*, 144, 159–160.

9. Blok, "Krushenie gumanizma," 110; Malevich quoted in Vassily Rakitin, "The Avant-Garde and Art of the Stalinist Era," in *The Culture of the Stalin Period*, ed. Hans Günther (New York: St. Martin's Press, 1990), 186; Baronov quoted in Blok, "Narod i intelligentsiya," in *Sobranie sochineny v vos'mi tomakh*, vol. 5, 318; Stalin quoted in Alexander Weissberg, *Conspiracy of Silence*, trans. Edward Fitzgerald (London: Hamish Hamilton, 1952), 501.

10. Fitzpatrick, *The Cultural Front*, 184; Golomstock, *Totalitarian Art*, 84; Zhdanov quoted in Régine Robin, *Le réalisme socialiste: Une esthétique impossible* (Paris: Payot, 1986), 87–88; Stites, *Revolutionary Dreams*, 124; Lenin quoted in Roy A. Medvedev, *Let History Judge: The Origins and Consequences of Stalinism* (New York: Vintage/Random House, 1971), 526.

11. For information on the discussion of the new Soviet art's "tendentiousness," see Robin, *Le réalisme socialiste*, 84. Mayakovsky's reference to "tendentious realism" is quoted in Medvedev, *Let History Judge*, 511; Mally, *Culture of the Future*, 162–164. Sheila Fitzpatrick argues that antiformalism was mandated less by Soviet policy than by a conservative "Soviet mentality" shared by members of the public and the various artistic professions (*The Cultural Front*, 214, 248–249). She also believes that the "cultural orthodoxies" to which members of the intelligentsia were made to conform were largely those of their artistic leaders (for example, those of Stanislavsky in theatre). There is some truth to these assertions, as attested by the (highly subjective) evidence in Mikhail Bulgakov's *Theatrical Novel* (*Teatral'naya roman* [n.p., 1937]; more commonly known in English as *Black Snow*). Bulgakov bitterly and comically depicts his difficulties in realizing his artistic vision of his play at MAT under Stanislavsky's uncomprehending direction. There was plenty of blame to be distributed among artistic leaders and government agencies. However, the boundaries of artistic taste and experimentation were set (or so the public was encouraged to assume) by Stalin and his bureaucrats.

12. Engels quoted in Golomstock, *Totalitarian Art*, 189–190; Herman Ermolaev, *Soviet Literary Theories 1917–1934: The Genesis of Socialist Realism* (Berkeley and Los Angeles: University of California Press, 1963), 169, 201; Robin, *Le réalisme socialiste*, 17, 21 ("epic"), 40, 72.

13. Ermolaev, *Soviet Literary Theories*, 142, 151–152, 157–158, 177, 229 n. 13; Daniel Gerould, "Gorky, Melodrama, and the Development of Early Soviet Theater," *Yale/Theater* 7 (Winter 1976): 33–44; Robin, *Le réalisme socialiste*, 59 (Tretyakov quote), 70.

14. Lane, *The Rites of Rulers*, 17, 22, 33. I am grateful to John Caemerer of Brown University for helping to clarify for me the "worthiness" theme in Soviet socialist realist fiction.

15. Medvedev, *Let History Judge*, 529.

16. From Soviet historian M. Y. Gefter's speech to the joint meeting of the

historiographical group and the methodological sector of the Institute of
History, 29 April 1966, quoted in Medvedev, *Let History Judge*, 517.

17. Propp, *Morphology of the Folktale*, 20, 22–23.

18. Yevgeny Shvarts, *Ten'*, in *Three Plays* (Russian-language edition), ed.
Avril Pyman (New York: Pergamon Press, 1972), 88 (all references are to
this edition of the play). Zamyatin, *We*, 180; Trotsky quoted in Sinyavsky,
Soviet Civilization, xii.

19. Boris Pasternak, *Safe Conduct*, trans. Beatrice Scott (New York: New Directions, 1931), 102; Herzen, *My Past and Thoughts*, 501; Wolfe, *Three
Who Made the Revolution*, 437 (Stalin "paper" quote), 578; de Jonge,
Stalin, 36 (quote by unnamed Soviet historian), 368 (Stalin "facts"
quote).

20. Modris Eksteins, *Rites of Spring: The Great War and the Birth of the
Modern Age* (New York: Anchor/Doubleday, 1989), 194–195; Robin,
Le réalisme socialiste, 56–59; Matei Calinescu, *Five Faces of Modernity*
(Durham: Duke University Press, 1987), 114 ("great"); Gladkov, *Ce-
ment*, 177–178 ("Euclideanism").

21. Les Essif, "The Iconic *Mise en Abîme* of the Space-Character Relationship in Contemporary French Hypersubjective Theatre" (Ph.D. diss.,
Brown University, 1990), 23 (quote); Golomstock, *Totalitarian Art*, 85–
86, 270–271; Bruno Taut, "Russia's Architectural Situation," unpublished manuscript, Berlin, 2 November 1929, in El Lissitsky, *Russia: An
Architecture for World Revolution*, trans. Eric Dluhosch (Cambridge:
MIT Press, 1970), 171; Herzen, *My Past and Thoughts*, 653.

22. Guy Debord, *Comments on the Society of the Spectacle*, trans. Malcom
Imrie (New York: Verso, 1990), 11–12, 16–17, 32; Nigel Moore, "The
Myth of Stalin: The Psychodynamics of Its Utopian Ideals," *Russian His-
tory* 11 (Summer–Fall 1984): 283, 299; Caryl Emerson, *Boris Godunov:
Transpositions of a Russian Theme* (Bloomington and Indianapolis: In-
diana University Press, 1986), 96, 140.

23. Eagleton, *William Shakespeare*, 30 (quote); Vsevolod Meyerhold, "Notes
at a Rehearsal of *Boris Godunov*," in *Meyerhold at Work*, 111; Clark,
"Political History and Literary Chronotope," 238; Herzen, *My Past and
Thoughts*, 145; Mandelstam, *Hope Abandoned*, 224.

24. See Emerson, *Boris Godunov*, 134–135, 242–243 nn. 118–120, for a
discussion of the theories behind and the implications of these textual
variants.

25. Golomstock, *Totalitarian Art*, 301; Stephen Orgel, *The Illusion of
Power: Political Theatre in the English Renaissance* (Berkeley and Los
Angeles: University of California Press, 1975), 87–88; Robert Conquest,
The Great Terror: A Reassessment (New York: Oxford University Press,
1990); Mikhail Bakhtin, "Forms of Time and of the Chronotope in the
Novel," in *The Dialogic Imagination: Four Essays*, trans. Caryl Emerson
and Michael Holquist (Austin: University of Texas Press, 1981), 84–258;
the wax figures in the cells are mentioned in Medvedev, *Let History
Judge*, 238; Eugenia Ginzburg, *Journey into the Whirlwind*, trans. Paul
Stevenson and Max Hayward (New York: Harcourt, Brace and World,

1967), 237; Herbert Blau characterized Meyerhold as being "seized by history" in *Take Up the Bodies*, 81.

26. W. J. T. Mitchell, *Iconology: Image, Text, Ideology* (Chicago: University of Chicago Press, 1987), 172, 181, 193, 202.

27. Bernice Rosenthal, "Preface," in *A Revolution of the Spirit*, ed. Rosenthal and Bonachevsky-Chomiak, xiii; Boris Uspensky, *The Semiotics of the Russian Icon*, ed. Stephen Rudy (Lisse, Belgium: Peter De Ridder Press, 1976), 53 (quote); Paglia, *Sexual Personae*, 29; Carmichael, *Stalin's Masterpiece: The Show Trials and Purges of the Thirties — The Consolidation of the Bolshevik Dictatorship* (New York: St. Martin's Press, 1976), 36, 62. The first "show trial" of the Bolsheviks' political opponents, the Socialist Revolutionaries, was staged in 1922.

28. Pipes, *The Russian Revolution*, 394; Trotsky quoted in de Jonge, *Stalin*, 270; Fyodor Dostoyevsky, *The Brothers Karamazov*, trans. Constance Garnett (New York: Signet/New American Library, 1957), 236; Poggioli, *The Theory of the Avant-Garde*, 138–139 ("technism").

29. Moore, "The Myth of Stalin," 285, 293, 296; Jonathan Levy and Phillip Whitehead, *Stalin: A Time for Judgement* (New York: Pantheon, 1990), 7.

30. Propp, *Morphology of the Folktale*, 84; Mikhail Bakhtin, *Rabelais and His World*, trans. Hélène Iswolsky (Cambridge: MIT Press, 1968), 450. See also Felicia Londré, "Evgeny Shvarts and the Uses of Fantasy in Soviet Theatre," *Research Studies* 47 (September 1979): 131–144.

31. Sinyavsky, *Soviet Civilization*, 93 (Yaroslavsky quote), 94 (Khrushchev image), 95; Nikolay Cherkasov, *Notes of a Soviet Actor* (Moscow: Foreign Languages Publishing House, 1953), 217; Golomstock, *Totalitarian Art*, 114; Stephen F. Cohen, *Rethinking the Soviet Experience: Politics and History since 1917* (New York: Oxford University Press, 1986), 101; Lane, *The Rites of Rulers*, 154, 182.

32. Jaubert, *Making People Disappear*, 36–37; Golomstock, *Totalitarian Art*, 194–195; Nikita Khrushchev, *Khrushchev Remembers*, trans. and ed. Strobe Talbot (Boston: Little, Brown, 1970).

33. Walter Benjamin, "The Work of Art in the Age of Mechanical Reproduction," in *Illuminations: Essays and Reflections*, trans. Harry Zohn (New York: Schocken, 1969), 224; Krupskaya quoted in Wilson, *To the Finland Station*, 551.

34. Ginzburg, *Journey*, 89; de Jonge, *Stalin*, 168, 349–350 (citing Maclean's statement from the British Foreign Office file 371 N 5720 250 38); Khrushchev, *Khrushchev Remembers*, 352.

35. Michael Sidney McLain, "N. P. Oxlopkov: A Critical Life in the Soviet Theater" (Ph.D. diss., University of Washington, 1982), 193–194.

36. Anton Antonov-Ovseenko, "Teatr Josifa Stalina," *Teatr* 8 (August 1988): 134 (quote); de Jonge, *Stalin*, 270.

37. Ermolaev, *Soviet Literary Theories*, 91–92; Carmichael, *Stalin's Masterpiece*, 4; Antonov-Ovseenko, "Teatr," 135; de Jonge, *Stalin*, 456, 458; Golomstock, *Totalitarian Art*, 26 (Tretyakov quote).

38. Rosalinde Sartorti, "Stalinism and Carnival: Organization and Aesthetics

of Political Holidays," in *The Culture of the Stalin Period*, ed. Günther, 62–63.

39. Materials in the H. W. L. Dana Collection, in the Harvard Theatre Collection.

40. Mandelstam, *Hope Abandoned*, 592 ("silence"); Clark, *The Soviet Novel*, 29 ("spectacle"); Vasily Grossman, *Life and Fate*, trans. Robert Chandler (New York: Harper and Row, 1985), 282.

41. Robin, *Le réalisme socialiste*, 92–93. On the avant-garde as a prelude to socialist realism, see Boris Groys, "The Birth of Socialist Realism from the Spirit of the Russian Avant-Garde," 122–148, and Rakitin, "The Avant-Garde and Art of the Stalinist Era," 178–189, both in *The Culture of the Stalin Period*, ed. Günther. This essay pursues the line of argument of Groys's book *Gesamtkunstwerk Stalin* (Munich: n.p., 1988).

42. On audience surveys, see Lars Kleberg, "The Nature of the Soviet Audience: Theatrical Ideology and Audience Research in the 1920's," in *The Culture of the Stalin Period*, ed. Günther, 172–195; Maxim Gorky, "On the Heroic Theatre," quoted in Gerould, "Gorky, Melodrama and the Development of the Early Soviet Theater," 35.

43. Lotman, "Concerning Khlestakov," 183; Wilde quoted in Ellmann, *Oscar Wilde*, 143.

7. THE *HAMLET* GULAG

1. Nikolay Okhlopkov, "Iz rezhissyorskoy eksplikatsy 'Gamleta,'" *Teatr* 1 (1955): 60, quoted in McLain, "Oxlopkov," 246; Aleksandr I. Solzhenitsyn, *The Gulag Archipelago* (New York: Harper and Row, 1974), 173–174.

2. As recently as 1986, a *Hamlet* essay appeared in the Soviet Union bearing the title "Not to Be?" (A. Minkin, "Ne byt?" *Teatral'naya zhizn'* 7 [1986]: 6); Billington, *The Icon and the Axe*, 354–355; Blok, "Stikhiya i kul'tura" (1908), in *Sobranie sochineny*, vol. 5, 351; Iurii M. Lotman, "The Poetics of Everyday Behavior in Eighteenth-Century Russian Culture," trans. Andrea Beesing, in *The Semiotics of Russian Cultural History*, ed. Nakhimovsky and Nakhimovsky, 86; Ju. M. Lotman, "The Theater and Theatricality as Components of Early Nineteenth-Century Culture," trans. G. S. Smith, in *The Semiotics of Russian Culture*, ed. Shukman, 143 n.

3. Billington, *The Icon and the Axe*, 354–355; Lidiia Ia. Ginsburg, "The 'Human Document' and the Formation of Character," trans. R. Judson Rosengrant, in *The Semiotics of Russian Cultural History*, ed. Nakhimovsky and Nakhimovsky, 189–190, 190 n. 2; Mochulsky, *Aleksandr Blok*, 233; Elliott, *New Worlds*, 12; Kozintsev, *Shakespeare*, 241–242; Herzen, *My Past and Thoughts*, 42–43, 59–60, 64–65, 333.

4. Jakobson, "On a Generation That Squandered Its Poets," 279–280, 288; Pasternak quoted in Monika Frenkel Greenleaf, "Tynianov, Pushkin and the Fragment: Through the Lens of Montage," in *Cultural Mythologies*

of Russian Modernism, 265; Pomorska, "The Utopian Future of the Russian Avant-Garde," in *American Contributions to the Ninth International Congress of Slavists* (Kiev, September 1983), vol. 2, *Literature, Poetics, History*, ed. Paul Debreczeny (Columbus: Slavica, 1983), 277, 379, 384–385; Paperno, "Pushkin," 33; Pyman, "Introduction," in *Alexander Blok: Selected Poems*, 2; Alexander Blok, "Religious Quests and the People" (1907), in *The Spirit of Music*, 27. For recent Soviet discussions of the fate theme in *Hamlet*, see O. Skorochkina, "V kakom kostyume khodit Hamlet?" in *V kontse vos'midesyatykh (na Leningradskoy stsene): Sbornik nauchnykh trudov* (Leningrad: Ministerstvo kul'tury RSFSR and LGITMiK, 1989), 88–89; and V. Gaevsky, *Fleyta Gamleta: Obrazy sovremennogo teatra* (Moscow: Soyuzteatr, 1990), 116.

5. Kozintsev, *Shakespeare*, 164, 226; Shattuck, *Marcel Proust*, 102; Richard Peace, *The Enigma of Nikolai Gogol* (Cambridge: Cambridge University Press, 1981), 175 (quote).

6. Mikhail M. Morozov, *Shakespeare on the Soviet Stage*, trans. David Magarshack (London: Soviet News, 1947), 11 (Sumarokov quotes), 13, 15–16, 20; Ernest J. Simmons, *English Literature and Culture in Russia* (New York: n.p., 1964), 206; Mikhail Morozov quoted in Joseph Macleod, *Actors Cross the Volga: A Study of the Nineteenth Century Russian Theatre and of Soviet Theatres in War* (London: Allen and Unwin, 1946), 265; Lazar Fleishman, *Boris Pasternak: The Poet and His Politics* (Cambridge: Harvard University Press, 1990), 218. I read the 1964 edition of Pasternak's *Hamlet* translation (Moscow: Khudozhestvennaya literatura).

7. Alma Law, "Chekhov's Russian Hamlet (1924)," *Drama Review* 3 (Fall 1983): 34; Billington, *The Icon and the Axe*, 515 ("pure," "unalloyed"); Paperno, "Pushkin," 39; Ivanov, "MKhAT Vtoroy," 224–226 ("world," "soulless"), 229, 229n.40, 231, 233 ("cross"), 234; Kozintsev, *Shakespeare*, 140, 156 ("ironclad"); de Custine, *Empire of the Czar*, 410. The Craig *Hamlet* is thoroughly covered in Laurence Senelick, *Gordon Craig's Moscow Hamlet: A Reconstruction* (Westport: Greenwood Press, 1982), 78. For a moving and intelligent discussion of Michael Chekhov's personal and theatrical existentialism, with specific illustrations drawn from his performances as Hamlet and Strindberg's Erik XIV, see Vladislav Ivanov, "Michael Chekhov and Russian Existentialism," in *Wandering Stars*, ed. Senelick, 140–157.

8. Joseph Macleod, *The New Soviet Theatre* (London: George Allen and Unwin, 1943), 152, 160–161 ("tombstone," "conditioned"), 162–163; Alma H. Law, "*Hamlet* at the Vakhtangov," *Drama Review* 4 (December 1977): 100–102 ("political" on 101); Nikolai A. Gorchakov, *The Theater in Soviet Russia*, trans. Edgar Lehrman (Freeport, N.Y.: Books for Libraries Press, 1972), 340–341; Juri Jelagin, *Taming of the Arts*, trans. Nicholas Wreden (New York: E. P. Dutton, 1951), 35, 327 ("flagrantly"); P. A. Markov, *The Soviet Theatre* (New York: G. P. Putnam's Sons, 1935), 92–93, 97; Andre van Gyseghem, *Theatre in Soviet Russia* (London: Faber and Faber, 1944), 102–105. According to Yesenina, Meyerhold, who attended the premiere of Akimov's production, was especially

taken with the beautiful actress Vagrina's bewitching interpretation of
Ophelia's mad scene. Evidently, he discussed his impression with Raykh,
who was then playing the would-be Hamlet Goncharova in Olesha's *A
List of Blessings*. The next day, Raykh told her daughter that her Hamlet
would be "a real madman." She probably meant by this that she could
bring greater skill to her performance than Vagrina. However, her statement also resonates with the deeper sense that the "madness" of the
actress-character playing Hamlet is more genuine than that of the actress
more traditionally cast as Ophelia. Since Meyerhold's production of Olesha's play premiered in June 1931 and Akimov's *Hamlet* in May 1932, it
seems clear that Raykh intended to improve rather than conceive a performance in light of the impression made upon her husband by Vagrina
(Yesenina, letter to K. L. Rudnitsky, 14 February 1983, 107).

9. M. S. Grigor'yov, *Sovetsky teatr: K tridtsatiletiyu sovetskogo gosudar-
   stva* (Moscow: Vserossyskoe teatral'noe obshchestvo, 1947), 323–
   335; de Jonge, *Stalin*, 223, 229–230, 242, 272–273; Eleanor Rowe,
   Hamlet: A Window on Russia (New York: New York University Press,
   1976), 155; S. Nikulin, *Vysotsky na Taganke: Pervye roli* (Moscow: Soyuzteatr, 1988), 49–50; Fleishman, *Boris Pasternak*, 222 (quotes); Kozintsev, *Shakespeare*, 146; Inna Vishevskaya, "Razmyshleniya o sovetskoy p'ese," *Teatr* (1992): 73, 81–82.

10. Nina Velekhova, "The Link of Time: Directing in the Soviet Union," *The-
    ater* 3 (Fall 1989): 30 ("own," "immature"); Billington, *The Icon and the
    Axe*, 358 ("new," "symbol"); Worrall, *Modernism to Realism*, 182; A. V.
    Bartoshevich, "Uroki 'Gamleta,'" in *Mir iskusstva*, ed. M. P. Kotovskaya
    and S. A. Isaev (Moscow: Gosudarstvenny institut teatral'nogo iskusstva,
    1991), 51 (quote).

11. Fleishman, *Boris Pasternak*, 218–219 (quotes).

12. Yevgeny Borisovich Pasternak, "Foreword," in *Boris Pasternak: Selected
    Poems*, trans. Jon Stallworthy and Peter France (New York: W. W. Nor-
    ton and Company, 1982), 41–42; Boris Pasternak, "Hamlet," "The
    Poems of Yury Zhivago," trans. Bernard Guilbert Guerney, in *Doctor
    Zhivago*, trans. Max Hayward and Manya Harari (New York: Pantheon,
    1958), 433 (quote); Mark Bly, "Lyubimov and the End of an Era: An
    Interview with Peter Sellars," *Yale/Theater* (Spring–Summer 1984), 9
    (Lyubimov's quote of Pasternak).

13. Boris Pasternak, *Stikhotvoreniya i poemy* (Moscow and Leningrad:
    Gosudarstvennoe izdatel'stvo khudozhestvennoy literatury, 1965), 463
    (quote); Poggioli, *The Poets of Russia*, 237 (quote); Billington, *The Icon
    and the Axe*, 562; Anna Akhmatova quoted in Mandelstam, *Hope Aban-
    doned*, 319.

14. Alla Demidova, *Vladimir Vysotsky, kakim znayu i lyublyu* (Moscow: So-
    yuz teatral'nykh deyateley RSFSR, 1989), 75–76, 80; Lioubimov, *Le feu
    sacré*, 121 ("irreplaceable"), 141–142; Marvin Carlson, *Theatre Semi-
    otics: Signs of Life* (Bloomington and Indianapolis: Indiana University
    Press, 1990), 85 ("icon"); Vysotsky quoted in Gershkovich, *The Theater
    of Yuri Lyubimov*, 109, 110, 129; also 118 ("singing"), 127–128.

15. Gaevsky, *Fleyta Gamleta*, 120; Gershkovich, *The Theatre of Yuri Lyu-*

bimov, 5, 109–110, 115–116, 124, 126, 128; Demidova, *Vladimir Vysotsky*, 87–89, 91–98, 101; Lioubimov, *Le feu sacré*, 95 (Meyerhold quote), 193; "Khudozhnik Pyotr Belov," *Teatr* 9 (September 1988): 132, 191; *zek* defined in the "Glossary" to *The Gulag Archipelago*, 641; Rowe, *Hamlet*, 158; Yutkevich, "'Gamlet,'" 85. In his productions adapted from Bulgakov's *The Master and Margarita* (*Master i Margarita*, Taganka Theatre premiere, 6 April 1977) and from the works of Gogol (*The Inspector's Recounting* [*Revizskaya skazka*], Taganka Theatre premiere, May 1978), Lyubimov demonstrated his affinity for "madmen" and his understanding of the madness of modern Soviet history.

16. Akimov quoted in Macleod, *The New Soviet Theatre*, 160; Kozintsev, *Shakespeare*, 146, 168, 228 (quotes); Aleksandr Blok quoted on corpses among the living in Yury Tynjanov, "Blok," 123, and in notes to Kornei Chukovsky, "A. A. Blok," 188n.13, both in *Blok: Essays and Memoirs*, ed. Vogel; Ginzburg, *Journey*, 70–71, 238–239, 341 (quotes); Mandelstam, *Hope against Hope*, 146, 153–154; Skorochkina, "V kakom kostyume," 89; Boris Pasternak, "Translating Shakespeare," trans. Manya Harari, in *I Remember: Sketch for an Autobiography*, trans. David Magarshack (Cambridge: Harvard University Press, 1983), 130.

17. Kozintsev, *Shakespeare*, 140, 156; Mikhail Shvidkoi, "The Effect of Glasnost: Soviet Theater from 1985 to 1989," trans. Vladimir Klimenko, *Theater* 3 (Fall 1989): 9 (Pasternak quote); Ivanov, "MKhAT Vtoroy," 219, 237–238; Nikulin, *Vysotsky*, 52; Ginzburg, *Journey*, 89, 234 (Juliya Nekrasov on "bliss"). The Taganka *Hamlet*'s oblique exegesis of Stalinist generational guilt anticipated by four years the first direct theatrical discussion of this theme in the Sovremennik Theatre production of Chingiz Aytmatov and Kaltay Mukhamedzhanov's *The Ascent of Mount Fuji* (*Voskhozhdenie na Fudziyamu*, 1975).

18. Demidova's Gertrude is described as "almost frighteningly sterile," with a cold, cruel intelligence, and as a "living corpse," in Gaevsky, *Fleyta Gamleta*, 124–125, also 117–119, 125 ("chimerical"), 126, 129 ("dirty"); Lyubimov, *Le feu sacré*, 193; Demidova, *Vladimir Vysotsky*, 82, 85; Yutkevich, "'Gamlet,'" 83; Gershkovich, *The Theatre of Yuri Lyubimov*, xii–xiii; Nikulin, *Vysotsky*, 49–50.

19. Nikulin, *Vysotsky*, 49 ("torn"), 50 ("tragedy"), 60 ("poor"); Gershkovich, *The Theatre of Yuri Lyubimov*, xiii ("adaptations"); Bartoshevich, "Uroki," 52; Lioubimov, *Le feu sacré*, 39–40 (Pasternak anecdote), 95–96.

20. Hedrick Smith quoted in Felicia Londré, "*Hamlet*" entry, in *Shakespeare around the Globe: A Guide to Notable Postwar Revivals*, ed. Samuel L. Leiter (Westport: Greenwood Press, 1986), 145.

21. Tatiana Tchernavin, *We Soviet Women* (New York: E. P. Dutton, 1936), 243 ("only"); Ginzburg, *Journey*, 79 ("cells"), 100, 104, 165 ("kennels"), 296, 316; Mandelstam, *Hope against Hope*, 162–163; de Jonge, *Stalin*, 214 ("gravedigger"); Yutkevich, "'Gamlet,'" 84 ("technological").

22. Mandelstam, *Hope Abandoned*, 592 ("silence," "unanimity"); Ginzburg, *Journey*, 296 ("suffer"), 316 ("careless"); Kozintsev, *Shakespeare*,

265; V. Berezkin, *Vadim Ryndin* (Moscow: Iskusstvo, 1974), 120–121, 131 (quote), 135, and Aleksandr Anikst, "Remarks at the Conference on Shakespearean Dramaturgy," 22 April 1962 (preserved in the archives of the All-Russian Theatre Society), both quoted in McLain, "Oxlopkov," 242–243, 245–248, 251–254.

23. Demidova, *Vladimir Vysotsky*, 80, 83–85; Lioubimov, *Le feu sacré*, 85; Nikulin, *Vysotsky*, 49–50; Kozintsev, *Shakespeare*, 236, 257 (quote), 265–266; de Custine, *Empire of the Czar*, 239 (quote), 498.
24. Pasternak, *I Remember*, 126, 149 (quotes); Demidova, *Vladimir Vysotsky*, 77–78, 83; Yutkevich, "'Gamlet,'" 88; de Jonge, *Stalin*, 272; Bartoshevich, "Uroki," 52 ("informer," "eyeless"); L. D. Trotsky, "O ranenom," *O Lenine, materialy dlya biografa* (Moscow: n.p., n.d.), 151–156, quoted in Tumarkin, *Lenin Lives!* 81; Viktor Shklovsky, *A Sentimental Journey: Memoirs 1917–1922* (Ithaca: Cornell University Press, 1984), 233 (quote).
25. Gershkovich, *Yuri Lyubimov*, 217.
26. de Vögué quoted in Simon Karlinsky, *The Sexual Labyrinth of Nikolai Gogol* (Cambridge, Mass.: Harvard University Press, 1976), 135; McLain, "Oxlopkov," 246; Worrall, *Modernism to Realism*, 183; Yutkevich, "'Gamlet,'" 83; Lioubimov, *Le feu sacré*, 39, 95–96; Demidova, *Vladimir Vysotsky*, 77–78, 80, 83; Micky Levy, "David Borovsky Designs for Lyubimov: Recent Productions at Moscow's Taganka Theatre," *Theatre Crafts* 7 (November/December 1978): 35, 57–58; Jakobson, *Puškin*, 42; Kozintsev, *Shakespeare*, 271; Bartoshevich, "Uroki," 51–52; George R. Kernodle, "The Open Stage: Elizabethan or Existentialist," *Shakespeare Survey*, ed. Allardyce Nicoll, 12 (1959): 1–7.

EPILOGUE

1. The Supreme Soviet of the USSR restored Lyubimov's citizenship in 1989. He resumed leadership of the Taganka Theatre in 1992, staging as the inaugural production of his new regime Nikolay Erdman's *The Suicide* (Anatoly Smelyansky, "Stanislavsky and the Modern Russian Theater," *Theater Three* 10/11 [1992]: 148–149). Michael Dobbs, "Yuri Lyubimov, Director in Exile," *Washington Post*, date unknown, F1–F6.
2. I rushed to see the Taganka production of *The Exchange* while it was in previews, having been advised that it would probably be closed by the authorities prior to its formal opening or else would have an abbreviated run. While this did not prove to be the case with this particular production, it had happened and would happen with other Taganka productions. In his staging of Molière's *Tartuffe* (Taganka premiere 14 November 1968), Lyubimov demonstrated that he could on occasion beat the government censors at their own game and wrest his theatre's fate from their fickle hands. Having been denied permission to stage the play by a puppet king and cardinal, who occupy gilt frames at either side of the stage, the Taganka's/Molière's actors assert that they will not offer a per-

formance but rather a rehearsal open to the public. This "open rehearsal" was the performance that I saw during the 1975–1976 season, when the Taganka's production of *Tartuffe* was still going strong, eight years after its (non)premiere. On the semiotic coding of theatre programs at the Taganka (with accompanying illustrations), see Nicholas Rzhevsky, "The Program as Performance Text," *Slavic and East European Arts* 4, no. 1 (Spring 1986): 97–114.

3. For a detailed discussion of Lyubimov's production of *The Exchange*, see Michael McLain, "Trifonov's *The Exchange* at Liubimov's Taganka," *Slavic and East European Arts* 3, no. 1 (Winter/Spring 1985): 159–169.

4. Unsurprisingly, Lyubimov later staged *Three Sisters* (Taganka premiere December 1981) to underscore the sentimental and at times ideologically driven theme of the mythic center and harmonious, beautified cultural memory. For a brief description of this production, which received significant critical attention in the Western press and scholarly journals, see Gershkovich, *The Theater of Yuri Lyubimov*, 100–105.

INDEX

263